Finches and
other seed-eating birds

The heads shown in this plate are taken from skins of adult male serins (genus *Serinus*), selected by the author, from the collection in the sub-department of Ornithology at the British Museum (Natural History).

1st row, left to right: Wild Canary (*Serinus canarius*), Serin (*S. serinus*), Green Singing Finch (*S. mozambicus*), St. Helena Seed-eater (*S. flaviventris*).

2nd row: Black-faced Canary (*S. capistrata*), Cape Canary (*S. canicollis*), Natal Linnet (*S. scotops*), White-bellied Serin (*S. dorsostriatus*).

3rd row: Streaky Seed-eater (*S. striolata*), Citril Finch (*S. citrinella*), White-throated Seed-eater (*S. albogularis*), Streaky-headed Seed-eater (*S. gularis*).

4th row: Brown-rumped Seed-eater (*S. tristriatus*), Alario Finch (*S. alario*), Yellow-throated Serin (*S. flavigula*), Grey Singing Finch (*S. leucopygius*), Yellow-rumped Serin (*S. atrogularis*).

Serins *(for the full caption see previous page)*

FINCHES
and other seed-eating birds

*An avicultural guide to
the seed-eating birds of the world*

by

ROBIN L. RESTALL
F.Z.S., M.B.O.U.

FABER AND FABER
3 Queen Square
London

First published in 1975
by Faber and Faber Limited
3 Queen Square London WC1
Printed in Great Britain by
Butler & Tanner Limited Frome
Colour plate printed by
The Curwen Press Limited London
All rights reserved

ISBN 0 571 10353 7

CONTENTS

PART THREE · ESTRILDIDAE

PART FOUR · PLOCEIDAE

ACKNOWLEDGEMENTS

I would like to acknowledge the assistance of the following people during the preparation of this book. Some of them answered individual queries, others a fair number; but in every case they helped to fill a gap in my experience and the literature: Mr. Frank Meaden, Mr. Derek Goodwin, Dr. C. J. O. Harrison, Mr. Herbert Murray, Dr. B. Lavercoombe, Mr. Claude Payne, Mr. Arthur Douglas, Dr. D. W. Snow, through whose kind auspices I was able to make innumerable sketches of skins at the sub-department of ornithology of the British Museum (Natural History); Mr. Fish and his staff in the library of the Zoological Society of London, who regularly produced photocopies of obscure references for me; Mr. Harry Lacey, who supplied dozens of superb photographs for me to choose from; Miss Maria Eugenia Perez Rivera, who willingly and happily converted rundown italic handwriting into immaculate typescript; finally, the patience and fortitude of my wife and children, who occasionally thought I had sunk into a pile of books and paper without trace. To them all a tremendous 'Thank you'.

But, of course, all the opinions and conclusions expressed in the following pages are my own, and any errors must be my own responsibility.

ROBIN RESTALL
Madrid, 1974

AUTHOR'S PREFACE

If we look at the world of birds as a kind of evolutionary tree, the topmost branches are reserved for a large group, nearly 700 species, of small- to medium-sized birds generally called finches. Seed-eating birds evolved comparatively recently when the seed-bearing plants of the Miocene came into dominance about 30 million years ago. Several other families already in existence, like the pheasants and pigeons, adapted their diets to take advantage of this great source of food. However, none of the new seed-eaters exploited the new niche as successfully as the finches. For as the seed-bearing plants spread, so did the finches. After the Miocene, the seeding grasses colonized every corner of the globe, except Antarctica, providing a livelihood for this new and successful group of birds which is truly world-wide.

Traditionally, the finches are classified into two large families based on their origin, and we see most textbooks presenting the New World Seed-eaters and the Old World Seed-eaters. The New World Seed-eaters have been given the family name Fringillidae, following Linnaeus, taking the name, ironically, from an Old World finch, the Chaffinch. What we normally call the finches (Goldfinches, etc.) are placed in a subfamily, Carduelinae, in the Old World family Ploceidae, which are the weavers. Personally, I find this beautiful simplification somewhat confusing and I must admit that I am rather gratified to find that just about every authority today has his own ideas as to how the seed-eaters should be arranged. Current scholarly thought is pretty much in line with the way in which I, personally, tend to look at the situation, and I feel this direction is most helpful to the aviculturist.

Currently, the trend is to recognize *four* families. The first, Emberizidae, embraces all the buntings and their allies. The second, Fringillidae, now becomes the family of the true finches, being comprised of all the Carduelines with the Chaffinch welcomed back to the fold. Thirdly, the waxbills and their allies are given family status as the Estrildidae and, finally, the sparrows, weavers and allied groups form the Ploceidae. The contents of this book are based on this system, which thereby becomes a method of presenting the seed-eating birds within a sound taxonomic framework. The motivation is that the average bird-keeper, who often knows little about taxonomy or systematics, might acquire an idea of the true relationship of the various families and subfamilies among the seed-eaters. I believe that it would have been misleading to have ordered the chapters under headings such as Finch, Waxbill, Bunting and Grosbeak, since these and various other collective names for seed-eaters have been so widely and miscellaneously applied to various species as to have little or no taxonomic significance. The danger of such a method would be that it carries the implication that all 'finches' are related, and may therefore be cross-bred. In this book it becomes clear that, for example, the Saffron Finch is a bunting and is not related to the Canary, which is a finch.

My personal philosophy as an aviculturist is that the hobby of bird-keeping will never rise much above the 'pet hamster' level unless its followers take active steps to increase the quality of their participation. I believe that to keep birds in cage or aviary simply as status symbols, or as variations on the goldfish-in-a-bowl syndrome, is not enough. The bird-keeper must recognize that he has living creatures in his care, the majority of which have been trapped in the wild and will be submitted to an artificial and controlled existence until they die. The bird-keeper has a responsibility to improve his hobby, to understand the needs of his charges so that each may live its life out in as happy and fulfilled a way as possible. This means knowing what they are and from where they come, how they live and, most important, why they live the way in which they do.

There can be many reasons for mixing various species in one enclosure: the commonest and least satisfactory of these is that the accommodation available to the bird-keeper is more limited than his ability to acquire new species. Next is that the keeper wants a decorative display. I do not intend to make any lists of 'ideal' or 'balanced' collections for such people. They are admirably catered for in *Cage and Aviary Birds* by D. H. S. Risdon. Reference to *balanced* collections would anyway be outside the scope of this book since so many species that are ideal for this purpose are not seed-eating birds. For example, in a nicely planted flight containing a pair of breeding buntings one could include (also breeding) pairs of doves and quail.

The best reason for adding more than one species to an enclosure is to make optimum use of the space available without in any way inhibiting the birds' natural behaviour. I would simply like to make a plea that, for the sake of the birds, do exercise restraint and don't keep too many birds in one enclosure.

The rules are simple. To begin with, *never* overcrowd. Next, try to achieve a balance in terms of ecology – the way in which the birds live and where. Some birds are naturally ground-dwellers, others are almost totally arboreal; some keep very much to cover, while others shun it and display themselves in the open. Some species are gregarious when not breeding but solitary when they are breeding; others are sociable all the year round and even breed in colonies. These are some factors to take into account. Two other factors to be considered are size and colour. Many large birds are peaceful and not at all aggressive and, in fact, may be safely kept with waxbills. However, their mere size will serve to make the waxbills sufficiently nervous to be put off breeding, behave unnaturally or maybe die young. Some male birds are aggressive in response to the colours of a competing male of the same species, so try wherever possible to segregate species by colour, not mixing red birds with other red birds, or blue with other blues, etc.

Most aviculturists take up bird-keeping from a fairly simple 'wouldn't it be nice' starting-point. Quite a few become hooked and develop passionate interests in various birds. Most people begin with a modest mixed collection and end up by specializing. Perhaps the most popular speciality is with parrots and parakeets, but large numbers of enthusiasts take up Australian Grassfinches, for example, or British finches. A few end up specializing in just one species such as the brilliantly coloured Gouldian Finch. The specialists have discovered that to breed wild birds is a twofold glory. On the one hand, it is evidence that the keeper is a master who is on top of his art, for only fit, healthy and happy birds that are given a proper diet will breed successfully. On the other hand, it is the most satisfying aspect of the great colourful world of aviculture. I do not see it as a triumph over nature but that one has been accepted as an accomplice of nature. And, in this ever-growing industrial, synthetic, controlled and progressive world, that is a good feeling.

There are other more objective arguments in favour of this attitude, primarily that of conservation. If bird-keepers try more and
more to breed their birds, the drain on natural wild populations
will be reduced. It will be reduced for two reasons. Firstly, because
replacements are increasingly available from within, and aviary-
bred stock itself tends to breed better. Secondly, if one is serious
about breeding, one cannot cram an aviary with birds. Overcrowding is the breeder's biggest single problem. *Ergo*, if the
demand for wild-caught stock is reduced, the hobby of bird-
keeping can become a little more respectable. Another aspect of
breeding that makes it particularly worth while is that breeders,
because they are proud and have something to say, tend to write
about their achievements. Less experienced people read these
notes with interest and thereby improve their own performances
as a result . . . and thus, the spiral continues upwards.

Generally speaking, there are two kinds of books for a bird-
keeper. The first has chapters on housing, feeding, sickness and
illness, acclimatization, starting and balancing mixed collections
and ends up with a representative selection of typical cagebirds.
Such books tend to be read well, once, and then gather dust on the
bookshelf. As the owner gains in experience so he acquires new
birds, or at least becomes interested in hitherto unknown species,
and he refers to his book for guidance. Unfortunately, he soon
ceases to refer to the book, for the few dozen species referred to
soon become familiar and well known. The second kind of book
for bird-keepers either reduces the introductory chapters to the
briefest of notes, or dispenses with them altogether, thereby allowing more space for birds and illustrations. These books are all very
well, but are invariably poorly illustrated, and never include
enough species.

The largest number of seed-eaters dealt with in any of the
contemporary avicultural handbooks is less than 150. There are
over 600 different species of birds imported into Britain in any
one year these days and probably as many as 200 of them are
what one might call seed-eaters. One would probably have to
span a ten-year period to raise this total to 300 and a twenty-year
period to exceed this figure. In this book, I have included practically every one of these species, plus a good many species to
which I have only found reference on one occasion, or have heard
about through friends. Some of these are birds that I have im-

ported privately myself, or conducted investigations by post to other continents to see if a given species is known in aviculture. As a result, this book contains reference to nearly 350 species.

In addition to including as many species as possible, I have included every alternative common English name that I can find. Most aviculturists scan the advertisement columns of *Cage and Aviary Birds* each week, and quite a few receive lists direct from importers and retailers. Many see the names of birds that they do not know, and for which they cannot find references in their handbooks. The index of this book is not a comprehensive glossary, but it is the result of twenty-six years of practical bird-keeping and research through a great deal of literature, resulting in over 700 common names being listed. I am sure that many readers will know other names. If they care to send them to me, care of the publisher, I will be very happy to include them in the next edition of this book.

This book is intended primarily to be used at two levels. For the experienced bird-keeper who knows how to keep birds, the entry under the species name will generally be sufficient to satisfy the reader whether the bird is of interest or not. For the beginner, there are two introductions prefacing the lists of species. For each family, there is a generalized introduction including comments on feeding, housing and breeding. Each subfamily then has its own introduction and subsequently each genus, supergenus, and homogenous group of genera has its own introduction.

The text for each individual species varies, and only follows a loose format. Some species are extremely well known, are dealt with adequately in all the books and do not justify traditional detailing; in these cases I have preferred to make my entry more anecdotal. With some rarely imported species, it has not been possible to write anything because the information simply isn't there. This is particularly the case with some South American species. If you know of some useful reference or, better still, have personal experiences of species that are woefully underrepresented here, I would be only too happy to hear from you. I will modify the text and give you full credit in the next edition.

I have no intention of writing long 'comprehensive' texts for each species. This would strain my resources to breaking-point, force me to plagiarize, increase the length of the text to un-economic limits and raise the price to an unacceptable level, and result in unavoidable inaccuracies and dogma. (Many references in the literature are based on single experiences and, because they do not take into account individual variations in behaviour and management, result in oversimplifications and dogmatic conclusions or generalizations. Where these exist as popular bird folklore I have offered my own experiences in contrast. Two examples are the peaceful nature of the Paradise Whydah and the aggressive nature of the Pin-tailed Whydah. I have found the reverse to be the case with both species.) What I have done therefore is to append two sections of references for further reading.

No list of books can be comprehensive, unless one quotes the British Museum archive in its entirety. Those bibliographies which are impressively long and 'comprehensive' are not really helpful, because they do not help the reader. I have, therefore, made a selection and given a short personal review of the relevance of each book to bird-keepers. I have included most of the books referred to by writers of articles, and by experienced bird-keepers in conversation. The list of breeding reports is as comprehensive as I can make it. It includes all the 'official' British reports, i.e. those published in *Avicultural Magazine*, plus a good few that appeared in magazines and publications that are usually ignored by the professional ornithologists. However, since my objective is to help the reader to find out more about the birds that he may be interested in, I have included interesting references from other countries that have appeared in the British press. I have also included a few long and interesting papers that are not essentially breeding reports. By using these two sections, the reader may find out a great deal about some species, and some experiences and opinions that may well differ from mine expressed here. This should encourage him to form his own opinions. Bird-keeping is like gardening, it is personal and quite different for each person. For the gardener, there are a dozen factors to make his experience with a given plant different from that of the next man – latitude, soil, altitude, wind, light, weather, kind of care, etc.; so it is with bird-men. This book is not a definitive work of reference to be used as a criterion by one and all; I will never live long enough to get the kind of experience that would require. It is one of those contributions, like soil or fertilizer, intended to help, or influence, or just provide a second opinion.

Part One
EMBERIZIDAE

1 · EMBERIZINAE

All the species found in the subfamily Emberizinae are entitled to be called buntings, although normally this is a term applied to the species in the *Emberiza* genus and one or two odd birds that look very much like true *Emberizae*. It is interesting to note that of all the seed-eating birds, it is perhaps the buntings that are most commonly mis-named – indicating the diversity of a group that includes birds called finches, sparrows, seed-eaters, cardinals and grassquits. In the introductory notes below, the word 'bunting' can be taken as a generalization that embraces the whole subfamily Emberizinae and not just the 'true buntings'.

Generally speaking, buntings are terrestrial birds, living close to the ground. Their habitats differ greatly, ranging from open grassland to broken scrub and all ranges of mesquite, to open woodland or forest clearings. It is unusual to find a bunting in dense forest or jungle, or in the higher levels of trees. On the other hand, they can be found in every geographical region, from the hottest to the coldest climates, from the driest to the most humid, from the seashore to the barren plateaux of the Andes. To the south, buntings can be found in the Tierra del Fuego, and, in the north, one finds the Snow Bunting breeding at the tip of northern Greenland, further north than any other land-bird. Despite this enormous variety of habitat, the buntings everywhere have tended to exploit the same ecological niche, and survive by foraging on the ground for fallen seeds.

Like most seed-eating birds, however, the basic diet of the adult bird is inadequate for nestlings and fledglings. For the first few days buntings feed their young almost exclusively on insects. Then, either rapidly or gradually, depending on the species, the diet is modified to include green or unripened seeds and, finally, ripened seeds. Most buntings will take any suitable insect that they happen to come across, at any time during the year, regardless of whether they are breeding or not. But it is only when babies are in the nest that they become truly insectivorous.

Many experienced aviculturists try to reject the artificial division of cage and aviary birds into 'softbills' and 'hardbills' (or insect-eaters and seed-eaters) since so many birds fall into an 'in-between' category. Buntings are rather like this for, while few if any will ever take more than just the occasional beakful of soft food, many will become mealworm addicts. I know several bird-keepers who have discovered that it is a mistake to keep buntings in the same aviary as insectivorous birds because there are some individual buntings who will take command of the mealworm tray and drive off all competitors until they are either utterly satiated, or the mealworms are all gone.

Buntings are individuals, although superficially they may all seem alike. A cage full of Red-headed Buntings is unimpressive. They lack the apparent intelligence of softbills, like Pekin Robins, or the personality of a bunch of parakeets, or the twittering charm of a cage full of waxbills. This, in my experience, is typical but false. Individuals vary tremendously and so do species. Of the hundreds of species of birds which I have kept, I can say that every bunting has been welcomed with pleasure. With every new bunting, one might have a bold, proud songster or a genteel and demure twitterer.

The variety of plumage is tremendous but, although many are brightly coloured, very few are gaudy. In an aviary they are seldom aggressive to other birds unless they are breeding, or are in breeding condition, or are in small or overcrowded quarters.

HOUSING

Buntings may be kept in cages, the bigger the better, and there should always be room enough for the birds to fly from one perch to another. Some individuals never seem happy in a cage and will make those distressing movements of the head as if looking for a way out, even after six months. If I cannot put such a bird in a large cage (minimum 4 ft. (1·2 m.) long, but 7 or 8 ft. (2·1 m. or 2·4 m.) would be much better) within a few days I prefer to release it. On the other hand, some specimens settle in like Canaries and warble contentedly, day in and day out.

If the diet is right, a male bunting will sing and come into breeding condition before the female, especially if kept indoors and subjected to an artificially long day (because of the electric light). Such a bird will, from time to time, attack the female and feathers will fly. These birds should have large quarters, or be separated.

Undoubtedly, however, buntings do better in outdoor aviaries. Most of them may be wintered outdoors but, of course, should have access to dry and draught-proof sleeping quarters. In a roomy, planted aviary they can be seen at their very best. The most successful aviary I have had for buntings (together with a few other species) was about 17 ft. (5·2 m.) wide and 11 ft. (3·4 m.) deep. The back half, about 5 ft. (1·5 m.) by 16 ft. (4·9 m.) was planted with cypress and apple trees, privet and a few smaller flowering shrubs and other plants such as chrysanthemums. The front half had two dead branches for perching and the ground was turfed. The lawn was cut regularly and was the favourite place for the resident buntings to forage over. I would broadcast a handful of seeds and mealworms over the lawn every day, thereby encouraging natural food-seeking behaviour.

FOOD

My recommendation is to supply a wide range of seeds in different bowls; plain Canary in one, small millet in another, large millet in another, Canary mixture (normal grade) in another, hemp and so on. If the cage has only two pots, one for seed and one for water, then it must be too small for any bunting and will only be suitable for a Canary or a Budgerigar. However, if for some reason the bird *has* to be kept in such a cage, then fill one pot with mixed millets and the other with a Canary mixture. Water must then be given in a bath which is hung over the open door. Feeding in this way enables one to buy in the most economical way and avoid waste. I had a male Red-headed Bunting who developed a passion for hemp. He would eat all the hemp from the pot of Canary mixture, then sit, so stupefied, that I could put my hand in his cage and pick him up. When he recovered his senses and, presumably, a little appetite, he would scatter all the remaining seeds about the cage in search of more hemp. I solved the problem by cutting out the hemp from the mixture, but it would have been better to have been able to place the bird in larger quarters, depositing the seed in separate pots and keeping the hemp ration low. One can have fun measuring how much of each seed a bird takes. In fact, serious research can quite easily be started in this way.

When breeding, the buntings will invariably require live food in the form of insects. Mealworms, whilst being the cleanest and most convenient food, are not good enough alone. In a roomy, planted aviary, let's say 5 sq. yds. (4·8 m.^{2}) of ground space with clematis and roses well covering two or three sides, mealworms alone might well be sufficient, particularly so with the New World buntings. It is unlikely, however, with the *Emberizae* and the breeder ought to be prepared to go out on daily sorties to dig up ants' nests for the pupae (which can be scattered over the ground of the flight), maintain a fruit-fly culture, supply blowfly maggots, or breed stick insects. A trick that I have used with success with insectivorous species, like thrushes and starlings, is to give the nestlings a shot of food, of my own preparation, with the aid of a plastic hypodermic syringe. A mixture of bottled high-protein baby-food, with a multi-vitamin/mineral complex added, plus a little fresh cream cheese is ideal. The risk of causing the parents to desert is higher with buntings, which are sensitive breeders, so only consider this as a last resort if you are prepared to hand-rear.

BREEDING

Typically, buntings build an open, cup-shaped nest, but some Central and South American species cover the nest over with a dome of one kind or another. The female normally builds, but the male may be close by, perhaps to stimulate her to greater industry, or even to help with an odd strand. The nest is generally built of fine bents, grasses, rootlets, moss and lichen, although there is obviously quite a bit of variation in such a wide-ranging group of birds. The nest is generally lined with a few hairs, or a little wool and the odd feather. It may be built in a bush or tree, but usually it is located low down and even on the ground among some species. The choice of site seems to depend less on a given norm than on security of support and concealment. Whilst a tree or bush will be typical for the group at one extreme, one can find the Reed Bunting nesting (among other places) in reeds over water, and, at the other extreme, the Snow Bunting in deep crevices among the rocks.

Eggs vary a lot in colouring but tend to be scrawled or blotched according to the species. Clutches range from two to six; incubation is twelve to thirteen days and the young will normally fledge in about twenty days. As a rule, the female alone incubates but both parents will join in rearing the young.

Buntings are often bred in confinement and most of them have been bred at some time. More often than not, the reason for failure is poor husbandry on the part of the keeper; either that, or lack of ambition. If one is serious in one's desire to breed buntings, one must set about the process logically and systematically. To begin with, one aviary per pair is to be recommended. This need not be over-large, and one as small as 9 ft. × 4 ft. (2·7 m. × 1·2 m.) could well suffice. Plants are definitely a great help, for they provide a natural source of insects, give a sense of security and protection, reduce risk of quarrelling with the next-door neighbours, and add to the attractiveness of the scene. They also provide cover for a pursued female and nesting sites. While buntings normally prefer to nest on or close to the ground, in an aviary they might well choose to build near the roof because, in such a small and restricted area as an aviary, suitable sites and adequate cover may be at a premium. To encourage the birds to breed in a specific site, one can place canary nest bowls or half-open boxes in judiciously chosen spots. Feeding should be arranged in such a way as to provide as little disturbance to the inmates as possible and, finally, one should try to keep to a set pattern of behaviour or routine. Do not suddenly become interested, standing by and watching, or start prying the minute nest building begins. Try to behave as always.

I mentioned above that one pair to one aviary is recommended when breeding, and as a generalization, this is true. The root of any trouble is usually territorial aggression on the part of the male. Some species will become aggressive to any similar-sized bird, others only to other buntings, or closely related or similarly coloured birds, and others only to their own species. Some are so gentle as to merely bicker with other males of the same species, if overcrowded. In the absence of specific data my advice is to assume that any species new to your collection will become territorial as the breeding season comes on.

TRUE BUNTINGS

The *Emberizae* and closely allied buntings are, on average, about the size of a sparrow. In the street or garden a sparrow looks small, but when placed in a cage with a few waxbills it suddenly looks positively bulky and the larger species look enormous. Normally, a bunting would not attack or even threaten a waxbill, but the waxbill does not know this and, under most normal conditions, the presence of such a large bird will put the waxbill sufficiently on edge as to significantly reduce the likelihood of its breeding.

Red-headed Bunting
(*Emberiza bruniceps*)

Description: *7½ in. (190·5 mm.). The head of the adult male is cinnamon, as is the throat and centre of upper breast; the upperparts are greeny brown, streaked with black, and the underparts are bright yellow. The females are dull, light brown birds, streaked lightly above with dark brown; there is a yellowish flush to the vent and undertail-coverts, and a distinct olive tone to the uppertail-coverts. Juveniles resemble females but are paler on the under-surfaces.*

Most writers cannot resist pointing out that the head of the male of this species is not red but at best can be described as chestnut. It is interesting to note that the birds are trapped in India where they over-winter and where they are invariably in fresh winter plumage. The edges of the feathers are paler, often a distinct fawn, and always obscure the colouring of the plumage as it appears by the spring. During the winter and early spring, the edges of the feathers gradually wear off leaving a much brighter and cleaner-looking bird. For some reason, however, this abrasion never seems complete in captive birds. In addition to suffering this handicap, typical of all *Emberizae* and most allied species, the Red-headed Bunting is extremely variable in colouring; I have had males in my possession ranging from orange-headed to a richness of chestnut that would be difficult to describe as anything but red.

It flies north-west from India to breed in an area ranging from Iran and Pakistan northwards through the Arals and the Urals to east of the Volga; so it is really a Russian bird. The Russian name for the species is Jaundiced Bunting, but this name is unlikely to be used in an avicultural context.

This species was the first bunting that I ever kept and there have been few periods when I have not had at least the odd male. I remember, one summer morning in 1962, I woke to hear a strange song that I had never heard before and could not recognize. After a few hours of careful stalking, I caught the performer in the act, to discover that it was the Red-headed Bunting. Edward Boosey once described the simple, descending abrupt song of this bird as 'scroogling', which isn't a bad word for it.

The Red-headed Bunting is probably the most commonly imported bunting, but males comprise an average of over 70% of most consignments. I have even seen shipments of 100% male birds. The sexes migrate in separate flocks, the males always leaving before the females. This natural segregation no doubt enables the native trappers to catch a more valuable haul, the singing males always fetching a better price than the non-singing, dull females.

Despite the fact that it is so commonly imported this species is not recorded as breeding in captivity until 1973. Two pairs were placed in an outside aviary at Chester Zoo in 1971. This enclosure, heavily planted with many shrubs and vines, measured 49 ft. 10 in. × 10 ft. 6 in. × 5 ft. 7 in. (15·2 m. × 3·2 m. × 1·7 m.) high. In addition to this superb flight there was a large shelter. One pair successfully nested in a bush of honeysuckle, raising the young on insects and regurgitated seeds.

though one school of thought (those who follow the geographic species concept) is inclined to regard them as being but races of one species, they are most definitely regarded in the world of aviculture as being different. I am of the certain opinion that the two birds deserve individual specific status, and I cannot see what purpose can be gained by insisting that they are con-specific. The Black-headed Bunting enjoys the rare distinction of migrating from east to west. Like its cousin above, it spends the winter in northern India but flies

Female and male
Black-headed Bunting
(*Emberiza
melanocephala*) : male
Red-headed Bunting
(*Emberiza bruniceps*)

Black-headed Bunting
(*Emberiza melanocephala*)

Description: *About 7½ in. (190·5 mm.). The head of the male is black, the body yellow, while the wings, tail and mantle are chestnut streaked with black; the fresh winter plumage is noticeably marked with brown scalloping caused by pale edging which abrades as the season progresses. The female is very similar to the female* bruniceps, *but is greyer on the head and mantle, and has the rump and uppertail-coverts rufous-yellow. Immature birds resemble the female but are browner, and more noticeably striped on the head and throat.*

The Black-headed and Red-headed Buntings are sibling species. Al-

westwards to breed from Iran along the Mediterranean to Italy.

Some writers have claimed that the song of this species is one of the most beautiful of the buntings, but I feel that this is something of an overstatement. Its song is quite similar to that of the Red-headed, but in all its notes, whether they be contact, alarm or song, it seems to me to be sweeter and softer. Males of one species do not normally respond to the cries of distress made by females of the other, but will often reply to their own kind.

It is a large bird, one of the largest of the buntings and, in my experience, one of the gentlest and most peaceful. I have kept singing males with every kind of companion, and in cages, and never once had any quarrelling. Since odd males are freely available, it can comfortably be added to the average mixed collection. Other names that I have come across for *E. melanocephala* are Royal Ortolan, Royal Bunting and Ortolan; in southern Europe all yellowy buntings are called 'Hortelano'.

Ortolan Bunting
(*Emberiza hortulana*)

Description: $6\frac{1}{2}$–$7\frac{1}{2}$ in. (*165·1–190·5 mm.). Adult male in summer has a grey head tinged with olive green, neck is darker and browner and back is brown streaked with black; throat and eye-ring are white to yellow — older birds being yellower; breast olive grey and rest of underparts brown; in winter the bird is lighter and duller due to new feathers having greyish edges. Females are a duller version of the male, a little paler and lightly streaked. Juveniles are typical miniature buntings but more heavily streaked all over.*

The Ortolan is famous throughout Europe as an epicurean delicacy. Although small and rare (rare in Britain anyway), they are considered to be very good eating in many countries, where they are netted in vast numbers, kept alive in darkened rooms and fattened on oats and millet. They soon become fat and are then marketed. In many parts of Spain they are considered to be the best of the *pajaros fritos* (fried birds) even though the practice of catching wild finches and larks, etc., for restaurant trade was outlawed in 1925. Although it is known universally as the Ortolan, or Ortelano, I have found it referred to as Garden Bunting in the literature.

I have managed to pick up a few Ortolan males in my travels, all in bird markets and all in terrible con-

dition. As each was restored to good health and fine plumage it was released. On one occasion, however, I was fortunate to come across a pair. It was early in November and I was searching the market for suitable birds to illustrate a lecture. The Ortolans were perfect for this, for both were in fresh winter plumage and I was able to demonstrate the weakness of so many book illustrations that only show adults in spring plumage. In this cage, the adult male looked more like the spring female, and the female, while looking astonishingly similar to the male, was much more streaked and indistinctly marked than the book would have led one to expect.

I kept this pair all through the winter and tried them on every type of seed. I expected them to like oats, but they were indifferent, their favourite seed being plain Canary! They, like every *Emberiza*, relished a few mealworms from time to time. The male sang sweetly and charmingly and both birds fattened up and became very fit by the spring. I was happy to pass them over to a friend of mine who was able to give them precisely the conditions they required. They were subsequently bred during the summer of 1973. To my mind, this is one of the loveliest of buntings and worth anybody's devotion.

I have kept odd males, in mixed company without any trouble whatsoever, but as an experiment I ran various other birds in with the pair in their cage. Both Ortolans were what one can only describe as irritable or snappy, and they had, for example, two feathers out of the tail of a male Chaffinch. The male was the more irritable of the two.

Corn Bunting
(*Emberiza calandra*)

Description: 7½–8 in. (190·5–203·2 mm.). *The biggest of the buntings, rather sombrely clothed in light greyish browns, pencilled and streaked with dark brown and black, but lacking any distinctive markings. A dark throat spot is sometimes noticeable.*

The field handbooks give no help in sexing these birds, but not much practice is needed to be able to tell the males as being bigger and bolder, and often quite noticeably so. The male is darker, or more boldly marked, and the thickening of the lower throat spots sometimes is very obvious and looks like a black *v*. One excellent pair that I had for a while were classic examples of how different the sexes can be, for the male was a good half-inch longer and it had the thickset profile of a fluffed-up Robin. It was tame and sang continually, whereas the female was shy and took flight readily. They were kept in a roomy flight-cage with other buntings and small finches and were very peaceful.

In the natural state, Corn Buntings are very territorial, males patrolling their area, continually singing from a few favourite singing posts, but they are said to be polygamous in certain areas. The polygamy appears to be a response to natural pressures and a surfeit of hens. It nests low down, and thoroughly conceals its nest: the female is most cautious and secretive about the whole affair. To encourage them to breed, one is advised to provide a naturally planted aviary with a couple of clumps of good dense cover.

Yellow Bunting
(*Emberiza citrinella*)

Description: 6½–8 in. (165·1–203·2 mm.). *Adult male has yellow head streaked with brown, underparts yellow with a light olivaceous-brown band across the breast; the mantle and upperparts are chestnut streaked with black. Female is similar but with weaker colouring and more heavily streaked. Juveniles resemble females but are browner and have darker streaking.*

This is probably the commonest British bunting and very common over much of Europe. Common names for this beautiful bird are Yellow-hammer, Yellow Ammer, Common Bunting and Scribbling Lark: the latter is derived from the pattern of the egg markings. The Yellow Bunting is that yellow and brown bird that pops up on a post and chatters out its song that has been so often paraphrased as 'little-bit-of-bread-and-no-che-ee-ee-se'.

It nests close to or even on the ground, a loosely formed cup of twigs and grasses, and may be encouraged to build in a tussock of grass that is protected from above by some shrub. It will nest in holes or openings in banks or slopes, suitably concealed, and might be inclined to accept a half-open box in a similar situation. When breeding, the female is pursued with above-average enthusiasm; and in an enclosure that is too small, or which lacks sufficient cover to provide protection, she runs the risk of serious damage ranging from scalping to murder!

In a collection of medium- to large-sized birds, the Yellow Bunting is an appropriate addition, more so if the enclosure is suitably spacious. I do not recommend it in a small flight. Although its colouring and song are quite appealing on a country walk, I find the latter soon becomes rather monotonous, and it would not come very high on my list as a song-bird for the house.

Cirl Bunting
(*Emberiza cirlus*)

Description: 6½ in. (165·1 mm.). *Adult male has the top of its head grey green, streaked with black, its back is rufous also streaked with black, the rump is greyish olive, re-maining upper-surfaces brown; there is a yellow line above and below the eye, a black line through the eye; chin, throat and side of throat are black; breast and underparts are yellow, with a light olive-grey band across the breast; sides of the breast marked with rufous. Females are typical but with finer and darker markings, breast brownish tinged at the sides; the superciliaries are yellowish. Juveniles resemble females but are paler below and more exten-sively streaked.*

Many books describe this as a common bird in England, but the only place in which I have found it to be truly common is north-western Spain. It is a beautiful bird, rather similar to the Yellow Bunting but, to my mind, more attractive. The male has a clear black eye-stripe and a black tail which reaches back to the nape. Arthur Butler said that in an aviary it was not aggressive, but 'sang rarely and was greedy'. R. B. Bennett also found it to be peaceful. An odd male I once had lived happily in the com-pany of some other buntings. A pair, on another occasion, shared a large cage with some serins and Skylarks and were perfectly peaceable and I never noticed the mild belligerence

often shown by an Ortolan or Yellow Bunting. I have found the species to be a model subject for an aviary, being calm, a little shy perhaps but quite steady, and the male can show off beautifully when in song. How-ever, when breeding them I would un-doubtedly treat them with the same care as the Yellow Bunting. Its song also is very similar to that of the Yellow Bunting but singularly lacks the final wheezing note. An alternative common name for the species in eastern Europe is the Truck-garden Bunting.

Yellow-breasted Bunting
(*Emberiza aureola*)

Description: 6 in. (152·4 mm.). *A male in spring plumage has a black face, chestnut on the back of his head, with the remainder of the upper-parts being chestnut streaked with black; the wings have a clear white bar, which is a very helpful identi-fication mark, especially on the female; the rest of the body is yellow with a chestnut band across the chest. Females lack the black face and chestnut head and are duller.*

Males of this very pretty bunting are occasionally available, females rather less so. It is a bird from north-eastern Europe ranging to Siberia and China, wintering in Burma and Malaysia where it is trapped. Males in fresh winter plumage do not re-semble the clean and brilliantly attired birds that decorate the field guides. It is quite distinctive, how-ever, because of its white wing-bar in particular. There is a clearly differ-entiated subspecies called the Eastern or Ussuri White-shouldered Bunting (*Emberiza aureola ornata*). It may also be called Willow Bunting.

I have only ever kept one specimen

of the species, a bird that had apparently been trapped locally in the Madrid province in Spain in 1971. A friend had reported seeing some a week or so previously, but this was so far outside the range of this Asiatic bird that I hadn't believed him. My bird never settled down, being nervous and restless at all times, so I passed it to a friend who found it to be an ideal inmate in a large planted aviary.

It first bred at Chester Zoo in 1971, only a few weeks after being released in the enclosure. Four pairs had been placed in the large Tropical House, which measures 240 ft. (73·2 m.) long, 200 ft. (60·9 m.) wide and 40 ft. (12·2 m.) high. In such an enclosure one can hardly regard the birds as being in captivity. The nest was built on the ground in a clump of asparagus; the male was only noticeably aggressive in defence of the nest-site, and the young were reared on a wide variety of insects with a little regurgitated seed.

Reed Bunting
(*Emberiza schoeniclus*)

Description: *6–7 in. (152·4–177·8 mm.). In summer the head of the adult male is entirely black, the hind neck and mesial stripe are white; underparts are white with a little black streaking, and upperparts are brown streaked with black. Females are heavily streaked on their heads but can always be told from males by the white superciliaries and white throat. Juveniles resemble females but are more extensively streaked below.*

A common bird of marshy areas, meres and broads, the Reed Bunting is the most widespread of all the European buntings. The distinctive black head markings with the white moustache line make it easily recognizable and, although the head gets particularly marked and mottled in winter, one can always tell the sexes apart. There is tremendous variation in size of bill according to where the bird comes from; the South European Reed Bunting (*E. s. intermedia*) has a stubbier and heavier bill; this race is also lighter in colouration. The species appears to be expanding its range in terms of habitat preference and can be found breeding in areas normally considered to be Yellow Bunting territory. Recent studies suggest that reduction of reed-bed habitat is forcing the Reed Bunting to look further afield and that, in doing so, it is competing, often successfully, with the Yellow Bunting. In some instances, it is replacing this near relative.

Evidence of adaptability in a species is always of interest in aviculture, because such birds are invariably more suitable for the inevitably artificial environment in which we place them. The Reed Bunting is, in fact, an easy bird, being undemanding, gentle in demeanour and not at all aggressive. I have kept quite a few of them from time to time, and have found them to be quiet and gentle, but unfortunately I have only kept males. I have heard the song only in the wild. It is a very simple and repetitious 'tweet, tweet, tweet, twitter' and of little interest to anything other than, no doubt, a female Reed Bunting. It is quite possible that Continental dealers handling the species may give it the name of Marsh Bunting.

Elegant Bunting
(*Emberiza elegans*)

Description: *About 6½ in. (165·1 mm.). Adult male is black on the top and sides of head, and cheeks, with a small crest; occiput entirely encircled by a yellow superciliary band; hind neck grey with brown streaks; back chestnut with light and dark streaks; rump grey, tail brown, throat yellow turning to white, which continues to the undertail-coverts, interrupted by a black band across the breast and brown streaks on the flanks. In the winter, the black is almost obscured by the brown edging on the new feathers. Females are paler and duller versions of the males. Juveniles resemble females, but are pale ochre instead of yellow.*

Elegant Bunting (*Emberiza elegans*)

This species is another bunting from north-eastern Asia that is only rarely imported into Europe. It is sometimes given the common name of Yellow-browed, or Yellow-throated Bunting. It is a very attractive bird, quite distinctive and elegant as its name suggests. It is found in Japan where, as a cagebird, it is held in high esteem for its song; however, oriental tastes in music are different from western ones, and a dramatic illustration of this is the fact that the common quail is often kept for its 'song'. In the case of the Elegant Bunting no information is available, but I suspect that it is, in fact, a pleasant song-bird (by western standards). It appears to be a typical bunting, and is a ground-nester — something to be remembered should one have a concrete and pebble-floored aviary with plants in tubs.

Once I found an odd male, the last of a batch of five (all males) that a dealer had received as part of a consignment of mixed Asian seed-eaters. I kept it in a large planted aviary along with a few other buntings, waxbills, starlings, etc. It was perfectly content and seemed to be ideal in such a collection.

Rustic Bunting
(*Emberiza rustica*)

Description: *5–6 in. (127–152·4 mm.). In adult males the top and sides of the head are black; there is a small spot on the back of the head, a strip behind the eye, and the underparts from the throat to the undertail-coverts, which are all white, relieved by a band of cinnamon-chestnut across the breast, with some streaks of the same colour on the flanks; upperparts are brown, streaked on the mantle and wings with black. Females resemble males, but are duller and paler, and the black on the head is marked with brown. Juveniles resemble females, but the breast-bar is almost entirely absent.*

One of the quietest and least offensive species of bunting that I have ever kept was a delightful pair of Rustic Buntings. They were included in the same aviary as the Elegant Bunting, and spent nearly all their time in the company of that individual carefully and methodically quartering the lawn. When not engaged in this activity, however, they perched together near the top of an exposed dead apple tree where they watched all about them with great interest. They were never nervous, but always kept their distance from me. I never once saw them enter the house to feed, and they survived, even thrived, on the seeds and mealworms that I broadcast over the lawn each day.

Another name for the species, though rarely used, is Tit Bunting, which probably follows the size,

Rustic Bunting (*Emberiza rustica*)

shape and demeanour of the bird. The black and white striped head of the male in breeding plumage makes it easy to distinguish from the less dramatically patterned female, but they are not colourful birds. The male sings rather sweetly and has a fluttering display performed on the ground. It is another ground-nesting species. It naturally takes a lot of small insects in its diet and my pair were always the first to the ground in the chase for mealworms each morning, easily beating the Spreo Starlings, who adored them. I doubt whether these or any other small buntings from the north of Europe would stay fit and in perfect condition if deprived of insect food permanently.

Little Bunting
(*Emberiza pusilla*)

Description: *4½–5 in. (114·3–127 mm.). A small bunting which is not easy to identify in both sexes, it is similar to the female Rustic and Reed Buntings. It can be distinguished by its chestnut cheek patches which are outlined clearly in black. The male can be identified by the bolder markings on its head.*

It breeds in the far north, from Finland due east to Siberia, and normally migrates in a southerly direction to spend the winter in Burma and India. It was with some surprise that I found some Little Buntings in a dealer's cage in Madrid one autumn. They had been trapped locally and were clearly off-course in their migration routing. We used the birds that I bought in a lecture to the local bird-watching club, where they aroused great interest. I did not keep them long before releasing them, so my experience is clearly limited. However, the avicultural literature never mentions them at all. In my experience they were quiet and calm little birds, and not in the least bit quarrelsome or argumentative. For those who appreciate quietly coloured birds, at least as a contrast to some of the brighter ones, this bunting would seem to be an excellent subject. The Little Bunting is also listed as Tiny Bunting. The song apparently is exceptionally sweet, being rather like that of a Robin.

Yellow-browed Bunting
(*Emberiza chrysophrys*)

Description: *About 7 in. (177·8 mm.). Adult male in summer has top and sides of head black with thin white stripe over top of head and* bright yellow superciliaries; rest of upperparts brown, dark streaks on back, paler edgings on wings and tail, tips of middle wing-coverts white, edges of outer tail-feathers white; below, white with mesial streaks either side of throat, ochreous tinge on side of breast, faint streaks on breast and flanks. In winter broad pale edgings tend to mask much of main colouration. Adult female is a duller version of male, browner above, greyer below. Juveniles resemble dull female but more noticeably streaked below.

This interesting bunting is rare in the wild and little is known about it. It breeds only in the central parts of east Siberia and winters in China. The nest in the wild has only been discovered once, and virtually nothing is known about its ecology, habits or diet.

The only record that I have of it in captivity is in the collection of Mr. Herbert Murray where it appears to be a fairly typical Asian bunting in its behaviour, being rather shy and keeping to cover. According to Dement'ev, its behaviour is typical; the song is described as pleasant, and its call a delicate whistling.

Grey-headed Bunting
(*Emberiza spodocephala*)

Description: $5\frac{1}{2}$–6 in. (139·7–152·4 mm.). Adult male in summer has head, neck, throat and breast grey with slight olive tinge, very faintly streaked; lores and chin blackish; back brown with blackish streaks; rump and upper tail-coverts brownish olive; wings and tail brown, light edging, outermost tail-feathers edged white; below, yellowish with some dark brown streaking on flanks; bill, irides and feet brown. Winter male has feathers on head and upperparts broadly edged with olive grey, below edged with whitish, almost obscuring the summer colouration. Adult female resembles male but is duller, paler, streaked about the head; below whiter and more heavily streaked on the flanks. Juveniles are a duller and paler version of female, young males being more boldly marked than young females.

An alternative name for this Asian species is Masked Bunting. There are several clearly defined races, differing from one another in the brightness and richness of the green and yellow tones. They breed over an area from central Siberia to Japan, Manchuria to Korea, and China to the Yangtze. The wintering grounds are north-eastern India across to southern China, and Burma to Vietnam. The bird described above is the nominate race from east Siberia. The Central Siberian Grey-headed Bunting (*E. s. oligoxantha*) differs in being lighter generally, lacking any greenish tone on head, and being whitish below with only a faint yellowish tinge. The Eastern Grey-headed Bunting (*E. s. melanops*) is richer in colouration, darker, greener on the head, richer yellow below and well streaked on the flanks. The Island Grey-headed Bunting (*E. s. personata*) is the richest in colouration of all, has a greenish rump; throat to belly bright yellow, lightly streaked.

At a casual glance this retiring and modest little bunting reminds one of a Hedge Sparrow, but is more upright, and is in fact a very attractive bird. I have not kept it, but Mr. Murray finds that his birds keep to low undergrowth, and seem to prefer the indoor aviary where the vegetation is thickest.

Chestnut Bunting
(*Emberiza rutila*)

Description: *About 6 in. (152·4 mm.). Adult male in summer has head to uppertail-coverts, throat to bib rusty chestnut; below, yellow, greyish on flanks streaked with yellow; wings chestnut, dull brown on flights and tail edged with rufous or lighter brown. Winter male has light edging to chestnut feathering. Adult female rufous brown above, tinged olive and faintly streaked with darker; rump and uppertail-coverts rusty chestnut; wings and tail brown with some rusty chestnut edging; below, light ochre with dark streaks, chestnut streaking on bib, breast to undertail yellow streaked with grey. Juveniles resemble paler female, wing-coverts are edged with ochre, not brown; underparts are whiter and less yellow. Immature males are more boldly streaked above than immature females, and lack any olive on head.*

The Chestnut, Rufous or Korean Bunting is a breeding bird of the southern part of east Siberia and northern China. Its status as a breeding bird of Korea is doubtful. It winters in southern China, eastern India, Burma and Malaysia. It is not a bird which I have noticed in dealers' cages ever, but I am grateful to Mr. Herbert Murray for describing the behaviour of a trio that he recently received. They appear to be very easy birds to maintain in good condition, taking a variety of seeds and being very fond of mealworms. Up till the time of writing, Mr. Murray's birds seemed peaceful. His two females seemed inclined to remain in the (heated) indoor aviary while the male remained outside. This was considered to be accidental 'as they are not very enterprising birds'. The male shows itself well and sits in prominent positions on occasions.

The male is a handsome bird, which differs from the Red-headed Bunting by its lesser size and being chestnut on all of its upper surfaces.

Common Rock Bunting
(*Emberiza cia*)

Description: *About 6 in. (152·4 mm.). The adult male has a grey head, palest on the face, embracing the neck and upper breast; irregular black stripes extending over the top of the head, above the superciliaries, through the eye and mesial stripe; the latter two join behind the cheek; upperparts chestnut heavily streaked with black; rump and lower body chestnut to cinnamon. Females are duller with darker heads and are lightly streaked on the upper breast. Males in winter are similar to females but are more distinctly striped on the head. Juveniles resemble females but are less clearly marked on the head.*

The Rock Bunting is a delightful bird found all over southern Europe, north Africa and eastwards, wandering as far as China. Numerous subspecies have been described. It is generally found in pairs in the foothills of the mountains, and an alternative name for it is Mountain Bunting. Another name that may occur in the literature is Meadow Bunting, but this is particularly inappropriate. The sexes look similar, especially in winter following the fresh autumn moult, but in fact the male has a more contrasting black and white striped pattern on the head, and it lacks all striations and streakings of the throat. It is not imported very often and invariably the words Rock Bunting in an advertisement refer to one of the African species.

I have had several of these birds, and kept them in mixed company, with larks and buntings. The males sang a great deal once settled in, not a particularly brilliant accomplishment, but a pleasant enough series of 'twees'. I have not seen a male chase or bully a female and have come to the conclusion that they are peaceable and, despite their non-gregarious behaviour in the wild, sociable.

name is derived from the seven thin white stripes on the head. In winter plumage, and in many dealers' cages, this little bunting looks far duller and more nondescript than the colour plates in field guides might lead one to believe. However, at all times of the year the body is a much richer cinnamon than that of the European Rock Bunting. It is widespread in Africa, running from Abyssinia down to the Cape and up to west Africa. Incidentally, the African Rock Bunt-

Cinnamon-breasted Rock Bunting (*Emberiza tahapisi*)

Cinnamon-breasted Rock Bunting (*Emberiza tahapisi*)

Description: *6½–7 in. (165·1–177·8 mm.). Closely resembles the above species, but is more strongly and brightly coloured.*

This species is often referred to as, simply, Rock Bunting, but occasionally dealers, always on the search for more exotic-sounding names, call it the Seven-striped Bunting. This latter

ings are often placed in a separate genus, *Fringillaria*, but most modern authorities feel that this is not justified and prefer the older name of *Emberiza*.

A fine male Cinnamon-breast is a handsome bird and an excellent guardian of his mate's honour, but it is not an aggressive bird. I have a note that, on one occasion when they bred in captivity, 'they took bread and milk, mealworms and termites virtually *ad lib*', together with seeding grasses and the normal run of seeds.

Like the common Rock Bunting, its preferred habitat is rocky hillsides spotted with mesquite and scrub, but this particular species appears to be more than usually adaptable; over its wide range it is remarkably constant and separate races are only recognized from Abyssinia.

Golden-breasted Bunting
(*Emberiza flaviventris*)

Description: $6\frac{1}{2}$ in. (165·1 mm.). The adult male has a black and white striped head, yellow throat and golden breast. Females are a duller form, and the head, where white in the male, is brownish white.

Like the previously mentioned species, this bird has often been accorded status in the *Fringillaria* genus, and occasionally is given the common name of Red-backed Yellow Bunting. It is primarily a South African bird but ranges northwards to Angola and Eritrea. It is very striking and attractive, but always seems to me to be an elegant and rather delicate bird, timid, and keeping to cover whenever possible; when it is searching the ground for food, it has a nervous crouching stance.

According to Skead, it has two songs, an all-the-year-round one which is simple and rather dull, and another, uttered in the breeding season, which is much more variable and accomplished. It was, no doubt, the former that made Butler describe it as insignificant and monotonous. The nest is built low down, practically on the ground, as with so many buntings.

It has a reputation for being delicate and difficult to acclimatize. This may well be true: often birds from South Africa do seem to be more difficult to begin with in Europe than races or allied species from the equatorial zone to the north. The Golden-breasted Bunting is a little more insectivorous than most, and the sudden change from natural diet to the hard seed and water of a dealer's cage must be something of a shock. Certainly, I recommend treating this species with some circumspection; be prepared to supply a few mealworms and/or maggots on a fairly regular basis. Some buntings will learn to take softfood, especially if mealworms are cut up over it, and in the case of this species I believe that it is well worth the effort. It has proved to be a good breeder, rearing several broods in a season, success being geared to supply of live food and to keeping one pair only to a flight to stop quarrelling.

Lark-like Bunting
(*Emberiza impetuani*)

Description: $5\frac{1}{2}$ in. (139·7 mm.). Heads of both sexes are buffy brown, streaked with olive brown; there is a faint superciliary and mesial stripe; above they are light brown with the streaks more pronounced; below is pinky buff, darkest on the breast. The sexes are alike, therefore, and juveniles resemble adults.

This rather inconspicuous little bunting looks very much like a pale buff version of almost any female bunting. It has the alternative common names of Pale Rock Bunting and Lark Bunting, since it is rather lark-like in its habits of running and crouching, and will jump up to snatch seed-heads from grasses. But it is also Canary-like in the way it rapidly settles again near by after having been disturbed. These birds come from South Africa and occasionally wander north into Rhodesia or Portuguese territory. It is a bird of dry open areas, particularly rocky ones, and is fond of hillsides. They are rare in captivity but, none the less, have been bred. They proved to be normal and satisfactory buntings in their behaviour and requirements. They began to feed seeds to their young at about ten days old. The breeding took place in a mixed aviary, some 20 ft. × 16 ft. (6·1 m. × 4·9 m.), with other buntings and waxbills, and no quarrelling or aggressive behaviour was noted.

Cape Bunting
(*Emberiza capensis*)

Description: *5–6 in. (127–152·4 mm.). Very similar to the European Rock Bunting, the grey of the head and the brown of the body being replaced by off-white; it has an olive-grey breast. The female closely resembles the male, but juveniles are duller and are streaked on breast and flanks. Two races that might be imported are* E. c. plowesi *and* E. c. smithersi. *The former resembles the nominate closely but is paler below, almost white, and is white on the throat. The latter is much darker than the nominate, more heavily streaked; below it is deep olive grey turning to light olive grey on the undertail-coverts.*

Sometimes called the Cape Rock Bunting, this rather dull-coloured and uninteresting-looking bird is occasionally available. It has a pleasant character, rather bold and confiding, and also is a reasonably accomplished songster. Its habitat preference is mainly rocky hillsides, but in fact it is found in many differing areas and at many altitudes in its native South Africa. It is nowhere near as dependent on insect food as its Golden-breasted cousin. Despite its undistinguished colouring, it is an excellent aviary subject and well worth the attention of a bunting enthusiast.

Crested Bunting
(*Melophus melanicterus*)

Description: *6½ in. (165·1 mm.). The adult male is glossy blue black with brown wings and tail, and a well-developed pointed crest. The female is brown above with pale edging to the feathers, whitish around the eyes, and yellowish white on the throat. She is a dull brown below with blackish streaks. Juvenile plumage is unrecorded.*

This bird is sometimes called Crested Black Bunting. It comes from India, south China, Upper Burma and Tenasserim. Its seasonal movements bring it to the lowlands, from 2,000 ft. (609·6 m.) down to sea-level, but it returns to the higher elevations to breed, where the male announces its presence with its loud whistling call from a vantage-point on top of a stone or tree. One very sweet note is a double call in which the bird seems to answer itself, creating the effect of two birds calling to each other with notes of an entirely different pitch. Caldwell describes watching a female busy building her nest. During her trips for building material, she uttered a beautiful warbling song otherwise never heard. These birds feed upon the ground in potato fields where they walk about like larks, or climb about the trunks of trees in search of insects, especially after small *cicadae*. The habits and conduct of this bird place it more properly with the larks than with the buntings.

Snow Bunting (*Plectrophenax nivalis*): adult male in fresh winter plumage

It is reputedly rather delicate in captivity, needing careful attention to begin with, being not terribly easy to acclimatize and needing rather more insects and/or insectile food than most buntings.

Snow Bunting
(*Plectrophenax nivalis*)

Description: *6½ in. (165·1 mm.). The adult male in summer plumage is white with the back, secondaries, wing-tips, centre and end of tail all black. In winter, the black is obscured by brown edges to new feathers. The head, breast and rump are also marked with brown. The female resembles the winter male with browner head. She is more regularly marked,* *is duller and the white below is dingy. Juveniles resemble females but are greyer. The tip of the bill is dark but not the black of the adult.*

The Snow Bunting is a romantic creature that captures the imagination of all bird-lovers, and aviculturists are no exception. It is a winter visitor to Britain, but a few pairs stay to breed each year in the Highlands of Scotland, usually above 3,000 ft. (914·4 m.). It is one of those handful of birds about which a whole book has been written. Despite its rather specialized way of life, it is in all respects a fairly typical bunting and, as if to make the point quite clear, has bred in aviaries from time to time. Breeding success to captive population level is high compared to most buntings, no doubt because, having paid a high price for a rarity, the owner is prepared to sacrifice more space, time and facilities to encourage breeding. It naturally nests in crevices and holes in rocky hillsides and a duplication of natural conditions is necessary; indeed, with most buntings plenty of close natural cover for the nest site is to be recommended. This species is also found in North America, breeding in parts of northern Canada and wintering as far south as the northern U.S.

The song is beautiful, having something of a Blackbird quality about it. The lovely black and white plumage is acquired in the spring without a moult, but after the breeding season there is a very heavy moult indeed, which, undoubtedly, calls for extra care in feeding.

Lapland Bunting
(*Calcarius lapponicus*)

Description: *5½–6½ in. (139·7–165·1 mm.). A male in summer plumage has a black head which is relieved by a fine white eyebrow stripe; the throat, breast and flanks are black; the remainder of the underparts are white; the hind neck is bright rufous, elsewhere it is rufous streaked with black. In winter, the black is nearly obscured with white. The female is a typical female bunting, but has a touch of bright rufous on the hind neck and has white underparts. She can also be told by the dark and irregular mesial stripe which extends to join the streaking on the sides of the breast and flanks. Juveniles are darker than adults; they lack the black on the crown, and are more heavily streaked below. The edges of body and head feathers are yellowish.*

This species is known as the Lap-

land Longspur in North America and, like the Snow Bunting, is circumpolar in its distribution. It has never been freely available, no doubt because it does not inhabit any of the traditional bird-trapping regions. Furthermore, being on the British List, it enjoys protection and can only be taken under Home Office Licence (like all other species in this chapter that appear on the British List). This may seem rather sad, because it is an attractive bird, said to be of a confiding nature and to have a delightful

Lapland Bunting
(*Calcarius lapponicus*)

and melodious song. One American says that a courting male will fly up to a height of about 30 ft. (9·1 m.) or so, then, setting its wings at an angle, will float down singing 'a liquid serenade'. I suspect that this is hyperbole brought on by the contrast of the song in an uncharitable country.

The Lapland Bunting's habitat is mossy heaths, open treeless areas and tundras, but it does not favour the barren extremes that attract the Snow Bunting. The food for the nestlings, and largely that of the adults when breeding, is mosquitoes, flies and moths. At all other times of the year the diet is composed of vegetable matter. They are excellent aviary birds, the cock particularly being lively and full of song. They spend a lot of time on the ground where the walking gait, furtive habit and rather cryptic colouring tend to make the bird rather inconspicuous.

AMERICAN SPARROWS

The buntings of North America are generally called sparrows, juncos or song sparrows. They are rare in aviculture since they are rigidly protected by U.S. law and few, if any, range south into Mexico or South America where they could be trapped. Being, in the main, sparrow-looking, I have no doubt that most of those trapped in Mexico are eaten. As far as our limited experience of them as avicultural subjects goes, they appear to be pretty typical buntings, and should be treated just like the *Emberizae*. One can, no doubt, contribute to general bird knowledge by writing about any experience with them.

Harris's Sparrow
(*Zonotrichia querula*)

Description: $7\frac{1}{2}$ in. (*190·5 mm.*). *Adults have a black crown, face and bib with grey on the side of the head; the body above is brown streaked with dark brown to black; below it is greyish, warmer on the flanks and sides of the breast, which are streaked. In winter the crown becomes grey. The sexes are alike. Juveniles have a cinnamon colour on the top and sides of the head, which is streaked blackish. The bib is vestigial.*

If I understand my National Geographic book correctly, Harris's Sparrow was discovered and named in 1834, but it was not until 1931 that a Mr. Sutton discovered a nest in Canada. It was placed on the ground, concealed by a shrub, and contained four eggs. This is interesting because, in the same year, W. Shore Baily bred the species in one of his aviaries in England. In his notes, he says that the first nest was discovered in 1907 but admits that no eggs were placed in a collection until 1931; these were his.

This is the only reference that I have of this bunting being kept by any aviculturist. It is interesting to note, however, that there were four birds in the aviary and that they appeared to cohabit without any trouble. Also, the aviary was planted and the nest was concealed in the base of a clump of nettles and tall grasses. The young were fed on spiders and other insects collected by the parents, and some mealworms, but were very quickly weaned on to a seed diet. It is the largest of the North American buntings, about the size of our Corn Bunting, and is unlikely to be imported as it is restricted to parts of the U.S. and Canada.

White-crowned Sparrow
(*Zonotrichia leucophrys*)

Description: $5\frac{1}{2}$–$7\frac{1}{2}$ in. (*139·7–190·5 mm.*); *length varies according to the race. The top of the crown is white, also superciliaries; there is a strong black stripe between the superciliaries and the crown; above, it is streaked with black; there are two thin white wing-bars; below, it is greyish. The sexes are alike. Juveniles lack the black and white striping, being brown and greyish.*

This North American bunting is sometimes referred to in the literature as White-crowned or White-eyebrowed Sparrow, or Song Sparrow. It migrates south for the winter and reaches Mexico, from whence the odd individual is sent to Europe. There is nothing particularly outstanding about the species other than its interest as a comparative rarity in captivity. The black and white striped head is fluffed out and the crest produced as the highlight of the display of the male. They feed and nest in bushy thickets. They were bred as long ago as 1904 by David Seth-Smith.

Lark Bunting
(*Calamospiza melanocorys*)

Description: $5\frac{1}{2}$–$7\frac{1}{2}$ in. (139·7–190·5 mm.). *The male in breeding plumage is black with large white wing-patches. In winter plumage it resembles the sparrowy female but retains sufficient black feathering on the throat and lower abdomen to be clearly identified. The female has white wing-patches that serve to distinguish it from other female buntings. Juveniles resemble the female but lack a clearly distinctive wing pattern.*

A pretty and distinctive bunting that ranges from the Rockies down to Texas but, in winter, wanders further south into Mexico. It is a bird of fairly open grassland. A fair amount of wild bird trapping is done in Mexico, but the bird trade is badly organized and most of any haul goes straight into the pot; only brightly coloured or celebrated song birds are saved for the market, the cause of much frustration to aviculturists who can buy only males and are thus unable to breed their birds.

The male Lark Bunting is, in fact, a fine singer, with a loud and varied song of musical notes, trills, buzzes and single notes often delivered in a jerky ascending song-flight. The nest is made on the ground under cover such as an overhanging plant, or tussock of grass.

Rufous-collared Sparrow
(*Zonotrichia capensis*)

Description: *6 in. (152·4 mm.). It is a typical American bunting, being brown above with a striped head, grey crown, black stripes, white superciliaries, black ear-coverts with white markings and rufous-orange patch on each side of the upper breast from which it derives its common name; the throat is white, the breast is grey and the underparts are white. Females are very similar, but are a little larger. Juveniles differ in having the underparts thickly spotted with dusky; the crown and back are rufous, streaked with black.*

The Rufous-collared Sparrow or Andean Sparrow is a bird of scrub and pasture-land, and is typical in its behaviour and needs. In fact, ranging over most parts of that continent from southern Mexico to the tip of South America, it suggests a fairly adaptable species. The male has a pleasant song, and becomes quite territorial when breeding. I found some of these birds in a pet shop once in Las Palmas and was immediately struck by their attractive colouring; the white eyebrow stripe and bright orange neck-patch accentuate a *svelte* and neatly groomed bird. We had three of them, two that I took to be males and one female which was slightly larger, and a little duller on the crown and back. They are very lively and alert birds, always on the move, and decidedly better off in an aviary than a cage.

It is occasionally imported and was bred in England around the turn of the century. Butler described it as being very pugnacious in the breeding season. The nest is generally placed on the ground, but if not is rarely more than a foot or two above it.

It has been bred by Mr. Murray, who found it to be a perfectly typical bunting except for its breeding behaviour, which was very secretive and nervous, and the parent birds defended their local nest area and nestlings with ferocious vigour. When several pairs were kept together, no breeding took place; but when separated, one pair to a flight (but sharing with other species), they settled down to breed. Several other breedings are on record from 1907 onwards. They were successfully bred some fifteen years ago when insects did not seem to play a major role in the diet, but they were available and must have been taken. A young male from the first brood was singing and chasing other occupants of the aviary around while its parents were busy with the second round. They have been successfully bred in a 4 ft. (1·2 m.) flight-cage.

Considerable confusion surrounds the nomenclature of this species, so much so that it is worth going into detail. From southern Mexico southwards, there is only one species of *Zonotrichia*, and that is *capensis*, normally known as the Rufous-collared Sparrow. This species is synonymous with *Z. pileata*, and where this latter scientific name is used the common name given is often Pileated Sparrow or Pileated Song Sparrow. In Chile the species is commonly called Chincol, but in Bolivia, Argentina and elsewhere it is generally called Chingolo, hence the commonly used English name of Chingolo Song Sparrow.

There are several clearly marked races of *Z. capensis*, another contributing factor to the confusion no doubt. The most likely race to be imported is the nominate, which ranges from Central America to Venezuela and northern Brazil. The Southern Rufous-collared Sparrow, *Z. c. australis*, is noticeable by its larger size ($6\frac{1}{2}$ in./165·1 mm.) and lack of lateral black lines on the crown; this race is probably the Chingolo Song Sparrow of some dealers. The Antofagasta Rufous-collared Sparrow, *Z. c. antofagastae*, is the smallest race ($5\frac{1}{2}$ in./139·7 mm.) and may be distinguished mainly by its size, having very broad black lines on the crown, and yellow-ochre barring across the undertail-coverts. There are probably another half dozen valid races, but I am sure that only a colour series plus measurement details would suffice to describe them all.

Fox Sparrow
(Passerella iliaca)

Description: $6\frac{1}{2}$–$7\frac{1}{2}$ in. (165·1–190·5 mm.). *The sexes are alike, but there are two distinct races. The eastern race has rufous upperparts, streaked with grey on top and on the back of the head and mantle; there are two slight white wing-bars; below, it is white, very heavily streaked with brown, a spot forming in the centre of the breast. It is similar to the Song Sparrow* (Melospiza melodia) *but is much larger. The western race is much darker above and not streaked. Below, the streaking is blackish to deep-chocolate.*

A correspondent once wrote to me describing an unidentified bird in his collection; it was finch-like, dark brown, sang well and clearly, and was distinguished by a habit of scratching with both feet at the same time. Eventually, we managed to identify it as a Fox Sparrow that had undoubtedly darkened over the years of living in captivity on an artificial diet. Melanism is not an unknown phenomenon in cagebirds. The species in which it seems most common is the Avadavat. In Spain, I have seen several melanistic Goldfinches, and I well remember a pair of Java Sparrows at the London Zoo that were almost totally black. It is not a well-understood process. Whatever the case, however, it is confusing when one comes across it in a species never seen before.

The Fox Sparrow is a fine songbird, ranking high among the Song Sparrows in this respect. They feed by kicking away leaves and vegetable debris, looking for seeds in the undergrowth of woodland edges. Small flocks move around in this way in the winter. It is said to be common in dense coniferous thickets and deciduous brush and is easily recognizable by the heavily streaked undersides. The sexes are alike, but there is considerable local variation in colouring and size of bill. With cautionary riders about possible aggressiveness when breeding, this bird seems to be a very interesting aviary subject.

Rufous-sided Towhee
(*Pipilo erythrophthalmus*)

Description: *7–9 in. (177·8–228·6 mm.); depending on race. Adult male has black head and throat, black back (with white spots on back, scapulars and wing-coverts on western birds, but with white spots restricted to tertiaries and base of primaries on eastern birds), rufous sides of body,*

white belly, long black tail white at tip. The female has head, throat and back brown. In most races the eye is red, but birds from Florida have white eyes. The bill is black. The race from Mexico has an olive back which contrasts strongly with the black head. Some twenty-four races are recognized. The juvenile bird is brown heavily streaked with dark brown below.

Anyone looking through the literature of North American seed-eating birds cannot fail to be interested in the buntings known as towhees. The appetite thus whetted, one is all the more disappointed by the total lack of mention of them in the avicultural literature. However, I came across a reference to the successful breeding of Oregon Towhees in 1955 by Mr. Payne. These birds were clearly such ideal aviary subjects, and bred so well, that they deserve a place in this book at least. Identifying *Pipilo* spp. is not very easy, but I soon traced this particular bird as a race of the Spotted Towhee, *Pipilo maculatus oreganus*, but then discovered that Spotted Towhees are now considered to be merely western forms of the Rufous-sided Towhee. Old American checklists give a distinct common name for every race of a species, but in the case of the present bird even the most ardent nomenclator of retailers would shudder at twenty-four alternatives!

Mr. Payne's birds bred successfully on several occasions, building a nest on the ground in typical towhee fashion. The nest was a skimpy affair but healthy young were reared, almost entirely on mealworms and gentles. There is no mention of any aggressive behaviour at all.

Slate-coloured Junco
(*Junco hyemalis*)

Description: $5\frac{1}{2}$ in. (*139·7 mm.*). *The sexes are alike. In the adult the plumage is slate grey, changing to a clean white belly and undertail-coverts; the outermost tail-feathers are white. It is, in fact, a very attractive bird. The juvenile is similar but has a pink flush to the flanks.*

We rarely see Juncos in Europe and I must admit to having no experience with them at all. However, a friend of mine once had some Slate-coloured Juncos. They turned out to be fairly typical and undistinguished buntings from an avicultural point of view. It is a bird of varied habitat and wide range, and can be found breeding in conifer forests in northern Alaska, right across North America to roadside scrub in the east. In the U.S., it is mostly only a winter visitor where flocks can be seen foraging in harvested fields, scrub and woodland margins.

Diuca Finch
(*Diuca diuca*)

Description: 7 in. (*177·8 mm.*). *The adult male is grey above; lores are black, sides of face and throat white; breast and flanks greyish and belly white with a spot of chestnut; undertail-coverts are white lines with chestnut; tail black. Females are similar but browner.*

These are pleasant and amiable birds, but rather unimpressively coloured. They soon settle down to life in cage or aviary, and prove to be rather sparrow-like in habit and behaviour. The country of origin is Chile and regrettably they are not often available. The Diuca Finch has bred in captivity. It is not a difficult subject to maintain in good condition.

Diuca Finch
(*Diuca diuca*)

Regarding diet, they are very open in their food preferences, taking almost anything that is offered, but will not rear their young unless an adequate supply of live food is to hand. They make a cup-shaped nest of rootlets, grasses, etc., but seem quite disposed to accept a half-open box. My only Diuca lives happily with some buntings and a Yellowish Finch, and is perfectly peaceable. It has a loud and very distinctive call-note, and a pleasant warbling little song.

CRESTED FINCHES

This is a small group of very attractive little birds that can be found in the northern parts of South America. They all have a loose crest, and carry red in their plumage, sometimes to a great degree. They have normal bunting requirements but do have a fondness for fruit, particularly when breeding.

Crimson Finch
(*Rhodospingus cruentus*)

Description: *About 5 in. (127 mm.). The head, back, wings and tail are a rich velvety black; chin, throat and upper breast are bright red, with a small crest of bright red on top of the head; underparts are a less intense red, fading to orange on the abdomen. The females resemble female sparrows and show no trace of crimson.*

Known in European cagebird circles more normally as the Rhodospingus Finch, but also listed as Purple-crowned or Ecuadorian Crowned Finch, this most attractive little bird is a very popular cagebird. It comes from equatorial South America and has been described as a breeding bird from Ecuador. It appears to be a fairly typical bunting in its behaviour and living patterns, apart from having an accelerated breeding system. It is found chiefly in scrub and bushy areas in preference to thick cover. It nests in low cover, building a large, untidy nest. The natural breeding season is remarkably short and timed to begin with the first flush of vegetation, all the Crimson Finches in the area going to nest simultaneously. The eggs are incubated for only eleven days and the young fledge only eight days later! The entire cycle, therefore, lasts only about three weeks, a remarkable adaptation to ecological limitations.

It is an excellent cage- and aviary-subject, being easy to cater for in most respects. It is much better to provide a roomy, planted aviary if breeding is intended, or a normal one if the birds are to be given a flight to themselves. They are fairly territorial when breeding and, if it is intended to breed them in a mixed collection, this should ideally contain only birds of the kind of constitution and colouring that will minimize possibilities of conflict. I would not regard them as really troublesome or aggressive birds. In addition to all the normal diet of softfood, seed and live food, Rhodospingus Finches may take extra fruit and canary-rearing food when breeding.

Pileated Finch
(*Coryphospingus pileatus*)

Description: *5½ in. (139·7 mm.). The adult male is grey above and lighter grey below, whitest on the throat, and has a scarlet crest edged with black. Females are similar, but there is a more bluish tone to the grey upperparts, and they lack the crest.*

Pileated Finches are very similar in habit and habitat to the Rhodospingus. They are cheerful and active birds and soon gain the affection of their keeper by the confidence they place in him, no doubt inspired by the mealworm tin. The male raises his crest readily at the slightest stimulus. They will breed fairly willingly, but especially in a planted flight, as they much prefer to nest in a patch of good cover. Incubation and fledging times are short, but the main difficulty with these birds appears to be with diet at a few days old because not all adults will accept mealworms or gentles for rearing, preferring smaller insects. In this case, one will just have to work a little harder,

Black-crested Finch (*Lophospingus pusillus*): the sexes are alike

supplying smaller mealworms, chopping them up and sprinkling over egg-food, etc. They are rather aggressive when young are in the nest.

Red-crested Finch
(*Coryphospingus cristatus*)

Description: *About 5½ in. (139·7 mm.). The adult male is reddish brown above and crimson on the rump and uppertail-coverts; crown is black on forehead and this extends along each side of a scarlet crest; throat, breast and abdomen are red. Females are similar, but less bright in colour. This is the same species that Haverschmidt lists as* C. cucullatus.

This is a charming, as well as a very attractive, bird. It is not imported very often, but is usually well in demand when it does appear. Apparently, it has been hybridized with a canary in an attempt to breed a red pigment into the latter. If this is true, it must cast some doubt as to whether the Crested Finches should be classed as buntings at all, or whether they should be considered as proper finches.

They are very lively and energetic and need a roomy cage or aviary in which to keep really fit. They are peaceful birds and willing breeders and have been bred successfully in the company of other birds, including others of the same species when a certain amount of chasing took place. In this case, I think that the breeding result might have been better, had there only been one pair of Red-crested Finches in the aviary.

Mr. Tielens noted some very interesting behaviour when his birds bred. The male would sit in longish grass, 'hidden but for his head'. He would open his bright red crest wide and utter a soft warbling note. The red apparently attracted a lot of insects which he jumped up and caught with unfailing accuracy.

Black-crested Finch
(*Lophospingus pusillus*)

Description: *5 in. (127 mm.). The adult male has a black crest, white superciliaries, and a black line through the eye. The upperparts are grey, blackish on the wings and tail; below is white with a black spot on the throat and a grey flush to the flanks. Females are similar, but have grey crests, and lack the throat-spot.*

This bird used to be called Pygmy Cardinal, and still is by some retailers, but now it is generally known as the Black-crested Finch – ironic, since it is a bunting. It is frequently available but is not often in demand because it is mainly black, grey and off-white. Its only distinction is its fine cardinal-like crest. It has a reputation for being aggressive in a mixed collection. Odd birds that I have kept have been peaceful enough and have lived cheerfully in the company of other birds.

I once saw an odd male in a Crystal Palace cage in a famous pet shop. It was obviously unwell and very unhappy, hunched up and seemingly trying hard to ignore the multitude of Zebra Finches and other noisy, lively birds around it. On inquiring the price, the retailer gave me the bird as a gift. It soon pulled round under better conditions and responded remarkably well to being released in a planted aviary. Within a week or two, it was as lively and as rumbustious as any Zebra Finch ever was, and gave me much pleasure.

The Black-crested Finch has been bred regularly for many years now, when it has proved to be fairly argumentative but not so much as to make isolation a necessity. Placing a true pair in a flight to themselves will, of course, make life easier for all concerned, and allow the proper regulation of live food, etc. The sexes are alike, but females may be told apart from the males as they lack the throat spot of the latter.

SAFFRON FINCHES

The Saffron or *Sicalis* Finches (sometimes *Sycalis*) from South America form a genus of eleven species. The Saffron Finch (*S. flaveola*) is the largest, most richly coloured with its orange-suffused yellow body, and is the most bunting-like. One of the smaller species, the Yellowish Finch (*S. citrina*), is sufficiently finch-like to appear to be a fairly typical serin. The larger species can be aggressive, especially when breeding, and should be treated just like typical buntings. The smaller ones are delightful in mixed collections or as individually housed pairs. Most of them seem to have been imported from time to time and, with the exception of the Saffron Finch, seem to cause the dealers some confusion in identification, and common names seem highly interchangeable. When in doubt, the retailer will resort to 'South American Wild Canary'! They are all particularly fond of millet seeds.

Saffron Finch (*Sicalis flaveola flaveola*): female above, male below

Saffron Finch
(*Sicalis flaveola*)

Description: *6 in. (152·4 mm.). Adult males have bright orange foreheads and crowns; sides of head are yellow; they are greenish yellow above, faintly streaked, clear yellow below. Females are similar to the males but duller; the yellow is less bright, the orange weaker; they are brownish above and greyish on the throat. Juveniles are like females but are streaked above and whitish below, yellow on the breast, flanks and undertail-coverts.*

The Saffron Finch is sometimes

called Brazilian Saffron Finch. It has been advertised in the past in small numbers, and seems to appear on the lists every year with unfailing regularity. It ranges over most of tropical South America. The first Saffron Finch that I ever saw was offered to me as a lad by a wily old Canary-fancier, who had been attempting to improve the colouring of his own stock by cross-breeding. I felt that a Saffron Finch would more likely become cross with a Canary than cross-breed with it. Claims of successful hybrids have been made, but I have never seen a substantiated report, and I doubt that it is possible. It is known as Wild Canary in Jamaica, where it was introduced around 1823 and, in fact, has been advertised as Jamaican Wild Canary on occasion. Although its common name is Finch, Butler considered the term Sparrow to be more appropriate, considering its habit and eggs. It certainly seems to be a fairly ubiquitous species, found in parks, gardens, farms, town, forest and bush, appearing to be somewhere midway between a Chaffinch and a House Sparrow in its behaviour.

It happily adopts old nests of other species, will accept a hole, or build its

Pelzeln's Saffron Finch (*Sicalis flaveola pelzelni*): female on the left, male on the right

own cup-shaped nest of twiglets and mosses. In an aviary, it will take to a half-open box or a Canary nest-pan. It is a willing breeder, once settled into suitable quarters, and is a good parent, rearing on a diet of seeds with a few mealworms and maggots. This is certainly a species which could fairly easily be established in confinement, and a determined breeder, with a range of small flights and a few pairs, could quickly establish a sound, self-perpetuating strain.

Saffron Finches are not aggressive, irritable birds, but on the other hand certainly have a tendency towards being rumbustious and rather bullying. The two sexes engage in a lively courtship. When breeding, they are not suitable birds for crowded aviaries or mixed collections in small aviaries.

Pelzeln's Saffron Finch
(*Sicalis flaveola pelzelni*)

Description: *5½–6 in. (139·7–152·4 mm.). The adult male is olive green above streaked with black; wings brown with yellow edging to feathers, rump grey; forehead is rich orange, and rest of body streaked slightly on sides of breast and flanks. Females are slightly smaller, browner above, more noticeably marked on the sides of the body and the throat is white.*

This is a race that is imported in a small quantity each year. It is a little smaller than the Saffron Finch and is told by the blackish streaking on its flanks. It will breed freely with *flaveola*, and can be accorded the same treatment in every way. It is an ideal aviary bird, but is said to be lethargic in a cage.

Orange-fronted Finch
(*Sicalis colombiana*)

Description: *4½–5 in. (114·3–127 mm.). Adult male has orange forehead; back, wings and tail bright olive yellow and underparts bright yellow. Females are greyish brown above, tinged with olive and faintly streaked; wings and tail are brown; below is dull white.*

Found in eastern Brazil and eastward to Peru, and also on Trinidad, this bird is smaller than the Saffron Finch. It resembles the latter but is a little darker, and might be advertised as Little or Lesser Saffron Finch. It has been given a common name of Orange-fronted Grassfinch and is recorded as inhabiting the grassy banks of the river Orinoco in Vichada.

Citrine Finch
(*Sicalis citrina*)

Description: *4–4½ in. (101·6–114·3 mm.). The head and lower back of the adult male are olive yellow; back is greyish olive broadly streaked with dusky; wings and tail are brown, and there is a distinct white patch on the inner web of the outer pair of tail-feathers. Females are like female sparrows but olivaceous on the rump and tinged yellow below. Smaller white tail-patches can be seen.*

This species is more olive-coloured above and is more heavily streaked with brown than the Saffron Finch. The female is browner and much less colourful. It comes from Guyana and Venezuela, where it inhabits open country in tropical and subtropical zones. I have no experience of the bird but believe that it is a typical *Sicalis* in avicultural terms. It may also be listed as Citrine Grassfinch, or Stripe-tailed Yellow Finch.

Yellowish Finch
(*Sicalis luteola*)

Description: *4½–5 in. (114·3–127 mm.). Adult male is pale olive on head and upper surfaces, streaked with blackish brown on the back and wings; superciliaries yellow; throat pale yellowish buff; rest of underparts yellow. Females are similar but browner above and weaker yellow below. Juvenile resembles female but is rather more noticeably streaked.*

This is a delightful little bird, irregularly imported but definitely available from time to time. It has been listed as Little Saffron Finch, Yellow Grassfinch, Field Saffron Finch, Misto Seed Finch, Yellow Finch, Grassland Yellow Finch, and Wild Canary, but it is under the last name that it has been most frequently advertised. In some books one may find it given the scientific name *S. arvensis*. It comes from Brazil and ranges southwards to the Argentine, Bolivia and Chile. It is rather similar in character and behaviour to a Grey Singing Finch, but in appearance it is rather like a European Serin (*Serinus serinus*), and I have no doubt that its serin-like qualities are the reason for it usually being called Wild Canary in the trade. In a planted aviary, it will rear young on the kind of diet given to Canaries when breeding, catching enough tiny insects to tide the young over the first few days. The Yellowish Finch enjoys the reputation of being the gentlest and best of the genus for a mixed collection. In a roomy flight this may well be, but I have kept it with buntings and sparrows, birds noticeably bigger, and under moments of stress there is no doubt that the Yellowish Finch can be quite tough. I would be inclined to treat it with the same respect as a *Sporophila*.

Citron-headed Yellow Finch
(*Sicalis luteocephala*)

Description: *6 in. (152·4 mm.). Adult male has forecrown and sides of head olive yellow; hind crown and nape grey; back brownish grey; throat, lores, around eye, and belly white (some lemon-yellowish wash around face); breast and flanks lightly streaked with greyish and olivaceous yellow; undertail-coverts lemon yellow; wings and tail dusky, edged bright yellow. Female very similar, but grey and yellow on head less clean. Juvenile resembles female.*

Citron-headed Yellow-finch
(*Sicalis luteocephala*)

These birds are not easy to identify and it took me many weeks to be sure that some *Sicalis* that I bought from a dockside dealer in Las Palmas were in fact *luteocephala*. De Schauensee is not particularly helpful, in fact it is the only member of the genus that has a white belly. According to De Schauensee it is a Bolivian bird, but according to the dealer that I bought mine from it comes from Brazil and is called Brazilian Canary, or

Brasileño. In a crowded dealer's cage they clearly had a penchant for plucking, and a lone Yellowish Finch in the same cage was plucked bald from forehead to rump: no doubt being smaller it somehow invited this action. Mine have since shown a tendency to pluck unless kept in a large flight-cage. They are very peaceful and show no signs of aggression to the other birds. I have tried them on every variety of seed and have found that they take about 90% small yellow millet, and they adore mealworms.

GRASSQUITS

The Grassquits are a small genus of South and Central American birds that have, at some time or another, been placed in the Fringillidae and the Ploceidae. If I have erred by following the current fashion of placing them in the Emberizidae, I hope that I shall be forgiven. They are small birds, about 4 in. (101·6 mm.) long, generally olive green above and greyish below. Their faces are usually black or blackish with yellow or orange markings. They are excellent aviary subjects and lend themselves well to domesticity. They have the great advantage of not being dependent upon live insects when rearing their young, feeding them almost entirely on regurgitated seeds.

Cuban Finch

(*Tiaris canora*)

Description: *Adult male 3½–4 in. (88·9–101·6 mm.). Head is black, graduating into olive green on the mantle and remaining upper surfaces, which are tinged with brown, with olive on the lower breast; there is a bright yellow crescent marking starting above the eye that continues around the face and broadens across the breast to almost meet on the breast. Female is duller, being brownish on the face, greyish on the crown, and having the yellow paler.*

The best-known member of the group, and known as Melodious Finch or Melodious Grassquit in America, it is now living on the reputation gained when it used to be frequently imported. Nowadays, it is rarely seen and most of the few offered are either aviary bred or the remnants of some strain. A true and compatible pair, settled in, can be relied upon to breed with regularity and efficiency; they have bred in cages on occasion. The natural nest is a domed structure, placed low down, and with an entrance tunnel low down at the side. The male is a belligerent husband and spends most of its time chasing rivals, and will not hesitate to take on a bird twice its size. The question of belligerency is very interesting in this species and I can give three clear, positive, but quite distinct examples: (a) colony breeding with some waxbills and mannikins present when lots of bickering and chasing took place but no blood was spilt; (b) aggressive male attacking anything within a few yards of its nesting area; (c) aggressive male being so obsessed with attacking other Cuban males in adjoining aviaries as to ignore nesting responsibilities altogether. As a generalization, I suggest treating them with some circumspection, and since advice in the literature is so varied, ranging from 'they are good colony breeders' to 'keep one pair to one flight', my advice is to treat every pair as individuals whose temper must be sampled and not divined. That it is a species suitable for domesticity seems to be undeniable. Silver placed it at the top of his personal list of foreign birds that could be easily domesticated, like the Zebra Finch, with little effort but rather more dedication.

Olive Finch
(*Tiaris olivacea*)

Description: *4½ in. (114·3 mm.). Adult male has golden-yellow chin and eyebrow mark, the rest of the head being black graduating to greyish olive on the body. Females are duller and have much less yellow-orange marking on the face and belly, and undertail-coverts are buff.*

Sometimes listed as Yellow-faced Grassquit, this is the most commonly imported of the group. It is found throughout Central America to Venezuela and the Greater Antilles, showing a preference for lush pasture-land. It is a cheerful but not very accomplished song-bird, and males will gather to hold 'singing contests'. The male will sit near the nest and sing regularly, warning off and chasing away other males. However, the aggression is quite ritualized and several pairs can safely be kept together and be bred on a colony system. Both sexes build the nest, which

is a domed affair built in a tussock of long grass or in thick herbage very near to the ground. They are not very dependent on live food when rearing and will probably rear on seeding grasses and egg food, etc., but I always offer a few mealworms, particularly if the aviary is not planted. It is a delightful and easy-to-keep little bird, perfect for a mixed collection, or specialization. Beginners should be aware that 'Cuban Olive Finch' refers to this species and not the Cuban Finch.

Four races of the Olive Finch (*Tiaris olivacea*): 1. *T. o. pusilla*; 2. *T. o. intermedia*; 3. *T. o. olivacia*; 4. *T. o. coryi*

Black-faced Grassquit
(*Tiaris bicolor*)

Description: *4–4½ in. (101·6–114·3 mm.). Black head graduating into olivaceous on entire body; belly whitish tinge. Female is a duller, drabber version.*

This is a tame and confiding little

bird that has a strong but not particularly sweet song and is rather sparrow-like in its habits. It looks very much like a dull Olive Finch that lacks any yellow on the face. It is common throughout Puerto Rico, the West Indies, Venezuela and Colombia. It is imported on the odd occasion and might have been bred, but no reports have been published. It seems to be a typical little grassquit and should be treated just like the Cuban and Olive Finches. I have seen it advertised as Black-faced Cuban Finch.

Jacarini Finch
(*Volatinia jacarini*)

Description: *4–4½ in. (101·6–114·3 mm.). Adult male is blackish, with a blue gloss on the head and upper parts. The female is brownish as are* *young males, but the latter will distinguish themselves by their song.*

This bird is known in ornithological circles as the Blue-black Grassquit and is distributed from Mexico to northern Argentina. They are lively and persistent singers, and will frequently combine the song with a dance which will take the male a foot or more up from his perch. Unlike the other grassquits, the nest is not domed but is a small shallow cup made of fine dead grasses. It is usually placed on or very near to the ground and the whole breeding cycle is very short; incubation is ten to twelve days and the young fledge in nine to ten days. It is a charming little bird which, whilst not being very beautiful and lacking a pretty song, is to be recommended as an excellent aviary subject.

SEED-EATERS

In the New World tropics, particularly in northern South America, there are a large number of small (about 4 in./101·6 mm. long) seed-eating birds known collectively as Seed-eaters. Most of these, some twenty-seven species, are in the genus *Sporophila*, and all have compressed conical bills, many looking like miniature Hawfinches, and some bills look distinctly parrot-like. They are very difficult to identify. They should not be confused with the larger African serins (*Serinus* spp.) which are frequently called seed-eaters by ornithologists and aviculturists alike. As cage and aviary subjects they are easy and undemanding; many species have been bred and, given reasonable conditions, there is no reason why any true pair should not become a breeding pair. On the other hand, they have little to distinguish themselves other than sometimes a pleasant song. Incidentally, in most species both sexes will sing.

They live almost exclusively on seeds, rearing their young on regurgitated green grass seeds, showing little interest in insects or fruit. Like grassquits they will normally take only millet seeds. When rearing they seem to need only seeds, hard and soaked, fresh seeding grasses, and they may be persuaded to take some soft food. Some pairs will take ant pupae, small mealworms and other insect food, and since diets in captivity are so rarely perfect, such luxury should not be denied them.

Sporophilae seed-eaters can be very pugnacious towards each other, especially during the breeding season, and if the risk of serious fighting is to be avoided, they should definitely be placed one pair to a flight.

White-throated Finch
(*Sporophila albigularis*)

Description: *4 in. (101·6 mm.). Adult male grey above with black head, white bib and black band across an otherwise white breast and underparts. Female is a dull greyish brown and rather drab. It is very similar to the White-collared Seed-eater, but the white of the throat does not surround the collar. The bill is yellow horn.*

This little bird comes from northeast Brazil. They have bred several times in captivity and have proved to be easy enough to look after, bringing up their young on a fairly simple diet. The nest is a shallow and flimsy little cup placed in a shrub or low tree. The young fledge in eleven to twelve days. The male is a pretty songster, but has been recorded as being very pugnacious in some instances.

White-collared Seed-eater
(*Sporophila torqueola*)

Description: *4 in. (101·6 mm.). Adult male has chin and throat buff; sides of neck white; lower breast cinnamon fading to white on undertail-coverts; rump cinnamon; remainder of plumage including band across chest black. Female is brownish olive above and yellowish below.*

1. Bluish Finch (*Sporophila coerulescens*); 2. Tobago Finch (*S. americana*); 3. White-collared Seed-eater (*S. torqueola*)

This little bird is the only member of the genus to range as far north as the U.S., but only as far as the lower valley of the Rio Grande in Texas. Birds from North America lack the white neck-patch, but birds from Central America may have the chin black. The typical bird from South America is the one described and illustrated. The species, which may be called Black-banded Finch, or Sharpe's Seed-eater, was first imported to England in 1895, but has appeared irregularly since then.

Lined Finch
(*Sporophila lineola*)

Description: *4 in. (101·6 mm.). Adult male glossy blue black above, including head and throat; there is usually, but not always, a white streak on top of the head; cheeks white, breast and underparts white also. Female is greyish olive above and paler beneath.*

Also called Lined Seed-eater, this bird is black above with lower back and rump grey. It has a white line over the middle of the crown from the base of the bill, white cheeks, black throat and is olive brown below. The female has olive brown in place of the male's black. It is found over most of northern South America. It is an easy bird in both cage and aviary and can be established in domesticity with little effort. It is a pleasant songster.

Lesson's Seed-eater
(*Sporophila bouvronoides*)

Description: *4 in. (101·6 mm.). Male glossy blue black above, including head and throat; breast and underparts white. Female greyish olive above and paler below.*

Generally called Black-headed Lined Finch in aviculture, this is rather a *non sequitur* since, if it is black-headed, it cannot be lined! In all other respects it is identical to the Lined Finch, but the females are indistinguishable. Apparently they range over similar habitat, but do not interbreed. Like the Lined Finch, it is a good and pretty songbird.

Chestnut-breasted Seed-eater
(*Sporophila castaneiventris*)

Description: *4 in. (101·6 mm.). Male is blue grey all over apart from a line of rufous chestnut from the chin that spreads down to form a patch on the breast. Female is olivaceous above and ochreous below.*

This bird is also listed as Chestnut-bellied Seed-eater, or even Chestnut Seed-eater which is misleading, since it has more grey than chestnut. It is a tiny little creature, quite waxbill-like in its delicacy. It is more a bird of open wasteland and pasture than many other seed-eaters that favour more lush grassland. It is not often imported. I had a pair for a while, but was not able to give them breeding quarters and soon passed them on. They were gentle and inoffensive birds and, like most seed-eaters, would do well in a planted aviary with a few waxbills and grassfinches for company.

Variable Seed-eater
(*Sporophila aurita*)

Description: *4 in. (101·6 mm.). Adult male mostly black with white rump, small white patch on each wing; white half-collar which is narrowest at the throat and broadest on side of neck; belly white shading to grey on flanks and undertail-coverts, banded with black. Female is olive above; paler olive on breast; buff on belly and undertail-coverts. Juveniles resemble adult female.*

This species may be known as Hick's Seed-eater. There is a black phase in which the white neck-patch is much smaller, and the rump is black. The Black Seed-eater, *S. corvina*, is almost certainly a race of *aurita*. Another race, *opthalmica*, has the chin and throat white, joining the neck-patch, and the white of the belly is much more extensive. The species ranges throughout much of the Central American peninsula and is a common and well-known bird in all kinds of open, bushy or cultivated areas where grasses abound; they often swarm along grassy roadsides and in the larger clearings, where they form loose flocks often in the

Three males of the Variable Seed-eater (*Sporophila aurita*): top, *S. a. aurita*; middle, *S. a. opthalmica*; bottom, black phase of *S. a. aurita*, not to be confused with *S. a. corvina*

company of other small seed-eating birds (*Tiaris*, *Sporophila*, etc.). I was lucky enough to keep a pair of Variable Seed-eaters for a season a few years ago, and placed them in a 20-ft. (6·1-m.) planted flight with a few other, larger birds of various kinds. The male sang quite cheerfully a great deal, and occasionally chased the female about. They were bold birds that came out into the open freely. In addition to the small seeds which they salvaged from the lawn they also pecked at the buds and leaves on the apple trees in the flight and, although they were the smallest birds present, were the most destructive in this respect. According to Skutch the song is inferior to that of *torqueola*. The young are apparently fed a mixture of soft green seeds and insects. The only breeding record I have is at San Diego Zoo in 1952, where the birds built a nest of dry grasses in a wooden box.

Collared Finch
(*Sporophila collaris*)

Description: *4½–5 in. (101·6–127 mm.). Adult male has white spot at sides of forehead, irregular white crescent below eye, remainder of top, sides and back of head black; nape and mantle black, wings and tail black with two buffish wing-bars, lower back greyish; rump white tinged with ochre; chin, throat and sides of neck white, bar across breast black, rest of underparts buff to cinnamon. Female brown above, paler brown below, wings greyish brown.*

The nominate race of this bird, *S. c. collaris*, has been called the White-breasted Finch. A slightly smaller race, *S. c. cucullata*, is distinguished by having a bold white spot between the lower mandible and the cheek; it

Seed-eaters, *Sporophila* spp: 1a. Tobago Finch (*S. americana*); 1b. *S. americana murallae*; 2a. Variable Seed-eater (*S. aurita*); 2b. *S. aurita ophthalmica*; 3a. Rusty-collared Seed-eater (*S. collaris*); 3b. *S. collaris cucullata*; 4. Half-white Finch (*S. leucoptera*); 5. White-throated Seed-eater (*S. albogularis*); 6a. White-collared Seed-eater (*S. torqueola*); 6b. *S. torqueola morelleti*; 7. Black-and-white Seed-eater (*S. luctuosa*); 8. Black Seed-eater (*S. aurita corvina*); 9. Black-headed Seed-eater (*S. melanocephala*); 10. Giant Black-and-white Seed-eater (*S. bicolor*); 11. Bluish Finch (*S. caerulescens*); 12a. Yellow-bellied Seed-eater (*S. nigricollis*); 12b. *S. nigricollis inspicua*; 13. Lesson's Seed-eater (*S. bouvronoides*); 14. Lined Finch (*S. lineola*)

tends to be browner above, particularly on the rump, and has been called Rusty-collared Seed-eater. It is a bird of humid scrubland and weed-patches bordering lagoons. It ranges from eastern Brazil downwards to the Buenos Aires region of Argentina.

I have not come across the species in captivity, and am forced to rely on Hopkinson who says of it, '. . . is included in Russ's List in *Bull.*, 1880, 680, and Decoux in the *A.M.* 1924, 116, says that *cucullata* "has been bred in Germany", almost certainly referring to Russ's record.' In a footnote the author then goes on to say, 'The Black-headed Finch, *S. melanocephala* (V), had a place in my original list on account of its inclusion in Russ's List of his first successes', but Neunzig (p. 238), writing on *cucullata* (= *melanocephala*), merely says, 'A pair nested in Dr. Russ's birdroom, . . . two eggs were laid, and the incubation was the same as that of the Grey Finch'. Neither this nor Russ's original account read quite like an account of complete success, and the matter is also complicated by the varying nomenclature. On the whole the evidence seems in favour of *cucullata* having been the species bred.

Ruddy-breasted Seed-eater
(*Sporophila minuta*)

Description: *3½–4 in. (88·9–101·6 mm.). Adult male top and side of head, back and uppertail-coverts brown; upperparts sometimes tinged with grey, occasionally upperparts entirely blue grey; rump and underparts orange chestnut. Female brown above, paler yellow ochre below; bill black.*

Possibly better named Dwarf Finch by the early aviculturists, this tiny species is sometimes not unlike the Chestnut-breasted, but it can be told apart by its slightly smaller size, olive-grey upperparts and ruddy chestnut rump. The female is more rust brown and more yellowish below than *castaneiventris*. It is a very common bird ranging over most of northern South America and the West Indies. It is perhaps the prettiest of the group and the male is also a good singer. It is not often imported but well worth picking up, should the opportunity occur.

Tobago Finch
(*Sporophila americana*)

Description: *4–4½ in. (101·6–114·3 mm.). Head and back glossy black with slight flecks of white on cheeks; rump white, sometimes mottled with black; wings black, sometimes with white edging to feathers; below, white with a broad black breast-bar. This may be broken or continuous. Throat may also be black, depending on race. The female is olive brown; bill black.*

This is a very popular cagebird in South America and is also known as the Variable Seed-eater. The male has a melodious song and a pleasing display flight; when the grey rump and back feathers are erect, the bird sings simultaneously.

Slate-coloured Seed-eater
(*Sporophila schistacea*)

Description: *5 in. (127 mm.). It is a dull grey bird with a small whitish strip on each side of throat; wings blackish with white edging on the wing-coverts, and whitish belly; bill yellow.*

It has a very pretty song and has been bred several times in captivity.

Seed-eaters, *Sporophila* spp.: 1a. Grey Seed-eater (*S. intermedia*); 1b. *S. intermedia bogotensis*; 2a. Slate-coloured Seed-eater (*S. schistacea*); 2b. *S. schistacea longipennis*; 3. Half-white Finch (*S. leucoptera*); 4. Dull-coloured Seed-eater (*S. obscura*)*; 5. Drab Seed-eater (*S. simplex*); 6. Cayenne Seed-eater (*S. frontalis*); 7. Chestnut-breasted Seed-eater (*S. castaneoventris*); 8. Marsh Seed-eater (*S. palustris*); 9. Chestnut-throated Seed-eater (*S. telasco*); 10. Chestnut Seed-eater (*S. cinnamonea*); 11. Reddish Finch (*S. bouvreuil*); 12. Ruddy-breasted Seed-eater (*S. minuta*); 13a. Plumbeous Seed-eater (*S. plumbea*); 13b. *S. plumbea whiteleyana*; 14. Grosbeak Seed-eater (*S. peruvianus*); 15. Dark-throated Seed-eater (*S. ruficollis*); 16. Pileated Seed-eater (*S. pileata*)

* Paul Schwarz in Venezuela believes that this species is a grassquit, and should be re-classified as *Tiaris obscura*.

Plumbeous Seed-eater
(*Sporophila plumbea*)

Description: $4\frac{1}{2}$–5 in. (114·3–127 mm.). *Grey above and on breast, whitish on throat and undertail-coverts; wings and tail blackish; bill grey or black.*

The Plumbeous Seed-eater is very similar to the Slate-coloured Seed-eater, but it is generally a little paler, noticeably paler below. It is a bird of open sandy grasslands, and it is not very common. It used to be much more frequently imported, like most seed-eaters, but we see it only occasionally now. It, too, is a fine song-ster. It is said to be quarrelsome in captivity, male and female always fighting, but in the wild it is naturally found in pairs. It is a free breeder, and is no trouble whatsoever to cater for.

Grey Seed-eater
(*Sporophila intermedia*)

Description: $4\frac{1}{2}$–5 in. (114·3–127 mm.). *Similar to* schistacea, *but one race from Colombia is noticeably darker.*

This bird is restricted to Colombia, Trinidad, Guyana and Venezuela. It can be told only by comparing two birds side by side, when *intermedia* will be seen to have smaller bill, longer tarsus, and nails dark instead of light. It is very rarely imported and I have no record of its treatment or behaviour in captivity. It is a bird of clearings and weedy pastures in tropical and subtropical zones.

Half-white Finch
(*Sporophila leucoptera*, formerly *hypoleuca*)

Description: 5–$5\frac{1}{2}$ in. (127–139·7 mm.). *Grey body, blackish on wings*

and tail, pale on throat. Female brown above, paler below; bill red.

Another species which is very similar to *schistacea*, but larger and with a reddish bill, is the Half-white Finch. This is also virtually unknown to modern aviculture, but is apparently fairly typical. It comes from Brazil where it is kept as a song-bird, but reports suggest that the song is repetitive and monotonous.

Bluish Finch
(*Sporophila caerulescens*)

Description: *About* $4\frac{1}{2}$ in. (114·3 mm.). *Adult male is bluish grey above, with white streaks on sides of throat, white below with black band across the breast. The female is olivaceous above, yellowish to white below.*

They are regularly imported in small numbers but, like many seed-eaters, appear to be rather male-heavy in the consignments, which is a pity because these birds are good breeders. They are quarrelsome among themselves when breeding, but not with other species. The male has a sweet but repetitive song.

Reddish Finch
(*Sporophila bouvreuil*, formerly *nigro-aurantia*)

Description: $3\frac{1}{2}$–4 in. (88·9–101·6 mm.). *Male is cinnamon coloured all over but for the wings, tail and crown, which are black. The female is brown, ochreous below.*

The Reddish Finch is a pretty bird from Brazil. It is one of the smallest and most attractive of the group, but rarely imported.

Guttural Finch
(Sporophila gutturalis)

Description: *4½ in. (114·3 mm.). Male of this Brazilian species is olivaceous above, pale on rump, with head black, and whitish below; black band across lower belly and yellow undertail-coverts. The female is a dull olive brown all over, darker on wings and tail, palest below.*

It is a very attractive little bird and settles in well enough. A pair and an odd male, which I kept together in a mixed collection of small seed-eaters, lived amicably without any quarrelling. They are imported fairly regularly in small numbers, though often there is a preponderance of males. I cannot see why they should not be bred regularly.

Grosbeak Seed-eater
(Sporophila peruvianus)

Description: *4–4½ in. (101·6–114·3 mm.). Adult male head and entire upper-surfaces grey with soft brown wash, darker markings on wing, slight white wing-bar and small white patch at base of primaries; throat and upper breast black with white crescent at side of throat; underparts dull white. Female similar to male but, in place of black bib, has greyish buff. Bill very large and decurved.*

This seed-eater is also listed as the Brown Grosbeak, and it is usually placed in the genus *Neorhynchus* all to itself on account of its rather large bill. In every group of seed-eating birds, where there is a great deal of speciation over similar habitat, as in the munias, Darwin's Finches, *Sporophila*, etc., there occur large-billed species. Among the seed-eaters, it is the present species that holds the title. Its plumage is reminiscent of a female House Sparrow, with the black bib of a male House Sparrow. The bill is a typical compressed conical seed-eater's bill, but twice the size, and has earned the species the common name of Parrot-billed Seed-eater. I had a pair in a mixed collection in a roomy outside flight for two years. To my regret they made no attempt whatsoever to breed and, with hindsight, I feel that I should have given them more cover and less company. I never heard the male utter a single note of song. They were perfect aviary companions, peaceful, gentle and slightly retiring and, although the bill looks ferocious, it certainly was not a weapon of offence. However, these birds were particularly destructive to branches and buds, particularly in a cage where they soon whittled off the bark from their perches like a pair of Crossbills. They apparently feed the young on soft green grass seeds, but I would be inclined to offer some insect food, as with all seed-eaters.

Cayenne Seed-eater
(Sporophila frontalis)

Description: *4–4½ in. (101·6–114·3 mm.). Adult male is olivaceous in colour, being darker above and strongly tinged with grey; it has white lines running through eye and above it, in an eyebrow-stripe; throat is white with grey moustachial stripes. The female lacks the white lines of the male and is yellowish below.*

The song is simple with both sexes singing, a not uncommon phenomenon in seed-eaters and some other species in this family. This, together with the fact that the female is distinctly coloured in her own right, makes it easy to assume that the two sexes are two males of distinct species. They were first bred in captivity about ten years ago by Mr. Partridge, who found them to be amiable with other birds, easy to keep and hardy. Unfortunately, they were quite destructive to growing plants, another character-istic of many *Sporophila*. They apparently fed the nestlings on insects to begin with, catching their own in preference to those supplied by the keeper.

WARBLING FINCHES

The genus *Poospiza* contains more than a dozen species of smallish buntings from central South America, about 4½–5½ in. (114·3–139·7 mm.) in length. A few species seem to be imported each year, but in small numbers. Those imported are not brightly coloured and this, combined with the fact that few dealers are able to identify them accurately, means that they tend to disappear into private collections, shrouded in anonymity. Unfortunately, there is virtually no reference to them in the literature. Furthermore, since the sexes are very similar in most species, and most species are quite alike, it is possible that, in a small mixed consignment, one might innocently buy two birds from different species in the belief that they were a true pair. Warbling Finches are delicately shaped and have been described as looking like something between a tit and a warbler, but having the song of a bunting. They tend to resemble *Sporophila* seed-eaters in plumage patterns but have noticeably more slender bills. They take the usual seeds, but need the addition of some fruit and insects in their diet if they are to be maintained in perfect condition. They certainly seem to be fairly easy birds to look after, and four of the five people who have ever written about them wrote with news of successful breeding. It has been suggested that a fit male will be spiteful towards the female, but reports indicate that a fit male in breeding condition will be aggressive to many other birds, particularly if they have similar colouring. An aviary devoted to one breeding pair seems to be desirable. I regret that I have no experience with them personally and that the literature is inadequate. Keepers with experience of the genus can certainly benefit aviculture by contributing notes on their personal observations.

Black, grey and white Warbling Finches: 1. Ringed Warbling Finch (*Poospiza torquata*), and 2. *P. t. pectoralis*; 3. Collared Warbling Finch (*P. hispaniolensis*); 4. Bonaparte's Warbling Finch (*P. bonapartii*)

Chestnut-and-black Warbling Finch
(*Poospiza nigrorufa*)

Description: $5\frac{1}{2}$ in. (139·7 mm.). *Adult male is grey above with a short, whitish superciliary that ends in a patch of cinnamon; lores and sides of head black; mesial stripe white; from chin to breast orange chestnut, white on belly; centre of tail black while two outer feathers white. Female similar, but duller and paler.*

This species is also called Black-and-rufous Warbling Finch. White's Warbling Finch, *P. n. whitei*, has the chin white, joining the mesial stripe, and the breast is a richer chestnut. These birds, about the size of a Canary, are excellent aviary birds that show themselves off well and fit into a mixed collection amiably. They were first bred by Allen Silver in 1937 (the race *whitei*), but unfortunately I have no details. They were again bred in 1955 in an unplanted

Warbling Finches: 1. White's Warbling Finch (*Poospiza nigrorufa whitei*); 2. Chestnut-and-Black Warbling Finch (*P. n. nigrorufa*); 3. Pretty Warbling Finch (*P. ornata*); 4. Red-rumped Warbling Finch (*P. lateralis*); 5. Black-capped Warbling Finch (*P. melanoleuca*); 6. Bay-chested Warbling Finch (*P. thoracica*); 7. Bolivian Warbling Finch (*P. boliviana*)

flight which was shared with a pair of doves. The young appeared to be reared almost exclusively on mealworms and gentles.

Pretty Warbling Finch
(*Poospiza ornata*)

Description: *About 5 in. (127 mm.). Adult male has forehead to back and lores to nape grey, rest of upperparts olive grey with two white wing-bars; superciliary stripe is cinnamon; from chin to belly it is cinnamon, becoming an intense chestnut on throat and breast, palest on undertail-coverts. Female is the same but paler. Juveniles resemble female but are more greyish and breast is streaked with grey.*

This bird is also called Cinnamon Warbling Finch. Unsuccessful breedings occurred with at least two breeders before the first recorded success in 1960, when the young were reared exclusively on live food. A detailed report from Sweden appeared in the *Avicultural Magazine* in 1972. The parents showed a marked preference for spiders and similar insects, only feeding mealworms and gentles as a second choice. The males of this aviculturist were all quite aggressive when breeding.

A male of this species is the only representative of the genus that I have in my collection. The dealer who sold it to me had kept it in the company of various mannikins (*Lonchura*), where it was restricted to a diet of small millet. It is currently housed with a motley mixture of finches, a Goldfinch, Wild Canary and Diamond Sparrow. It is perfectly peaceable and has never shown any signs of aggression to my knowledge.

Ringed Warbling Finch
(*Poospiza torquata*)

Description: *About 5 in. (127 mm.). Adult male is dark grey above, blackish on forehead, lores, and sides of head; there is a white superciliary, and a small white crescent beneath the eye; chin and throat, breast, flanks and belly are white, but there is a narrow black band across the breast and the undertail-coverts are chestnut. The female is similar but a little duller and the breast-band is narrower and grey.*

A subspecies, *pectoralis*, lacks the white crescent beneath the eye, and has a broader black chest-band. It is a lively and pleasant species, which would probably breed if given the opportunity. Boosey also mentioned Bonaparte's Warbling Finch (*Poospiza bonapartii*) but gave no details. It is very similar to the Ringed Warbling Finch, *P. torquata pectoralis*, but lacks any white on the wings. The Grey-and-white Warbling Finch (*Poospiza melanoleuca*) is better named the Black-capped. It is smaller, with a black head, grey upperparts, and white from chin to undertail. It is clear that any aviculturist with any experience with the Warbling Finches can make a genuine contribution to our knowledge of these birds by sending their notes to an avicultural publication.

Ringed Warbling Finch (*Poospiza torquata*)

SIERRA FINCHES

While researching for this book, I came across a reference to the Orchard Finch. It was a species that I had not heard of and could not trace by its common name. Eventually, I found it mentioned by Butler, in *Aviculture*, and ran it to earth as the Mourning Sierra Finch. This was my introduction to the genus *Phrygilus*, a group of ten buntings from South America that ranges from the southernmost tip of the continent, up the western side of the Andes to Venezuela. They appear to be fairly typical buntings. They are altitudinal migrators, moving up into the higher ranges as spring develops, when they breed. They descend as the winter sets in and, no doubt, reduces the supply of food. They flock in winter but pair off to breed in summer. They nest low down in a sheltered and protected spot. The basic diet is seeds, but they probably all feed the young on insects when rearing. Dr. Mansell bred his Orchard Finch in 1915 and was successful in breeding it at liberty the following year. He describes how the cock would recognize him at some distance and fly to him to beg for mealworms to take back to the nest.

Butler described three species: the Orchard Finch, Gay's Finch and the Alaudine Finch. I have included some descriptions below in the event of any of these interesting birds being imported nowadays. Inspired by my discovery I put some inquiries in hand that eventually resulted in two separate shipments of *Phrygilus* being prepared for me in Santiago de Chile, but on each occasion despatch was thwarted by bureaucratic inefficiencies inevitable, I suppose, considering the politico/economic state of the country at the time (late 1972). At the time of writing (late 1973) I have managed to obtain one pair of Sierra Finches only. I have gathered from Chilean friends in Madrid that several of the Sierra Finches are popular cagebirds and are often kept for their song. They are apparently quite easy to keep in good condition on a diet of seeds. It is unclear whether they have been bred in captivity in Chile.

Ash-breasted Sierra Finch
(*Phrygilus plebejus*)

Description: *About 5½ in. (139·7 mm.). Adult male grey above, striated with black; pale grey superciliary, eye encircled by whitish; below, greyish white, paler on throat, undertail white. Female similar but more heavily streaked above and faintly streaked on breast and flanks.*

The Ash-breasted Sierra Finch may also be called Lesser or Little Plumbeous Finch, or Grey Finch. It ranges down the Andes from Peru to the Argentine where it is a characteristic species of the high-zone Andes. It is most numerous above 13,000 ft. (3,963 m.), although nests have been found as low as 3,000 ft. (914 m.). The nest appears to be a bulky, untidy effort reminiscent of that of the House Sparrow and has been found under the eaves of a house, and in rock crevices.

totally ignored mealworms, and not touched any fruit or soft food.

Patagonian Sierra Finch
(Phrygilus patagonicus)

Description: *6–7 in. (152·4–177·8 mm.). Adult male has a dark blue-grey head, olive-green mantle, deep chestnut back and yellow-ochre rump; throat is paler blue grey and underparts yellow ochre; wings and tail black, edged with dark blue; bill brown above, white below. Female smaller, browner and duller.*

This species is similar to *Phrygilus*

Black-headed
Sierra Finch
(Phrygilus atriceps)

This is the only species of *Phrygilus* that I have kept, and I only have two birds, believed to be a pair. In a cage they maintain an edgy peace, but in a small flight they are decidedly quarrelsome – they rose in the air bickering and chirruping like fighting House Sparrows, even as I released them from their travelling box. I would not trust them in a small enclosure with nervous birds, or breeding birds.

I have tried them with all kinds of seeds, but find that they prefer hemp and small sunflower, then take Canary and big white millet. They have

gayii, but any doubts can be resolved by bill colour. Its favourite habitat is heavily vegetated river bottoms, well tangled with seed-bearing plants and vines, and not surprisingly it chooses to nest there as well.

Black-headed Sierra Finch
(Phrygilus atriceps)

Description: *About 7 in. (177·8 mm.). Adult male has entire head and throat black; mantle to rump olive brown; ochreous uppertail-coverts; wings dark grey with black flights; tail black; breast and flanks ochreous yellow, whitish on belly and undertail. Female has head, throat and upper breast dusky grey, otherwise duller edition of male.*

The Black-headed, Black-hooded or simply Hooded Sierra Finch is a bird of high country, ranging up to 17,000 ft. (5,181 m.), and rarely descending below 6,000 ft (1,828·8 m.). It ranges from south-western Peru, through western Bolivia and Argentina, and much of Chile. In habits and requirements it seems to be rather similar to the Grey-headed Sierra Finch, and indeed was once considered to be a race of that species. However, it is more adaptable to differing habitats and more versatile in choice of nest site. In Chile it is a prized cagebird, popular for its colour and its song.

Band-tailed Sierra Finch
(*Phrygilus alaudinus*)

Description: *About 6 in. (152·4 mm.). Adult male has head and upper body entirely grey, lores brown; below, belly to undertail white; central tail feathers brown, rest of tail feathers have broad white band on centre of inner web. Female grey above with buff and brown bar on wings; below whitish striated with greyish brown, centre of belly and vent white. Bill yellow.*

It is a native of the Andes from Chile to Ecuador. It is also listed as Alaudine Finch, and is known locally as the Platero, Yellow-bill, or White-tailed Finch, but may appear in the literature as Lark-like Finch. This is a low-country bird, not going above 6,000 ft. (1,828·8 m.). It is easily identified by its yellow bill, and

banded tail – the latter only noticing when the bird flies, which it is reluctant to do. It is a ground-frequenting species, hopping about picking up seeds of bushes and weeds. The nest is placed on the ground and is usually hidden in the middle of a clump of long grass.

Mourning Sierra Finch
(*Phrygilus fruticeti*)

Description: *Male 7 in. (177·8 mm.); slate-grey, streaked with black above, a white wing-bar, brownish on wings and tail; below, face, throat, centre of breast and belly black, sides of breast pale grey streaked with blackish brown, remaining underparts grey; bill yellow. Female 6 in. (152·4 mm.); lacks black frontal marking of male and is whitish on face and buff on breast lightly streaked with brown and has two white wing-bars; bill flesh-colour.*

This is Dr. Mansell's Orchard Finch. It is also listed as Mourning Finch and Black Finch. It ranges from Peru and Bolivia down to Chile and Patagonia. It was apparently imported from time to time and was a good cagebird, being easy to maintain on an all-seed diet. It is a species of semi-open hillsides with small trees and seed-bearing bushes. It forages among thicker vegetation in the ravines and valleys, but comes into the open to utter its Greenfinch-like song.

Plumbeous Finch
(*Phrygilus unicolor*)

Description: *6–7 in. (152·4–177·8 mm.), depending on the race. Male entirely plumbeous grey, paler on the lower parts, white on undertail; wing and tail feathers black edged with* grey. *Female streaked brown and black above; below greyish white, broadly streaked with brown.*

Ranges from Venezuela to Tierra del Fuego, and known locally as the Mountain Diuca or Lead-coloured Finch. At the northern end of its range it is a bird of high altitude, above 9,000 ft. (2,743 m.), but occurs lower down as one goes southwards until it occurs at sea-level at the southern extreme. It is an extremely shy nester, hiding the neat hair-lined cup of grasses and moss in cracks of drystone walls.

Grey-hooded Sierra Finch
(*Phrygilus gayii*)

Description: *6 in. (152·4 mm.). Adult male, slate-grey head, paler on chin and throat, back orange sienna becoming yellow on the rump, uppertail-coverts dark blue grey; wings and tail blackish with the feathers edged with grey; under-surface bright yellow, white on vent and undertail. Female is slightly smaller and browner, paler on the head, and indistinctly streaked and paler underneath. Bill, lead grey.*

It comes from Chile and western Argentina and was referred to as Gay's Finch by Butler, but is probably better called Grey-headed Sierra Finch, and is called Fat-eater locally. This handsome bird nests among dense vegetation bordering mountain streams, or in crevices among rocks on the ground in the absence of suitable cover.

CARDINALS

These lovely birds are great favourites in aviculture. They are cheerful but not very accomplished songsters. Most of them have been bred in captivity and have proved to be enthusiastic and easy breeders. They are hardy and are good mixers in a collection, neither fighting each other nor attacking other species. Even in a modestly roomy aviary various cardinals have bred in mixed company without causing trouble. The Green Cardinal is perhaps the exception to this remark and is best kept in a flight of its own when breeding. It can be seen that the cardinals are fine birds for the beginner starting with a collection of medium-sized birds.

They can be maintained on an all-seed regimen but will do better on a more varied diet. In fact, the menu suggested by Rutgers gives us a good idea of what can be offered: oats, berries, universal food and such green food as lettuce, chickweed, and twigs with young buds on them, also wholemeal bread, mashed potatoes, apples, hemp seed and sunflower seed. Ants' eggs and live insects must be freely given during breeding and rearing. The exclusive feeding of mealworms will inevitably lead to rickets and weakly developed feet.

Dominican or Pope Cardinal
(*Paroaria dominicana*)

Description: *7–8 in. (117·8–203·2 mm.), from nape of neck to tail, grey with some blackish markings and a little white mottling on the mantle; sides of neck white joining on to white breast and underparts; head and throat crimson red. The sexes are alike, but males may be seen to be slightly larger or bolder. Juvenile birds are slightly smaller and are duller both above and below; they have brown heads.*

This bird comes from eastern Brazil where it inhabits forest clearings, scrub, parks and gardens. It seems to be something of a Brazilian equivalent of the North American Virginian Cardinal in its ubiquity and lack of fear of man. It has a loud and cheerful, but not particularly elegant song which is uttered throughout the day by a male in breeding condition, but most frequently in the early morning. It is also listed as Red-headed and Red-cowled Cardinal. A scientific synonym for the species is *P. larvata*.

It is regularly imported and is not expensive for such a fine bird. However, the sexes are impossible to tell apart (though perhaps the red of the throat is more extensive on the male, and the mantle scapulars are whiter) and this undoubtedly results in many 'pairs' being birds of the same sex. In my experience a true pair are willing breeders, and not aggressive even when breeding in a mixed collection. Some writers urge caution in this respect.

Red-crested Cardinal
(*Paroaria cucullata*)

Description: *7½ in. (190·5 mm.). Very similar to the Pope, but the back is a lighter and more even grey. The head is bright scarlet and both sexes have a fine soft crest. Juveniles are duller with greyish-brown head and vestigial crest.*

Mr. Risdon suggests that the male can be told by the greater frequency with which it will raise and depress its crest. I think that this should not be taken as a guide in a dealer's cage, but might well be the case if one is able to watch over a prolonged period under fairly natural conditions. Females are held by some to be smaller, slimmer and to have less extensive red on the head. I am certain that the red of the head can fade over successive moults, particularly in seed-fed, cage-kept specimens. The day before writing this page I watched a cage of newly imported birds in a pet shop and they had absolutely dazzling scarlet heads. When compared to the average seed-fed bird a few years later the latter will be seen to have a vermilion head. By contrast, incidentally, the head of the Pope is crimson, i.e. not so bright or light, but it does not fade.

Red-crested Cardinals breed freely in captivity. I have a note (I know not from where) that it first bred in Florence in 1836, and seems to have been bred regularly in Europe ever since. When breeding it is inclined to be aggressive and should either be housed apart or with larger birds. Incidentally, I believe that this species is also known as *Paroaria coronata*. It has been hybridized with both the Pope and the Yellow-billed Cardinals.

Yellow-billed Cardinal
(*Paroaria capitata*)

Description: *6½ in. (165·1 mm.). Adult male bright carmine head with black bib; above white nape, rest of upperparts black, below pure white; bill and feet yellow. Female has head duller and has greyish back. Juveniles are light brown to buff on the head, brown throat and grey bill.*

This species resembles the Pope Cardinal but is noticeably smaller, and its lighter build makes it much more bunting-like. It is rather brighter in colouring and can be distinguished readily by its black bib and yellow bill. It also has the advantage of being sexually dimorphic. A friend of mine once bought a pair of these birds as 'Brown-headed Cardinals'. The 'male' was in fact an adult female, while the 'female' was a juvenile male. They successfully bred before the male had gained full colour, but what a surprise in due course. Butler in fact mentioned that the immature *capitata* had once been described as a distinct species and given the name *P. cervicalis*. I can well believe it.

It is a good aviary bird, being sociable and never displaying any of the aggression sometimes attributed to its bigger cousins.

Red-capped Cardinal
(*Paroaria gularis*)

Description: *7½–8 in. (190·5–203·2 mm.). Adult male head crimson; lores, lower throat black (the race P. g. nigrogensis has top of head black and throat entirely red, with a black stripe through the eye); the red of the head joins immediately on to the black nape; rest of upperparts blue black; below, white. Females are similar. Juveniles are like adults but dull black; head brown and the throat is buff; bill black above, white below.*

It is a forest species ranging from southern Venezuela, the Guianas, southward to Brazil, Peru and eastern Bolivia, covering the Amazon basin. De Schauensee places it in the genus *Coccopis*. It reminds one more of a black-throated Pope Cardinal than a yellow-billed and has in fact been advertised as such in the past, but it is rarely imported. The race *nigrogensis* has also been imported in the past when it was presented as a separate species and called Black-cheeked Cardinal. Both the black-chinned and the red-chinned races have been successfully bred in captivity.

Green Cardinal
(*Gubernatrix cristata*)

Description: *7½ in. (190·5 mm.). Adult male upperparts olive green streaked with blackish. Tail yellow with two centre feathers black, crest, chin and throat black. Superciliary and sides of throat bright yellow, breast greenish yellow, rest of underparts bright yellow. Female duller, yellow on face is replaced by white, underparts duller yellow. Juveniles resemble female but are duller.*

This is an excellent aviary bird and is a firm favourite among aviculturists and exhibitors alike, for it is a remarkably steady bird in a cage once settled and will stand proudly and sing in defiance at an audience just like any cock Canary. It has been bred on many occasions and undoubtedly a breeding strain could be developed if the strain on the breeder didn't prove too much to supply enough live food. In terms of pugnacity they are about equal to the Red-crested Cardinal, i.e. when breeding they are much better kept to themselves unless either their companions are bigger, or suitably different, e.g. Quail.

II · CARDUELINAE

Within this subfamily one encounters all the finches of avicultural fame, the most celebrated of course being the Canary. It is superfluous to repeat the notes included in the preface to this family, as they serve equally well here.

SERINS

The serins are an extremely homogenous genus, probably originating in the Ethiopian region and in fact the majority of species are restricted to the African continent. Basically they are yellow or yellow-to-white birds marked or streaked with black and greens. The exception to the rule is the Red-fronted Serin. Several species have brown in their plumage. The basic difference between the serins and the essentially similar siskins is that the former are grass seed eating, while the latter are tree seed eating; there is, however, a point where it is arguable which genus any particular species belongs to. For example, the Citril Finch is generally portrayed in field guides as being serin-like, and it is currently included in the *Serinus*, but there can be little doubt in the minds of those who have studied its behaviour in the field that it is a siskin. Accordingly I have included those species of doubtful status at the end of this section.

Serins are noted as song-birds, although performances are very variable between species. They are commonly kept as song-birds wherever they occur and a popular pastime among bird-keepers of every region is to cross-breed the local serins with domesticated varieties of Canary to create variations of song. Not only are such hybrids easy to produce, but hybrids between various species of serin have been produced with almost equal facility. Hybrids are most easily bred by introducing a male of the wild bird in a roomy cage with a female, domestic Canary. The young of most if not all of these cross-breedings appear to be fertile, demonstrating how closely related the genus is.

HOUSING

They all make excellent and interesting aviary subjects and add colour to a mixed collection. They will breed in mixed collections, often making the attempt when conditions really are not favourable at all, and individuals from different species have hybridized in this way. Because of their preferences for live food when rearing they are much more ideally housed in aviaries, where they are either alone or are not competing with similarly fed birds. Also I believe that a planted enclosure is much more to the advantage of the birds.

I have kept many of these species in a cage, but have no doubt that they do better where they can fly. A cage about 3 ft. (914·4 mm.) long should be regarded as a minimum, and for the larger species such a cage should only be temporary accommodation.

To say that they can winter out-of-doors is a generalization that cannot help anybody, since in itself that statement needs defining, and anyway my winter may not be yours. With some exceptions, I would say that these birds *may* be left out-of-doors all the year round providing they have access to a roomy enclosed shelter that is draught-proof and, ideally, has a heating system that keeps the temperature inside above 40° F. or 5° C. (some authorities maintain that 50° F. or 10° C. is a safer minimum). In this, as in much else in aviculture, birds are individuals and some will be quite perky at freezing point while others within the same species will look quite miserable.

FOOD

As with the buntings in the previous chapter I wholeheartedly recommend supplying seeds in individual pots, canary in one, millet in another, etc. With the exception of the *Passerinae*, these birds may take larger seeds and can be offered sunflower, hemp, wheat, oats and other larger seeds that may be available locally. Do not ignore the smaller ones, however. I have watched a Pyrrhuloxia pick up maw. In an aviary it is advisable to encourage natural food-seeking behaviour by scattering seeds on the ground of the flight. Some individuals will take lettuce or spinach with relish, others not at all; chickweed is a better bet but is not always available. A halved orange may be sampled, sweet apple and pear may be relished, but all soft food is a matter for trial and error. They all take some live food, and mealworms will usually be gobbled up. Like the true buntings the cardinals and related species have a tendency to become mealworm addicts and should never be given them *ad lib*. The biggest danger with a heavy hand for mealworms is that the parent birds will refuse to feed anything else to their nestlings. I know from personal experience that mealworms are an imperfect rearing food, and youngsters deprived of everything else during the first week will be imperfect and generally either die, or suffer from rickets and other symptoms of vitamin-D deficiency.

The best solution of course is to provide rearing birds with as varied a diet of live food as possible, grasshoppers, young locusts, spiders, caterpillars, worms, ant pupae, maggots and, ultimately, mealworms. If one is unable to obtain a supply of anything other than mealworms (maggots are usually available commercially, but few birds will take them if there is a supply of mealworms) one must try various ruses to improve their quality by dripping multi-vitamin and mineral complexes on them, for example. One breeder I knew would put the mealworms free from bran or any food overnight, then give them thinly sliced wholemeal bread that had been damped with multi-vitamin; while the mealworms were still eating this (i.e. their food was barely ingested let alone digested) they would be given to the birds.

BREEDING

All the birds in this group build cup-shaped, open nests usually made of leaves, twiglets, straws and grasses, and the cup itself is lined with finer, softer material. The nests are placed in cover, maybe in a bush or leafy tree, and usually fairly near the ground, an exception being the Evening Grosbeak that will build its nest up to 60 ft. (18·3 m.) above the ground. In an aviary, however, it is generally more accommodating. Saltators and tropical grosbeaks lay only two-egg clutches, other grosbeaks lay four, while other genera produce three to five eggs.

In an aviary they normally prefer to build their own nest but might well take to a half-open box or the discarded nest of another species. I have persuaded various cardinals to breed by placing an old Blackbird's nest in a concealed position, in an open box that had been placed on its side and in a roof corner with a restraining cross-piece.

Most of the males are fairly aggressive while breeding, although
in my experience aggression has been reserved for the same or
allied species. In general, however, I do not consider this an
aggressive group.

SALTATORS

These are the largest birds in the group, the biggest being the
Black-headed, which is 10 in. (254 mm.) long. They come from
Central America ranging south to the Argentine. They are the
least colourful of the subfamily; the sexes are not only alike but

Saltators: 1. Streaked Saltator (*Saltator albicollis*); 2. Buff-throated Saltator (*S. maximus*); 3. Greyish Saltator (*S. caerulescens*); 4. Black-headed
Saltator (*S. atriceps*); 5. and 6. Orange-billed Saltator (*S. aurantiirostris*)

in several species the female sings as well as the male and a true
pair will engage in duetting frequently. Apart from the field notes
of Alexander Skutch there is hardly any reference in either avicultural or ornithological literature that will provide guidance for
the person wishing to keep saltators. The sexes of each of the
species are alike, and it is virtually impossible to tell which is male
or female. For this reason anyone hoping to breed them is advised

to buy more than two birds, thereby increasing the chances of obtaining a true pair. A further advantage of keeping more than two saltators is that natural social and intersocial behaviour is more likely to occur. The saltators have a reputation for being dull and lethargic, but as nothing is published they provide an excellent opportunity for anyone with experience of them to contribute to our knowledge by writing up, and publishing notes in the avicultural press.

Saltators are more vegetarian and frugivorous in the wild than most buntings, often taking a large amount of berries and other fruits. However, they do not take much fruit in captivity. They do take insects and undoubtedly feed young nestlings on insect food to some degree. They are also said to relish mealworms. But it seems very likely (Skutch tends to support this) that the young are fed on soft seeds, berries and fruit to a large extent, and are vegetarian by the time they fledge. There is obviously great room for study here.

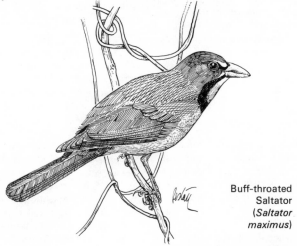

Buff-throated
Saltator
(*Saltator
maximus*)

Buff-throated Saltator
(*Saltator maximus*)

Description: *About 8 in. (203·2 mm.). Greyish head otherwise olivaceous above; white superciliary stripe and black moustachial stripe which in some races joins across the breast completely encircling a buff throat; remaining underparts pale grey becoming buff at undertail-coverts. The sexes are alike, but it is possible that the black breast-bar of the male is broader than that of the female.*

This bird is not the largest of the saltators, despite its Latin name, but none the less is also called Great Saltator. It is a gentle and retiring bird which only draws attention to itself by its song. In birds that Skutch studied the male was overbearing to the female, always occupying the feeding-table to take banana alone, and forcing the female to wait its turn – except when young were in the nest. Other species were grudgingly admitted but not welcome. It ranges from Panama to the south of Brazil, and is occasionally imported. It is one of the boldest of the genus and, despite its lack of bright colouring, it should be an interesting and rewarding addition to a collection. It is a cheerful and very persistent songster.

Black-headed Saltator
(_Saltator atriceps_)

Description: _About 10 in. (254 mm.). Very similar to the above species, but where_ maximus _is grey on the head_ atriceps _is black, and the upperparts are not so greenish._

This species ranges from Mexico to Panama and is rarely available.

Greyish Saltator
(_Saltator caerulescens_)

Description: _A large bird, about 9 in. (228·6 mm.), similar to the Buff-throated but has a darker head, the white eyebrow-stripe is not so clearly defined, and there is also a little white below the eye; back is much greyer; black bill is heavier._

It has a similar range and habitat to the Buff-throated, being found from southern Mexico downwards, throughout most of Central and South America to the Argentine. It is a bird of open woodland reported as being common in shrubberies, plantations and woodlands. It feeds on berries, fruits and insects and appears to be a perfectly typical member of the genus. It is probably imported in small numbers from time to time, but I must admit to never having seen it.

Orange-billed Saltator
(_Saltator aurantiirostris_)

Description: _About 8 in. (203·2 mm.). Ashy-grey above with white superciliary stripe, sides of face and throat black; fawn coloured below; bill orange._

The species ranges over much of Uruguay, Paraguay and the Argentine. It used to be imported from time to time and odd specimens were exhibited at shows and zoos, but it has not made many appearances in recent years.

Streaked Saltator
(_Saltator albicollis_)

Description: _6½–7½ in. (165·1–190·5 mm.). One of the smaller of the genus. Above, it is entirely dull olive green tending to greyish; below, it is white streaked with grey or olive, there is a black moustachial streak; bill black._

The Streaked Saltator ranges from Costa Rica to Peru, and across to Venezuela. It is also found on the Lesser Antilles. It is a good songster, and in this it resembles the Greyish. While the aforementioned species will all choose a high and exposed song perch from which to broadcast their presence, the Streaked Saltator is content with a branch little more than head height from the ground. It does, however, have a song flight, singing on the ascent but plunging swiftly and silently to the ground. It is a very retiring and secretive bird, rarely showing itself out of cover, and at a hint of danger will stay hidden away. It is no doubt an easy bird to maintain in captivity, taking seeds and fruits, like any saltator, but its dull colouring and hide-away nature would commend it only to the real enthusiast.

RED CARDINALS

The subfamily has always taken its name from the generic name for the true Cardinals, currently listed by Peters as *Cardinalis*, but previously as *Richmondena* and *Pyrrhuloxia*. The Red-bird, or Common Cardinal (*Cardinalis cardinalis*), is the best known of the genus; it ranges over much of North and Central America and adjacent islands, and has been introduced elsewhere, notably Hawaii where it breeds all the year round and is a real pest to the fruit-growers. It is a small genus, comprising only three species; the other two are rarely imported and have proved to be less successful in aviculture, requiring more care and attention than their widespread and ubiquitous cousin.

They take a wide variety of seeds, of various sizes including hemp and sunflower, enjoy a little fruit such as sweet apple and berries of rowan and cotoneaster, and will eagerly accept mealworms.

Virginian Cardinal
(*Cardinalis cardinalis*)

Description: *8–9 in. (203·2–228·6 mm.). Adult male bright red all over with well-developed crest; forehead, lores and bib black. Female yellowish brown, paler below, flushed with red on head, wings and tail, and retaining black face. The bill is red. Juveniles are similar to the female but duller; bill dusky.*

This bird is normally listed as *Richmondena cardinalis*, but current systematic thought considers it to be sufficiently closely related to the Pyrrhuloxia as to place it in the same genus. It has a multitude of common names. In American literature it is known simply as the Cardinal, at other times it is called Common Cardinal, and it is sometimes listed as Scarlet Cardinal, Crimson Cardinal or Virginian Nightingale. It is essentially a bird of the south-western States of the U.S. and northern Mexico, the latter from whence avicultural supplies come. It is a dearly loved bird in the U.S., enjoying a combination of the status of the European Blackbird and Robin combined.

It is a fine song-bird which, combined with its brilliant colour, makes it an ideal cagebird. However, the red colour will fade with successive moults unless some colour agent is included in the food. Incidentally it is very fond of sunflower seed. The name 'Nightingale' stems from its tendency to sing at night-time if there is moonlight or a bright street-light, but the song is not quite comparable with a Nightingale. The female also sings during the breeding season.

It has been bred on several occasions, and only needs reasonable room for manœuvre – preferably a planted flight – and a regular supply of live food.

Phoenix Cardinal
(Cardinalis phoenicea)

Description: $7\frac{1}{2}$–8 in. (190·5–203·2 mm.). Adult male has head including crest and underparts vermilion; back, wings and tail rose red; forehead, lores and bill black. Female, crest vermilion, sides of head grey, upperparts sandy grey, throat white, breast grey, rest of underparts cinnamon-buff; face mask black as male; wings brown edged with red, tail dull rose; bill bluish flesh.

The male of this species is remarkably like the Virginian Cardinal, but is a little smaller and the black around the bill is less noticeable. The bill itself is more heavily decurved, being just like the bill of the Pyrrhuloxia (*P. sinuata*). It can also be found in the literature as Venezuelan Cardinal and Vermilion Cardinal. It tends to travel badly and is in greater need of careful acclimatization than its more common cousin. Once settled it is a perfectly typical cardinal. It comes from Venezuela, Colombia and Trinidad, and is rarely imported. I have only seen it advertised twice in the last ten years.

Pyrrhuloxia
(Cardinalis sinuata)

Description: 9 in. (228·6 mm.). Male, large but slender and delicate in build; grey-brown washed with rose pink, stronger on tail-coverts, and underwings particularly bright; face bright rose as is tip of the long crest; throat, breast and belly flushed with rose. Female brownish grey with reddish crest, buff breast and flushes of red on wings and tail. Juveniles resemble the female.

Virginian Cardinal (*Cardinalis cardinalis*); Pyrrhuloxia (*C. sinuata*)

Despite attempts in avicultural literature to call it Rose Cardinal it has stuck to its tongue-twisting scientific name which stems from the Greek, meaning crooked-billed flame-coloured one. The bill is a strangely hooked thing. It is rarely imported. A male that I had lived contentedly with some buntings and sparrows and pottered around picking up various seeds. It was content to sit quietly on a high and secluded perch just watching the world go by, but would respond so immediately to the sight of a mealworm that it was invariably first to the tray. It is a shy bird by nature. I have no doubt that a pair could be induced to breed in a roomy, secluded and quiet aviary.

AMERICAN GROSBEAKS

If one tries to sit down to define a grosbeak it is only a matter of moments before one is in the thick of the debate on the systematization of the Passerines. In this section I am including only those New World species that are listed in Peters' checklist as being in the Cardinalinae. They are less than a dozen in all. They are all fairly large thickset birds with heavy bills, generally of open woodland, woodland verges or scrub, often brightly coloured and good if not quite accomplished song-birds. They are not really suitable cagebirds but do settle well in aviaries where they prove to be easy enough to cater for and most species have been bred at some time or another. They are mostly hardy and may be kept out-of-doors all the year round providing they have access to a dry and draught-proof shelter. In addition to seeds they have a liking for fruit and green food like fresh-growing buds.

Rose-breasted Grosbeak
(*Pheucticus ludovicianus*)

Description: *7–8 in. (117·8–203·2 mm.). Adult male, in summer, head, neck and back, wings and tail black; rump white, sometimes flushed with pink; a deep V-shaped patch of rose pink on breast, rest of underparts white; two white wing-bars. Female dark brown above, streaked with tawny and blackish; rump brown; two white wing-bars; below, buff to white flushed pink on breast and heavily streaked. Female has under-wing-coverts yellow. Juveniles resemble female but young males not so heavily streaked and show pink underwings. In winter the male loses much of his brilliance and resembles the female but retains rosy underwings and a touch of red on breast.*

This is a delightful species, with charming manners and attractive displays in which the male shows all the rosy parts of its plumage. A shortened version of the song is given as the male chases the female and, once paired, they frequently indulge in a bill-touching 'kiss'. The male has a fine song, frequently given by moonlight. It will also share in the brooding of eggs and young and even sing during the process, an unusual occur-rence. They take not only seeds but also relish fruit and insects. In spring they take a fair amount of buds and blossom. They come from the eastern half of the U.S., wintering in the south, as far as northern South America.

Black-headed Grosbeak
(*Pheucticus melanocephalus*)

Description: *7–8 in. (177·8–203·2 mm.). Adult male, in summer, head, nape and remainder of upperparts black; some orange on rump; two white wing-bars; below tawny orange, yellow on belly, palest under tail. Female resembles female Rose-breast but is yellower below, and less strongly striped. Juvenile resembles female.*

Application of the geographical species concept dictates that the Black-headed and Rose-breasted Grosbeaks are con-specific, simply races of the one species. The Black-headed is a bird of the western half of the U.S., and where the ranges of the two overlap they hybridize and intermediates may be found.

Not surprisingly, it is similar to the Rose-breast in behaviour and in the treatment it requires in captivity. It is an excellent aviary subject and has been bred on many occasions.

Blue Grosbeak
(*Guiraca caerula*)

Description: $6\frac{1}{2}$–$7\frac{1}{2}$ in. (165·1–190·5 mm.). *Adult male, in summer, bright purplish blue all over relieved by black forehead, lores and chin, and two brown wing-bars; in winter the blue is obscured by brown except for lower back, rump and tail-coverts which retain the blue. Female is smaller, olive brown above with dusky wings and tail, greyish on rump; occasional blue wash on upper surfaces. Juveniles resemble female, young males show more blue.*

This lovely bird ranges from the southern parts of the U.S. south to Nicaragua and Costa Rica. The birds from the U.S. winter in Panama. It can always be distinguished from the Indigo Bunting by its superior size (being over 1 in. (25·4 mm.) longer), the much heavier bill and the chestnut wing-bars. Indeed, it has an alternative name of Chestnut-shouldered Blue Grosbeak. Its usual habitat is rough overgrown hedgerows, and woodland edges. It is frequently found in orchards and gardens where the bright finch-like song will call attention to the territory of a male, particularly in the early morning and late afternoon. While the beak is suitably adapted for cracking the stones of fruit it takes a fair amount of live food and seems to be particularly fond of grasshoppers when rearing. It is occasionally imported, but most 'Blue Grosbeaks' advertised are the following species.

Brazilian Blue Grosbeak
(*Cyanocompsa cyanea*)

Description: $5\frac{1}{2}$–7 in. (139·7–177·8 mm.). *Depending on race, or locality, adult male, overall bright blue, lightest on rump, black on forehead, lores and chin; abdomen and tail black. Female brown, yellower above, warmer on wings, tail and underparts. Juvenile birds resemble the female.*

This species, also called simply Blue Grosbeak and Ultramarine Grosbeak, can be distinguished by its greater size and heavier bill from the Indigo Bunting. It is a brighter blue than either the foregoing or following species. It ranges over most of South America except west of the Andes and is the commonest of the grosbeaks in captivity. It is regularly imported (though females unfortunately do not show up with the frequency of males) and has been bred on several occasions. Decoux records the female as being a pleasant songbird in its own right, sounding rather like a Robin Redbreast. But undoubtedly the male is the dominant songster, singing frequently throughout the breeding season. When rearing they will take germinated seed and rearing food in addition to mealworms and other live food. Insects do not play the critical role found in many other species.

Blue-Black Grosbeak
(*Cyanocompsa cyanoides*)

Description: 6–7 in. (152·4–177·8 mm.). *Adult male, dullish blue black all over, brightest on forehead and crown; bib black, wings and tail blackish. Female uniform reddish brown, darker on wings and tail. Juvenile birds resemble the female, but young males soon show some blue colouring.*

Whereas the Brazilian Blue Grosbeak is a bird of open woodland and scrub, this species is a bird of dense forest and jungle. It is larger than its relative but duller blue, and the black of the face is restricted to the chin. However, both species are very variable both in size and colouring and might be confused. I do not know if it has been imported and have no record of it in captivity, but it strikes me as being a species that would adapt well to life in an aviary and should breed providing it is not crowded and has plenty of cover. According to Skutch the young are reared almost entirely on regurgitated vegetable matter, mostly maize, with insects playing a very secondary role. Such welcome news to the aviculturist must enhance the species' desirability considerably.

Blue-black Grosbeak
(*Cyanocompsa cyanoides*)

Yellow-bellied Grosbeak
(*Pheucticus aureoventris*)

Description: *8½–9½ in. (215·9–241·3 mm.). Adult male, head, throat, breast and back black; wings black with inner wing-coverts and base of primaries white, lesser wing-coverts*

yellow; tail black, tip to outer feathers white, uppertail-coverts spotted white; lower breast and belly bright yellow spotted on sides with black; sometimes throat and breast also yellow, spotted with black. Female similar to male but throat spotted black and white and breast black and yellow. Sometimes the female has its throat and breast yellow, spotted black, as does the occasional male, but it may be distinguished then by its yellow superciliary.

It is perhaps the largest of the grosbeaks. Despite its great size it appears to be a peaceful bird in an aviary, but I have no record of it having bred. It undoubtedly takes the larger seeds like sunflower and maize and may be offered cherries and other fruit with stones, or simply the stones. It is also listed as Golden-bellied Grosbeak or Black-backed Grosbeak.

Yellow Grosbeak
(*Pheucticus chrysopephus*)

Description: *8–9 in. (203·2–228·6 mm.). Adult male, entire head and underparts bright golden yellow, undertail-coverts white; mantle black spotted with yellow, lower back and rump greenish yellow; wings and tail black with large white spots. Female similar but streaked with dusky on top of head, rump spotted black, wings and tail brownish.*

This bird has been described as the Mexican Yellow Grosbeak, and it ranges southwards from Mexico to Venezuela. The Venezuelan race *P. c. chrysogaster* has been called the Venezuelan Yellow Grosbeak. It has been imported from time to time, although the latest reference that I have is pre-war. It was bred in Scotland in 1917, but the only details I can find for the species are for isolated males. These appear to be ideal aviary inmates.

Green Grosbeak
(*Caryothraustes canadensis*)

Description: 7½–8 in. (190·5–203·2 mm.). *Adult, head, back and tail yellowish green; flight feathers blackish edged with yellow green; mask and upper throat black; below, bright yellow tinged with olive on flanks. Sexes appear to be alike. Juvenile is not described.*

The species seems to be sufficiently distinctive and attractive to warrant inclusion. It is common in the savanna forest of the interior of northern South America, living in the treetops in loose flocks. Recorded food is insects and berries.

Dickcissel
(*Spiza americana*)

Description: *6 in. (152·4 mm.). Adult male has head grey; back brown streaked with darker brown, wings blackish with brown edges, rump and upper tail-coverts greyish, tail dark brown with paler edgings, the lesser wing-coverts are chestnut; chin white, mesial stripe yellow, centre of throat large black patch with white on either side, breast yellow, rest of underparts buffish white darker on flanks. Female lacks throat-patch or may have a few vestigial black feathers, is browner on the head, may be streaked on breast and flanks, and is generally paler. Immatures resemble female but young males are usually yellowy on breast.*

The Dickcissel takes its name from its call, which may be described as *dick-dick-ciss-ciss-ciss*. It is a breeding bird of the North American grasslands ranging from around the U.S. side of the Great Lakes to Texas and South Carolina. In August most Dickcissels gather into flocks of several hundred birds and migrate to Mexico or as far as the northern countries in South America for the winter.

The nest is placed on or near the ground and is built entirely by the female, who also does the incubating and all of the feeding of the nestlings. The babies are fed mainly on insects, the parent birds becoming particularly fond of grasshoppers, but once fledged they become almost totally seed-eating. According to reports of the species in the wild there is a large proportion of infertile eggs among the clutches laid.

I have no notes on the species in captivity, and regret that I have never seen it alive. It has been bred, by Teschemaker in 1911, but I have no details. It appears to be a fairly typical bunting both in behaviour and requirements in captivity, and although it is considered to be closely related to the cardinals and grosbeaks I would treat it much as an *Emberiza* bunting.

PASSERINA BUNTINGS

We come now to a group of six American buntings that together form the genus *Passerina*; however, the diligent researcher may well discover them listed in *Cyanospiza*. They are sometimes referred to as the tropical buntings in North America. The beautiful bright colouring of the males has guaranteed the everlasting attention of the Mexican bird-trappers who net them as they arrive in Mexico to sit out the winter in comfort if not safety. The females are dull coloured, generally brown but with bluish or greenish suffusions, and hence land in the pot. Consequently, the greater number of birds that are imported into Europe are all males.

Lazuli Bunting
(*Passerina amoena*)

Description: *5 in. (139·7 mm.). Adult male, head and upperparts blue, distinctive wing-bar white, breast cinnamon and underparts white. Female is brown where male is blue, has white wing-bars, buff underparts; it has bluish tinge on wings and tail. Immature resembles female.*

By the same token that the Red-headed and Black-headed Buntings are considered to be con-specific, as are the Rose-breasted and Black-headed Grosbeaks, so the geographical species concept rules that the Lazuli Bunting is con-specific with the Indigo and Varied Buntings. Indeed, it could be that not only these three but also the Nonpareil Bunting are all but races of one species. I personally find this a little hard to swallow. The Lazuli is a peaceful bird. Unfortunately I have kept only males, but these have been model members of a mixed collection, sharing happily with Tanagers and Parrot-finches. One of my birds had the misfortune to be murdered by a Spreo Starling (the latter was the male of a true pair) who, having been a mild-mannered creature hitherto, might well have taken exception to the Lazuli's colouring which, being bright blue above, cinnamon breast and white belly, is not too dissimilar to that of the Spreo.

In a report of several breeding attempts, one of which was successful, the author remarks that the Lazuli Buntings shared their aviary with a Zosterop, Avadavat and two Red-eared Waxbills. There appears to have been no conflict or aggression on behalf of either parent and they seemed to be model parents. Like many buntings the weakness to get fixed on to mealworms is very prevalent, and these two birds were inclined to feed mealworms almost exclusively, even though their breeder also supplied ants' cocoons, maggots and flies. The parents took fair amounts of Sluis universal brand of soft food.

It is a bird from the western half of North America, ranging from Canada down to Baja California; eastwards it reaches Oklahoma. It is a very adaptable species and is found in a wide range of habitats – in moist coastal forests, or among the aspens, willows and wild rose thickets along the rushing mountain stream, or in the brush of a burned-over field. In California it has been seen at 10,000 ft. (3,048 m.) in King's Canyon National Park and below sea-level in Death Valley. Such fairly typical bunting behaviour suggests an ideal aviary bird, which it is, for in addition to this and to being very attractive the male is an active and energetic song-bird. It is not a lovely song, but wouldn't the world be boring if it were populated only by Nightingales?

Indigo Bunting
(*Passerina cyanea*)

Description: *6 in. (152·4 mm.). Adult male, in summer, indigo blue all over, black lores and wing-spots; in winter, blue is largely obscured by rich brown, paler below, but sufficient blue retained to distinguish it from the female. Female is brown with paler lightly streaked underparts, blue flush on wings and tail. Juveniles resemble female, young males resemble winter male.*

Males in fresh autumn plumage, females and young birds are all pleasant but insignificant brown birds, though males can usually be

Indigo Bunting (*Passerina cyanea*)

told by the amount of blue on wings and tail. In spring, however, the males become a rich blue, varying in shade and intensity a little but generally deserving their common name. It is an eastern counterpart of the Lazuli Bunting occupying the same ecological niche from Canada down to the Gulf Coast, and ranges westwards as far as Arizona. Where its range overlaps with that of the Lazuli the two are often found to hybridize, though nobody seems keen to prove that they are con-specific, I'm happy to say. It is easily the most persistent and irrepressible songster of the *Passerinae* singing throughout the breeding season from the first rays of dawn until long after other birds have stopped for the night. One male I had delighted us, and the neighbourhood, by uttering his song during the night, especially if disturbed by sudden noise or light. The breeding song normally lasts until around August and is then replaced by a gentle sub-song.

In contrast to the Lazuli I have found the Indigo Bunting to be a bit of a bully, not really aggressive, but a fit male will chase other birds off its perch, or away from a favourite sun-bathing area, or away from the meal-worm tray. One male I had simply gorged himself to death with meal-worms due to an overenthusiastic helper leaving half a pound out.

There are various members of the Canary fancy who are devoted to producing new colours, red being the biggest obsession. For some strange reason the idea is nearly always to begin by producing a fertile hybrid then, by keeping to a strictly controlled breeding plan, gradually eliminate all the characteristics of the original shot of new blood except that of colour. This singularly unsuccessful and laborious plan is never given up. Following it, several attempts have been made to produce a truly blue Canary by crossing it with an Indigo Bunting. Despite a few claims of successful breedings, there is no evidence that a hybrid has ever been bred, and even were it possible it would certainly be infertile.

Varied Bunting
(*Passerina versicolor*)

Description: *5–5½ in. (127–139·7 mm.). Adult male, purple crown and rump, back of head and nape vermilion, reddish-purple back and throat, blue-black wings and tail. Female greyish brown, paler below with bluish grey on wings, tail and rump. Juvenile resembles female.*

Varied Bunting (*Passerina versicolor*)

Also listed as Painted or Versicoloured Bunting, this species replaces the Lazuli Bunting along the southwestern border of the U.S. where it breeds in Arizona and Texas: it is mainly a Mexican species. It is not very common in its native habitat, and spends most of its time on or near the ground in open country among brushy pastures, in mesquite chaparral, or in streamside thickets. It is a retiring bird, quickly dropping into cover at a sign of danger but emerging as soon as it is passed to stutter out its bright song, as if to say, 'I wasn't really afraid of you anyhow!'

It is not commonly imported and females are even rarer on the dealers' lists. The female can be told apart from the male even when the male is in fresh autumn plumage, when it appears much browner and duller. It is a delicate species, sensitive to begin with, and must be acclimatized with a degree of common sense. It needs a little more insect food than the aforementioned *Passerinae*.

Nonpareil Bunting
(*Passerina ciris*)

Description: *5–5½ in. (127–139·7 mm.). Adult male has head, nape and sides of neck purplish blue, back yellowish green, rump purplish red, and underparts vermilion. Female is greenish above, olive yellowish below. Juveniles resemble the female but are greyer.*

Called Painted Bunting in the United States, the French colonists called it *nonpareil* – without equal – and this is its common name in Europe. Spanish colonists called it *mariposa pintada* – painted butterfly. It is the most colourful of the genus and regularly imported in small numbers. If the reader hasn't wearied of me saying it by now when referring to this genus I must repeat that females are not often available. What this means to a serious aviculturist is that if he hopes to be able to breed them he must specify carefully that he wants a *true* pair, i.e. male and female, and not simply two birds. It is a sad fact that many retailers receive birds that they are unable to identify, or they simply do not realize that the sexes are different (and with many species the sex differences are often rather subtle).

The male retains his bright colouring all the year round and is thus clearly identifiable. He is territorial in behaviour, like the Indigo Bunting, and will argue and fight any perceived rival for his mate or home territory. It is less insectivorous and less delicate than the Mexican members of the genus and in this respect is like the Indigo and Lazuli. One problem with it is that the beautiful red of the plumage tends to fade and become yellowy, but this is unlikely to occur in a roomy planted aviary. In any case a course of colour feeding will correct the deficiency.

Rainbow Bunting
(*Passerina leclancheri*)

Description: *5 in. (127 mm.). Adult male, sky blue above, greenish on mantle; crown and tail turquoise green; ear-coverts and sides of neck cobalt; sides of face and underparts golden yellow, orange on breast. Female olive green, yellower below, bluish on tail.*

A beautiful bird from Mexico which is regularly available, it is always in demand and rarely fails to delight the purchaser on its arrival. However, there are several negative aspects of the bird. To begin with it is quite delicate on arrival and needs careful acclimatization; once acclimatized, however, it is reasonably hardy. It is not much of a songster, being more of a twitterer. It is the most insectivorous of the genus and does not seem to last very long without the regular addition of some insects into its diet. They do have the reputation of skulking in bushes and in general providing their eager owner with some disappointment. One correspondent hadn't seen his Rainbow Bunting for over two months and finally organized a careful search through the aviary to find its body, only to discover it happy and well.

I solved this problem by keeping mine in a planted aviary that lacked all shrubs or dense cover, being grassed with annual flowers and two or three apple trees. It seemed happy enough and eventually became quite steady and bold. Bold enough to escape somehow. I sat in a deck-chair watching its endeavours to get back into the flight and, while I was calculating the best way to help it achieve its objectives, a Magpie dropped like a bolt from a near-by horse chestnut and neatly caught it in its beak. The Magpie's performance would have done credit to a Sparrowhawk. I clapped my hands and ran, and retrieved the hapless Rainbow, which promptly expired in my hand.

Alternative names for the species are Leclancher's and Orange-breasted Bunting.

Rose-breasted Bunting or Rose-bellied Bunting
(*Passerina rositae*)

Description: *About 5½ in. (139·7 mm.). Adult male is very similar to male Indigo Bunting but has more purplish wash to head and white eyering; differs in having breast, belly and undertail-coverts bright rose pink, deepest and most intense on breast, sides of breast and flanks streaked with blue. Females are similar to the female Indigo.*

This sixth and last member of this genus of brilliantly coloured and beautiful birds is a complete mystery to me. It is not mentioned in the literature at all and has never been imported into Europe to my knowledge. However, to the reader who comes across mention of *six* species, but can never find more than five in the literature, I feel that it is well worth including a description. According to the skins in the British Museum of National History, it is found only in south-west Mexico.

I am indebted to my friend Mr. Arthur Douglas of Dallas, Texas, for the following lines (personal communication): 'Rosita's Bunting is from the semi-arid Pacific lowlands of Chiapas and Oaxaca. No doubt odd ones appear in the markets in Guadalajara and Mexico City. The one I had was a female. She seemed fairly hardy, always quick to fly out when I opened the pop-hole to the flight on still winter mornings. Kenton Lint (San Diego Zoo) had a male. He mentioned to me that its colour had faded (as would be the case with a Nonpareil Bunting). These buntings are coarser about the beak and head than the other Mexican *Passerinae*.' According to Margaret Lappe Wheeler it is found in a very restricted area, but 'fortunately is abundant along the highways passing through the steep wooded slopes as they drop from the interior highlands to the Pacific coastal plain' (*A Bird-Watcher's Guide to Mexico*).

Part Two
FRINGILLIDAE

INTRODUCTION

The total number of true finches varies according to which checklist one looks at, but there are roughly 120. Personally, I prefer to see the Chaffinches regarded as proper finches and not as buntings, but they differ from the Cardueline finches sufficiently (they have no crop, and have other anatomical and behavioural differences) to fully justify having their own subfamily, Fringillinae. These diferences have never been fully appreciated by bird-fanciers, and vain attempts are regularly made to produce hybrids between the Chaffinch and a Canary.

Finches are tree-dwelling birds, and belong much more to the forests than buntings. They are sociable birds, some even breeding in loose colonies, and most of them sing during a display flight. They are invariably attractive birds, often brightly coloured; the sexes are usually dimorphic, and in such cases the female is usually a duller, cryptic version of the male.

The three species of the Fringillinae are restricted to Eurasia, but the Carduelines range all over Eurasia, throughout Africa where they are most numerous, and in North and South America, but only two or three species have reached the Philippines. No finches occur naturally in Australia or the Pacific Islands apart from those introduced by man.

The Goldfinch is a favourite cagebird all around the world, and many thousands are trapped for this purpose in countries where it is permitted. In Britain it is protected, but a few are taken under licence each year. Its close relative in the United States is also a bird much appreciated by aviculturists, but it is also protected and is rarely seen in our aviaries. Another great favourite is the Siskin. There are twenty siskins ranging from Asia right across Europe, throughout Africa, to North and South America, and they are remarkably similar to each other both in appearance and behaviour. The siskins all have long sharp beaks adapted for feeding on tree seeds. Their close relatives, the serins, have shorter and less sharp bills more suitable for picking up seeds from the ground. They are mainly African birds. The best known of the genus is the Wild Canary from the Canary Islands, which has now become domesticated and is perhaps the most popular cagebird in the world.

A unique group of birds are the Crossbills with their strong bill with overlapping tips, a perfect tool for prying seeds out of tough pine-cones. They are rarely found away from conifer woods. Another group with distinctive bills are the Hawfinches, their large and heavy 'nut-crackers' being able to crack a cherry stone. The species are well spread out, one in Japan, another in China, our own well-known European bird, and a fourth is found in North America.

Finally, there are some reddish finches, many in the genus *Carpodacus*, from Europe, Asia and North America. In Europe, there is the familiar Linnet, the closely related Twite, and the circumpolar Redpoll. All of these are familiar cagebirds. Less familiar are the Rosefinches. They all have an unhappy reputation of losing their red in captivity, unless fed very carefully or given some colouring agent in their food prior to and during the moult.

HOUSING

Finches do well in cages, but the cage must be big enough for the birds to be able to fly about, as they are very active and agile. The most convenient size of cage in my experience is about 4 ft. (1·2 m.) long, and if they are to be kept permanently in a cage, one 6 ft. (1·8 m.) long is very good. They will often breed in a roomy cage whether wild-caught or 'domestic'. Of course, they do much better in outdoor aviaries – those with pink or red in their plumage have a much better colour, and breeding results are most likely to be good.

Being rather more sociable than buntings, finches can be kept more than one pair to a flight and many keepers tend to keep one pair each of several species in each enclosure. There are exceptions to what might be thought as a general rule here. For example, Hawfinches are frequently regarded as being sensitive and delicate breeders, and are given a secluded flight to themselves. Serins are sociable and easy-going birds, but the males can get quite pugnacious when breeding, and some of the larger African species are better off segregated. Goldfinches can be a problem in a mixed collection since a male will be very willing to service a soliciting female of another species, who is in fact

soliciting her proper mate while he is vainly displaying a short
distance away. Accidental hybrids between Goldfinches and
several other species have occurred in this way. The solution is
to keep the Goldfinches in an enclosure where such mishaps are
unlikely to occur.

In nature, the finches rear their young on a diet largely composed of insects, and for this reason planted outdoor aviaries are
very suitable for breeding. Many British bird-fanciers keep their
breeding finches in one large aviary that is 'planted wild', allowed
to become a semi-jungle of blackberry bushes, roses, Russian
vine, chickweed and other weeds. It is functional, but not very
sightly, and it doesn't take very much foresight and planning to
produce something just as functional, but a little more pleasing
to the eye.

FOOD

The basic diet obviously is seed, and whereas the staple seed for
the estrildines and ploceids is millet, the staple for finches is
Canary seed and all finch mixtures are based on this. In addition
they are given niger, teazle, hemp, linseed, rape, maw and gold
of pleasure. With a wide variety of seeds to choose from, it is very
convenient to buy a commercially prepared British Finch Mixture
and supplement this with a ready-made weed mixture in a separate
pot. One can experiment to find the birds' preferences by buying
seeds separately and giving each in its own pot. It is not a bad
idea to offer some seeds known to be favoured by particular birds
in individual pots, in addition to a basic mixture. Some examples
in my experience: I have found the European Serin to thoroughly enjoy lettuce seed; I have given mirabella (a small plum)
stones to Hawfinches, sunflower to Greenfinches, alder seeds to
siskins, and pine-cones to Crossbills. Green food is recommended.
Most species will take chickweed whenever it is available, especially
when breeding, and I have found various serins and siskins to take
large quantities of the buds, flowers and seeds. Lettuce is a favourite and will be nibbled, as will some other green vegetables. Soft,
sweet apples and pears may be given. Wild berries such as rowan
and cotoneaster will be eagerly taken by many species, particularly
the larger ones, and a few will take raisins and sultanas. Soft food
will be taken by most individuals and every keeper seems to have
his own formula ranging from crushed biscuit and egg yolk, to

complicated concoctions containing crushed insects and honey.
One might prefer to offer a commercial brand. Soft food, or egg
rearing food, is certainly to be recommended when the birds are
rearing. Wild birds may be encouraged to try it if it is sprinkled
over with a little maw, or a few mealworms chopped up.

BREEDING

Finches often build beautifully compact, cup-shaped nests that
are normally placed in the branches of trees or bushes. There are
many occasions where Redpolls have nested on the ground, but
this is usually at the northernmost limits of their range where the
birch and other plants are so stunted or small as to offer no advantage. The nests are built of twigs, grasses, rootlets, moss and
lichens, and the cup is lined with fine roots, wool and hair, down
and sometimes feathers. It is made by the female, although the
male may be in evidence near by as if to supervise, or exhort its
mate to greater efficiency by singing.

The eggs are bluish or greenish, normally spotted or streaked
with reddish or brown markings. An average clutch is four to six
in most species, three to four in Crossbills, but the Brambling has
a large clutch of six to seven. The incubation lasts about fourteen
days and is normally done exclusively by the female although
there are exceptions, notably the Bullfinch. The Carduelines feed
the nestlings by regurgitation, while the Chaffinches and Brambling
feed directly. An interesting aspect of finch behaviour that is
frequently commented upon is the fact that there is little or no
nest sanitation. It is difficult to see the survival value of this;
however, it should be remarked that during the first few days
after hatching the nests are kept clean, and at least one species,
again the Bullfinch, maintains this until the young fledge.

When breeding is hoped for the best kind of nesting facility to
offer is a secluded and sheltered corner, a cluster of heather or
evergreen branches, or hang-up open boxes or Canary nest-pans.
Many breeders arrange nest-sites under cover, and fix Perspex
or a similar material across the roof of the flight where birds are
nesting. This serves to protect from rain, cats and other defects
of nature. I have hung Canary nest-pans on walls that have had
clematis growing up them, and a most natural and attractive cover
has been produced. Many finches will breed in cages, especially
if the cage is roomy, has no other occupants, and the nest-site is

sheltered. Some will even breed in normal Canary double-breeder cages and hybrids with a Canary are quite simple to produce.

All finches need some insect food when rearing young, although it is possible to rear on a non-insect diet. If the breeder is intent on beating nature at its own game, and hopes to rear on a non-live food diet, the proteins and vitamins, etc., must be provided in some way. Fresh seeding grasses, seeding chickweed *ad lib.*, soaked seeds, and egg rearing food will all be useful, but some extra additive like Squibb's Vionate sprinkled over the seed or mixed with the soft food will be invaluable. If the adults refuse to feed the young without insects one must supply maggots in quantity, some mealworms, and all the natural insects available like spiders, caterpillars, etc.

I · FRINGILLINAE

CHAFFINCHES AND BRAMBLINGS

Of the three species making up the subfamily two are very well known to aviculture. The Chaffinch, in fact, is one of the commonest birds in Europe, and a few years ago was considered by some authorities to be the commonest bird in Britain. It is a creature of almost every habitat one can encounter in Europe, but it does not wander far from trees. The Brambling, the northern cousin, is most familiar to us as a winter visitor. In times of particularly hard winters in northern and eastern Europe we enjoy the Brambling invasions, when the winter flocks are swelled by the tens of thousands of extra birds driven further south-west than normal in their search for food. These two species have frequently been hybridized, but all attempts to cross-breed either with a Canary have failed. This is not surprising when one realizes that they are not so closely related as superficial similarities might suggest. The Blue Chaffinch is virtually unknown to us. It has been mentioned by Butler, but I get the impression that no specimens have been imported for some fifty years now, at least since the war.

All three species will take seed normally throughout the non-breeding seasons, but in the wild become extremely insectivorous during the breeding season. In my experience with Chaffinch and Brambling a good-quality British Finch Mixture is really all that is needed, although I have often given plain Canary in a separate pot. They will readily take alder, beechmast, and most tree seeds. Green food is not greatly appreciated, although a little lettuce and chickweed may be nibbled. When rearing, a wide variety of live food is desirable and a diet of mealworms and/or gentles will only suffice if supplemented with additives and a good-quality rearing food. The adults might be persuaded to take an insectile mixture.

Chaffinch
(*Fringilla coelebs*)

Description: *About 6 in.* (*152·4 mm.*).
*Adult male in breeding plumage,
forehead to nape and side of neck
slate-blue; superciliary, side of head,
chin to breast rich pinky brown fading
to whitish on belly and undertail-
coverts; mantle chestnut; rump olive
green; tail blackish, outer edges white;
wings, scapulars grey, shoulders
white, greater wing-coverts dark grey
with white tips, flights dark, edged
with fawn on secondaries, white patch
on primaries; bill steel blue; in winter,
bill is horn coloured and plumage is
duller. Female is dark ashy brown
above, paler below, but is unmis-
takably a Chaffinch by its distinctive
wing-barring which is the same as
the male's. Juveniles resemble the
female.*

There are several races of the
Chaffinch. None has attained any
significance in aviculture (unlike the
Bullfinch and Goldfinch, for
example), and the various Continental forms are insufficiently distinct to
warrant special attention. There are,
however, some races from north
Africa and the Atlantic islands which
are quite distinctive from the
European birds. *F. c. spodiogenys*
was called Algerian Chaffinch by
Butler, but according to Etchecopar
and Hue it is restricted to Tunisia;
it has the head, scapulars and uppertail-coverts slate blue, the mantle
and rump olive green, below it is
yellowish buff. The African Chaffinch, *F. c. africana*, is similar to
spodiogenys but is darker and has
more green on the back. The Madeiran
Chaffinch, *F. c. maderensis*, at one
time thought to be a distinct species,
is similar to *spodiogenys*, but it has
sides of face yellowish buff and

mantle and scapulars dull green.
Visitors to the Canary Islands who
leave the beaches long enough to
get up into the mountain forests may
see *F. c. tintillon*. This race is dark
blue above, with olive rump; the lores,
cheeks and underparts are warm
peach buff. This is the only one of the
races that I have any knowledge of
at all. It is occasionally kept in the
Canaries but is not considered to be
of much interest, for although it will
settle down to cage life and has a loud
and cheerful song, it will not cross-
breed with a Canary and this is the
criteria applied by the Canary Is-
landers to all finches. Butler received
some of the Madeira Blue Chaffinches in 1895 and over a couple of
years with them decided that they
were tamer and less excitable than
the British bird. The song of his male
developed well, and the call-note was
distinct. He was unsuccessful in
breeding them, despite some near
misses, and recommended use of
large quantities of chickweed.

Blue Chaffinch
(*Fringilla teydea*)

Description: *6½ in.* (*165·1 mm.*). *Adult
male is almost entirely slate-blue,
with a white circle around the eye;
paler below; wings darker and browner
and have characteristic bar markings
of the Chaffinch, only not pure white;
bill steel blue. Female, less vivid blue
washed with green, particularly
above. Juveniles resemble female;
young males soon show blue but do
not attain rich blue of maturity until
second year.*

This beautiful bird is also called
the Teydean Chaffinch after the area
of Tenerife where it abounds in the
upland pine forests. I made efforts to
obtain some when in the Canaries

and was told by the bird-fanciers there that it was available if one was patient, but that it didn't make a good cagebird as it remained nervous and never really settled to cage life. Furthermore, it suffered the mortal sin of refusing to breed with a Canary. Butler mentions it in *Aviculture* but gave no indication of its qualities in aviculture. Meade-Waldo imported some at the turn of the century and successfully bred them in an outdoor aviary. He stated that the males' song was more prolonged and had more volume than the British Chaffinch, and his male was very aggressive. In fact, during the breeding it failed to assist the female in rearing, and stole food from her that was intended for the chicks. This does not agree fully with what I have heard, but I certainly would not attempt to breed it in an open mixed aviary.

I am indebted to my friend Mr. Arthur Douglas for the following lines (personal communication): 'The Blue Chaffinch was described as "very rare" in 1913 when Alfred Ezra showed one at the L.P.O.S. National Show. This bird is illustrated in *Bird Notes*, March 1913. The Zoo had one about 1907. Hubert Astley bought four in Puerto Orotava about 1912. Meade-Waldo seems to have been the first importer about 1894. Apparently they bred in a large cage in Breslau Zoo about the same time (*Avicultural Magazine*, 1912, pp. 195–7). Meade-Waldo was the first breeder in England (1905).'

Brambling
(*Fringilla montifringilla*)

Description: *6 in. (152·4 mm.). Adult male in breeding plumage, head to mantle glossy black; rump white; uppertail-coverts dusky, edged white; tail black; mantle and lesser wing-coverts orange; median wing-coverts white; greater wing-coverts black edged white orange; flights black, pale edges, chin to breast orange, whitish to undertail-coverts, blackish flecks on flanks; in winter edges of black noticeably orange brown; breast duller also. Female resembles eclipsed male but is duller above and less strongly flecked on the head. Juvenile resembles female.*

The Brambling is also called the Bramblefinch, Mountain Finch and Royal Chaffinch, and is noteworthy for its lack of song. It is a bird of the forests of northern Europe and Russia, only visiting Britain as a winter migrant and wandering as far south as North Africa in 'explosion' years.

As an aviary subject it requires the same treatment as the Chaffinch, with which it has hybridized on many occasions. Those hybrids that I have seen were very attractive, but some enthusiasts maintain that this is the loveliest of the finch hybrids. Producing such useless creatures, however, can have little value apart from that of curiosity. I have found wild-caught Bramblings to be much steadier than wild-caught Chaffinches; they settle down very quickly indeed, but they have sometimes struck me as being rather dull.

II · CARDINALINAE

INTRODUCTION

This subfamily consists entirely of New World species and, with the exception of the *Passerina* buntings (a genus which most aviculturists would be more inclined to include in the Emberizinae), are all fairly large birds. Most of the saltators and many grosbeaks are the size of a thrush, but their bill shape and bulky body-size leave no doubt that they are seed-eaters. As a group they tend to be birds of forest margins rather than deep forest dwellers. Some are very widespread in their choice of habitat, like the Virginian Cardinal which is found in parks and gardens, deserts, and swamps.

The males are reasonably accomplished song-birds, though some – notably the Virginian Cardinal – are more accomplished than others. Generally speaking, however, they have acquired fame as cagebirds on account of their brightly coloured plumage. Females tend to be dull coloured. They are frequently sociable but not noticeably gregarious, and all are solitary nesters. When breeding, the male takes a secondary role, helping to build the nest but leaving the female to do all the incubating (there are exceptions). It will feed the incubating female on the nest, and help to rear the young. Many species in this subfamily stay paired throughout the year.

Essentially they are South American birds, their centre of distribution being tropical America, but species have radiated outwards and extended their distribution southwards to the Argentine and northwards to the borders of Canada. The Virginian Cardinal is an interesting case in hand which is clearly extending northwards year by year and has been doing so for a hundred years. The Rose-breasted and Blue Grosbeaks are also extending northwards, but being less hardy migrate back south each winter.

I have found most serins to be wilder and less confiding than siskins, and young aviary-bred birds acquire the attitudes of their parents very quickly. Those birds that do settle down are usually willing to breed, but, while there are plenty of records of breedings without any live food being supplied, one should consider them to be semi-insectivorous when rearing. Normally they will not breed on an all-seed diet, but the addition of seeding grasses and chick-weed, a good egg-rearing food and perhaps an insectile mixture will often prove to be sufficient. Prebendary Sweetnam made endless experiments with Bengalese as foster-parents in the 1920s and 30s and successfully produced young of several species of *Serinus* in this way. Whether these fostered young in turn bred successfully is another matter, and there is no record of this. My suggestion is that domestic Canaries make very much more appropriate foster-parents and any problem from imprinting will be minimized, or negated. Similarly, hormone deficiencies arising from badly balanced feeding will also be avoided.

Serins can be very aggressive when breeding. Any aviculturist who has kept adult pairs of *Serinus* spp. in small aviaries that contain mixed collections will have his story to tell of territorial aggression by the male serin. The solution is clear: either keep the birds in an enclosure (or cage) to themselves, place them in a large and uncrowded aviary, or ensure that the companion species are able to protect themselves. In other words don't keep serins with waxbills.

Canary
(*Serinus canarius*)

Description: *About 5 in. (127 mm.). Adult male, from forehead to lower back, uppertail-coverts, and tail grey, streaked with blackish; wings similar but feathers edged with yellowish; lores, superciliaries, side of neck, cheeks, chin to belly and rump, yellow; ear-coverts and mesial stripe grey; flanks yellow streaked with black; undertail-coverts whitish. Female similar but noticeably less yellow on side of head and greyish streakings occur on side of breast; wing-barring clearer and lighter. Juveniles resemble female but have* much less yellow and are generally duller.

At one time the Wild Canary was considered to be a race of the European Serin (*S. serinus*), being what one would expect an island race to be, larger and duller, but it is now considered to be a valid species in its own right. I have kept both birds together and have no doubt at all that *canarius* is a good species. It occurs in the Canary Islands, the Azores and Madeira. When the Canaries fell to Spain, the colonizing Spaniards soon brought the bird back to the peninsula and its popularity rapidly spread. Incidentally, the bird takes its name from the Islands and not the other way round. The Islands were so named by the Spaniards because of the wild dogs they found there. (*Can* is dog in Spanish.)

When in the Gran Canaria I learned that the local bird-keepers are practically fanatical about Canaries and are always trying to produce 'improved' versions (a favourite is *La Belga*, the variety known as Belgian Fancy) and will attempt any kind of cross-breeding to achieve this end. The favourite cross is with the Hooded Siskin, where the prime object is the red hybrid, but song variation is almost more important. A few of the more traditional older fanciers prefer to cross a male Wild Canary (*El Canario Montesino*) with a domestic female, and get their birds by one of two methods. The first is to trap them, the second is to take a clutch of eggs and place them beneath a broody domestic Canary. For purity of song I would prefer the former, but they opt for the latter.

Serin
(*Serinus serinus*)

Description: 4½ in. (114·3 mm.). *Very similar to Wild Canary (above) but is noticeably smaller, has a more 'cobby' shape, and smaller bill; yellow of forehead, sides of neck, chin to breast and rump of adult male is much brighter. Female is much more heavily streaked than female canarius. Juveniles resemble adult female but are less distinctly streaked, and more marked about the face. Young females usually have the streaking of the breast right across while young males have a lighter strip down the middle.*

The Serin can only be described as being a delightful bird; it is very common over much of southern Europe and its butterfly-like courtship-display flight is a familiar sight in town and country. They bred every year in a pine tree in front of my house and in a birch behind when I lived in Madrid, and the competition between rival males was a delight. They would respond to the challenge of my caged birds, and alight with intent to combat before me as I stood watching. It is the smallest of the European finches (though not the smallest serin), and ranges over the whole of western Europe and the Mediterranean littoral, but is not resident in either Scandinavia or Britain.

I have found it to be rather delicate when first trapped, requiring quiet and plenty of small seeds (mine have always loved lettuce seed); young birds are particularly delicate during the moult, and it is not a good traveller. However, once acclimatized and established it proves to be a hardy and long-lived bird.

St. Helena Seed-eater
(*Serinus flaviventris*)

Description: 5½ in. (139·7 mm.). *Adult male, forehead and superciliary, cheeks, chin to undertail-coverts bright yellow; crown to uppertail-coverts, lores and ear-coverts in a stripe joining the neck, mesial stripe, olive green streaked with black; rump washed with yellow; wings and tail blackish, feathers edged with white. Female greyish olive above, heavily streaked with dusky drab; wings dusky drab, the feathers edged buff, on yellowish green; below it is dull buff streaked with dusky on breast and flanks. Juveniles resemble a more densely marked female, young males soon show some yellow.*

This lovely serin comes from South

Africa where it is known as the Yellow Canary: it was introduced to the island of St. Helena, from which it takes its common avicultural name. An alternative common name is Yellow-bellied Seed-eater and Butler mentions Marshall's Canary. It is not often imported, but when it is available it proves to be very popular, being renowned for its strong clear song which several writers have described as being like that of a Skylark, but I have found it to be a little mechanical and repetitive. The female also sings when breeding, a softer version of the male's song. Male hybrids with a Canary are popular song-birds.

There are several records of successful breedings, including in cages, and three points emerge with clarity: firstly, that the male can be very aggressive and can damage its own mate if in too confined a space; secondly, that the male plays little or no part in the rearing of the young (and thus may be removed to an adjoining cage or enclosure); thirdly, that a little animal-protein is a great help and should be given as a supplement to half-ripe seeds when rearing.

Green Singing Finch
(*Serinus mozambicus*)

Description: *4½–5 in. (114·3–127 mm.). Adult male resembles St. Helena Seed-eater (above) but may be distinguished always by its smaller size and yellow rump. Female resembles the male but has an indistinct necklace of black spots across the throat. Juveniles resemble female but are paler and have light brown streaks on the breast.*

This very popular cagebird is over much of Africa south of the Sahara, from Senegal to east Africa and then southwards to eastern South Africa. It is known in South Africa as the

Green Singing Finch (*Serinus mozambicus*): two outer birds are females; centre one male

Yellow-eye Canary, but other names include Icterine Canary, Yellow-fronted Canary, Shell or Shelly, and Mozambique Serin. It is a ubiquitous and confiding little bird that may be found in town (breeding in trees in the street), park, or uninhabited country. It is not at all aggressive unless breeding in confined crowded quarters as its territorial requirement is restricted to the immediate vicinity of the nest. It breeds on a loose colony system and singing males definitely benefit in their performance by competition with each other. It is quite insectivorous when breeding and is best kept in a planted aviary for this reason, although it has been suggested by some writers that a good rearing food and unripe seeds will suffice.

Sulphury Seed-eater
(*Serinus sulphuratus*)

Description: *6–6½ in. (152·4–165·1 mm.). Adult male has superciliary, stripe between mesia and ear-coverts, chin and throat yellow; rest of body green, yellowish on belly, flecked and streaked above with black. Female very similar but has less distinct and less extensive yellow on face; belly to undertail-coverts paler. The bill is large and conical, and is horn to flesh. Juveniles resemble female but have black bill.*

The species is also called Sulphur-coloured Seed-eater, Brimstone Canary and Bully Seed-eater, the latter possibly deriving from the shape of the bill. It is a big bird, one of the largest of the serins. It is a bird of the southern third of Africa ranging from Kenya, Uganda and Angola downwards to the Cape. The race most likely to be imported would be *S. s. sharpii*, which is smaller than the nominate and is very easy to confuse

with the St. Helena Seed-eater. However, there are two points that help to reduce the risk of mistaken identity: the first is that *flaviventris* has the forehead yellow, whereas *sulphuratus sharpii* has the green of the crown extending to cover the forehead; the other is that the female *flaviventris* is quite distinct.

Sulphury Seed-eater (*Serinus sulphuratus*)

They are birds of bush and shrub country, often occurring in and around villages and gardens in towns. Apart from the usual seeds it also favours buds and berries (remember the clue of the Bullfinch-bill?) and when either is in season is more likely to forage in gardens. The male has a loud and sweet song and, like many serins, the female also sings when breeding. The young are reared almost exclusively on vegetable matter, and insects do not play a significant role. The species has been bred, but records are few and far between. It appears to be fairly amiable, but its size and bill would make it a formidable opponent for any small finch. I would keep it alone or with larger birds.

White-bellied Serin
(*Serinus dorsostriatus*)

Description: *5 in. (127 mm.). Adult male very similar to male* mozambicus, *but has longer tail, and belly to undertail-coverts white. Those I have seen have been paler above than* mozambicus. *Female is earth-brown above, streaked with dusky; uppertail-coverts yellow; wings and tail blackish, feathers edged with white or yellowish; below buff, paler on belly to undertail; blackish stripe running through eye, mesial stripe also blackish, and blackish streaks on breast. Juveniles resemble female, lack mesial stripe, are more heavily streaked on breast; young males have yellowish wash.*

This little bird is a fairly typical serin, occurring in scrub and open bush country in East Africa where it is locally common. It appears to be rarely imported and there are no records in the literature. I have a suspicion that males might be taken for a race of *mozambicus* and females sold as something else. It is undoubtedly worth special attention should it occur. It is said to have a fine song.

Natal Linnet
(*Serinus scotops*)

Description: *About 5 in. (127 mm.). Adult male essentially green all over with yellow superciliary, throat, and centre of belly; heavily streaked with black, the forehead, lores and chin being completely black. Female similar but duller below, being more heavily streaked, and lacks black chin and yellow throat-patch. Juveniles resemble female but are duller.*

Natal Linnet is only the avicultural name, for elsewhere it is known as Striped Canary, Grass Shelley, Sundevall's Seed-eater, or Forest Canary. It is a South African species, not very well known as it is a bird of forest canopy and, because of its cryptic colouring, is not often noted. It rarely wanders away from the thick tree-cover that it loves.

It feeds on tree seeds, buds, and soft parts of new leaves. The only reference I have for the species breeding in captivity is in *Foreign Birds* in 1955 which contains two reports. In one the pair shared a flight with about sixty other birds; they were model inmates but apparently quarrelled with the only other serins present. Several young were reared on a diet of mixed seeds, chickweed, dandelion, seeding grass-heads and boiled egg. In the other case the birds bred in a cage, and were successfully reared on 'the usual canary seeds, and egg and biscuit food'.

Cape Canary
(*Serinus canicollis*)

Description: *5–5½ in. (127–139·7 mm.). Adult male, forehead, crown, sides of head, chin to undertail-coverts yellow; neck and nape pale grey; rest of upperparts olive yellow, streaked with grey; rump unstreaked. Female duller than male; grey extends to crown; mantle grey streaked with dusky; below duller yellow; grey on side of neck extends across breast and may meet, otherwise as male. Juvenile resembles female but is grey to buff on head and throat, streaked with dusky.*

This distinctive bird cannot be confused with any other serin. It comes from South Africa and is described by Skead as having a confiding nature and 'comes readily to the environs of human habitation around farmsteads, and into towns. It is a favourite cage-bird both by virtue of its pleasing appearance and its delightful song.' It is a ubiquitous bird that may occur singly, in small flocks or very big ones, in open country or woodland. It is a lovely song-bird, being very Canary-like and strongly reminiscent of the Roller Canary whose song consists of a series of rolling trills and warbles.

Cape Canary (*Serinus canicollis*)

They generally breed in loose colonies with, for example, twenty pairs spread over about six trees forming the colony. Other species of serin often join such a colony, the Green Singing Finch being the commonest. Territorial aggression is restricted to the immediate vicinity of the nest. Cape or Grey-necked Canaries are occasionally imported, and according to Rutgers are delicate on arrival but soon become active and cheerful once settled down. They certainly make lovely additions to a collection.

Black-faced Canary
(*Serinus capistrata*)

Description: $4\frac{1}{2}$ in. (114·3 mm.). *Adult male, forehead, lores, superciliary, ear-coverts to chin black; broad yellow band edging black face; from throat to undertail-coverts yellow; upperparts green streaked with blackish on mantle and wings. Female greenish all over, yellowish below, streaked with blackish above and dusky from chin to breast. Juveniles resemble female, more heavily streaked.*

Black-faced canary (*Serinus capistrata*)

This bird comes from the Congo, and little is known about it in its natural habitat. The only reference that I have in fact is a breeding report from Northern Rhodesia (Zambia) in 1961 (*Foreign Birds*): the researcher will be confused since in error part of the report refers to the species as White-faced Canary. These birds bred successfully in a 16-ft. (4·9-m.) flight shared with about thirty other waxbills and finches: no mention is made of any aggression. The young were successfully reared on fresh and dry seeds, termites, apple and lettuce. The author made a point of stating that little interest was shown in the termites and that the parents would probably have reared without them, but the apple and lettuce were taken readily. A point of interest is that the male fed the young in the nest, while in many serins the male does not share in this duty until the young fledge.

Yellow-crowned Canary
(*Serinus flavivertex*)

Description: *About 6 in. (152·4 mm.). Adult male, forehead, crown golden yellow; lores, cheeks and ear-coverts, neck, olive green; nape to lower back and wing-coverts green streaked with black; rump and uppertail-coverts, yellow green also streaked; wing black with two yellow bars on coverts; tail black edged with yellow; chin to belly yellow, washed with greenish along sides of body; lower belly white. Female similar, duller because more heavily streaked, light streaking on head and underparts. Juvenile browner above than female and more heavily streaked all over.*

This is a bird of the highlands found both above and below the forest belt, where it is usually found in small groups. It comes from east Africa and Ethiopia, is said to feed on weed seeds and has 'A soft tinkling song, reminiscent of a European Goldfinch'. I regret that I know nothing about this species.

Red-fronted Serin
(*Serinus pusillus*)

Description: *5½ in. (139·7 mm.). Adult male, forehead and crown vermilion red; remainder of head black becoming streaked over a pale yellow base; rump and uppertail-coverts,*

belly and undertail-coverts less covered with black. Female similar, but red less extensive, and rump more heavily streaked. Juvenile resembles female but red of head is replaced by cinnamon brown, and rest of head brownish.

The Orange-fronted, Gold-fronted or Red-capped Serin is a mountain bird that ranges from Turkey across to the Himalayas and up into Tibet. In the winter it may be found in small flocks, ten to thirty, and often consorts with Twites and Goldfinches in

Red-fronted Serin (*Serinus pusillus*)

the foothills and valleys. During the summer it moves up to high groves of pine and birch or rocky steppe overgrown with barberry and juniper. It feeds on weed seeds, being particularly fond of the seeds of the common mugwort, alder and birch. It is not a familiar bird in aviculture but has been imported – probably trapped on the southern side of the Himalayas in northern India. In my experience it is a typical serin in its behaviour, but it clearly has some needs that ordinary aviculture does not satisfy. My own pair died after a year during which they seemed to be doing very well. Inquiries showed that other bird-keepers who have kept them also found them short-lived. Clearly they deserve special study.

S. pusillus is the only serin that naturally has red in its plumage. Some old males are suffused with red over much of the wings and body, including the rump. When one remembers that inter-*Serinus* hybrids are apparently all completely fertile it seems obvious that if a red Canary is to be produced by mixing blood it should be with this species, and not with the Venezuelan Hooded Siskin which is no more than 75% viable (see Hooded Siskin). However, it is such a lovely bird, completely tame and peaceful, that it deserves every effort on establishing it in captivity.

Streaky-headed Seed-eater
(*Serinus gularis*)

Description: *6 in. (152·4 mm.). Adult is drab ashy brown above streaked with black and white on head from forehead to nape; superciliary white; cheeks dusky; chin to undertail-coverts white; breast tinged with ashy brown. Sexes alike. Juvenile streaked noticeably on mantle and breast.*

This must be one of the least interesting serins to look at. It is a quiet and rather retiring species and might well be regarded in general as a species for the enthusiast. It does, however, have a pleasant song. Canary-like but a little quieter. It is a wide-ranging bird, being found over most of Africa south of the Sahara and is fairly common in bush and light woodland, and is frequently seen in and around towns and villages.

I have no record of it being imported into Europe, but I have no doubt that it has been. The only mention I have of it in aviculture is of Hawkes, who bred it successfully

in Mozambique in 1957. No details were given. However, it is known to rear its young at least partially on insects. Praed and Grant mention that at times it congregates into large flocks and does damage to both corn and fruit.

White-throated Seed-eater
(*Serinus albogularis*)

Description: *About 5½ in. (139·7 mm.). Adult male, from forehead to lower back drab heavily streaked with brownish black; rump yellowish; uppertail-coverts pale yellow edged with dusky; superciliary white; chin to undertail-coverts white, breast washed with pinky grey. Female resembles male but rump is more olive, less bright. Juveniles resemble adult female.*

The White-throated is sometimes called Thick-billed Seed-eater, which indicates that it has a much heavier bill than normal for a serin. In this case it is like that of the Bully Seed-eater. It may be confused with *S. gularis*, but may always be distinguished by the yellow rump; also, in most races of *gularis* the bill is a normal small serin-bill. It is a bird, not particularly attractive, that might just be advertised as a Yellow-rumped Serin (but this is the common name normally used for *S. atrogularis*) as its rump is sometimes a bright lemon. It is a bird of dry country in South Africa and South-West Africa, and some five races are recognized; the further into South-West Africa so the paler and larger the races become. The largest is *S. a. crocopygia*; it is the palest, and has the brightest yellow rump, equal in the female.

The White-throated Seed-eater is not a common bird in captivity, but it has a very pleasant song and appears to subsist mainly on seed and vegetable matter, but feeds the young on a mixture of insects and seeds. Butler's only remark about it is that 'it has a very powerful beak and can bite severely'.

Alario Finch
(*Serinus alario*)

Description: *5–6 in. (127–152·4 mm.). Adult male, entire head, throat and broken line extending from throat down either side of breast, black; black of head divided from chestnut of remaining upper-surfaces by white; primaries black; rest of underparts white. Female head light greyish brown, faintly streaked with dark brown; elsewhere, above a dull version of male; below pinkish buff, dark*

Alario Finch (*Serinus alario alario* and *S. a. leucolaema*)

on chin, washed brown on sides of breast. Juveniles resemble female but are more heavily streaked on head, and streaked lightly on throat and breast.

The Alario Finch, or Black-headed Canary, comes from South Africa. A distinct race, *S. a. leucolaema*, is found in South-West Africa and Orange Free State. It may be distinguished by the male having white superciliary and white chin and throat-patch; the female differs by having a much paler throat. It is a tame and confiding species often seen around farms and homesteads and is a favourite cagebird. Unfortunately, being a South African bird it is not often available. It has a pretty soft warbling song, and is said to be somewhat of a mimic. There are several reports of it breeding in captivity when it has reared on a diet of seed, weeds and seeding grasses. On one occasion, when ant pupae were supplied in quantity the parent birds ignored them. Both parents feed the young. It is many years since the species was represented in my collection, and a lone male we had was a model inmate, never showing any aggression to waxbill or munia.

Brown-rumped Seed-eater
(*Serinus tristriatus*)

Description: *5–5½ in. (127–139·7 mm.). Adult male, forehead to nape streaked black and white; rest of upperparts ash grey streaked with black; lores, superciliary, side of head black; chin white spotted black; throat white; breast white streaked ashy; rest of underparts white. Sexes similar but female duller black on head, and duller on belly. Juvenile brownish, streaked darker, and paler edges on wings.*

Also called Mennell's Seed-eater, this is a bird mainly of Rhodesia and Mozambique; little is known of it in the wild, but according to Praed and Grant it is a species of woodland or wooded rocky hillside. It takes seeds, naturally, but also fruits and small berries, the mistletoe being a favourite. It takes some insects when rearing and is said to have an 'attractive' or 'sweet' song. I have no avicultural reference at all.

Streaky Seed-eater
(*Serinus striolatus*)

Description: *About 5½ in. (139·7 mm.). Adult, buff, heavily and clearly streaked with dark brown all over; superciliary whitish, chin and belly white; some yellow suffusion sometimes occurs around forehead and throat. Sexes alike. Juveniles difficult to distinguish but more finely streaked below.*

This is a common species in high country, up to 14,000 ft. (4,267·2 m.), over much of East Africa from the Sudan to Tanzania. It is often seen in gardens, where it apparently does a bit of damage, presumably to buds and flowers, and is known locally as 'Sparrow' (Praed and Grant). I have not noted its occurrence in captivity, but cannot see why it shouldn't turn up from time to time.

Yellow-rumped Serin
(*Serinus atrogularis*)

Description: *4½in. (114·3 mm.). Adult, ash-brown above, streaked dusky; rump bright lemon yellow; uppertail-coverts ashy edged whitish yellow; below buff white streaked brownish black, chin whitish, throat heavily streaked. Sexes alike. Juveniles are paler.*

Sometimes called Yellow-rumped Seed-eater or Black-throated Canary, this lovely little bird is widespread over Africa from Arabia through East Africa to the Cape and up to Angola. Within this wide range it is irregularly distributed, preferring lightly wooded country. There are seven or eight distinct races and much racial variation: most races have the spots on chin and throat much blacker than the nominate, and are greyer.

This species is regularly imported in small quantities and, because of its similarity to the Grey Singing Finch, is sometimes advertised as Yellow-rumped Grey Singing Finch. It is similar in habit, is boisterously energetic and lively. Males will chase each other about and compete, singing lustily, but never doing any damage. Of course they should not be kept more than one pair to a flight unless the enclosure is fairly roomy. They are said to be very fond of flower seeds. In the only detailed breeding report that I have the birds were given '. . . mealworms, maw seed, soaked millet sprays, seeding grasses and a seed mixture of panicum and canary'. It is a good singer, even by serin standards, and can stand alongside the Grey Singer in this respect.

Grey Singing Finch
(*Serinus leucopygius*)

Description: *4½ in. (114·3 mm.). Adult, ash grey above, streaked dusky; rump white; chin to breast ash grey; belly, undertail-coverts white. Sexes, alike. Juvenile more heavily streaked above, and also streaked below.*

This species ranges from Senegal across to the Sudan, and is the West African analogue of the Yellow-rumped Serin. It is a common bird of dry bush, but is also found around farms, villages and in gardens. By virtue of its small size and lack of any bright colour it is one of the least significant of the serins. It is also possibly the smallest. However, it distinguishes itself by being probably the finest songster of them all, and more than repays for its keep by its performance. One problem with it is that the sexes are difficult if not impossible to tell apart and if one simply buys 'a pair' there is always a chance of getting two females. However, this should not deter anyone from trying it. Along with the Green Singing Finch it is the commonest species to be imported. Males will chase each other tirelessly, stimulating each other to even greater outbursts of song, but in my experience no serious damage is ever done. Of course, if two males and one female were kept in a cage or small aviary there may be serious

Grey Singing Finch (*Serinus leucopygius*)

trouble. They are good breeders, and a planted flight is recommended; the young will be reared on seed, grass and chickweed seeds, and Canary-rearing food. I have crossed it with a Border Canary with no difficulty, but like many serins it has cross-bred with other serins.

Yellow-throated Serin
(*Serinus flavigula*)

Description: *4½–5 in. (114·3–127 mm.). Adult has chin white; throat yellow, upper breast black (forming a bar); middle breast yellow; lower breast to undertail-coverts white;*

above like Yellow-rumped Serin. Sexes alike. Juvenile unknown.

This species is a very attractive variant on the small grey serin theme. I know it only from museum skins, but it comes from Abyssinia and may crop up in mixed consignments so is worth recording here. Virtually nothing is known of it.

South African Siskin
(*Serinus tottus*)

Description: *5 in. (127 mm.). Adult male, head green streaked with olive brown; back and wings brown, flight feathers tipped white; rump yellowish olive; uppertail-coverts olive tipped white; tail olive grey tipped white; chin to undertail-coverts yellow. Female similar but has yellow less intensive; streaked with brown on throat, rump brownish. Juveniles resemble adult female.*

There are two distinct races of this South African bird. The nominate, *tottus*, I have described above; it may be given the common name of Cape Siskin as it comes from the Cape region. The other race, *symonsi*, may be called Mountain Siskin, which is found in the mountains of Lesotho and Natal. This race may be distinguished by the lack of any white flecking on the upperparts, and brown flanks and belly of the male. The female lacks all yellow and is brown all over, paler below, and generally streaked. Either race may be called Brown Canary.

The species has a sharp-pointed siskin-like beak, and has been placed in the genus *Spinus* at some time but is now considered to be a serin. It feeds in bushes and on the ground, but less on the ground than most serins, and takes seeds, buds and insects. It has been reported as rearing the young entirely on insects (Skead), but this needs confirmation. Butler says of it (in 1925), 'The Totta Siskin (*C. totta*) from South Africa is also rather dull coloured, but has been far more frequently imported than the American species, though its song is certainly inferior. Messrs. Stark and Sclater evidently considered it more nearly related to the serins than the siskins.'

Citril Finch
(*Serinus citrinella*)

Description: *5 in. (127 mm.). Adult male, forehead, superciliaries, cheeks, chin and throat yellow; crown to nape and sides of neck grey; mantle greenish grey streaked dusky; rump olivaceous-yellow; wings and tail black, edges of medium and greater wing-coverts yellow, flights and tail edged white; underparts yellow-washed on breast and flanks particularly with grey. Female greyer and more heavily streaked above. Juvenile browner above and buffer below, streaked all over.*

The Citril is something of a mystery, for despite its appearance in every European field guide nobody seems to know anything about it. Allen Silver once wrote about some that he received from Germany (where it has been bred a few times): he bought the pair that Teschemaker bred, together with the young, and passed them on to somebody interested in Canary genetics. He said '. . . later heard nothing as to how the birds fared, but suspect they lost them in due course as they were not experienced bird-keepers. I am afraid if caged and treated exactly as Canaries they would sooner or later lose them.' It is a shame that Silver never explained why he was of that opinion.

Citril Finches are birds of high country and mountainside, and are generally associated with spruce and firs. I have watched them above the tree-line in the Spanish Guadarramas in summer. Their staple diet is the seed of spruce and fir, but they are recorded as taking the petals of apple blossom, buds and shoots of flowering shrubs, dandelion seeds (and many other weed seeds) and a few insects. Unlike Mr. Silver I would expect them to thrive on sensible Canary treatment.

GOLDFINCHES, SISKINS AND GREENFINCHES

Three finches that are very well known in Europe are the Goldfinch, the Siskin and the Greenfinch. They appear to be quite distinct from each other in shape, colouring and habit, and most books will place them each in its own genus, the Goldfinch in *Carduelis*, the Siskin in *Spinus* and the Greenfinch in *Chloris*. Current systematists, however, regard all three as being members of one genus, *Carduelis*, and when one studies an array of museum skins from around the world it is easy to see that *Spinus* and *Carduelis* are impossible to separate, and the Asian forms of the Greenfinch fall neatly in between the two.

There are a large number of species in the genus, but few of them appear in our aviaries. Members of the British Bird Fancy show an active interest in the Russian forms of some *Carduelis*, notably the Goldfinch since the northern birds are larger, and when cross-bred with the smaller British birds are a short-cut to improving bulk. Of course there is a negative corollary, in that the larger birds are not so brightly coloured: this is the privilege of the southern races. Apart from this aspect, foreign bird-enthusiasts tend to regard foreign siskins as something in between a 'real' foreign bird – such as a weaver, waxbill or Pekin Robin – and a British bird. This is very unfortunate, for the siskins are, without exception in my experience, most rewarding birds indeed. They settle very well in captivity, are very easy to maintain in good condition in cage or aviary, are willing and cheerful song-birds and are not difficult to breed. This last remark needs to be qualified of course, for although the occasional wild-caught bird will breed in a Canary double-breeder, most prefer quiet and seclusion. If cage-breeding is hoped for this should be roomy, 6 ft. (1·8 m.) long I suggest, and the nest-tray should be shielded by some heather or hessian. In a planted aviary, most specialists in these birds are inclined to let the enclosure run wild, and actually encourage tangled growths of brambles and weeds, especially thistle, shepherd's purse, groundsel and chickweed. Chickweed is the most popular green food, and a lush bed of it should be cultivated and protected as gold. When rearing the normal finch, seeds should be maintained, with soaked and germinated seeds added. In addition to the chickweed, egg-food or finch-rearing food may be given, and many keepers have their own formulas. One may enrich a proprietary brand with an excellent additive like Squibb's Vionate, or a simple multi-vitamin like Abidec or Paladec, and crumbled yolk of hard-boiled egg. Insects are a moot point and no doubt are a natural help; personally I have never given more than either mealworms or maggots. Some breeders go to lengths to collect aphids, blackfly, etc., while others make it a point of honour to avoid all live food.

European Goldfinch (*Carduelis carduelis*), male left, female right

European Goldfinch
(*Carduelis carduelis*)

Description: *5 in. (127 mm.). Adult male has frontal mask, forehead to bib, crimson; crown to upper nape black, forming a crescent that curves round to sides of neck; between red and black is white; nape whitish becoming cinnamon on back; breast and flanks washed pale cinnamon, belly and tail-coverts white; wings black with bright yellow* Carduelis *wing-bar; tail black; white tips to flight and tail-feathers. Female very similar. Juvenile olivaceous, paler on belly; streaked dusky; wings and tail blackish with characteristic yellow wing-bar. Intermediate immatures are greyish on head.*

The Goldfinch ranges from Britain eastwards to central Asia, and southwards to North Africa. It is prized as a cagebird in many countries on the Continent where it is kept in tiny cages and has a fairly limited life-span. About a dozen subspecies are recognized, and these divide roughly into two groups, those with a black crown (over most of Europe, North Africa and the Canary Islands), and those with a grey crown which are found in the mountainous regions of the eastern extreme of the bird's range in Asia. Throughout most of its range it is a bird of lightly wooded or cultivated areas, and is particularly noted in the autumn and winter when twittering flocks of adults and 'grey-pates' move about the countryside descending happily on waste ground to devour the thistle seeds. They are very difficult to sex in the field or in a crowded cage, but in the hand are easy. The fine rictal bristles on either side of the gape will be seen to be light in a female, black in a male; the red of the 'blaze' extends beyond the eye in a male but stops half-way in a female; finally the white areas, especially the rump, are more flecked with brown in a female. In an aviary the Goldfinch is a ready mixer, living amicably with other species and rarely bickering. The male is a great one for singing and courting, and has lightning-fast reactions when confronted with a soliciting female. Many a male serin or Canary (or come to that, Redpoll, Greenfinch or Bullfinch) has been thwarted by a speedy male Goldfinch dashing across to service the ready female responding at last to the efforts of its proper mate. I know of several unexpected mules and hybrids turning up in this way. Mules, of course, are easy to produce for this reason, but the Goldfinch is also a fairly easy bird to breed in a roomy cage.

Siberian Goldfinch
(*C. carduelis major*)

Description: *5½ in. (139·7 mm.). As for Common Goldfinch but entire plumage lighter; brown patches on breast less brownish, lighter, and occupying a smaller area; underparts much lighter, ochre-brown tinge scarcely noticeable.*

This bird is a race of the Common Goldfinch, but is bigger and less brightly coloured. It should be bred for its own sake and not cross-bred with the British race, *britannicus*, which in my opinion only serves to dilute the characteristics of each.

Grey-headed Goldfinch
(*C. carduelis caniceps*)

Description: *6 in. (152·4 mm.). Differs from Goldfinch in being grey from crown to lower back, thus lacking all black on head and brown on back.*

There are several grey-headed races. The one that I have mentioned here is referred to by Butler as the Eastern Goldfinch. Its range extends south-east to touch the northernmost parts of India, where it is probably trapped more frequently than one would gather from the advertising. They have been advertised as Himalayan Goldfinches: I was too late to buy any, but the dealer told me that 'they were not as pretty as the British Goldfinch and were not very popular. As they were slow-movers I won't take them again.'

American Goldfinch
(*Carduelis tristis*)

Description: *About 5 in. (127 mm.). Adult male in breeding plumage is bright lemon yellow with black cap, wings and tail, the wings having a noticeable white bar; uppertail-coverts white; out of colour the male loses black cap and yellow is replaced by olive yellow tinged with brown. Female resembles eclipsed male but lacks the latter's bright shoulder-patch. Juvenile resembles female but is duller and browner.*

American Goldfinch
(*Carduelis tristis*)

This lovely bird appears to have very similar habits to our European Goldfinch, and in most ways is its North American counterpart. It seems to have a similar behaviour-pattern in captivity and will settle well, delighting its owner with its song, and will breed tolerably easily. It has undoubtedly been bred several times in captivity, both in its native U.S. and in Europe. It is said to rear its young almost exclusively on vegetable matter, feeding only a little insect food. American bird correspondents have voiced the opinion that the European bird is more attractive. It's all a matter of taste, and scarcity certainly enhances desirability in the market place. This bird may be listed as American Siskin.

Lesser Goldfinch
(Carduelis psaltria)

Description: *4–4½ in. (101·6–114·3 mm.). Adult male, top of head black; sides of head and back dark olive green streaked with black and soon graduating into black wings and tail; wings have white bar; lower side of face, chin to belly yellow. Female similar but lacks black cap, and is faintly streaked below. Juvenile greyer and duller than female.*

There is a form of this bird which has the entire upper surface black, from forehead to tail, relieved only by the white wing-bars. It is known as the Arkansas Siskin or Goldfinch, or may be called Green-backed or Dark-backed Goldfinch. It ranges throughout the U.S., through Central America to northern South America. The race that I have seen came from Central America and had the entire head black. This bird was bred in the San Diego Zoo in 1952 when the parents took over a deserted Zebra Finch nest in a wooden box, and successfully reared four youngsters. They were referred to by the Zoo as Colombian Siskins.

Yarrell's Siskin
(Carduelis yarrellii)

Description: *4–4½ in. (101·6–114·3 mm.). Adult male, lores and forehead to nape black; back olive green; wings and tail black, former with yellow bar; sides of face and entire underparts lemon yellow. Female lacks black cap, is browner on wings and tail. Juvenile duller version of female.*

Yarrell's Siskin (*Carduelis yarrellii*)

This attractive siskin comes from southern Venezuela and eastern Brazil. It is listed by De Schauensee as Yellow-faced Siskin, and is said to be a bird of open country and shrubbery. It has a smaller bill than most siskins, which may denote ground-feeding habits. Butler found them delicate and his died early on: Rutgers says that they may arrive in a weak and delicate condition, and 'need much care and plenty of insect food to become acclimatized'.

**Hooded, Southern, or
Black-headed Siskin**
(*Carduelis magellanicus*)

Description: *5 in. (127 mm.). Adult
male, entire head and throat black;
neck and back olive yellow; wings
black with bright yellow bar; tail
black; rump, uppertail-coverts and all
underparts yellow. Female, head to
rump olive grey, streaked with
greenish, below grey, belly white;
wings and tail as male. Juvenile dull
version of female.*

There are several black-headed
siskins in South America, which may
be confused with this bird. I have
already mentioned the black-headed
form of *C. psaltria*, which may be
distinguished by its dark green back.
C. ictericus is very similar but
has a greener and duller breast.
It may be called Hooded or Black-
headed Siskin. The Thick-billed
Siskin, *C. crassirostris*, may be told
by its larger and heavier bill, and
bigger size, being a good $5\frac{1}{2}$ in. (139·7
mm.). The Saffron Siskin, *C. siemeradzkii*, is smaller, only 4 in. (101·6
mm.), and has the underparts bright
saffron yellow. Finally there is *C.
notatus* from Mexico with extensive
black head, black wings and an
orange tinge to breast and flanks.
However, it seems that the Black-
headed Siskin, *C. ictericus*, is the
species normally imported. It is unfortunately not very popular as it only
differs from the European Siskin in
having the head black, is rather delicate until fully acclimatized, is never
as hardy as our native bird, and is
more expensive. On the credit side it
must be said that it is a lively bird
with a sweet Goldfinch-like song. I
have no record of it having bred in
captivity.

European Siskin
(*Carduelis spinus*)

Description: $4\frac{1}{2}$ *in. (114·3 mm.).
Adult male has lores, forehead and
forecrown black; back yellowy green
with black streaks; rump and uppertail-coverts yellow streaked faintly;
wings and tail black, edged with
yellow or white, wings carry clear
yellow bar; chin normally black (but
much diminished in winter and may
not be present in younger males);
throat to breast and flanks yellowish
turning to white on belly and undertail; flanks streaked with black.
Female lacks black on head, is more
grey-green above, much less yellow on
breast and is more regularly streaked.
Juvenile like female but duller and
more developed streakiness.*

The Siskin is found over most of
the British Isles and ranges westwards through Europe until it peters
out in western Asia. A pocket of
distribution is found in China. It is
much given to wandering and irregular
migrations according to the weather
in its native north, the aspen and
birch crop, and population explosions.
It is remarkably homogeneous, and no
races are recognized. The male is a
cheerful and persistent songster and,
in a mixed collection of newly
trapped birds in a dealer's cage, it
will certainly be the Siskin who begins singing first. Anyone who has
kept a Siskin cannot fail to be en-
chanted by it, for it is the cagebird
par excellence. My first experience
with the species was only a few
years ago when I bought a single,
newly trapped young male in a street
market in Spain. I ran it in a small
cage – about 30 × 20 × 20 in.
(762 × 508 × 508 mm.) – with a
female Border-type Canary, more
out of idle curiosity than serious am-

Siskins: 1. Black-headed Siskin (*Carduelis ictericus*); 2. Thick-billed Siskin (*C. crassirostris*); 3. Saffron Siskin (*C. siemeradzkii*); 4. Black-chinned Siskin (*C. barbatus*); 5. Himalayan Greenfinch (*C. spinoides*); 6. Yellow-rumped Siskin (*C. uropygialis*); 7. Lesser Goldfinch (*C. psaltria*); 8. Yarrell's Siskin (*C. yarrellii*)

bition. Within no time the Siskin was feeding the Canary and so I gave them a nest-pan and some nesting material, and within a week the Canary was sitting on five eggs. Four of these hatched and grew into fine healthy mules. Before they fledged I opened the cage door and allowed the parents the run of the bird room. The Siskin was a model parent, as tame and steady with me as was the Canary. They reared exclusively on mixed seeds, dry and soaked, and a pile of freshly picked chickweed each day. I have since kept many Siskins, and have found the females more difficult to steady down than the males. In my experience they love the seeds of alder and birch, and a bunch of branches hung up in the flight will provide a lot of interest, and nutritious food.

Black-chinned Siskin
(*Carduelis barbatus*)

Description: $5\frac{1}{2}$ in. (*139·7 mm.*). *Adult male crown deep black, upper-parts dark greenish, streaked with black, wings black with two yellow bars and yellow patch; tail black with yellow patches at base; chin and upper throat black, rest of under-parts yellowish green, whitish around vent. Female lacks black on head and chin, is less yellow below, undertail white.*

The Black-chinned Siskin is called variously Canary, Goldfinch or Siskin in South America. It is by far the most widespread and common siskin in Chile, living at low alti-tudes and frequenting orchards, gardens, parks, and cultivated areas around town and village. It is a popular cagebird and is the Chilean counterpart of the European Siskin and Goldfinch in one. It is rather like a larger and boldly marked European Siskin in appearance, and would no doubt be viewed by fanciers of *C. spinus* with considerable interest.

Yellow-rumped Siskin
(Carduelis uropygialis)

Description: *5½ in. (139·7 mm.). Adult male head, neck and back black (maybe finely scalloped with green on the back); rump, breast, belly and undertail canary yellow; uppertail-coverts yellow marked with black; wings black with wide yellow bar; tail black edged yellow at base. Female similar but black less dense, and yellow not so bright.*

This is a strikingly coloured bird, in my opinion one of the most attractive of the entire subfamily. In its native South America, it is another Andean species, it may often be called the Mountain Canary. It has a sweet song, remarkably like that of a European Goldfinch, and the combination of colouring and song make it a prized cagebird. I do not know whether it has been bred in Chile or the Argentine, but I have been told that it is occasionally cross-bred with a domestic Canary.

The only nests described in the wild have been placed in inaccessible cracks high up on cliff faces. Whilst it may occasionally wander down the valleys to lower levels, it is essentially a bird of the high plateaux.

Black Siskin
(Carduelis atratus)

Description: *6 in. (152·4 mm.). Adult male completely velvety black, with double yellow wing-bar; vent and undertail-coverts, patch at either side of tail at base yellow. Female similar but both black and yellow duller.*

This beautiful bird, possibly even more striking than the Yellow-rumped Siskin, ranges from southern Peru through Bolivia and Chile to Argentina. It is another bird of the Andes, generally occurring from 6,000 ft. to 16,000 ft. (1,828·8 m. to 4,876·6 m.). It appears to be identical in its habits to the Yellow-rumped bird.

Hooded Siskin (*Carduelis cucullatus*)

Hooded Siskin
(Carduelis cucullatus)

Description: *4½ in. (114·3 mm.). Adult male, entire head and throat black; rest of body scarlet red; wings and tail black with red edgings; bright red wing-bar. Female lacks black head, mainly greyish above, washed with red, bright red rump; grey on sides of head, whitish on lores; throat and breast red; flanks grey; belly white. Juveniles are a duller, faintly streaked version of the female.*

The Hooded or Red Siskin is practically unique among the *Carduelis* in having such a lot of red in its plumage. It is officially protected in its native Venezuela, but there is a thriving trade and consequently a high market price ranging from £40 to £60 for a male bird. The males are in demand among Canary-breeders all over Europe, who see the species as the way to produce a truly or naturally red Canary. Unfortunately this desire is based on an imperfect opportunity, since the *Carduelis* and *Serinus* are sufficiently distinct genetically for a cross-breeding to be only 75% viable. The non-viable 25%, which, by the Laws of Mendel, would be the red hybrid are produced by the female Canary as dead-in-shell. This was demonstrated statistically and graphically by C. H. Rogers in *Cage and Aviary Birds. If* it will ever be possible to produce a red Canary (meaning a form of *Serinus canarius* with an admixture of another species), then logically the other partner in the mating has to be *S. pusillus*. Some of these birds have the body totally suffused with red, and a *pusillus* × *canarius* cross should be 100% viable.

Personally I find the Hooded Siskin a delightful bird in its own right, and a true siskin in behaviour and all its attributes. I have heard of breeders attempting to establish domestic strains of the species in order to take advantage of the great demand. This is all to the good, because one day the Venezuelan government will be sufficiently well organized in its natural resources control to stop exportation, and we will see the Hooded Siskin no more. Among the many successful breedings is the interesting record of two Hooded Siskins being raised successfully by Bengalese, at San Diego Zoo in 1952.

Yellow-bellied Siskin
(*Carduelis xanthogaster*)

Description: 4½ in. (114·3 mm.). *Adult male velvet black all over except for belly, flanks (which are streaked with black), undertail-coverts and yellow wing-bar. Female has black replaced by dull greyish olive; below dull yellow, centre of belly white.*

Yellow-bellied Siskin (*Carduelis xanthogaster*)

This is a beautiful and striking bird from Colombia, Venezuela and Ecuador where it is a bird of the bushy or lightly wooded mountain slopes. I have been thwarted several times in my attempts to obtain this bird and so far know nothing about it.

Greenfinch
(*Carduelis chloris*)

Description: 6 in. (152·4 mm.). *Adult male, mainly dull olive green, greenish yellow on breast and rump; lemon-yellow wing-bars and sides of tail. Female duller, browner, and much less yellow. Juvenile is similar to female but paler and lightly streaked.*

The Greenfinch is one of our larger finches, and is common over much of Europe. It has a similar distribution to the Siskin, ranging from Ireland to the Urals and Russian Turkestan. Its diet is varied, mainly because its large bill enables it to husk seeds of a wide size-range, but when confronted with a choice it generally prefers the larger seeds. In the wild it will take elm, yew, hornbeam, rose and bramble. On waste or cultivated land it will show a lot of interest in charlock, persicaria and burdock. In captivity it can be readily satisfied with a good supply of sunflower, and a sure way of keeping Greenfinches as regular visitors to a bird-table is to be lavish with it.

The male Greenfinch is a persistent songster, and will pour out its offering for hours on end. Personally I find the long-drawn-out wheeze at the end of the song-burst unattractive, and decidedly unpleasing when heard for the hundredth time in an afternoon. However, the Greenfinch is thriving in aviculture; it is well and truly established as a reliable breeding bird and there are hundreds of self-perpetuating strains in Europe today. The reasons are twofold: firstly, the ability and willingness of the bird to breed in captivity and rear strong healthy young on a diet that does not include live insects. Secondly, the interest created by the colour varieties that have been established by skilled breeders, most noticeably fawn, dilute and the beautiful lutino. The Greenfinch is renowned, or infamous, for the reason that large numbers (maybe 40%) of newly weaned young birds die inexplicably round about the moult time. The arguments rage about causes, and every breeder has his own pet theory, preventative and solution. Personally I have no idea as to the reason. However, there is evidence that *if affected birds are caught early enough* and given large doses of total vitamin complex and mineral trace

Common Greenfinch (*Carduelis chloris*): the two outer birds are males

elements, etc., the mortality is reduced dramatically. The first noticeable signs are a ruffing, or erection of the feathers at the nape of the neck.

Like all the European finches the Greenfinch has been the partner in many cross-breedings. One of noteworthy interest perhaps is a Purple Finch (*Carpodacus purpureus*) × Greenfinch produced by George Lynch in 1954.

Chinese Greenfinch
(*Carduelis sinica*)

Description: *5½–6 in. (139·7–152·4 mm.). Adult male, lores black; forehead, chin, throat and sides of head dull lemon yellow; crown to nape grey; back cinnamon, washed blackish; rump yellow; wings black with bright yellow bar; tail black; breast cinnamon, paler on rest of underparts. Female similar but duller, much less yellow on head.*

The thing that struck me about this bird when I first saw it was its similarity to a Goldfinch, despite its grey-to-yellow head, and size and shape belonging to the Greenfinch. Its status as a true species is in doubt, and it might possibly turn out to be a race of *chloris*. It is an easy bird to maintain in captivity, and will thrive on a normal diet of mixed seeds, but has a great love of thistle. It breeds fairly readily, and one breeder in South Africa has established a fine strain. None the less there is a great need for data about its behaviour, song, etc., and careful comparisons with the Greenfinch are most welcome.

Japanese Greenfinch
(*Carduelis kittlitzi*)

Description: About *5½ in. (139·7 mm.). Adult male dark olive green all over, lighter and more yellowish on belly and rump; wings blackish with bright yellow bar, tail black edged yellow. Female duller, paler and greyer.*

Nothing appears to be known about this bird and I cannot trace it in aviculture apart from vague hearsay references. From the skins I have studied it looks very much like a typical siskin with a Greenfinch-like bill. Any information published would be most welcome.

Himalayan Greenfinch
(*Carduelis spinoides*)

Description: *5 in. (127 mm.). Adult male, superciliary, crescent below eye, chin to undertail, and band around neck and rump bright lemon yellow; remainder of body greenish brown to black, darkest on head; wings and tail · slightly browner, wing-bar bright yellow; bright yellow patch outer edge of base of tail. Female similar but duller and less yellow on wings.*

Whereas the above-mentioned Greenfinches were previously placed in *Chloris* this siskin was placed in *Hypacanthis*, under which genus one is most likely to find it if searching field literature for reference, although in even earlier literature it appeared under *Chrysomitris*. It is often referred to as Himalayan Siskin, and I have come across it described as Sikkim Siskin. It ranges from Pakistan across the southern side·of the Himalayas through northern India, Nepal, Sikkim, to south-eastern Assam and western Burma. It breeds at levels between 8,000 and 11,000 ft. (2,437 and 3,351 m.) but winters lower down.

It is longer and more brightly coloured than the European Siskin, and is found in woodland; occasionally, however, small parties are seen in gardens. Teschemaker successfully reared two broods in 1914 and Shore Baily raised two broods of Goldfinch × Himalayan Greenfinch hybrids in 1919. They appeared to be good parents and no mention is made of any aggression.

Tibetan Siskin
(*Carduelis tibetanus*)

Description: *4–4½ in. (101·6–114·3 mm.). Adult male bright yellowish green on the head with blackish green superciliary, and similar stripe below eye; streak through eye yellow, cheeks and mesia olive green; back and mantle olive lightly streaked with dusky, rump yellow; wings olive green, greater wing-coverts brown edged with yellow, flights and tail brown edged with greenish; below, throat and breast bright yellow, flanks yellowish green streaked with brown, remaining underparts deep yellow washed with olive on flanks. Female similar on head to male, but entire body more noticeably streaked brownish and yellow areas are paler. Immature resembles female, but more extensively streaked; the belly and undertail-coverts are more white, whiter on females.*

The Tibetan Siskin is a Himalayan species that is found only in Nepal, Sikkim, the south-eastern corner of Tibet and south-western Sikang. It breeds at high altitudes (14,000 ft./ 4,269 m.), in juniper bushes close to the ground, and feeds on grass, and other seeds and berries. It winters south to north-eastern Burma from whence the odd specimen may be available. It appears to have been available fifty or sixty years ago, but virtually nothing occurs in the literature. Shore Baily mentions that Teschemaker's birds bred very freely, and a show report in 1919 describes them as 'really attractive and beautiful birds'. They appear to be rather like the European Siskin in their requirements in captivity, though this is pure supposition. They may be listed in the genus *Chrysomitris* in early literature, and have also been called Sikkim Siskin.

BULLFINCHES

There are some five species of Bullfinch comprising the genus *Pyrrhula*, and for convenience I have included in the same section the *Rhodopechys*, which includes the Trumpeter Bullfinch. The only species familiar in aviculture is the Common Bullfinch, which is of course very well known and deservedly popular. In Germany it is a traditional cagebird, where it is frequently hand reared and taught to whistle tunes. Such accomplishments are an advance on the natural performance of the bird, for it is a poor songster normally. All of these birds are attractive and interesting, but in my opinion the British race of the Bullfinch is the loveliest.

It is a cause of great sadness that its depredations in the orchards ensure its wholesale persecution and destruction.

Bullfinch
(*Pyrrhula pyrrhula*)

Description: *6–7½ in. (152·4–190·5 mm.). Adult male, entire top of head, lores, forecheeks, and bib black; nape to lower back grey; wings black with bright white bar; rump white; upper-tail-coverts and tail black; sides of head, throat to belly rosy red; undertail-coverts white. Female dull browner version of male. Juvenile resembles female but lacks black cap.*

Some ten subspecies of the Bullfinch occur, and some of these even coexist with others in certain localities, but this is evidently secondary overlapping of ranges, an insufficient ground for regarding such forms as distinct species. Besides, cross-breed-ing between such subspecies has been known to occur. However, for commercial reasons the pet trade persists in regarding the more popular races as distinct species, and one has some sympathy with this.

The nominate race, *pyrrhula*, becomes the Siberian Bullfinch of the trade, or East European or Northern Bullfinch. It is a longer and larger bird, not as bright red on the breast as the British Bullfinch, *pileata*. The Japanese Bullfinch, *griseiventris*, has the red restricted to the face, the rest of the underparts being grey. The race which actually comes from Siberia is *cineracea*, which is called the Grey Bullfinch which has *all* the red replaced by grey. Sizes are variable, the European races are about 6 in.

Bullfinch (*Pyrrhula pyrrhula*)

(152·4 mm.), and the Northern bird is about 7 in. (177·8 mm.). The Japanese is about 6 in., but another race, *cassini*, the Kamchatkan Bullfinch which we never see since it only comes from the Russian peninsula of Kamchatka, is 7½ in. (190·5 mm.). It is, incidentally, coloured like a pale Northern Bullfinch.

It is perhaps foolish to say that one bird is preferred over all others, but the Bullfinch is my personal favourite. It has a delightful rounded shape, and the smooth *svelte* plumage that may also be found in the Java Sparrow. The red colour is quite variable, and is naturally at its richest and deepest in fully adult wild males. In captivity many breeders cross the Northern Bullfinch with the British to increase the size of their birds, but in doing so lose richness of colour (though some deny this) and compensate by providing red pepper-colour food, or one of the cantha-xanthin derivatives in the diet. Other breeders keep their birds in planted outdoor flights and provide plenty of natural colour-rich items, like rowan-berries. One friend of mine maintains a strain of pure Northern birds bred in this way and I must say that they are the equal of any British Bullfinch in colour. Bullfinches breed well, and readily in captivity, and are frequently bred in cages. In a mixed collection they can be rather aggressive when breeding and best results are obtained if they are given a small enclosure to themselves. Use of live food when rearing is not critical, but in my opinion much better than not. In the absence of live food the egg-rearing food must be very well balanced.

Red-headed Bullfinch
(*Pyrrhula erythrocephala*)

Description: *5½ in. (139·7 mm.). Adult male, forehead, lores, small spot behind eye, forecheek, and chin black; rest of head, neck, throat and breast orange red, pale to greyish on the cheeks; belly greyish; undertail-coverts white; back grey; wings black*

Bullfinches: 1. Red-breasted (*Pyrrhula erythaca*); 2. Brown (*P. nipalensis*); 3. Common (*P. pyrrhula*); 4. Orange (*P. aurantiaca*); 5. Red-headed (*P. erythrocephala*)

with greyish bar; rump white; upper-tail-coverts and tail black. Female similar to male, but orange red is replaced by yellowish green, underparts browner.

This lovely bird is one of four Bullfinches that are found in the Himalayas, ranging from Kashmir to Bhutan. The Orange Bullfinch, *P. aurantiaca*, is very similar to *erythrocephala* but has a richer, more tawny orange that extends to back and belly. The Red-breasted Bullfinch, *P. erythaca*, also has the black mask of the other two but has the rest of the head grey, uniform with the back, and has a bright red breast. The last of the quartet is the Brown Bullfinch, *P. nipalensis*, which has the mask dark brown, and the rest of the plumage brown. These are birds of mountain forests that breed at elevations of from 6,000 ft. (1,828·8 m.) to 11,000 ft. (3,352·8 m.), descending to 3,500 ft. (1,066·8 m.) in winter. None the less it is surprising that they do not find their way to the Calcutta bird-market rather more often than they do. Butler mentions the Red-headed species, and says that it was kept by Astley and Ezra, and appeared at the London Zoo in 1914. It does not seem to have appeared in Britain in recent years, and any account of it, or any of the other Himalayan Bullfinches, would be most welcome.

Trumpeter Bullfinch
(*Rhodopechys githaginea*)

Description: 5 in. (*127 mm.*). *Adult male in breeding plumage, head, back, breast and flanks ash brown with rosy edges; rump, rest of underparts whitish brown with rosy edges, particularly pink on belly; wings and tail dark brown with pale edges and*

reddish suffusion or edging intermingled; in winter pink or red is lost, leaving the bird an irregular sandy colour; bill red, brighter in summer. Females are less pink and lack any grey on the head, and have the bill duller orange red. Juveniles are dull sandy brown all over, darkest on wings and tail, paler below; bill brown.

The Trumpeter Bullfinch is found on the Canary Islands, where it is known as the Moro, and ranges over much of north Africa eastwards to Iran, and possibly through Pakistan to reach north-western India. It is a bird of rocky outcroppings and low-grade mesquite in desert country. Its song is a prolonged tremulous twittering, interspersed with chirps and croaks. In display the male throws its head back, raising the open bill vertically and uttering a sound from which the common name is derived. They are said to feed largely on buds, leaves and seeds of desert plants with some insect food, especially when breeding. In captivity, they are easy to maintain on a simple seed diet with a little lettuce or chickweed given at intervals. It is a remarkably steady bird in a cage, and seems to develop a personality like that of a tame lark rather than of a finch. I

Trumpeter Bullfinch (*Rhodo-pechys githaginea*)

have four wild-caught birds at the moment, and all are more or less finger tame. A caged male will raise the feathers of its occiput erect, drop its wings and charge at a finger tip thrust between the cage wires.

Meade-Waldo reared four rounds, three of six and one of four, from a single pair. The young were apparently fed entirely on Canary seed, spray millet and shepherd's purse, all regurgitated. A pair that I brought back from the Canary Islands was bred in a cage by Dr. Harrison in 1973. The nest was built on the cage floor. In Gran Canaria, where it is a popular cagebird, it is said to cross-breed with a Canary. However, I have not seen one of the hybrids. The lovely rosy flush of a male in breeding plumage is lost in captivity, and the plumage in cage-kept birds becomes darker and greyer. Birds kept in an outdoor aviary are better. The colouring is probably dependent on some constituent in the natural diet of the birds in the wild. In captivity I am sure that some colouring agent is necessary. The lovely vermilion of the bill is never lost.

CROSSBILLS

The Common Crossbill is a popular cagebird among the enthusiasts for European finches: its tame and confiding habits – almost parrot-like in some ways – have ensured it a body of devotees. The other Crossbills are not seen so often, but require the same treatment. They are peaceful and tolerant of other species but become aggressive to other Crossbills when breeding, and it is not advisable to have more than one pair to an enclosure. They have bred in cages, but breed more readily and freely in an aviary, and are liable to come into breeding condition at any time. Crossbills can be very destructive. I have heard that if given plentiful supplies of fir-cones they satisfy the working urge and leave the perches and woodwork alone, and I've no doubt that this is normally true, but one pair that I had were loose in the bird room and, although I hung up fresh pine branches, with cones attached, every week, they still did a great deal of damage to the window frames, curtains, etc. It is unfortunate that Crossbills never seem to retain or, if aviary bred, develop the crimson colouring found in some wild birds. Colour feeding is not a complete solution – though some devotees will deny this – and there are often strong arguments at bird shows. Perhaps the most endearing aspect of the Crossbill for me is its tameness, for it will often become sufficiently tame to take a fir cone from the hand, or a sunflower seed. One pair of Spanish Crossbills that I had simply adored mealworms, but this addiction is not common, and most breeders concentrate their efforts on diet supplementation by collecting fresh whole fir-cones, preferably kept on the branch, and nestling Crossbills in the wild are fed exclusively on regurgitated fir-cone seeds. Finally, one must mention the bill, that extraordinary adaptation for extracting seeds from fir-cones. The cross-over only happens as the birds mature, and immature Crossbills have the same kind of rather heavy bill that a Greenfinch has, and young Crossbills in fact closely resemble Greenfinches. They also have this frightful weakness that kills them around the moult. The symptoms are the same, a kind of 'going light' that Canaries sometimes get, and it seems to be incurable. As with Greenfinches (I suspect), the only hope is to catch the ailing birds as early as possible and give large doses of total multi-vitamin/mineral complex.

Common Crossbill (*Loxia curvirostra*)

Common Crossbill
(*Loxia curvirostra*)

Description: *About 6½ in. (165·1 mm.). Bright red plumage, with brownish tones on scapulars; wings, longest uppertail-coverts, and tail brown; belly and undertail-coverts greyish. Female has red replaced by greenish yellow. Juveniles brownish grey, darker above, streaked with darker, browner on wings; juvenile male after first moult becomes yellowish orange red.*

Also known as Spruce Crossbill or Red Crossbill this species has a great range from Finland to north Africa, Ireland to Japan, Alaska to Newfoundland, to Mexico. Some twenty races are recognized, but their differences are complicated by the tremendous individual variation in colours within a stable population. Some males, for example, may take years before they acquire the bright red adult plumage, some may stay yellow-orange for ever. It has a habitat preference for pine, larch, silver fur or spruce, but shows a preference for spruce and often for spruce mixed with birch and alder. Crossbills inhabiting isolated spruce forests have the smallest bills; those inhabiting isolated pine woods the largest. In any case they are birds of mature coniferous woodland, where the large trees are well spaced out and bear seed freely. They are seldom found in younger, more uniform stands where the seed crop is smaller and less certain. The Scottish Crossbill, *scotica*, is a race of dubious standing. It is a larger bird with a bigger, heavier bill.

Parrot Crossbill
(*Loxia pytyopsittacus*)

Description: *6½–7 in. (165·1–177·8 mm.). Adults and juveniles extremely similar to* curvirostris, *but bill is larger and heavier, and head is also proportionately heavier.*

Some authorities consider the three races of this Scandinavian bird to be simply races of the Common Crossbill; others maintain that the Scottish Crossbill is not a race of *curvirostris* but of *pytyopsittacus*. It is a bird of pine woods and is very rarely found away from mature pines. For the dedicated enthusiast, the species preferred is the Scots pine, *Pinus sylvestris*. The bird may often be referred to in fact as Pine Crossbill.

Like the Common Crossbill it rears its young exclusively on regurgitated seeds, but becomes quite insectivorous *after* fledging and often during as well as after weaning. According to Bannerman it will stuff itself on various species of chermes. It may well be that this post-fledging change of diet provides the clue to the juvenile mortality problem, and one should give mealworms and gentles, or better still chermes, to avoid the disaster.

Two-barred Crossbill
(*Loxia leucoptera*)

Description: *5½–6 in. (139·7–152·4 mm.). Adult male generally bright red, with green bases to the feathers of the mantle, causing a brown patch; wing-coverts blackish brown with two white wing-bars; tail brown; lower belly and undertail-coverts white. In female, red is replaced by greenish-yellow, dark shafts more noticeable. Juveniles brownish with dark streaks.*

This lovely, smaller bird, sometimes called White-winged Crossbill, is a rare visitor to Britain from the Continent, and is a rare entrant for the dealers' lists. It is smaller, but with a cleaner more positive colouring and the male is a fine songster. However, not only is it said to be just like the Crossbill in its needs, but is more readily tamed, and has a more attractive song (according to Dement'ev, not unlike the song of Eversmann's Warbler).

Pine Grosbeak
(*Pinicola enucleator*)

Description: *8–9½ in. (203·2–241·3 mm.). Adult male generally red; from crown to uppertail-coverts bases of feathers are dark; belly and under-tail-coverts greyish; wings brown with two narrow white bars; tail brown, pale edges. Female has red replaced by olive green on body and yellowish grey on head and throat. Juvenile similar to juvenile Crossbill, only larger, and develops reddish orange after first year's moult.*

The European Pine Grosbeak (*P. e. enucleator*) is the largest of the European finches, but loses this title to the Asian Hawfinches. In fresh autumn plumage it looks greyer, but as the greyish tips abrade away, so the red becomes brighter and stronger. There are eleven races recognized which between them range from Norway eastwards to cross the Bering Strait into Alaska, and thence throughout Canada and much of the U.S. Throughout its range it is a bird of the northern coniferous forests and it is very trusting of man because, it is said, it has no experience of him. It is a popular cagebird. In Sweden, where it is called *dumsnut* (silly idiot), it is often trapped and kept as a song-bird, for the male is an excellent songster. Lord Lilford kept several and remarked on how very tame they became, and Butler says they were just about the tamest birds that he ever kept. Butler also remarks on the loss of red after the first moult in captivity. They have been bred by St. Quintin, and probably other breeders, but I have no details. Unfortunately it is rarely available.

ROSEFINCHES

These finches are delightful birds, being readily adaptable to life in captivity, settling down well, often singing sweetly, and often breeding with no complications. They lack popularity, however, simply because the red in their plumage is ephemeral, and will largely disappear with the first moult in captivity. This can be very disappointing. Colour food in some form is needed if something of the former glory is to be retained and this is not always very satisfactory. Rosefinches comprise the genus *Carpodacus*, and representatives may be found both in the New World and the Old. Most of our Rosefinches today are North and Central American birds trapped over-wintering in Mexico. The Eurasian species do not attract much attention from dealers, but the occasional pair does show up now and again.

House Finch
(*Carpodacus mexicanus*)

Description: *5½ in. (139·7 mm.). Adult male has front of head (except lores, which are light brown), chin to breast, and rump crimson, rest of upperparts dark brown with pale edges to feathers giving a streaky appearance; below buff, streaked with dark brown. Female lacks all crimson, having it replaced by the streaky brown. Juveniles resemble female but are more heavily and intensely streaked, most noticeably on breast and flanks.*

This is the Blood-stained Finch of Butler, and birds from different parts of the U.S. have different common names according to race or locality. It was bred by George Lynch in 1956, and he described his birds as coming from Canada and lacking the colour of southern races (but these birds must have been moulted in captivity prior to being obtained by the breeder) and calls them North American House Finch. They were bred in 1951 at San Diego Zoo, and Mr. Lint identified his birds as being of the race *clementis*, and called them San Clemente House Finch. It is sparrow-like in habit and habitat, wandering about the streets of western towns searching for food, and flocking to sunny fields to pick up weed seeds. It is considered a pest in some areas because of its liking for fruit and buds, and may do considerable damage. Mr. Lynch's birds reared their healthy young on a diet of mixed seeds, soaked teazle, chickweed and gentles: classic finch-breeders' fare. They did not take any egg-food, although it was available and taken by other birds present.

Purple Finch
(*Carpodacus purpureus*)

Description: *5½–6 in. (139·7–152·4 mm.). Adult male has entire head, breast and rump rosy red; back heavily streaked brownish red; below whitish. Female similar to female* mexicanus *but has paler ground colour, whitish below, and streaks are more clearly defined; superciliary is whiter. Juveniles resemble female but are duller.*

The Purple Rosefinch, as it may be called, is more vinous or rosy red than the House Finch and may readily be separated by its white belly. It ranges over most of the U.S., wandering a great deal when not breeding, taking berries and fruit in summer and autumn, and weed and grass seeds in winter. It was successfully bred by Mr. Lynch in 1958, both parents consuming large amounts of chickweed, and possibly Canary-rearing food also.

Cassin's Finch
(*Carpodacus cassinii*)

Description: *6½ in. (165·1 mm.). Both sexes intermediate between Purple and House Finches in plumage characteristics. Male has less extensive red bib, and contrast between red crown and brown nape noticeable. Size is diagnostic, and wing-tips extend nearly to tip of tail.*

This is a bird of the mountain forests of western North America and is not at all well known in captivity.

However, it winters to central Mexico and is worth mentioning here because of its similarity to the other two American Rosefinches.

Common Rosefinch
(*Carpodacus erythrina*)

Description: *6 in. (152·4 mm.). Adult male, entire body dull crimson, largely mixed with brown on back and flanks, brightest on rump and chin to breast; below it gets paler, fading to whitish on undertail-coverts; wings and tail brown edged rufous. Female olive brown streaked with darker, wings and tail feathers edged with ochre. Juvenile a streakier version of female.*

A popular common name for this bird is Scarlet Grosbeak, and I have also seen Rose-breasted Finch and Caucasian Rosefinch, the latter for the race *kubanensis* which is found in northern India and may also be called Indian or Himalayan Rosefinch. This is the race that is imported by the pet trade, and differs from the European race by being paler red, more a pink, particularly below. It has a weak song, reminiscent of a Goldfinch. I once kept three of these birds in a small mixed aviary and found them to be rather dull and uninteresting. They have a very wide range of habitat, from Finland and Germany to Outer Mongolia and Kamchatka, to India and Thailand. It has been bred in captivity, and one report says that in addition to the usual seeds the parent birds took some paddy rice, groundsel and chickweed, and a few mealworms. Rutgers suggests that rearing birds will take bread and milk and Canary-rearing food.

Great Rosefinch
(*Carpodacus rubicilla*)

Description: *8 in. (203·2 mm.). Adult male has body rich carmine red with small silky, silvery-grey spots on head, throat and breast; red of uppertail- and lowertail-coverts is more like pink; wings and tail dark brown, feathers edged with pink. Female grey brown, faintly streaked; wings and tail-feathers dark brown with pale edges; uppertail-coverts grey. Juvenile resembles female but is duller.*

I have described the western race, which may be called Caucasian Large or Giant Rosefinch, but it is much more probable that the Central Asian Giant Rosefinch, which could also be called Severtzov's Rosefinch, *severtzovi*, would be imported. This race is paler than the nominate from the Caucasus and the red has a pink or purple tinge, not carmine. The light spots on head and breast are larger and the back is brownish. The female is much less brown, and more grey. Some of these birds have been imported in recent years, but I have not noticed any mention of them in the literature. They eat a wide variety of tree seeds but seem to have a great fondness for juniper, birch and sea buckthorn. The lovely red will be replaced by a shiny golden straw-yellow on the first moult in captivity unless the diet includes a colouring agent.

Pink-browed Rosefinch
(*Carpodacus rhodopeplus*)

Description: *About 7 in. (177·8 mm.). Adult mainly brownish above, head, neck and back streaked with blackish and overlaid with a rosy wash; superciliary and cheeks are bright rosy;*

rump feathers tipped rosy, wings brown edged with crimson brown, median coverts tipped rosy pink, greater coverts and tertiaries tipped pink, throat feathers pointed and tipped with glistening pink, rest of underparts dark rosy red, faintly striated. Female drab all over, darker above and marked with dusky, below rich buff lightly striated with black, superciliary pinkish. Immatures resemble the female, although young males have a more clearly defined eyebrow.

This species is also called the Spotted-winged Rosefinch. It is restricted to the Himalayas and occurs between 10,000 ft. (3,048 m.) and 15,000 ft. (4,572 m.). The birds descend to lower country in the winter and occur in Nepal, Sikkim and as far as northern Burma. Like many if not all of the truly Himalayan species they are extremely rare in captivity. The only information that I have of them is taken from the report by St. Quintin in the *Avicultural Magazine* of 1916–17.

St. Quintin's birds nested in a yew bush only a few feet away from a nesting pair of Bullfinches. The nest was similar to that of a Greenfinch, but maybe slightly smaller and deeper. Three youngsters were reared, being fed on a diet consisting mainly of insects, for which the parent birds hunted industriously. No attention was paid to bundles of seeding weeds hung up for the Bullfinches. These birds appeared to be peaceful but were described as being 'shy and most reclusive, and are not particularly interesting birds to keep'.

LINNETS

Acanthis is a small genus of some half dozen birds, brownish, and often with a patch or two of red. They are gentle, unobtrusive birds, quiet, inoffensive, sweetly singing, and with a little loving care steady breeders in cage and aviary. They are, it seems to me, birds for the connoisseur. They seem out of place in mixed collections and showplace or decoration aviaries, but they are most satisfying birds to keep.

Linnet
(*Acanthis cannabina*)

Description: 5½ in. (139·7 mm.). *Adult male in spring, forehead and forecrown carmine red; rest of head and neck grey; back cinnamon chestnut; tail-coverts blackish brown with broad ochreous edges; wings blackish with brown edges, and white leading edge to primaries (forming a white patch when wing is closed); tail blackish with white edgings; underparts light brown, pencilled on throat and streaked on breast, with large patch of carmine red on breast; male in fresh autumn plumage has red largely obscured by brownish-grey edges to new feathers which eventually abrade away. Female lacks any red and is more noticeably streaked than male. Juvenile similar to female but white edgings to tail and wings are rusty-ochre.*

Linnet (*Acanthis cannabina*): male

The Common Linnet is found over most of Europe and western Asia, but there are seven races recognized in all, the differences being very slight. Perhaps the only one worth mentioning is the Turkestan Linnet, *bella*, which is lighter in general tone, has the cinnamon tones on back purer and brighter, and the red colour on the breast more intense and extending further. This race may occasionally show red colouring on the uppertail-coverts. In the wild the Linnet feeds on a wide variety of weed seeds and other seed matter, and rears its young on insects and regurgitated seed. I have bred it in a small planted aviary giving only seeds, chickweed and Canary-rearing food on some occasions, and on others I have supplied gentles and maggots as well. Males that are kept in roomy well-planted flights show the best colour, but aviary-moulted birds never achieve the intensity of colour that some old wild males have.

Redpoll
(*Acanthis flammea*)

There are seven clearly defined races of the Redpoll, and since they are invariably given individual

Mealy Redpoll (*Acanthis flammea flammea*): the two centre birds are male

nomenclature and treatment in aviculture – and often in the field guides also – I will describe those that occur in aviculture, separately.

Mealy Redpoll
(*A. f. flammea*)

Description: 5½ *in.* (*139·7 mm.*). *Adult male in fresh autumn plumage, crown red, neck and back whitish with broad grey-brown streaks, and pinkish tinge to uppertail-coverts; wings and tail dark brown with whitish borderings and a white wing-bar; chin dark brown, more or less covered by whitish edges to feathers; throat and breast white with pink-red tinge* *of varying intensity, rest of underparts white, faint streakings on flanks; in spring, the edges wear off leaving the red brighter, chin-spot cleaner and back darker. Female similar to male but lacks any red on breast, this being replaced by pale brown streaked with dusky. Juveniles resemble dull female but lack red on head.*

The Northern, Common or Mealy Redpoll is not a British bird but comes from Scandinavia, and thence eastwards through Russia to Siberia. The larger and heavier-billed forms have been given separate race status as Holböll's Redpoll (*holboelli*) by some taxonomists, but it is now generally considered to be synonymous.

Greenland Redpoll
(*A. f. rostrata*)

Description: *6 in. (152·4 mm.). Larger and darker than the Mealy, and it also has a heavier and slightly larger bill.*

This bird is not easily acquired at all, though it does occur as a winter visitor from Greenland, and may be taken under Home Office licence. It has been recorded as breeding in Scotland.

Lesser Redpoll
(*A. f. cabaret*)

Description: *About 5 in. (127 mm.). Altogether a smaller bird, and generally browner with less grey about the plumage; wing-bar fawn or ochreous, as opposed to white in the foregoing races, and pink of breast less extensive.*

Many adult males may be found breeding in the wild without any, or with very little, red on the breast at all, so the lack of this should not be taken as an indicator of female sex, and of course it may well disappear altogether after a moult or two in captivity. It is the race resident in Britain and is the one most frequently offered for sale. I find the Lesser a more attractive bird, but the extra size makes the Mealy a better commercial proposition, since size and bulk are important factors in show competition. I would like to quote R. B. Bennett on the race: 'Unpretentious in appearance, the Redpoll is nevertheless a vivacious little bird, rather smaller than a Goldfinch.... Its confiding ways have long made the Redpoll a favourite with bird-lovers, for it is indeed an affectionate and altogether desirable bird for cage or aviary. The song is simple, pleasant and twittering, though not particularly musical.... In an aviary or cage it will mix and breed freely; in fact, it was with Redpolls I had my very first success in breeding British birds. I was then nine years old, and my Redpolls reared their brood in a double breeder.' I have found them very easy to breed in a small planted aviary, and have supplied nothing more than all the usual British Finch seeds, plus chickweed and a commercial brand of Canary-rearing food.

Arctic Redpoll
(*Acanthis hornemanni*)

Description: *5½ in. (139·7 mm.). Exactly like Mealy Redpoll in all sexes, but ground plumage-colour much whiter and all feathers have a whiter edge; pink of breast is greatly reduced in male; rump is clear white in both sexes but may be tinged with pink in males.*

According to the geographic species concept, which regards the Black-headed and Red-headed Buntings as one species, and many American seed-eaters, including practically the entire genus *Passerina*, the Arctic, Hornemann's, Coue's or Hoary Redpoll is simply another race of the Common Redpoll, *flammea*. This is because natural hybridization occurs at some points of the species' range. I have an aviculturist's tendency to regard different birds as being different, and this usually overcomes zoologist desires to assert discipline. I must point out that Dement'ev considers it to be con-specific. It hardly makes any difference because it requires the same treatment as its relative.

Twite
(*Acanthis flavirostris*)

Description: $5\frac{1}{2}$ *in. (139·7 mm.).*
Adult male in autumn plumage,
generally rusty ochre with dark
brown centres to feathers, uppertail-
coverts more or less pinky red, long-
est uppertail-coverts ochre with dark
brown centres; centre of breast to
undertail-coverts ochreous to white;
wings and tail dark brown to black
with white edges to primaries and
tail; bill yellow; in spring uppertail-
coverts are redder and bill becomes
grey. Female similar to male but
uppertail-coverts brownish grey, and
generally slightly paler. Juvenile like
female but duller, and uppertail-coverts
greyer.

The Twite may be called Mountain
Linnet (since it replaces the Linnet at
higher altitudes) or Mountain Redpoll
(not logical since it has no red poll).
It is an unobtrusive bird, more common than sightings would suggest,
that is found in Britain, Norway and
Lapland, and then it disappears until
it recurs in Turkey and again in Asia.
The Turkestan Redpoll in fact differs
significantly in that it is less tawny,
has rump and uppertail-coverts clear
pinky red, and the breast is strongly
spotted with black. Butler says of the
Twite that he found it 'greedy, selfish,
and quarrelsome'. I regret that I have
not kept it, and all the breeding reports that I have read refer to it as
being kept in a small planted aviary to
itself, or in a large 'British Bird Communal Aviary' where there is plenty
of space, and lots of wild entangled
herbage. In either of these situations
one can hardly tell how 'greedy,
selfish' a bird is, and it would have
to be exceptionally quarrelsome. It
requires the same treatment as the
Linnet and the other European
finches, but does need a little more
care and solitude when breeding. It
does not breed readily in a cage.

Warsangli Linnet
(*Acanthis johannis*)

Description: $5\frac{1}{2}$ *in. (139·7 mm.).*
Adult male, forehead and super-
ciliary, sides of face and underparts
white; rump and lower flanks chest-
nut; blackish-grey stripe through
eye; top of head, mantle, scapulars
grey; wings and tail black. Female
has less white on forehead, is paler
grey above, slightly browner and
faintly streaked; tips of secondaries
and secondary coverts white; less
chestnut on rump. Juvenile is
brownish above, spotted with dusky,
including rump; below, white spotted
blackish including flanks.

This virtually unknown bird is
placed in the genus *Warsanglia* by
some authorities. It could well be that
it is misplaced in *Acanthis*, but until
some more detailed observations and
studies are published we shall not
know. Apparently it is a bird of high
juniper forest in north-east Africa,
where it feeds on grass seeds and has
been seen feeding on *Salvia* plants. I
mention it here to suggest that any
reader with experience of it would do
well to submit his observations to one
of the recognized journals. It is quite
likely that it has been imported, but
I have never seen it on offer.

HAWFINCHES

The Hawfinches form a small genus of probably nine species. They are large birds, 6–9 in. (152·4–228·6 mm.) long, and characterized by their large and powerful beaks which are beautifully adapted for cracking open fruit stones, such as cherry and olive. They are seldom imported, and even the European Hawfinch is so rarely available that it never appears in the advertisement columns. Avicultural references are few and far between and there is clearly a splendid opportunity with any of the species to make worthwhile contributions to the literature by relating personal experience.

European Hawfinch
(*Coccothraustes coccothraustes*)

Description: *7 in. (177·8 mm.). Adult male, lores and bib black; rest of head cinnamon; neck grey; mantle chestnut; lower back and rump grey; uppertail-coverts cinnamon; broad white wing-bar; flight feathers black with violet tinge (ends of secondaries three-pronged shape); tail black to brown with white terminal spots; below, vinaceous greyish brown; bill yellow in winter, steel grey in summer. Female duller and rather more greyish, secondaries also grey without sheen. Juvenile yellowish brown on head and body, streaked above and flecked with brown on flanks; young female may be told from male by grey secondaries.*

The Common Hawfinch, or European Grosbeak as it may be listed, ranges from Britain in the west, eastwards to Japan. Throughout the northern parts of this great range only the nominate race is found, but in the southern parts some four other races have been defined. Since a couple of these may find their way on to the market it is worth describing them.

Spanish Hawfinch (*C. c. buvryi*).

European Hawfinch (*Coccothraustes coccothraustes*)

The rump is not yellowish brown but pure grey, the white on the tip of the tail is narrower.

Indian Hawfinch (*C. c. humii*). Easily distinguished from *cocco-*

thraustes by lighter general colouration, and by brown-ochre uppertail-
coverts, light rufous-brown underparts
with centre of belly grey.

Hawfinches are shy and timid birds
that dive into dense cover at the
slightest sign of danger. In captivity
they may become quite steady and
tame, and will often take mealworms
from their keeper's hand. Such tameness, however, does not significantly
improve their propensity to breed, and
success may only be gained
(unless one is endowed with great
luck) by providing the birds with
either a roomy, well-planted and uncrowded aviary, or a smaller but still
well-planted aviary to themselves.
By well-planted I mean with plenty of
thick cover for the birds to retire to,
and in which to build their nest. They
may desert very readily and must be
left in strict solitude. I am inclined to
agree with Bennett that one should be
prepared to hand-rear the young if
desertion is obvious, but the corollary
of this of course is that one should
not pay such nervous attention that
the result is to frighten the birds. They
naturally take plum, cherry and stones
of similar fruit and these may be
collected in the autumn to be given
during the winter. When rearing they
will take some soft food, such as
peas, lettuce and chickweed, soft buds
from fruit trees may be relished, and
a fair quantity of live food is needed.
The facilities afforded by a well-
planted aviary will tend to offset any
deficiencies in given diet.

Chinese Hawfinch
(*Coccothraustes migratoria*)

Description: *7–8 in. (177·8–203·2
mm.). Adult male, entire head black
with bluish metallic tinge; upperparts
greyish brown; uppertail-coverts white,*
*wings black with white bar, longest
tail-coverts and tail black; below
greyish off-white with pink-ochreous
wash to sides of breast and flanks;
bill yellow in winter, in summer
yellow with black base. Female lacks
black on head, head brownish and
tail dark brown.*

This species may be mistakenly
listed as Japanese Hawfinch, but a
more appropriate alternative is the
ornithological Black-headed Hawfinch. It may also be called the Lesser
Black-headed Hawfinch. In its feeding
habits this bird appears to be similar
to the Common Hawfinch, and is believed to feed its young entirely on
insects. However, in direct contrast
to the Hawfinch, it is said to be confiding and tame in the presence of
man. It appeared regularly ten to
fifteen years ago, but the source of
supply seems to have dried up rather
and I cannot remember seeing it for
some time. Several failed breeding
attempts have been recorded, usually
in small mixed aviaries, but it has
been bred, when the young were
reared on seed, soft food and
maggots.

Japanese Hawfinch
(*Coccothraustes personata*)

Description: *9½ in. (241·3 mm.).
Adult male, crown, forehead, lores,
front part of cheeks and chin black
with blue metallic glint; wing black
with steel-blue metallic sheen and
white bar; tail black; entire body
vinaceous grey, whitish on belly.
Female similar, maybe a little duller,
and less metallic shine on wings.
Juvenile lacks black head, body
faintly streaked with white.*

Even by Hawfinch standards this
is a very large bird; Russian records

Japanese Hawfinch (*Coccothraustes personata*); European Hawfinch (*C. coccothraustes*); Chinese Hawfinch (*C. migratoria*)

of birds from China go to 10½ in. (266·7 mm.)! If a European Hawfinch can crack an olive stone with a pressure of 160 lbs. (73 kg.) one shudders at the strength of this one. Alternative names are Greater Black-headed Hawfinch, Japanese Masked Hawfinch and Black-headed Hawfinch. Its natural diet appears to be mainly cedar nuts, but in summer it becomes quite insectivorous, taking a lot of caterpillars and beetles. According to Rutgers it is peaceable in an aviary, and does not use its massive bill as a weapon of attack.

White-winged Grosbeak
(*Coccothraustes carnipes*)

Description: *About 8½ in. (215·9 mm.). Adult male, head, neck, back, breast, upper belly, dark steel grey; back, rump, uppertail-coverts and edges to greater wing-coverts and secondaries, belly, flanks and undertail dingy greenish yellow. Female lighter, steel grey replaced by ashen grey, dark streaks on cheeks. Juvenile, like female but streaked all over head, upper back and breast.*

This bird is also known as the Juniper Hawfinch. It ranges from eastern Iran across through the Himalayas and up into China, and may be found in forest country on the mountain slopes. In winter it descends to lower elevations and thus may find its way to the Calcutta bird-market. It is a large bird, shy and wary as most Hawfinches, but when disturbed flies off noisily. It is a greedy and gluttonous eater and, while it tends to feed almost exclusively on the nuts of juniper berries, will also take rowan. Dement'ev has commented that in the city of Przhevalsk in winter, they pick up grains dropped in the market place, like sparrows.

Black-and-yellow Grosbeak
(*Coccothraustes icteroides*)

Description: *About 8 in. (203·2 mm.). Adult male, slaty black above, flecked with grey; throat, breast, thighs, and uppertail-coverts black; wings and tail black edged pale yellow; belly to undertail-coverts bright yellow; bill olive green. Female similar to male but flecked with yellow above, and a black patch at centre of belly. Bill horny green.*

My only reference for this bird is M. Decoux, writing about grosbeaks in *Aviculture* in 1925. He says, 'I have never seen this bird alive. A few examples have at long intervals been seen in the collections of zoological gardens, notably in that of the Zoological Society of London. Miss Hawke had a young one, hatched in her aviary, successfully reared by a pair of Hedge Accentors in 1914. Habitat, throughout the Himalayas to Manipur and Western China.' According to Whistler who lists it under an earlier name, *Perissospiza*, it is a bird of spruce and silver fir forests breeding between 7,500 ft. (2,286 m.) and 9,000 ft. (2,743·2 m.), descending to around 4,000 ft. (1,219·2 m.) in the winter. It keeps mainly to the upper levels of the trees, feeding on shoots, buds and fir-cone seeds, but does descend to the ground to poke around the undergrowth for berries and seeds. If they are kept in an aviary with a concrete floor or in a cage they appreciate being given a freshly cut turf to sort over, and this may be sprinkled with seed, especially sprouting seeds.

Allied Grosbeak
(*Coccothraustes affinis*)

Description: *9 in. (228·6 mm.). Adult male very similar to Black-and-yellow Grosbeak but has thighs yellow (black in* icteroides*), and upperparts are more orange. Female is distinct, having yellow of the male replaced by brownish green. Bill in both sexes is grey.*

The Allied Grosbeak might well be mistaken for a Black-and-yellow Grosbeak unless either the retailer or buyer realizes that the thigh colour is a diagnostic, as is the silver-grey bill. They, too, are birds of the Himalayas, but of even higher elevations, occurring in the silver fir and birch forests at 10,000 ft. (3,048 m.) and 11,000 ft. (3,352·8 m.). They are mainly ground-feeders, taking fallen seeds, shoots and buds, etc., but they also take fir-seeds and buds.

They are rarely available in captivity but are occasionally offered and deserve attention. They soon settle

down, appear to be peaceable with other large birds, but should be handled with care as their large bills can give quite a nasty bite. They will take the usual seeds but also enjoy sunflower, hemp, wheat and oats. They can be given fresh green food and may enjoy fruit: they relish mealworms and maggots. Allied Grosbeaks also appreciate a fresh sod of soil and grass unless kept in a planted aviary, when the ground may be broadcast with mixed seeds.

Evening Grosbeak
(*Coccothraustes vespertina*)

Description: *7–8½ in. (177·8–215·9 mm.). Adult male, yellow forehead and superciliary stripe, crown, nape, sides of head, chin, throat black soon fading to dusky and thence to yellow on back, scapular rump, and all underparts. Secondaries and innermost wing-coverts white, rest of wings, uppertail-coverts and tail black. Female is greyish tinged with yellow on sides of neck and breast. It has the black and white wings of the male, but has an additional white spot at base of primaries and centre of tip of tail. Juveniles resemble female, but young males lack the second white wing-spot of the female.*

The generic name for the species used to be *Hesperiphona*, which was taken from the Hesperides of Greek mythology who resided only in the west, but for many years now the Evening Grosbeak has ranged eastwards across the U.S. An early observer believed that the species only lived in dark places, leaving them at evening – hence the common name. It is a bird of conifer forests but feeds mainly on the seeds of box elder and maple trees, chokecherry and dogwood. The large bill is beautifully developed for dealing with the large seeds or stones of such trees' fruits. It breeds mainly from western Canada southwards through the mountainous ranges to New Mexico. It winters in the southern States, mainly southern California and South Carolina; since it is not a common wanderer south of the U.S., it is rarely imported into Europe. However, it has appeared and has been bred. Mr. Payne successfully raised two young cocks to maturity in 1956 in a roomy aviary that contained parakeets, love-birds, starlings and quail. By way of live food they were given mealworms and gentles. It is likely that this was insufficient, since a young female that fledged suffered from foot deformities indicating vitamin-D deficiency (rickets). I have experienced similar problems when breeding cardinals which would only feed on meal-worms. In such a case one is faced with two possibilities: the first is to sprinkle the mealworms with a mineral/vitamin powder such as Squibb's Vionate, and hope that sufficient is taken by the birds; the second is to supplement the food given to the nestlings by a limited amount of hand-feeding. Care must be taken not to dull the appetite of the nestlings too much, or the stimulus of begging to the adults will be re-duced and they may stop feeding altogether.

Part Three
ESTRILDIDAE

I · ESTRILDINAE

We come now to the waxbills, a remarkably uniform group of little birds. Indeed they are the smallest of the seed-eaters and a large number of them are between $3\frac{1}{2}$ in. (88·9 mm.) and $4\frac{1}{2}$ in. (114·3 mm.) long. They are great favourites in captivity and are perhaps the best-known cagebirds on a worldwide basis. The popular name 'waxbill' stems from the colour of the bill, which in many – but by no means all – species is sealing-wax red. They are frequently brightly coloured but, if not, their tiny size and distinctiveness give them an exotic quality that makes them most attractive. However, they are not known as song-birds and, with a few exceptions, are never kept for this reason alone. The sexes are

Upper left pair: Gold-breasted Waxbills (*Amandava subflava*). Centre pair: Common Firefinch (*Lagonosticta senegala*). Lower left and far right: Red-eared Waxbill (*Estrilda troglodytes*)

usually similar, and sexual dimorphism while being common is rarely dramatic.

They are native to the tropical parts of the Old World, are non-migratory and generally resident wherever they occur, although a great deal of wandering takes place in times of drought. They are birds of open grasslands, reedy marshland, or forest edges and clearings. They are ground-feeders, taking seeds from the growing grasses and sedges or picking up ripened seeds that have fallen to the ground.

Waxbills are gregarious little creatures and flock at all times of the year. When not breeding, however, they are much more sociable and large flocks comprising several species can be found.

Most waxbills, being birds of open grassland or arid scrub country in tropical regions, are fairly adaptable. Faced with sudden shortage of water, sharp changes of temperature from night to day, they have an adaptability of habitat based on a solid grounding of a hard-seed diet that makes them ideal cagebirds. Those that have developed more specialized ecologies – especially the forest waxbills – are seldom seen in captivity, and usually require more careful attention. Another indication of the adaptability of the group is shown by the frequency with which colour mutants occur. Fawn Cordon-bleus have been established in Australia, buff St. Helena waxbills have occurred, yellow Firefinches looked like being established but faded out, and many other sports have been reported.

HOUSING

Waxbills may be kept in cages, quite small ones compared with most other species, and will live out long and contented lives under quite simple conditions. A cousin of mine bought a pair of Red-eared Waxbills when he was ten years old and they lived happily in the kitchen, in a tiny box-cage that must have measured little more than $15 \times 8 \times 8$ in. ($381 \times 203 \cdot 2 \times 203 \cdot 2$ mm.). They met an unhappy end the year that my cousin was called up for military service some nine years later, victim to a new cat in the household.

Waxbills seldom become aggressive towards each other, do not frequently become fat or sluggish, and in general are fairly easy birds to keep in a cage. Overcrowding can cause problems, the most noticeable one being that of plucking. Some species seem to be more prone to pluck each other than others and I suspect that the non-stop nearness of other waxbills presents an allo-preening *super*-stimulus that results in a *super*-response. In this case both pluckers and plucked must be rehabilitated in more suitable quarters. The smallest cage permissible must enable the inmates to *fly* from one perch to another. A cage that allows the bird to get everywhere by hopping is too small. Box-cages (enclosed with only wire at the front) are ideal for waxbills, and they undoubtedly do better in them. In a roomy cage, and properly cared for, they may even breed. I remember Peter Pope telling me how he had cage-bred Avadavats to the tenth generation.

I once kept a flock of mixed Blue waxbills in a garden aviary that had a planted flight some 20 ft. (6·1 m.) long. They behaved very naturally in this and seemed extremely happy. They were a lovely sight to see combing the closely cut lawn. In an outdoor aviary care must be taken to see that they roost sensibly, and most keepers will drive the birds into the house or shelter every evening at dusk. Usually they quickly acquire the habit and will put themselves to bed. If left out at night they often roost in the open and become liable to night attacks by cats and owls. Settling an aviary full of panicky tiny birds at 2 a.m. in the pitch dark is no joke.

Since waxbills are naturally ground-feeders they can be encouraged to indulge in natural food-seeking behaviour by the broadcasting of a handful of millet seeds over the floor of the flight each day.

FOOD

Individual species vary in their preferences, but most of them will take a large proportion of millet in their diet. Various millets can be supplied in separate pots, as can small Canary seed and other small seeds. I generally supply one bowl or hopper filled with a mixture of whatever is available locally by way of small wild seeds including lettuce, maw, rape, teazle, plantain, etc. There are several commercial mixtures of wild seeds, weed seeds, British Bird Mixture and others that one can buy and use in this way. In addition they can be given millet sprays, fresh seeding grasses (the favourite is usually *Poa annua*), cuttle-fish bone, which should be crushed; some birds will take lettuce and peck at soft sweet apple. Soaked seeds are readily taken all the year round.

BREEDING

Waxbills build spherical nests with a side entrance, placed in a shrub fairly low down, usually within a few feet of the ground. In several species the nests are placed in thornbushes, others in close proximity to hornets' or wasps' nests, and others close to the nest of an ant that is particularly vicious. This is not a symbiosis, since neither of the protecting hosts seems to gain any benefit from the waxbills. It seems that the ants do not harm the nestling birds in any way. The nests are made mainly of dry grasses, with fresh green grass added. The interior chamber is lined with soft seeding grass-heads, some fine rootlets, hair and a few feathers. There is often a porch protruding over the entrance hole, and sometimes a short tunnel. Some male birds will build a small, unlined chamber above the nest proper in which to roost. This is called a cock's nest.

They appear to form very stable pairs which in some species may be bonded for life. Both sexes share the nest building, the incubation and the care of the young birds. The eggs are white. Incubation lasts about twelve days. The nest is not kept clean after the first week, the nestlings defecate on the sides of the nest chamber and these quickly dry giving little or no smell. It is desirable to take down a nest once used and replace it with a new one. This will allow the birds to go to nest again immediately, and the keeper to disinfect the used nests. The juveniles mature very quickly and some species may begin breeding at a few months old, sometimes before full adult plumage is acquired.

There is considerable variation among the courtship displays, but all are recognizable as estrildrine. The male may bob up and down or make some stiff-legged jumps, curtsey, swing from side to side, or have some combination of two or more of these. The brighter-coloured areas of the plumage are fluffed out to present the most dramatic impact on the female. In many species the male may hold a stem of grass in its beak and incorporate this in the display. The female may even take hold of the grass, or pick up a bit of her own. The song is usually a melodious run of high-pitched trills, quite audible in most waxbills, but, in contrast, the song of most munias has a reach of only a few feet.

When breeding, most species of waxbill require live food and soft-food supplements, and most successful breeders have developed their own techniques. Most waxbills find the skins of meal-worms and blowfly maggots too tough to break. Many of the larger species will take them, or try to, but the smaller ones won't. Mealworms may be cut up and sprinkled on top of egg-food; maggots should be pricked with a pin before giving. Anglers' bait-supply firms will sometimes supply a very small size of maggot called a 'feeder'. (These are too small for putting on a fish hook, but a handful sprinkled in a run will whet the fishes' appetites.) The most reliable source of live food for breeding waxbills is a healthy culture of white worms (if the birds will take them), but ant pupae (ant 'eggs') are excellent if a regular supply of nests can be found.

Breeding in a richly planted aviary with rambling roses, clematis, runner beans and other suitable plants providing a source of insects is a good solution, and many waxbills are reared successfully in such surroundings each year with little or no help from their keepers.

The technique that I and other breeders have employed is to get the birds accustomed to taking soft food, whether it be bread and milk, sponge-cake and honeywater, Canary-rearing food, or home-made egg-food. This should always be provided fresh daily and may be sprinkled lightly with millet or maw, and chopped mealworms. If one bird is introduced that will take soft-food, the others will usually follow suit. It is important to accustom the birds to such dietary supplements *before* breeding is seriously under way.

The most popular nest receptacle is a large wicker-basket nest-box of the kind commercially available. These will be used to roost in all the year round. It is normal to place a few more nests in the aviary than pairs of birds, to reduce the risk of quarrelling. It is also normal to place the nests at approximately the same height to avoid some nests (the higher ones for example) having greater appeal. Soft grasses, stuffing, hair, dog combings, feathers, all will be used in nest building. Sometimes the male will build a 'cock's nest' on top of the nest proper.

In a well-planted aviary a pair of waxbills might elect to build their own nest. This is a sphere-shaped affair, sometimes the size of a melon, with an entrance hole on one side. The eggs are invariably white, and a clutch will usually be from four to six, but up to ten is not unheard of. Incubation is eleven to thirteen

days but may be up to seventeen. Both parents work at building
the nest, brooding the eggs, and feeding the young. The nestlings
have luminous globules inside their mouths. The real purpose of
these is not clear, but they must have some stimulating effect
on the parental feeding behaviour. Since the gape pattern is
different in every species it makes it difficult to transfer nestlings
from the nest of one species to another when, for some reason
or another, fostering-out is necessary.

ESTRILDA WAXBILLS

These are the typical waxbills, or 'true' waxbills if such a term
can be used. They have been described as differing from their
relatives in the genera *Amandava*, *Uraeginthus* and *Lagonosticta*
in the following way: they can cling to grass stems with much
greater agility, habitually feed by clinging to growing grass heads,
hold their food down with their feet, build more elaborate nests,
make conspicuous side-to-side wagging movements of the tail
that are more deliberate than similar movements made by other
waxbills. Finally, the sexes are alike, though not identical. They
are a remarkably homogeneous group. Nearly all of the genus is
imported fairly regularly, and it includes some of the commonest
waxbills found in captivity. They tend to be a little delicate on
arrival and certainly should not be put out-of-doors until the
intemperate changeability of winter and early spring is past, mid
May being a rule. Most keepers of *Estrildae* bring their birds
indoors for the winter, and I certainly would not recommend
leaving them out unless they have a warmed and draught-proof
shelter in which they can happily spend all day if need be. I don't
believe that the cold as such can harm them so much as long and
damp nights. Considering the number of birds imported each
year there are too few breedings reported, but I think that this is
mainly due to the fact that they are usually kept in overcrowded
mixed collections for decorative purposes. They will breed readily
enough if kept under ideal conditions. The black-faced/black-
cheeked members of the genus are rather difficult in captivity
and should only be kept by experienced aviculturists. On the other
hand, I feel that the St. Helena, Red-eared and Orange-cheeked
Waxbills are particularly suitable for beginners.

St. Helena Waxbill
(*Estrilda astrild*)

Description: *4–4½ in. (101·6–114·3 mm.). Adult male, brown above, greyish on head, closely and finely barred with dusky; crimson stripe through eye (eye-ring is fawn); sides of face, chin and throat white washed with pink, rest of underparts finely barred with dusky white and pale brown; centre of lower breast and belly red; lower belly and undertail-coverts black; bill red. Female has less extensive red and black underneath. Juvenile has thinner eye-streak; bill black.*

The bird I have described is the nominate race *E. a. astrild* from southern Africa. However, up to a dozen races have been described and no doubt several are imported. The most widespread race from east Africa, *E. a. cavendishi*, is browner and has most of the plumage suffused with pink. Most West African races seem to be paler and more clearly barred. One race, *E. a. rubriventris*, has a marked crimson wash on the uppertail-coverts.

This species is known universally in avicultural circles as the St. Helena Waxbill, but in field books it is generally called simply Waxbill or Common Waxbill. Bannerman has a *penchant* for giving individual races their own common names and comes up with the Cape Verde Islands Waxbill, Gaboon Waxbill, Kemp's Sierra Leone Waxbill and Cameroon Waxbill. No doubt an exhaustive search of the literature could produce more.

Rosy-rumped Waxbill
(*Estrilda rhodopyga*)

It is also possible to find the species listed as *Estrilda estrilda*. It is distributed widely over Africa south of the Sahara, in grass country, where it moves around in small flocks – occasionally large ones – and can be found in and around villages, gardens and cultivated regions as well as in remote areas. It is tame and has no fear of man.

A few years ago it was introduced in Portugal and appears to have established itself successfully. Flocks of up to 300 birds or more have been seen, including immatures, in widely differing locations.

It is the largest of its genus, noticeably larger than the two species following. The three together may be termed collectively 'The grey waxbills'. A fit bird has a smooth *svelte* plumage and is very attractive indeed. They are not difficult to sex. Adult males tend to be aggressive when breeding or in breeding condition, and a true pair are best kept in a small enclosure to themselves. If they are kept in mixed company it is best to avoid including other grey waxbills. It has been bred on many occasions and has hybridized with allied species, and with the African Silverbill.

Rosy-rumped Waxbill
(*Estrilda rhodopyga*)

Description: *4 in. (101·6 mm.). Adult male very similar to St. Helena Waxbill above but has rump and upper-tail-coverts crimson. Central tail-feathers also edged crimson, as are inner secondaries; below it is buff, barred slightly on sides of body and sometimes on undertail-coverts; bill blackish or deep sepia. Female very similar but red of eye-stripe slightly smaller and white of throat less extensive. Juvenile birds lack crimson eye-stripe.*

This species is often listed as Crimson-rumped Waxbill or Ruddy Waxbill, and sometimes as Sundevall's Waxbill after the man who first described it. It is an East African bird, not very common, apparently preferring low-lying scrub country or old cultivations. It is infrequently imported but does appear on the dealers' lists most years. Once it has settled in it does well and will breed willingly. The erratic nature of the supply has often meant that if one bird of a pair dies within the first year or so the remaining bird will pair up with another species of 'grey' waxbill, frequently with the Red-eared, and in this way hybrids have been produced. This species is one where, if breeding is honestly considered, more than one pair should be obtained at the outset. They were successfully bred in 1965 when the only addition to the normal diet of seeds was a supply of maggots.

Red-eared Waxbill
(*Estrilda troglodytes*)

Description: *3½–4 in. (88·9–101·6 mm.). Adult bird very similar to St. Helena but smaller, with two impor-*

Red-eared Waxbill
(*Estrilda troglodytes*)

tant distinctions: Red-ear has rump and tail black (latter with white edging to outer feathers) and undertail-coverts buff; bill red. Sexes are very similar and brighter, bigger red belly patch of male is not always apparent; but pink suffusion of a male in breeding condition is more extensive than the female's. Juvenile birds lack eye-stripe and have a black bill.

This coquettish, tiny bird ranges from the West African coast across to the Sudan. More than any other species the Red-ear typifies for me the whole group of birds known as waxbills. Half a dozen in a cage are alert and vivacious, constantly flicking their tails from left to right and keeping up a continual high-pitched squeaking contact note. They also show off well in an aviary, unless feeding, when they hop around the ground like miniature mice and are very difficult to see. On account of their low price and the uncertainty of sexing, it is advisable to buy more than one pair, unless space really is at a premium. They are very sociable and will roost clumped together side by side, unless a suitable nest is available. They are not easy to breed as they are nervous birds and will quickly desert a nest, but if looked after properly will breed as successfully as any other waxbill. The species has hybridized with Rosy-rumped, Gold-breasted and Orange-cheeked Waxbills.

Other names for the species are Black-rumped, Grey, Pink-cheeked and Common Waxbill. The last name should not be used, as it is more normally associated with *E. astrild*. A favourite name in the trade is Pink-cheek.

Orange-cheeked Waxbill
(*Estrilda melpoda*)

Orange-cheeked Waxbill
(*Estrilda melpoda*)

Description: *4 in. (101·6 mm.). Adult male has top of head grey, from hind neck to upper rump warm earth brown, lower rump and uppertail-coverts crimson; tail blackish; sides of head bright orange; below, throat whitish, centre of belly whitish sometimes flushed yellow, rest of underparts pale grey; bill red. Sexes are alike but female a trifle duller and may be smaller. Juveniles are buffish below and have a blackish bill.*

The combination of grey and orange on the head makes this a very beautiful little bird. It is a native of West Africa, ranging eastwards as far as Zambia and being found in flocks in well-watered grasslands, feeding upon seeding grasses. It is freely imported every year and there are no signs of the supply diminishing yet. The problem of sexes being similar was solved neatly by the bird-dealers in one street market that I visited on the Continent. They sold every Orange-cheek as a male and every Red-ear as the female of the same species! It is not a difficult bird to breed and every year reports of successes by novices appear in the avicultural press. It has hybridized with many other waxbills and with grassfinches and munias.

Fawn-breasted Waxbill
(*Estrilda paludicola*)

Description: *4 in. (101·6 mm.). Adult male, brown above, greyish on head; back finely barred, somewhat indistinctly, with darker lines; rump and tail-coverts scarlet, tail blackish with feathers edged scarlet near base and indistinctly barred; chin and throat whitish becoming buff on breast and belly, yellowy fawn on flanks; sometimes a flush of red on the lower belly; bill red. Female never has red on belly and red of rump and tail-coverts less uniform or extensive. Bill of juvenile black.*

It is a bird of West and South-west Africa, usually being found in grassland, but occasionally in wooded country and forest clearings. Like other semi-woodland waxbills it seems to be averagely insectivorous when rearing and otherwise is apparently a perfectly normal waxbill in captivity. Not surprisingly is better known in

Fawn-breasted Waxbill (*Estrilda paludicola*)

South Africa where it has been bred, and has hybridized with the Orange-cheeked Waxbill. It is rarely imported into Europe and presents a perfect opportunity for specialization, and discovery.

Yellow-bellied Waxbill
(*Estrilda melanotis*)

Description: *3½–4 in. (88·9–101·6 mm.). Adult male, forehead to upper mantle grey, mantle and wings olive finely barred with brown, rump and uppertail-coverts scarlet, tail blackish; face, including upper throat, black; lower throat, and sides of neck, breast and flanks light grey; lower breast, belly and undertail-coverts yellowy buff. Upper mandible of bill black, lower crimson. Female lacks the black face, being pale grey instead. Juvenile similar to female but is duller, has olive rump, uppertail-coverts dull red and bill black.*

The above description is of the nominate bird, *E. m. melanotis*, from South Africa. Another race, *E. m. bocagei*, from Angola is similar but is darker and more strongly barred.

south as a separate species, and call it Dufresne's Waxbill. The usual common name is reserved for the two yellow-bellied races from east Africa. Incidentally *kilimensis* is slightly smaller than *quartina*.

Both East African and South African birds have been bred in captivity, but require a steady supply of small insect food while the nestlings are small. They are lively birds and extremely attractive with their yellow, grey, olive and scarlet. They always seem to me to be rather delicate and (while I have not kept the black-faced

Dufresne's Waxbill
(*Coccopygia melanotis melanotis*)

The former is occasionally available, the latter probably not. There are two races from East Africa that lack the black face altogether and have a much brighter yellow belly. The juvenile of these two races, *E. m. quartina* and *E. m. kilimensis*, is distinguished by having the rump and uppertail-coverts orange, and the bill black. Some royal confusions have resulted through misapplication of field notes in avicultural literature. In addition to Yellow-bellied Waxbill the species is also known as Swee. However, most bird-fanciers insist on regarding the black-faced bird from the

species) one does not think of leaving them out of doors all the year round. In fact I would say that they are ideal for a well-lit indoor flight. They are peaceful and sociable little birds, well suited for a small mixed collection.

The species is sometimes placed in the genus *Coccopygia*.

Black-crowned Waxbill
(*Estrilda nonnula*)

Description: *About 4 in. (101·6 mm.). Adult male, finely barred dark grey above, greyish white below with a black cap and a rather broad black*

Black-cheeked Waxbill (*Estrilda erythronotos*): male

tail; *flanks, lower rump and upper-tail-coverts rosy-crimson; bill black with some longitudinal red marks. Female is paler and browner grey above, more suffused with grey below. Juveniles are similar but are dull brown above, buffish below, with no red on the flanks, and have the bill black.*

Black-headed Waxbill
(*Estrilda atricapilla*)

Description: *4 in. (101·6 mm.). Remarkably similar to Black-crowned but differs by having vent and under-tail-coverts black also, the red of the flanks is more extensive. Juveniles can be told by blackish underparts.*

Black-cheeked Waxbill
(*Estrilda erythronotos*)

Description: *4–4½ in. (101·6–114·3 mm.). Adult male has entire head and throat grey, darkest on crown; lores, behind eye, sides of face and chin*

black. *Hind neck, back and scapulars vinous brown faintly barred with dusky, secondaries and ring-coverts barred black and white; rump and uppertail-coverts crimson; throat to breast vinous indistinctly barred, flanks and belly red; vent and under-tail-coverts, tail and bill black; eye red. Female very similar but paler red on flanks and brownish black below tail and vent. Juveniles are greyer on throat and breast, duller on flanks and have the eye brown.*

I have grouped these three species together since they are remarkably similar in avicultural terms, and since I have not kept any of them I have had to resort to the literature for reference. All three are rarely imported, but any writer with experience of them is clear in his opinion that they are delicate on arrival, and are extremely difficult to maintain in good condition for long. In South Africa, however, the reverse seems to be the case and they are kept and bred in aviaries where they appear to

Black-cheeked Waxbill
(*Estrilda erythronotos*)

be about equal to other estrildines in their requirements. This is exactly paralleled by the Gouldian Finch where there are strong robust strains to be found in Australia and this 'delicate and difficult' species behaves like any other grassfinch. I think that it is a combination of climate and availability of natural food.

They are undoubtedly insectivorous to a greater degree than any other member of the genus (they are forest birds, and it seems to be a rough and ready rule that the more forest-dwelling an estrildine the more specialized its food requirements are). Wharton-Tigar successfully bred the Black-crowned in 1936 (there is a delightful photograph in the *Avicultural Magazine* for that year of the four youngsters, looking just like a group of miniature Bullfinches). These birds seemed to take mainly ant pupae,

fresh seeding *Poa* grass-heads, and a little soaked seed. Goodwin found them very difficult, and his took mainly millets (dry and soaked, and large quantities of maw). The expert Danish aviculturist Nørgaard-Oleson has kept two distinct races of the Black-crowned. He found them delicate enough to become egg-bound in an outdoor flight in October, but when brought indoors they soon recovered and reared healthy youngsters on a diet of seeds, especially grass and thistles, also mealworms and midge larvae. Bannerman describes them as travelling through the foliage of trees and shrubs, presumably searching for insects, and being observed on the ground eating small seeds, ants and other insects.

Greatest success seems to have been achieved with the Black-cheeked, and Rutgers suggests that Bengalese can be used with good effect as foster-parents. My thoughts about Bengalese are expressed in the notes for that species, but it is worth adding here that the Bengalese can only be used with genuine efficiency if they take and feed a well-balanced diet of the kind that the natural parents might well feed.

It also seems clear from the literature that these three waxbills do best in a large well-planted outdoor flight, with plenty of sunshine and a well-lit, warm and dry shelter to retire to. Indeed I would go so far as to suggest that unless one has such a facility it might be unwise to keep the birds.

AVADAVATS

These three species are sometimes placed in the genus *Estrilda*; however, whilst each is quite clearly a distinct species from the other two they are regarded as being more closely related to each other than to the other waxbills. They have certain behavioural differences in common. To the bird-keeper, through, they can be regarded as being fairly typical waxbills.

Red Avadavat
(*Amandava amandava*)

Description: *3½–4 in. (88·9–101·6 mm.). Adult male in breeding plumage bright red with brown flight feathers and blackish lores, tail and belly. Each wing-covert and tertiary has a terminal white spot and there are tiny white spots on the back, breast and flanks; when not breeding the male moults into earth brown above, retaining the red rump, below to yellowish buff; some white spots are retained on the wings; bill is red. Female resembles the eclipsed male; however, eclipsed males usually retain some odd red feathers about the body, and are rarely as neat and svelte as a female. Juvenile birds resemble the female, are duller on the rump and have a black bill.*

These birds are trapped in great numbers all over their native India, where the males are kept in tiny cages as song-birds. They are generally sent to Europe from Calcutta where the dealers have a habit of spraying them with vegetable dye to compensate for their dull colouring when 'out of colour'. The three colours used are cerise, yellow and lime green. (This treatment is also given to Silverbills and immature Spice Birds.) Personally I think that far from enhancing the appearance of the birds it ruins it. Alternative names for the species are Strawberry Finch, Tiger Finch, Red Munia, Bombay Avadavat or Red Waxbill. Often it will be listed simply as Avadavat. The song of the male is a series of clear liquid notes on a descending scale. I do not find it at all musical, but very sad. It is usually uttered by an unmated male.

In my experience it is an easy bird to maintain and has bred frequently, not requiring very much in the way of live food and being reasonably undemanding. Pope bred it in a cage to at least ten generations as an exercise to prove that it could be domesticated if anyone was interested, but nobody seemed to be impressed by his achievement. Undoubtedly, such a cheap bird in such free supply will continue to be kept in overcrowded small mixed collections for decoration until such times as the governments of India, Malaysia and Indonesia begin restricting the drain on their wildlife resources. Doubtless the Avadavat will then receive the attention of the serious breeders. It is a hardy bird; I have kept it out of doors all the year round without heat and the males in this collection never moulted more than about half of their nuptial plumage before once more becoming all-over red.

There are two subspecies besides the nominate. One, invariably called Strawberry Finch, Chinese Avadavat or Cochin Avadavat, *A. a. punicea*, is smaller, noticeably richer and brighter in colour and peppered with white spots. It is a lovely bird, well worth serious attention. Another race is called Golden-bellied or Yellow-bellied Strawberry Finch, *A. a. flaviventris*, and is very rarely imported.

All three races have a tendency to melanism, and males will become darker and blacker as the years go by. Sometimes they will produce white feathers. Birds kept in outdoor aviaries are invariably free from such aberrations; they usually only occur with birds deprived of sunlight and kept on an all-seed diet. One male *punicea* that I know of grew progressively darker and duller until one year, inexplicably, it moulted into a brilliant nuptial plumage quite the equal of any freshly caught bird.

Green Avadavat
(*Amandava formosa*)

Description: *4 in. (101·6 mm.). Adult male olive green above, with black tail; below, it is much paler, yellow on breast and belly, flanks are barred black and white; bill red. Female is similar but noticeably duller. Juvenile resembles female, has black bill and much-reduced flank markings.*

This species may be listed as *Stictospiza formosa*, and may be called Formosa Green Avadavat (which is ironic since it is only found in central India) or Green Munia. It is not often imported and has a reputation for delicacy, particularly on arrival. However, once acclimatized and settled in it is hardy, though not so hardy as its more widespread cousin, and should be brought in for the winter. It has a tendency to feather-plucking, and in this habit is second only to the Lavender Finch. Thus, affected birds should be separated and housed in roomy quarters. It has bred on several occasions and has proved to require a good supply of small insects when rearing, but can be taught to take rearing food.

Golden-breasted Waxbill
(*Amandava subflava*)

Description: *3½–4 in. (88·9–101·6 mm.). Adult male, earth brown above, including wings, sometimes olivace-* *ous; bright crimson stripe from lores to over and behind eye, uppertail-coverts scarlet, tail blackish; throat is yellow or golden and the underparts are golden orange to orange red; sides of breast and flanks strongly barred with dark grey; bill red, culmen black. Female lacks the eye-stripe and is paler below, with greyish tinge. The southern race, A. s. clarkei, is slightly larger, more extensively yellow below with the orange less diffused. Female is yellower below than the female of the nominate race. Juvenile birds are brown above, lacking red rump and eye-stripe, no*

Golden-breasted Waxbill
(*Estrilda subflava*)

barring on flanks, buffish underparts, bill blackish.

Other names for this lovely tiny bird are Orange-breasted Waxbill (not to be confused with Fawn-breasted) and Zebra Waxbill. Dealers list the southern race as Giant, Clarke's, or South African Golden-breasted Waxbill, and double the price. It is a tame and confiding little bird, seen in flocks over most of Africa south of the Sahara in grassland and cultivation. It is said to have the habit of sliding down a grass stem to look for fallen seeds. The spherical nest with its side entrance is usually built low down, often in a thornbush, but the species' *penchant* for adopting the old nest of a weaver or similar species and re-lining or renovating it, encourages it to adopt the aviculturist's basket.

The problem of finding suitable live food for such a small bird has often bothered aviculturists, who find that the skins of mealworms and maggots are too tough for the bird to cope with. In a small confined aviary, particularly indoors, the keeper must pursue white worm cultures and dig up every ants' nest in the vicinity and try every ruse to feed soft foods. However, in a large planted aviary they have been bred successfully with no other extra provided than chopped-up mealworms. I have found it to be an utterly delightful bird to keep, but rather delicate, with a very quick response to cold damp weather conditions, which necessitate it being brought indoors.

BLUE WAXBILLS

The three species that are known generally as blue waxbills on account of their colouring are well known in aviculture. The Cordon-bleu has been an old and familiar favourite for most of this century, but the other two have only been infrequently imported until comparatively recently, when they have made regular appearances on the importers' lists. To the specialist they are individual and distinct species, but to many an aviculturist they differ from each other only in their colouring. I once had a collection of a dozen or so blue waxbills, with all three species represented. Some were wild caught, but others had been bred in captivity. I placed them in a large outdoor planted aviary that had a large well-lit house attached. They made a delightful sight, generally staying together as a homogeneous unit and all roosting together in an apple tree in the centre of the flight. Trying to get them to roost in the house would drive me to distraction; they simply wouldn't. Notwithstanding owls and cats I eventually allowed them to roost out at night, but by the end of November I transferred them to a smaller enclosure so designed that I was able to get them all indoors in one swoop and then shut the trap door.

One problem with these birds that has been discovered by Goodwin is that when unmated single birds, such as two males, 'pair up' – as often happens in many mixed collections with various species (I once had a Pekin Robin 'paired' to a hen Canary) – the eventual appearance of a suitable mate is most unlikely to break the unnatural bond. I had two male Cordon-bleus firmly 'paired' up and a lonely unmated female who wandered about calling plaintively all the time in quite a distressing way. When a similar situation occurred with some Red-eared Waxbills of Goodwin the birds 'flocked' out of the breeding season and when the spring came round again males and females paired up naturally. It might be possible to hypothesize from this that blue waxbills pair for life, and *Estrilda* waxbills only for a season. I don't know the answer to this, but it is certain that one cannot assume that simply to put a male and a female together (of any species) is to establish a breeding unit.

Cordon-bleu
(*Uraeginthus bengalus*)

Description: *4½–5 in. (114·3–127·0 mm.). Adult male, earth-brown above, from forehead to upper rump, lores and around eye, throat, breast, flanks, rump and uppertail-coverts powder blue; tail greenish blue; from centre of breast to undertail-coverts pale brown; claret crescent on cheeks and ear coverts; bill rose-madder, sometimes mauve, with blackish tip. Female very similar but slightly duller, bill may be greyer, and lacks red ear-patch. Juveniles resemble female but are paler and have much blacker bill.*

The tail of the Cordon-bleu is longer than that of most *Estrilda* waxbills (but similar to the other blue waxbills) so the size indicated above is a little misleading. The races from East Africa are a little larger than the nominate bird from West Africa, and lead dealers to advertise them as Giant East African Cordon-bleus. Most field books describe this species as Red-cheeked Cordon-bleu, as they reserve plain Cordon-bleu for *U. angolensis*. It is a common species, tame and not shy in the presence of man, and can frequently be found in small parties feeding on or near the ground, in and around villages. It is wide-ranging, being found in most of West, central and eastern Africa.

Being a freely imported species, not expensive, and beautiful as well, it suffers the fate of all similar birds – namely that of ending up in over-crowded collections of waxbills and mannikins. Such birds rarely breed and those that do make the attempt rarely succeed. However, in a planted aviary with little direct competition for the available insects Cordon-bleus are bred each year. Of course, a serious and dedicated attempt will result in proportionately greater success. My own success with the species was a long time ago and the parent birds raised their young with little help from me. They have reared young with only mealworms and gentles as live food, but are much happier with whiteworms or ants' eggs in addition or in preference. A healthy brood of Bengalese and Cordon-bleu hybrids was raised on an all-seed diet, most of the feeding being done by the Bengalese.

Cordon-bleu (*Uraeginthus bengalus*)

Blue-breasted Waxbill
(*Uraeginthus angolensis*)

Description: *4½–5 in. (114·3–127 mm.). Adult male resembles female U. bengalus, but blue is more extensive, bill is greyer and brown is of a greyer tone. Female has less extensive and weaker blue, but this is a subtle distinction when compared to the female bengalus. Flanks are blue. Juvenile birds are paler, bill blackish, and lack blue on the flanks.*

In aviculture this species is invariably known as Blue-breasted Waxbill, but, as mentioned above, in ornithology it is known as Cordon-bleu. Its habits and ecology are very like those of the Red-cheeked Cordon-bleu; most of its calls are also similar and its displays are identical. In fact, Delacour considered the two to be con-specific, but later writers generally hold them to be separated, and aviculturists who have kept the two in captivity find that they do not naturally interbreed, neither are there any reports of natural hybrids occurring in the wild. The geographic species concept therefore suggests that they are not con-specific.

In captivity it is considered to be hardier than the Cordon-bleu, and breeds more readily, but since I have given all three species identical treatment, and in so doing must have hit the common denominator, I think that they are pretty well alike.

Blue-headed Waxbill
(*Uraeginthus cyanocephala*)

Description: *4½–5 in. (114·3–127 mm.). Adult male, entire head powder blue, also throat, breast flanks and uppertail-coverts; tail darker, greeny blue; mantle, back and wings a warmer brown than either of the other species; bill reddish pink with black tip. Female similar to U. bengalus but slightly paler both of brown and blue. Should it be necessary to separate it with absolute certainty in the face of apparently identical plumages, the second primary of the females of bengalus and angolensis are notched on the inner edge while that of cyanocephala is perfectly even. A practised eye, however, can distinguish from the more upright stance of the latter species and its generally slightly bigger size. Juveniles are much paler blue than young of the other species and the blue is more restricted.*

They are extremely beautiful little birds and have proved to be as easy, if not easier, than *angolensis*, to keep and breed. They breed very reliably indoors providing a variety of live food is supplied, but in planted aviaries out-of-doors have reared healthy and sound youngsters on seed, egg-food and chopped-up mealworms. And no doubt they were able

Heads of male Blue Waxbills: Cordon-bleu (*Uraeginthus bengalus*); Blue-breasted Waxbill (*U. angolensis*) and Blue-headed Waxbill (*U. cyanocephala*)

to find additional tiny insect life during the first few, critical days after the young hatch. Goodwin has described how the parent birds, particularly the male, of this and the Blue-breast have searched his indoor aviary exhaustively on the first day, no doubt looking for the kind of small live food that it would take in the wild and only taking whiteworms, gentles and mealworms reluctantly. The moment when the young waxbills hatch, and for the following forty-eight hours, is when the keeper should really make an extra effort, and ants' eggs, greenfly and small green caterpillars are undeniably valuable adjuncts to the food available.

The Blue-headed or Blue-capped Waxbill has been hybridized with the Cordon-bleu and apparently the hybrid males had both the blue head of one parent species male plus the red cheeks of the other.

GRENADIERS

There are two grenadier waxbills, formerly given a genus of their own (*Granatina*) but now aligned more closely with the blue waxbills. Their colouring gives them a truly exotic and delicate appearance, and while they are as exotic as that word might mean to the reader they are not among the hardiest of waxbills and are about equal to the Cordon-bleu in delicacy. They are quite large, about 5 in. (127 mm.) or so, and are more pugnacious when breeding than the *Estrilda* or *Uraeginthus* waxbills. Males, particularly, can be aggressive and the best breeding results seem to have been obtained when a pair have been given an enclosure to themselves. They are undoubtedly difficult when first imported and need to be acclimatized carefully with full attention being given to both temperature variation and diet. They are fairly typical in their dietary requirements, taking a large proportion of millet seeds and having a fancy for seeding grasses, soaked and sprouting seed, and small insects. They need a regular supply of live food if they are to be maintained in fine condition for long, but access to an open planted aviary may alleviate this need. They love spray millet and

Purple Grenadier (*Uraeginthus ianthinogaster*): female on the left, male on the right

this can be soaked and allowed to germinate, especially during breeding. Like so many waxbills they are reluctant to rear their young exclusively on mealworms and maggots but have done so in the past (by exclusively I mean the only form of live food) taking egg-food, bread-and-milk sop, and other supplements. The two species have hybridized with each other.

Violet-eared Waxbill
(*Uraeginthus granatina*)

Description: *5–5½ in. (127–139·7 mm.). Adult male has body a rich, dark chestnut brown with tail and throat black; a short deep blue stripe runs from the forehead to above the eye; sides of face beautiful rich lustrous violet; upper and lower tail-coverts cobalt blue; bill, eye and eye-ring red. Female similar but much paler colours. Juveniles are sexually dimorphic within a couple*

of weeks of leaving the nest. Young male resembles female but has colours of adult on face, and has eye red. Young female resembles adult but has facial area buff, eye brown.

This is a South African bird of dry thorn scrub country and may be found even in quite arid areas. It moves around in small parties and is often found in the company of Blue-breasted Waxbills. It is thought that as an adaptation to the drier areas it has developed a reliance on termites as an alternative source of water. Later on in this book is a section devoted to brood-parasitic whydahs, one of these – the Shaft-tailed Whydah – parasitizes the Violet-eared Waxbill. Other names for the species are Grenadier, Common Grenadier or Grenadier Waxbill.

Purple Grenadier
(Uraeginthus ianthinogaster)

Description: *About 5½ in. (139·7 mm.). Adult male, mainly dark reddish brown; there is a crescent of blue feathers above and below the eye, underparts royal blue scalloped irregularly with the brown of the rest of the body; uppertail-coverts bright violet blue; tail black; bill red. Female similar to the male, but whitish around eyes, and below the brown feathers have white spots and scallops. Juvenile birds resemble the female but lack the white around the eye and the spots on the underpart.*

There are three races of this bird, but the differences are, in my opinion, too subtle to enable identification from words unless two, or ideally the three, races are before one at the same time. It is a secretive but not particularly shy or retiring bird and is tame in an aviary. It feeds near or on the ground, frequently beneath bushes and aloes. In its turn it is parasitized by the Fischer's Whydah.

They were first bred by Boosey in 1958, who reported that they only took a few maggots and mealworms. However, the outdoor flight was apparently overgrown with nettles and weeds, and the two youngsters were fine specimens. However, when

Canon Lowe raised a hybrid the male parent, the Purple Grenadier, was apparently an excellent parent and fed a large amount of mealworms. There seems to me to be no doubt, though, that to simply get some young birds 'on the sticks' is not enough. Allen Silver was a stickler in his belief that a breeding should not be recognized until the young birds had over-wintered, or moulted into adult plumage. There's a lot to be said

Violet-eared Waxbill (*Uraeginthus granatina*)

for that attitude. However, evidence from experiments with Bullfinches in Germany suggests that, unless a baby bird is fed correctly, despite the fact that it could well develop into an apparently healthy adult, it can be an imperfect parent and/or might never actually breed. For this reason I believe that one should give as wide and full a diet as possible for rearing birds.

FIREFINCHES

The firefinches are an interesting group of reddish-brown waxbills from Africa, only one of which is well known and regularly imported, *L. senegala*, although it might be argued that with the inclusion of the Lavender Finch this figure could be doubled. They are birds of the brush, but can often be found living in and around villages and cultivated areas. Small groups can be seen at most times of the year hopping around picking up minute seeds on the ground. They feed in the open but prefer to have dense cover always at hand to retreat into at a sign of danger.

Firefinches: 1. Black-bellied Firefinch (*Lagonosticta rara*); 2. Bar-breasted Firefinch (*L. rufopicta*); 3. Brown Firefinch (*L. nitidula*); 4. Common Firefinch (*L. senegala*); 5. Black-faced Firefinch (*L. larvata*); 6. Dark Firefinch (*L. rubricata*)

They are not particularly hardy in captivity, and do not seem to be particularly long-lived or prolific breeders; the two species mentioned above have the most successful record, but all will do well if cared for properly. There are many races among the (probably) seven species, and much confusion about identity. I trust that my notes and sketches will serve to clarify the issue a little. Firefinches are parasitized in the wild by the Viduine whydahs known as Combassous. Apart from the work of Nicolai in Germany, this phenomenon has been little studied and practically nothing of value has appeared in the English language. Turn to the whydah section of this book for further details.

Common Firefinch
(*Lagonosticta senegala*)

Description: *3½–4 in. (88·9–101·6 mm.). Adult male, rose-red on head, breast and rump; back brown, suffused with red; wings and tail dark brown; lower belly and undertail-coverts light brown; a few fine white dots on the side of the breast; bill red; orbital eye-ring pinky white. Female has lores and uppertail-coverts red; rest of body brown, with small white spots on sides of breast; bill red. Juveniles lack red lores, breast spots, and have the bill dusky, but otherwise resemble the female.*

This is the most frequently imported of the genus and is usually referred to in avicultural literature as simply Firefinch. Synonyms are Senegal Firefinch and Red-billed Firefinch. It is the widest-ranging of the firefinches, being found from the west coast to the east of Africa, south of the Sahara, and down to South Africa. It is a bird of the savanna country, of dense scrub and thorn thicket, but is absent from the drier parts of the country. It must be one of the commonest birds of Africa.

They make a nest of dry grasses, old rags, and any reasonably suitable material, which is usually a loose ball with a side entrance. The cup is generally lined with feathers and some of these are used by the outgoing female to camouflage the hole. Firefinches will nest in thatches, under awnings, in nooks and crannies and will readily accept a nest basket. They are parasitized by the Combassou (*Hypochera chalybeata*), so the first step in breeding the latter is to establish some breeding firefinches. They will breed fairly well in captivity providing that small insects are available. Several hybrids have been recorded, including the Lavender Finch and the Golden-breasted Waxbill.

Common Firefinches are reasonably hardy and have wintered out-of-doors, but in my opinion no waxbills should be submitted to such spartan trials unless there is a dry and draught-proof shelter in which to retire, and where the temperature does not fall below 50° F. (10° C.).

Dark Firefinch
(*Lagonosticta rubricata*)

Description: *4½ in. (114·3 mm.). Adult male, dark earth brown above; uppertail-coverts and base of tail claret red; tail black; face, throat, breast, belly and flanks red with a few clear white spots on flanks; thighs, vent and undertail-coverts black; bill slate grey; inner edge of second primary notched; there is also a pink orbital eye-ring. Female is similar to the male but is a paler, rather more buffish red below. Juveniles resemble the female, but the red is only faintly present on young males and there are no white dots on the flanks. The eastern races of this bird have the entire head washed with red in both sexes, that of the male being darker;* haematocephala *is probably the brightest of these.*

The Dark Firefinch is also known as the African Firefinch and the Ruddy Waxbill, and all three names must be known to the researcher when avicultural records are studied, since scientific names are only occasionally used. There is a race with a pinkish bill from Angola (*landanae*) to which Praed and Grant have accorded full specific rank and called the Pale-billed Firefinch. Its status is still under debate.

This species looks like a giant

Common Firefinch, with all the markings a bit bolder and stronger. The female is just like a male *senegala* in colouring and extent of red. It is no doubt quite possible that the presence of a female *rubricata* in with a group of *senegala* could result in problems of identification for the *senegala* females.

They have been bred on various occasions and have fed young rearing almost exclusively on live food for the first week to ten days. Birds bred in African aviaries seem to have taken termites exclusively, but in England have fed on small white-worms, small mealworms and ant pupae, etc.

Second primary of Firefinches as a diagnostic aid: A. Notched, as with *L. senegala, L. rubricata, L. larvata, L. landanae, L. vinacea* and *L. rara.* B. Without notch as *L. rufopicta, L. caerulescens, L. jamesoni, L. nitidula* and *L. perreini*

Jameson's Firefinch
(*Lagonosticta jamesoni*)

Description: *4–4½ in. (101·6–114·3 mm.). Adult male, extremely similar to* rubricata *but generally differs in being paler earth brown above and washed with rose-pink; below the red is more rose. Female is also similar to the female* rubricata *but is paler with subspecific variation; in both species the only certain means of identification is by looking at the*

second primary which is not *notched in* jamesoni, *and this is the only way that juveniles may be identified.*

The literature is peppered with stories of frustration on the part of keepers who are seeking a male or a female *jamesoni*, and how every bird that turns up inevitably proves to be a *rubricata*. It is possibly imported more often and gets disposed of as a 'Ruddy Waxbill' or 'Dark Firefinch'. I cannot see why it should not be equally available since it has roughly the same distribution, but, whereas *rubricata* is a bird of both wild country and cultivated or inhabited areas, *jamesoni* is rarely seen around towns or villages. This is probably reflected in the trappers' behaviour.

In South Africa and Rhodesia they appear to have bred without any difficulty, but large natural aviaries and adequate supplies of termites are no doubt relevant factors. In Europe they have proved to be demanding when rearing young and cannot be relied on to rear on mealworms and gentles. Undoubtedly a richly planted aviary would be a great asset for the keeper.

Bar-breasted Firefinch
(*Lagonosticta rufopicta*)

Description: *4–4½ in. (101·6–114·3 mm.). Adult male, from top of head to lower back, wings, earth-brown; lower rump and uppertail-coverts dark red, tail black; forehead lores, sides of head, throat and breast vinous red; belly and flanks various grey; undertail-coverts buff; there is a broad band of white marks across the breast that form more or less broken bars. The sexes are alike, and the bill is red. Juveniles are brown below, washed with reddish; bill dusky.*

Brown Firefinch
(*Lagonosticta nitidula*)

Description: *4½ in. (114·3 mm.). Adult male, earth brown from forehead to uppertail-coverts, perhaps slightly greyer than* rufopicta*; lores, sides of head, throat and breast vinous red, the latter spotted brightly and profusely with white* (red does not suffuse over flanks and belly as in rufopicta)*; flanks and belly are grey; undertail-coverts buff; bill dusky purple, reddish on lower mandible. The sexes are very similar, but the female is slightly less red on the breast.*

I have placed these two birds together since many authorities consider them to be con-specific, with *nitidula* being a race of *rufopicta*. As the two are visually distinct I think that it is sensible to maintain the common names as they are most normally used. In this way, one will avoid the kind of confusion that resulted in a lot of crossed lines in correspondence in *Foreign Birds* during the 1950s when aviculturists in three continents had bred one or the other and kept correcting each other on nomenclature.

According to Praed and Grant, *nitidula* is a 'rather local species, shy and normally found in swampy thickets and reed beds, coming out into open ground to feed'. In direct contrast they describe *rufopicta* as 'another town-dwelling Firefinch, found freely in villages and equally tame and fearless, with the habits of the Red-billed species'. The contrasting behaviour of the two seems to be the same in captivity, with Brown Firefinches being much more retiring to begin with.

Once settled in, however, both birds seem to be good breeders, providing of course that they have small insects in adequate supply the first two weeks.

Black-bellied Firefinch
(*Lagonosticta rara*)

Description: *4½ in. (114·3 mm.). Adult male has entire head, throat, breast and flanks vinous red; mantle dark brown, washed with vinous red; rump and uppertail-coverts dark red; wings dark brown; tail blackish; belly and undertail-coverts velvet black; no white spots on breast or flanks; bill black above, red below. Female has top and sides of head grey; lores red; chin a light grey and breast a paler red; lower breast suffused with grey; in other respects it resembles the male. Juveniles are sooty brown with red rumps; the young male is suffused with red.*

This species may be listed in some books as the Black-bellied Waxbill, *Estrilda rara*, and some writers consider it to be an intermediate between the firefinches and the *Estrildinae*. It is local throughout its range from the Cameroons in west Africa across to the Sudan and Kenya. However, it is apparently common in Uganda, and is a bird of the grass country. Sir Richard Cotterell received a pair in 1960, and placed them in a garden aviary to themselves. After wintering indoors with some other waxbills they were once again placed in this aviary. The grass was cut short, leaving a few big clumps of long grass, and it was in one of the latter that they built a nest and reared two broods of youngsters. The first brood took large quantities of ant pupae, plus of course whatever they could find in the aviary, and the fledglings proved to be strong and sturdy birds. The second brood were less lucky with the time of the year and had hardly any ant pupae, instead they were given mealworms. Like breeders of other species of firefinches, Sir Richard found them to be very wasteful with mealworms, eating only the head and a bit of the body. The young of the second brood were later leaving the nest and slower to moult into adult plumage. In his report in the *Avicultural Magazine* in 1962, Sir Richard says, 'I think perhaps the secret of breeding these and similar birds is to give them an aviary of their own, so that *all* the natural insect life is available for one pair only, to rear their young.' I fully agree with this.

Black-faced Firefinch
(*Lagonosticta larvata*)

Description: *About 4½ in. (114·3 mm.). Adult male has lores, cheeks, chin and throat black; top of head brownish grey (sometimes washed with red); nape, sides of neck and breast maroon red; mantle and wings dark brownish grey; uppertail-coverts maroon red; flanks grey, often washed with maroon and spotted with white; belly and undertail-coverts grey and black or simply black; bill grey. Female is dusky earth brown above with maroon uppertail-coverts and blackish tail; below pale brown, dusky on flanks, washed with vinous and spotted with white; bill grey. Juveniles resemble adult female.*

There are several distinct races of this species, some of which are accorded full specific status by some authorities: for example *nigricollis*, which looks like a Black-tailed Lavender Finch since it is a much more uniform grey all over its body, including the breast, but has the same back, rump and tail markings as

larvata. Another very distinctive race is *vinacea*, where the maroon and grey of the body is replaced by a pinky-vinaceous grey. In this race the rump and uppertail-coverts are also vinous, but of a richer hue than on the body, and inclining to crimson.

It is a shy and silent bird found in heavy grassland, among bamboos, or woodland verges and clearings, usually feeding on the ground and presumably taking small seeds. They seem to be particularly fond of bamboo. Hopkinson brought some *vinacea* back to England in 1912 and found

Black-faced Firefinch (*Lagonosticta larvata*); Black-headed Waxbill (*Estrilda atricapilla*)

them to be more difficult to acclimatize and settle than most waxbills, but once fully adjusted they appeared to be hardier.

The Vinaceous Firefinch was first bred in England in 1963 by Sir Richard Cotterell, who kept them in a planted aviary along with some Blue and Black-cheeked Waxbills. They successfully reared a first brood, apparently almost exclusively on ant pupae. A second brood, however, was given only mealworms and the nestlings eventually died through being fed on millet seed; the parents ignored the mealworms very soon and completely ignored insectile food.

Lavender Finch
(*Lagonosticta caerulescens*)

Description: *4–4½ in. (101·6–114·3 mm.). Adult male, clear blue-grey above; below, similar but paler; rump, upper and lower tail-coverts and tail crimson; throat and upper breast whitish; usually a few white spots on flanks; lores black with small black spot behind eye; bill black, reddish at base. Female very similar but a little smaller and grey, slightly dusky by comparison.*

Bates placed this species in the genus *Lagonosticta* in 1934 and was followed by several authorities, including Bannerman. It has been called Lavender Firefinch and Lavender Waxbill. It may be listed as *Estrilda caerulescens*. It is normally listed by bird-dealers as plain Lavender Finch. It comes from West Africa. There is no doubt that it is more insectivorous than most of the *Estrilda* waxbills decribed above, an indication quoted by Hopkinson of its affinity to the *Lagonosticta*.

Lavender Finches have a reputation for delicacy on arrival and should not be placed out-of-doors without some circumspection. However, once settled in and thoroughly acclimatized, they prove to be as hardy and easy to handle as all the other regularly available waxbills, and will often attempt to breed in a mixed collection. Breeding success is not easy to come by unless small insects are available while the nestlings are tiny. Most breeding records indicate that ants' eggs and chopped-up mealworms are sufficient. It has hybridized with the Orange-cheeked Waxbill.

This species is the worst feather-plucker that I know, and they should never be overcrowded or kept for long in a small cage if this is to be avoided.

Black-tailed Lavender Finch
(*Lagonosticta perreini*)

Description: *4–4½ in. (101·6–114·3 mm.). Adult, like a darker* caerulescens *but has chin, tail, undertail-coverts and bill black; lacks any white spots on the flanks. Juveniles are duller.*

This bird is rarely imported as it comes from South Africa. It is a bird of woodland and open grassy areas in woody country, never straying far from cover. It appears to be more delicate than its northern cousin, and might be more insectivorous in its dietary needs. It has been bred, but the young were difficult to rear. I have no experience with the species at all and would advise approaching it with care. It is regarded as a sub-species of *caerulescens* by many authorities.

CRIMSON-WINGS

There are four species in the genus *Cryptospiza*. They are beautiful birds, better known on the Continent than in Britain, and those specimens that have arrived here have all been via Continental dealers as far as I know. Very little is known about their behaviour in captivity, and references in the literature are woefully few. They are birds of the mountains of central and eastern Africa, and can be found in the grasses bordering woodland and the grassy clearings in the dense shrubberies alongside mountain streams. At the slightest disturbance they disappear into the thickest woodland and remain hidden. Even when feeding in the open, they stay in the shadow of the trees. They will apparently venture into millet plantations on the hillside, but not more than 100 yds. (91·5 m.) from cover.

The nest is fairly typical, being a spheroid of grasses with a side entrance, lined with feathers and fine grass-heads. The food in the wild is recorded as being seeds of various grasses, but in captivity they will take mealworms, ant pupae and other small insects. The three species described below have all been imported at some time; the fourth, Shelley's Crimson-wing (*Cryptospiza shelleyi*), is a very shy bird of impenetrable jungle found only on the Virunga Volcanoes and the Ruwenzori Mountains. I do not believe that it has ever been imported.

Red-faced Crimson-wing
(*Cryptospiza reichenovii*)

Description: *About 4½ in. (114·3 mm.). Adult male has lores and patch round eye scarlet; rest of head to upper mantle dark olive-brown; rest of upperparts except innermost webs of tertiaries, primaries and tail, crimson; latter blackish brown; below is a paler olive; flanks crimson. Female very similar to male but lacks any red on the face, and is paler around eye and chin. Juveniles resemble the female but have no crimson on flanks and less extensive crimson on mantle and uppertail-coverts. Bill black.*

This is the most widely distributed species, ranging from the Congo and the Cameroons to Rhodesia and Mozambique. It is quite common but rarely seen owing to its love of the dense shade provided by the forest, which has given rise to an alternative name of Forest Finch. Other names are Red-eyed and Reichenow's Crimson-wing. They do well in an aviary and have proved to be as easy to cater for and to breed as, for example, twin-spots and pytilias. They are particularly active in the early hours of the morning and at dusk.

Abyssinian Crimson-wing
(*Cryptospiza salvadorii*)

Description: *About 4½ in. (114·3 mm.). Resembles female reichenovii but can be distinguished by being a lighter tone of olive, the upperparts being a more reddish crimson and the absence of crimson on flanks. Female is similar but paler yet. Juveniles have mantle olive and less red on uppertail-coverts. Bill black.*

This bird is also known as Salvador's Crimson-wing, or Crimson-backed Forest Finch. It ranges from the Congo into southern Ethiopia. It should be treated as the other crimson-wings.

Jackson's Crimson-wing
(*Cryptospiza jacksonii*)

Description: *About 4½ in. (114·3 mm.). Adult male has head, sides of face, sides of neck, mantle to upper-tail-coverts, and wing-coverts bright crimson-red; wings and tail blackish; nape of neck an irregular triangle of dark slate grey; chin to undertail-coverts slate grey; flanks may be marked with crimson. Bill black. Female is very similar to male but red of head less extensive, the grey forming a clear collar, and often reaching up on to crown. Juvenile has entire head grey.*

This beautiful bird is also known as Dusky Crimson-wing or Jackson's Forest Finch. It has a very restricted range on Mt. Ruwenzori, occurring between 6,000 ft. (1,828·8 m.) and 8,000 ft. (2,438·4 m.). It ventures forth to feed on millet and other grasses, retreating into dense forest undergrowth at the slightest cause. None the less it has been trapped and sent to Europe, but nothing has been published. Despite their exclusiveness, I suspect that they should be treated like the other species.

BLUE-BILLS AND SEED-CRACKERS

The genera of infrequently available and little-known birds that deserve much more attention are *Spermophaga*, the blue-bills, and *Pirenestes*, the seed-crackers. Those that do turn up appear to be the tail-enders of Continental shipments, are frequently odd birds, and are very expensive.

Both are birds of dense forest undergrowth, being seen in similar conditions to the crimson-wings – along the grass verges of woodland, into which they will instantly beat a hasty retreat. The seed-crackers have a marked preference for wetter conditions and are found in swamps and clearings in high-rainfall forests. However, in some areas blue-bills and seed-crackers are found sharing the same habitat. Little is known about the dietary needs and no hypotheses seem to exist for the function of the enormous bills, for they certainly take, even seem to prefer, many tiny seeds. They love ripening rice, but such a large bill is not necessary for this. In captivity they have accepted live food willingly.

Red-headed Blue-bill
(*Spermophaga ruficapilla*)

Description: *5½–6 in. (139·7–152·4 mm.). Adult male has entire head, chin to breast, flanks and uppertail-coverts crimson-red, rest of plumage black; bill, mother-of-pearl blue with cutting edges and tip red; black eye-ring. Female has head duller red; mantle dark grey; belly grey profusely spotted with white; spots tending to form bars on vent and undertail-coverts; bill as in male. Juvenile sooty above; brownish black below.*

This species ranges from Angola to Tanzania; the race, *S. r. cana* from north-eastern Tanzania, has the black replaced by dark grey, lighter in the female. They take small seeds, enjoy soaked and sprouting seeds very much and will take larger seeds up to hemp, oats and sunflower, which may be soaked. Mealworms and other live food may be offered. No doubt live food is necessary should they attempt to breed. I am sure that a secluded and densely planted aviary is necessary for breeding to even be attempted.

Red-breasted Blue-bill
(*Spermophaga haematina*)

Description: *About 6 in. (152·4 mm.). Adult male has chin to breast and flanks bright red, rest of plumage black; bill pearly blue with red tip; white eye-ring. Female has chin to breast and flanks duller red, head grey suffused with red, especially on face, rest of plumage dark grey, spotted with white on lower breast, and grey part of flanks. Juvenile sooty above, brownish below.*

The Red-breasted Blue-bill is listed by some writers as Blue-billed Weaver. It comes from West Africa where it is occasionally found alongside the Black-bellied Seed-cracker. Wostendiek found that it preferred small and soaked seeds, soft food and insects to dry or large seeds. This was a contrast to the Red-headed Blue-bill, which readily took large seeds as well.

Black-bellied Seed-cracker
(*Pirenestes ostrinus*)

Description: *About 5½ in. (139·7 mm.). Adult male has entire head, chin to breast and flanks, uppertail-coverts scarlet; tail reddish; rest of plumage black. Female is brown,*

Black-bellied Seed-cracker
(*Pirenestes ostrinus*)

where male is black. Both sexes have sharply angled (straight edges) blue-black bill, and a yellow eye-ring. Juveniles are wholly brown with red only on uppertail-coverts and tail.

There is wide variation of bill size. Chapin suggested that the very large-billed types are primarily birds of the edges of the range, living in patches of woods in the savanna, · while the small-billed birds live in heavy forests, mainly in the scrubby growth of clearings. Therefore, Rothschild's Seed-cracker (*P. rothschildi*) and the Large-billed or Great Seed-cracker (*P. maxi-* *mus*) are all synonymous with *P. ostrinus*. This and other species of seed-cracker should be treated like blue-bills.

NEGRO-FINCHES

Earlier in this section I mentioned that the forest-living waxbills have generally developed a more specialized ecology, and are either more insectivorous or have some other food requirement that sets them apart from the normal *Estrilda*. The Negro-finches of central Africa form just such a group, and have evolved into an existence almost entirely in the tropical forest canopies. The genus, *Nigrita*, contains four species. Very little is known about them in their natural state, but they are believed to feed on seeds, fruit and insects. Three of the four species are associated with palm trees, particularly the Oil Palm (*Elaeis guineensis*), and they are known to feed on the highly nutritious oily husk of the orange-coloured fruit. They are likely to be seen at any height, feeding in, on or among flowers, frequently in the company of sunbirds. There might possibly be a symbiosis between the two, with the Negro-finches taking insects disturbed by the nectar-feeding sunbirds, but this is pure hypothesis.

Their breeding season is more attuned to the natural seasons than that of the ground-feeding waxbills, which are more affected by the ripening of grass-seeds. The nest is a large untidy ball of fibres, moss and leaf-strips, lined with soft grasses and grass-heads. The songs are said to be 'simple but melodious', quite loud, and are given throughout the year.

There is no mention of them in the avicultural literature, and they are rarely imported. I cannot remember with certainty ever seeing any on offer, but that they are available from time to time is shown by those that appear at bird-shows on occasion. On hearsay evidence alone, I would say that they are not so difficult as one might suppose and I suggest that in addition to a normal seed diet they should be offered fruit, and mealworms and gentles. It is almost certainly necessary to provide a little softbill mixture, on which a few mealworms can be cut up.

Grey-headed Negro-finch
(*Nigrita canicapilla*)

Description: *About 6 in. (152·4 mm.).
Adult has forehead, around eye, sides
of face and neck black edged with
whitish grey; wing-coverts are black
with white spots; wings, tail and
underparts entirely black; bill black,
eye vermilion. Sexes are alike. Juvenile is sooty black with faint wing-
spots, eye blue, and dark horn bill.*

This species is said to be tame and
inquisitive, and may be encountered
in pairs or small parties in the open
parts of forests, generally near water.
It is the largest of the genus. This is
the only Negro-finch that I have seen
in captivity.

White-breasted Negro-finch
(*Nigrita fusconota*)

Description: *4½–5 in. (114·3–127
mm.). Adult has mantle and wings
earth brown; rest of upperparts glossy
blue-black; chin, throat, sides of neck
and rest of underparts white; eye
brown; bill black. Juvenile has head
dusky brown where adult is black.*

I have a vague recollection of seeing this species advertised some years
ago, but have no knowledge of it in
captivity.

QUAIL-FINCHES

Another rather aberrant genus of African waxbills that has
developed a rather specialized way of life is *Ortygospiza*. This one
is even smaller than the last and contains two species. They are
thought to be very closely related to the avadavats, but have been
kept apart by reason of their much more terrestrial habits. There
are some physical differences too, for the Quail-finches have
evolved longer and stronger legs, shorter tails and louder voices.

They are birds of bogs, marshland and wet grassy areas, where
they can be flushed in small flocks or family parties. They stay

Quail-finches: *Ortygospiza atricollis atricollis, O. a. muelleri, O. a. fuscata*

close to the ground, quail-like, then rise with whirring wings only to drop back to earth a few yards further on. They build spherical nests of grasses, which are placed on the ground usually among grassy tussocks. They are believed to live entirely on grass-seeds. They are interesting aviary birds that generally stay on the ground, although one pair I had used to perch a great deal. They run around a lot, and are apt to fly upwards suddenly if taken unawares, and for these reasons I suggest that they need quite a roomy aviary, definitely with a natural floor. They are fairly good breeding birds.

Quail-finch
(*Ortygospiza atricollis*)

Description: *3½—4 in. (88·9—101·6 mm.). Adult male has forehead, face and throat black; rest of upperparts, including wings, earthy brown; small white chin-spot; chest, breast and flanks are barred finely with white on earth brown; centre of breast and belly orange brown; undertail-coverts paler; when breeding, bill is red; out of season, upper mandible turns black. Female is a paler and duller replica of the male. Juveniles resemble paler females, but lack the barring below.*

I have described the nominate race, which is the most widely distributed from Senegal to the Sudan and, I believe, is the one most commonly imported. It is the race that I have always received. It is also the dullest. There are several races, and two that I have seen show the range of variation the species has. *O. a. muelleri* comes from East Africa; it is slightly greyer above, and the bars on breast and flanks are wider and more clearly pronounced. It has a white crescent above and below the eye. This, or other similar races with white eye-markings, is the Quail-finch that is usually illustrated.

Another race that I have seen is *O. a. fuscata*, which has been given full specific rank by some authorities, with the name *O. gabonensis*. This may be called Gaboon Quail-finch, Black-chinned Quail-finch or Bar-breasted Weaver-finch. It is a much more strongly coloured bird, all the markings in both sexes being darker and richer. It ranges from Gaboon through the Congo to Zambia. The South African Quail-finch of the dealers is either *muelleri* or a South African race *digressa* which is virtually identical. All of the races described here are slightly larger than the nominate and are occasionally graced with the appellation 'Giant' by retailers as an excuse for charging a higher price.

In courtship the male Quail-finch flies up to a great height, uttering a clicking sort of song, finally plummeting back to earth. This aspect of the breeding cycle is not indispensable, however, for they have bred on several occasions. A fit and healthy pair will breed under fairly uninviting circumstances, and have built nests on the floor of indoor flights, unplanted enclosures, and even large cages. However, to increase the chances of a completely successful breeding, they should be kept in a planted and uncrowded flight. Birds in my care have built nests in tussocks of grass, and laid eggs, but overcrowding and inter-ference from Chinese Painted Quail in too small an area put the Quail-finches off. They are said to be mildly aggressive when breeding, males being particularly antagonistic to other male Quail-finches. In my experience of only ever having one pair to an enclosure, they appear to be model inmates, and have never attacked any other waxbills.

They should be fed as all waxbills, and when breeding is definitely under way, should be offered chopped meal-worms, small maggots, etc. In a well-planted flight, they might well find enough live insects among the grass, but the inclusion of ant pupae and some shovelfuls of leaf mould and freshly pulled sods will undoubtedly make a contribution.

Locust-finch
(*Ortygospiza locustella*)

Description: *About 3½ in. (88·9 mm.). Adult male, forehead, sides of face, chin to breast bright red; wings dark brown with edges of all feathers golden orange; top of head to rump dark sienna brown, spotted on mantle, scapulars and tertiaries with white; uppertail-coverts bright red; tail dark brown; belly and rest of underparts blackish brown; bill red, but when not breeding upper mandible is black. Adult female has no red on frontal area at all and red of uppertail-coverts is very restricted; throat to belly buff; flanks and undertail-coverts barred whitish and dark brown; above, it resembles the male. Juveniles resemble the female, but are duller and browner below; bill brown.*

These lovely little birds remind one of an Avadavat, and look like what one might imagine as an Avadavat and Quail-finch hybrid. They are sometimes called Marsh-finch, a name derived from their narrow preference for marsh and bog country. The name Locust-finch stems not from feeding habits, but rather because, when a flock rises from the ground to alight further on to resume feeding, they very much resemble locusts.

I cannot accept the view that they only feed on grass-seeds, particularly when breeding, but in a planted aviary with plenty of grassy tussocks and undergrowth they are very likely to find all the insects they need. Un-doubtedly, the provision of ant pupae during the early days of rearing nestlings would be invaluable. I have no record of a successful breeding. In all respects they should be treated like the Quail-finch.

TWIN-SPOTS

The twin-spots are a group of waxbills that are found in scrub country over much of Africa, south of the Sahara. They are attractive birds that are regularly imported, although in small numbers, and are fairly expensive when compared to the more commonly imported birds. They have always been popular with aviculturists and there are plenty of breeding references in the literature. The name twin-spot derives directly from the fact that the white spots on the underparts are always a subterminal pair, although they rarely appear to be paired when looking at a bird.

Peter's Twin-spot
(*Hypargos niveoguttatus*)

Description: *About 4½ in. (114·3 mm.). Adult male, crown and nape brownish grey, mantle to upper rump and wings brown washed irregularly with crimson; uppertail-coverts deep crimson, tail blackish heavily washed with deep crimson; lores, sides of face, sides of neck and breast crimson; lower breast to undertail-coverts black with clear white spots on breast and flanks. Female has head greyish brown, buffish on face; rest of upperparts as in male; chin buff. throat, sides of neck and breast paler crimson; rest of underparts grey, spotted as in male. Bill blue with black tip. Juveniles are like female above, or paler; below russet, blackish at centre of belly.*

These are quiet little birds of East Africa that frequent bushy country bordering rivers or forests. They are said to be tame and inquisitive, feeding off the ground along paths through bush near water, picking up grass- and weed-seeds. They are satisfying birds to keep in captivity, are not aggressive, and will breed well with a minimum of live food. In a recent report, the adults took dry and soaked seeds, a little softfood, and maggots. In another report, again both dry and soaked seeds, some mealworms and 'picking up ants'. Hybrids have been produced with the Rosy Twin-spot. Alternative names for the species are Red-throated Twin-spot and Peter's Spotted Firefinch.

Rosy Twin-spot
(*Hypargos margaritatus*)

Description: *About 4½ in. (114·3 mm.). Adult male exactly like male niveoguttatus, but the deep crimson is replaced by a vinous pinky mauve; spots fractionally bigger and pink; bill black, blue at base. Female resembles male above, but pink of face and breast is buffish grey; centre of breast and belly white; side of breast, flanks and undertail-coverts blackish, profusely spotted with white. Juveniles resemble female, but young males have pinkish tinge on throat, and spots are pinkish.*

The Rosy Twin-spot, also known as Verreaux's Twin-spot, comes from the eastern side of South Africa and Mozambique. It is occasionally available, has been bred and requires similar treatment to Peter's. It is reputed to be more delicate and needs more live and soft food. Wostendiek has considerable experience with twin-spots and recommends regular supplies of mealworms. In a planted flight I consider this to be unnecessary, but in winter a few mealworms each week will no doubt be beneficial – this applies to all the larger waxbills.

Green-backed Twin-spot
(*Mandingoa nitidula*)

Description: *About 4½ in. (114·3 mm.). Adult male has lores, around eye to chin orange red; uppertail-coverts golden olive, remainder of upperparts, neck, throat and upper breast, undertail-coverts olive green; lower breast, belly and flanks black, heavily spotted with white; bill black, tip red. Female slightly paler than male; lores and around eye pale orange; less red on bill. Juvenile is duller olive, rump olive, lores buff; below, grey without any spots.*

The bird I have described is the nominate race, *M. n. nitidula*, from Mozambique. There are two other races that are sufficiently different to warrant description, and they have been given separate common names in aviculture. One is Schlegel's Twin-spot (*M. n. schlegeli*) from West Africa, which is the most colourful race. Around the eye it is bright tomato red; chin to breast reddish orange. There is a golden wash on mantle and wings, and the uppertail-coverts are orange. The female is golden olive from chin to breast and is a richer orange around the eyes than the female *nitidula*. The second is Chubb's Twin-spot (*M. n. chubbi*), which comes from East Africa; it is bright red around the eyes, chin to breast golden olive, sometimes washed with orange; uppertail-coverts are dull orange. The back, wings and tail are lightly washed with yellow. It may also be called Hartlaub's or the Marsabit Twin-spot.

They are birds of forest-edges and thickets, inconspicuous and retiring. They feed mainly on the ground. They have proved to be hardy birds, well suited to life in captivity, but are very active and should be kept in an aviary or as roomy a cage as possible. They take a variety of seeds and will readily accept some mealworms. They are not aggressive, but have a tendency to pluck if kept in a confined area for long. Wostendiek has stated that immature birds, which are not sexually dimorphic, may be easily sexed as the rump of a male is always shiny and that of the female is always dull. They have been bred in South Africa.

Brown Twin-spot
(*Clytospiza monteiri*)

Description: $4\frac{1}{2}$–5 in. (114·3–127 mm.). *Adult male has entire head grey with a red diamond-shaped spot in the centre of the throat; mantle and wings brown; rump and upper-tail-coverts scarlet; tail browny black; below, breast to undertail-coverts orange brown profusely spotted with white, becoming bars under the tail; eye red; bill black with a blue patch at base of lower mandible. Female resembles male but has a white throat-patch. Juvenile birds are brown below with no spots; eye brown.*

This beautiful bird is also known as Monteiri's Twin-spot. It comes from central Africa, from Nigeria to Angola, but not including the Congo basin. They are said to be shy birds, appearing in pairs of small parties in secondary forest growth or in clearings, feeding on long grass. Little is known about its habits in the wild. In captivity, it is also reputed to be shy; nevertheless, it has been bred several times in South Africa. It requires some live food when rearing.

Dusky Twin-spot
(*Clytospiza dybowskii*)

Description: *About $4\frac{1}{2}$ in. (114·3 mm.). Adult male has entire head and neck, nape and breast slate grey, mantle, rump and uppertail-coverts crimson, tail bronzed black; lower breast to undertail-coverts blackish grey with white spots on breast and flanks. Female resembles male but has entire underparts slate grey with rather more, and smaller, spots on breast and flanks. Juvenile plumage is unrecorded but is likely to be a duller version of the female's, without spots.*

Little is known of this species, which is also called Dybowski's Twin-spot, and might be listed as Red-backed Twin-spot. It ranges right across west Africa from Sierra Leone to the Sudan, and is a bird found in high wet grasslands. It is recorded as being easy to trap by baiting the nets with termites.

PYTILIAS

This genus of four species is one of the more sought-after of the waxbills. They are larger birds than the average estrildine and, whilst being sturdier and quite hardy once properly acclimatized, are by no means easy subjects. They tend to be a little belligerent at times and may be quite aggressive when breeding. It is recommended that breeding pairs be given planted enclosures to themselves, although they certainly have bred successfully in mixed collections. They are parasitized by the *Steganura* whydahs, rearing the young whydah along with their own young as part of the family. Therefore it is of interest to keep a pair of the lovely Paradise Whydah with a pair of Melbas. They will not rear young without life food, but reports vary enormously and, in a well-planted aviary, it is likely that young will be successfully reared with just a few mealworms and maggots.

Melba Finch
(*Pytilia melba*)

Description: *5 in. (127 mm.). Adult male has forehead and front of crown, mesial stripe, chin and throat vermilion; lores, around eyes, to upper mantle and sides of neck grey; mantle and wings olive green; lower rump, uppertail-coverts and tail crimson; breast golden, washed with red of throat; lower breast and flanks grey, barred strongly with white, bars often breaking up into spots. Female has red of head replaced by pale grey, and is paler above; chin to breast pale grey, highly spotted with white; rest of underparts as male. Juveniles resemble the female but are browner above and have no clear barring below.*

The Melba Finch is also listed as Green-winged Pytilia. There are four clearly distinct races which may be given separate common names. The race I have described above is *P. m. melba*, which is found in the southern third of Africa. The Uganda Melba Finch, *P. m. grotei*, comes from Ruanda, Uganda and Nyasaland, and differs from the nominate in having much paler grey lores, less red suffusion on the breast (instead, it may have olive suffusion) and slightly less barring below. The Sudan Melba Finch, *P. m. soudanensis*, comes from East Africa, the Sudan to Tanzania, and has the lores red. The breast is well suffused with yellow and there is a red wash on the wings. All three of these races are parasitized by the Paradise Whydah, *Steganura paradisea*. The Senegambian Melba Finch, *P. m. citerior*, ranges from Senegal to the Sudan and is a much lighter bird, the grey being paler; there is a pale grey wash on the mantle, and it is the only race with red ear-coverts; the breast is clear yellow and the barring below is weak and mainly on the flanks. It is parasitized by three races of the Broadtailed Whydah, *Stenagura orientalis orientalis*, *S. o. kadugliensis* (sometimes called Yellow-naped Paradise Whydah) and *S. o. aucupum*.

Orange-winged Pytilia
(*Pytilia afra*)

Description: *4½–5 in. (114·3–127 mm.). Adult male has forehead, sides of face and chin, rump, uppertailcoverts and tail crimson; rest of body olive grey; there is a lot of olive suffusion on wings with edges of greater wing-coverts and flight feathers bright orange; breast to undertail-coverts barred irregularly with off-white. Female has red of face replaced by pale grey; barring below more noticeable and extends to throat. Juveniles resemble female but slightly duller.*

This species has a wide distribution from the Sudan down to Mozambique and across to Angola. It is fairly common, being found in scrub and semi-open country feeding on the ground. It is parasitized by the Broad-tailed Whydah, *Steganura orientalis obtusa*. Sometimes called the Golden-backed Pytilia, this species has proved to be a free breeder when kept under ideal conditions. For example, in a large planted aviary in South Africa, with unlimited quantities of termites being given, one breeder produced twenty young in one season. By contrast, they have been bred in small aviaries in England, in the company of other waxbills, when the only live food provided was maggots and, in one report, the keeper only gave ant pupae, which appeared not to be taken at all.

Aurora Finch
(*Pytilia phoenicoptera*)

Description: *4½ in. (114·3 mm.). Adult male has entire head, back, rump and all underparts French grey, lower breast to undertail-coverts barred with white; wings brown with large patch of crimson, uppertailcoverts and tail crimson. Female rather browner and paler. Juvenile browner with crimson much duller.*

This bird is also known as the Red-winged Pytilia. The race *lineata* from Abyssinia has a red bill; *emini* from the Sudan and Uganda has a black bill; the nominate *phoenicoptera* from West Africa also has a black bill. It may be seen feeding on the ground, taking grass-seeds, but it is a fairly arboreal bird and spends more time in the trees than most waxbills, according to Bannerman. The race *lineata* was bred by Langberg in Denmark, and he gave it the name Red-billed Aurora Waxbill. His birds shared an 8 ft. (2·4 m.) indoor flight with some Yellow-rumped Mannikins and Verreaux's Twin-spots, and successfully reared young on a diet of mixed seeds, softfoods, mealworms and mosquito larvae. Cotterel bred *emini* and, in his report, called it the Crimson-winged Waxbill. His notes include a comment that the female also sang. His pair shared a 12-ft. (3·6 m.) planted flight with a pair of Dufresne's Waxbills and reared young on a mixture of seeds. During the early days some ant pupae and a few grasshoppers were accepted, but mainly the form of live food was the mealworm.

Yellow-winged Pytilia
(*Pytilia hypogrammica*)

Description: *About 4½ in. (114·3 mm.). Adult male has face, ear-coverts and chin, rump, uppertail-coverts and tail scarlet; rest of body is slate grey with some whitish barring on belly, flanks and undertail-coverts; wing-coverts and flight feathers strongly edged with golden yellow. Female lacks red on head. Juveniles resemble slightly duller female.*

Some authorities consider this to be a race of *P. afra*, but I don't share this opinion. It is a little-known bird of dry grasslands. In captivity it should be treated as for the other Pytilias.

II · AMADINAE

MANNIKINS AND MUNIAS

The mannikins and munias are widely distributed throughout the Old World tropics and subtropics. Generally speaking, they are highly adaptable birds, living in dry, arid, and semi-arid to well-watered, open, semi-cultivated or cultivated grasslands. Their staple diet is grass-seed of all kinds. Water may well be in short supply and the only food that will be available all the year round is seed – sometimes green and milky and sometimes dry and hard. To survive, therefore, they have to be hardy and adaptable and this is why they adapt to life in captivity so well. In fact most of the birds in this chapter are probably easier to keep than any others in this book.

Most mannikins are gregarious and will live happily in the company of their own kind. Gregariousness is a function of habitat with this subfamily and has survival value. There is greater safety in numbers because of the confusion caused by a predator, when all scatter in every direction at once. A few mannikins are not so gregarious, though I doubt if any are solitary. These tend to defend their nest more vigorously, and to commandeer food supplies as if they were personal property. Of course there are always individual birds who contradict every rule and confound their keeper, but there is usually a good reason for aggression. A few reasons include: too few nesting-sites, or not enough in the better/preferred places, food in too small a pot or area, overcrowding, the best/most preferred perch being too small, or only one female present. Generally, one can say that mannikins are extremely equable birds and are only likely to become even mildly obstreperous when breeding.

Mannikins are, by and large, too dully coloured for anyone to want to form a collection entirely of them, and they are usually only additions to a much wider collection. As such they are perfectly satisfactory. I do recommend buying them in quantity; they behave more naturally and are more likely to breed when maintained in small flocks, and also one is more likely to get good pairs, as most mannikins are polymorphic and one can never pick out a male and female with certainty. I have only given descriptions for juveniles where they differ noticeably from the norm. Practically all juvenile mannikins are dull olive brown all over, paler below, with the bill black.

HOUSING

Mannikins do well in cages, especially roomy ones with bunches of twigs for perches. Some keepers maintain that most mannikins do better in cages, especially Bengalese, but I disagree. All birds do better in aviaries, especially planted ones. However, if they have to be kept in cages I suggest a box-cage, only open at the front, not less than 30 in. (762 mm.) wide, 20 in. (508 mm.) high and 15 in. (381 mm.) deep. Ideally the cage should be longer, 6 ft. (1·8 m.) being very suitable. Twigs can be arranged at each end, and food and water may be placed in the centre. Many mannikins have a tendency to grow long toenails. This is not because of incorrect diet, as has been suggested in some quarters; it is in fact as nature intended and enables the bird to cling to upright grass-stems rather more efficiently. In an aviary they become a liability as they can get hooked up on the wire mesh and so the unfortunate individuals should be netted and the nails carefully trimmed. It should be noted that vertical perches are desirable, and this should be borne in mind when planting an aviary. Suggested plants are bamboo, golden rod, sunflowers and ox-eye daisy. Golden rod is very useful as it can be cut and dried and used for perching in due course.

BREEDING

Most, if not all, of the species mentioned in the following notes have been bred in captivity. Unfortunately records are hopelessly inadequate and the free use of exotic-sounding common names, with no scientific name to specify the bird, results in confusion and no little frustration for the searcher through the literature. All of these birds weave typical estrildine nests, a ball of grasses lined with softer grass-heads, etc. They all readily take to the commercially produced raffia or wicker nest-baskets, which will also be used for roosting. I prefer to use the largest size of these baskets because the inside can be more easily cleaned, nests can be inspected, fingers inserted, infertile eggs or dead young can be more easily removed. More important, most birds prefer them. A roll of wire mesh is an acceptable substitute. The birds can be encouraged to take up nest-building if a twist of dry grasses is inserted. A pile of grasses and feathers, short lengths of wool, dog combings, etc., may be hooked together and hung up in a corner.

FEEDING

Various millets and small Canary seed are best given in separate pots to avoid wastage. Millet on the spray will be taken eagerly as a rule, and all seeding grasses are picked over, the favourite being *Poa annua*. I regularly dig seed-gleanings into various corners and these will germinate and grow. One can plant millet and Canary-seed in pots and place them in the aviary when ready, but they should be supported to a stake to prevent the birds breaking them with their weight. In an unplanted aviary or cage it is a good idea to give a freshly pulled sod from time to time. Cuttle-fish bone should be crushed, and should always be available, as should sand or grit. Many mannikins will learn to take bread-and-milk, soft food and egg-rearing food. When breeding they should be given soaked seeds and freshly germinated seeds. Some birds will take a few maggots and mealworms, and ant pupae, etc., may all be taken, but there are many records of breedings occurring where no live food was given. It is a good thing to give a multi-vitamin solution in the drinking water, and water should be given in a big enough bowl to satisfy the many eager bathers in the group.

CUT-THROATS

There are two species in the genus *Amadina*, birds of bush and desert, common and gregarious. They make good cagebirds, but the commoner and more freely available Cut-throat is an ideal cagebird, particularly suitable for beginners.

Cut-throat
(*Amadina fasciata*)

Description: *4½–5 in. (114·3–127 mm.). Adult male, greyish fawn above, barred and speckled with black; chin and lores buff; a band of crimson runs from ear-covert across throat to other ear-covert; below, various fawn with a chestnut patch on the belly; flanks irregularly barred with black and speckled with brown. Female slightly paler; lacks red throat-bar; brown belly patch vestigial or not present. Juveniles resemble less clearly marked and lighter adults.*

The Cut-throat takes its dramatic-sounding name from the red bar across the throat. It ranges from Senegal across to the Sudan, Kenya and Tanzania. There is an East African race, *A. f. alexanderi*, that is slightly larger and has broader barring both above and below. It is sometimes advertised as Alexander's Cut-Throat, but some dealers cannot resist 'Giant East African Cut-throat', while other names are Abyssinian or Ethiopian Cut-throat. Females are rather more delicate than males, and seem shorter-lived in captivity. There are many collections that sport the odd male, the female of the pair having quickly succumbed. Once acclimatized, however, it is a reliable breeding bird, and will cheerfully rear on a diet lacking in live food, but chances of successfully rearing the young will be considerably enhanced if some live food is given. It has bred in cages on several occasions, and is one of the few species that could no doubt be domesticated if enough people took it seriously. A male in breeding condition can be a nuisance and be spiteful to other small birds. A really fit bird that is breeding will cheerfully attack birds much bigger than itself. I do not recommend keeping Cut-throats with waxbills that are breeding.

Red-headed Finch
(*Amadina erythrocephala*)

Description: *About 5 in. (127 mm.). Adult male has entire head dull red, rest of upperparts earth brown with whitish spots at ends of upperwing-coverts and tertiaries; below, breast and flanks barred black and white suffused with rufous on flanks and lower breast; belly and undertail-coverts off-white. Female lacks red on head, being pale earth brown, otherwise resembles male but is more finely barred. Juveniles are duller, less clearly marked versions of the adult.*

This is a bird of dry open country from Angola down through western parts of southern Africa. It prefers to adopt a used nest of a weaver and reline it, and will use a hole in a tree, or under the eaves of a house. It is a less interesting bird than its cogener, being less colourful, noticeably less active, and to my mind rather dull. It is definitely more difficult to breed, requiring peace and quiet, little companionship and good conditions. With me it has never progressed past the nest-building stage. However, many people think of it as a Red-headed Cut-throat and, because of its scarcity value, are prepared to persevere with it in preference to the other. The two species have hybridized on several occasions.

JAVA SPARROWS

There are two species in the genus *Padda* and according to many authorities they are sufficiently distinct in their anatomical and behaviour patterns to warrant this separation from the *Lonchurae*. Personally, I'm not so sure, and I would prefer to see *Padda* absorbed into *Lonchura*.

Java Sparrow
(*Padda oryzivora*)

Description: *5–5½ in. (127–139·7 mm.). Adult male has entire head black with a large white cheek-patch; lower throat, breast and upperparts are French grey; tail black; lower breast and flanks pinky grey; belly and undertail-coverts white. Sexes are alike, but breeding male has base of pink bill swollen and redder than female.*

Java Sparrow (*Padda oryzivora*)

The Java Sparrow naturally comes from Java and Bali, but has been introduced into other islands and other continents by man. It has often managed to establish itself but has nowhere spread dramatically like certain other introduced species. It is a bird of rice fields and bamboo, populations concentrating into hungry flocks as the rice ripens. Its other common names, Rice Bird, Rice Munia, Paddy Bird, all reflect this. The Java Sparrow was a popular cagebird long before it arrived in the west, and was domesticated – or very nearly so – by the Japanese. There are well-established free-breeding strains of white and pied birds, the latter known as Calico for some obscure reason. Despite their large size they are gentle birds and will not harm the smallest waxbill, but it has to be said that their presence might sufficiently unnerve waxbills as to reduce the latter's breeding efficiency. They do, however, make good companions for Budgerigars.

Timor Sparrow
(*Padda fuscata*)

Description: *5–5½ in. (127–139·7 mm.). Adult male has entire head black with a large white cheek-patch; lower throat, breast and upperparts are brown; tail black; lower breast, flanks and undertail-coverts white, separated from the brown breast by a black band. The sexes are alike.*

The Timor Sparrow, Munia or Rice Bird is very rarely imported and I only have one reference for it. Interestingly enough, this is a breeding report where it was called Brown Mannikin. The keeper provided plenty of live food, but this was never touched; large quantities of green food were eaten, particularly chickweed and seeding grasses.

MUNIAS

The remaining species in this section are all very closely related. The remarks for the Amadinae in general apply equally to all of these birds.

Pectoral Finch
(*Lonchura pectoralis*)

Description: *4–4½ in. (101·6–114·3 mm.). Adult male, from forehead to uppertail-coverts greyish brown; wings brown with white terminal on wing-coverts; tail dusky; lores, sides of face, ear-coverts, chin and throat purplish black, separated from grey above by a fawn streak; breast white faintly barred, which becomes irregular, barring more noticeable on flanks; rest of underparts vinous brown. Female browner on face; breast-barring more noticeable; otherwise resembles male.*

This species has certain behavioural differences that have led some authorities to classify it in its own genus, or subgenus of *Heteromunia*, but I am inclined to favour keeping it in *Lonchura*. It has also been called Pectoralis, Pictorella, White-breasted Munia or Finch. It is found only in tropical northern Australia, where it is a bird of open country and savanna and is most completely adapted to life in dry, arid country. It is a ground-feeder, taking fallen seeds, but is equally adept at picking seeds from growing grasses.

They are rare birds in aviaries these days, but before the war they were occasionally available. They are not easy breeders, but once a pair have really settled in, in a roomy and planted aviary, they will quite possibly rear a healthy family. They are naturally semi-insectivorous when rearing and although they have reared young without the aid of live food being given (in planted aviaries) the addition of a few mealworms and maggots for the first couple of weeks will definitely be acceptable. It has hybridized with the Yellow-rumped Munia.

Indian Silverbill
(*Lonchura malabarica*)

Description: *4½ in. (114·3 mm.). Adult has forehead to rump dusky brown; uppertail-coverts white; wings and tail dark brown; lores, sides of face, chin to vent pale fawn, lightly flecked on sides of breast with tan; undertail-coverts white. Sexes alike.*

Also known as Silverbill, Common Silverbill, White-rumped Munia and White-throated Munia, the species range over the entire Indian sub-continent from Afghanistan to Ceylon. It is a bird of open country, living almost entirely on grass-seeds. It is trapped in large numbers, and is often sprayed with a vegetable dye by the Indian vendors to 'enhance' its appearance. It is illegal to advertise artificially dyed wild birds so it is quite possible that some coloured Silverbills might turn up in response to an advertisement. The dye tends to wear off with bathing, but in any case will disappear at the next moult. The colours are cerise, bright green, and yellow.

It really is difficult to sex these birds, and a male can only be told with certainty by its song and dance.

They are free breeders, will rear young on soaked seeds, green seeds and hard seed, and a regularly breeding pair will usually act as foster-parents. They are peaceful and easy-going gregarious little birds.

I once placed a pair in a flight that was used as a holding aviary for young Budgerigars. There was a hole

Indian Silverbill
(*Lonchura malabarica*)

beneath the eaves, gnawed by the Budgies, which the Silverbills adopted apparently as a roost. To our surprise five young Silverbills appeared one day, and two months later another three. These birds were reared on hard seed, with maybe a little lettuce and chickweed as the only extra. It has hybridized with many other munias and grassfinches, as well as the occasional waxbill.

African Silverbill
(*Lonchura cantans*)

Description: *4–4½ in. (101·6–114·3 mm.). Adult has entire body pale sandy brown, faintly barred, darkest on wings and tail, lightest on belly and undertail-coverts. Sexes alike.*

Dr. Bannerman called this species the Warbling Silverbill, a reference to the bird's vocal accomplishments, which are scarcely more noteworthy than any other munia. For some unexplained reason there has been a tendency to regard it as but a race of *malabarica*, but the kind of discipline that has to be employed on this would inevitably result in the fifty or so munias being reduced to about five species. It is a bird of savanna, being common around villages and cultivations but also ranging deep into desert country. It ranges from Senegal across to East Africa. In my experience it takes a full season to settle in before breeding is attempted but, like its Indian relative, will breed freely under reasonable conditions. It will also rear young on a non-live food diet. It is a very lovely bird but admittedly is one for refined tastes. Its quiet colouring shows off best in a well-planted roomy flight, with some more colourful species to set a contrast.

Pearl-headed Silverbill
(*Lonchura caniceps*)

Description: *4½ in. (114·3 mm.). Adult has head grey, sides of face and throat speckled with white; mantle and all underparts vinous biscuit; rump and uppertail-coverts white; wing-coverts grey; wings and tail black. Sexes alike. Juveniles like duller adults without white spots on head.*

This species may be listed under the genus *Euodice*, *Odontospiza*, or even *Pytilia*, and as its specific name was pre-empted by *Munia* (now *Lonchura*) *caniceps* (now considered to be a race of *L. maja*) it may be listed as *griseicapilla*. It has the alternative common name of Grey-headed

Pearl-headed Silverbill (*Lonchura caniceps*)

Magpie Mannikin
(*Lonchura fringilloides*)

Silverbill. It is a species from East Africa, and little is known of its natural behaviour or habitat. In captivity it has proved to be a typical munia and will breed quite well providing that conditions are not too difficult. Although it may rear young on a simple diet, it has always been offered, and has accepted, live food and reared successfully as a result.

Description: *4½ in. (114·3 mm.). Adult has entire head, patch on sides of breast, rump, uppertail-coverts and tail glossy blue black; mantle brown with black centres to feathers with white quills, wings dusky; underparts white; black and brown markings on flanks. Sexes alike. Juvenile is dusky brown above; uppertail-coverts and tail black; below pale buff.*

The Magpie Mannikin is the largest of the African munias; it ranges from Senegal across to East Africa and down the eastern half of the continent to the Zambesi. They are lively birds frequenting cultivated areas and gardens, hopping around the ground in flocks and often in the company of other munias.

It has the reputation of being aggressive in captivity, and is not usually recommended for inclusion in collections of waxbills. However, I have found that it is only while breeding – or attempting to breed – that it really has the inclination to throw its weight around. To avoid problems, and also to greatly improve the chances of a successful breeding, it is better to either give them a flight to themselves (they are unlikely to breed in a cage) or restrict their companions to larger and peaceful species. They should be given a few mealworms or maggots when rearing.

Bronze-winged Mannikin
(*Lonchura cucullata*)

Description: *3½ in. (88·9 mm.). Adult has top of head, sides of face, shoulder of wing and patches on flanks glossy bottle green; chin to upper breast bronze black with a glossy green wash; nape, mantle and wings greyish; uppertail-coverts barred greyish and black; tail black; below, white; flanks and undertail-coverts barred with black. Sexes alike.*

The Bronze-winged Mannikin is also known as Bronze-wing, or Bronze Mannikin, or may appear as Swainson's Bronze Mannikin. It ranges from the coast of West Africa across to the Sudan, and the race *scutatus* ranges from Abyssinia down to the Cape. The latter may be distinguished by its browner shading on head and bib, and lack of green patch on the flanks. It was previously in the genus *Spermestes*. It is a tame and cheerful little bird, feeding on the ground in flocks around villages and cultivated areas just like tiny sparrows. It is very prolific and large flocks gather at the close of the breeding season, moving around the countryside to take seeding grass as it ripens. It is an excellent aviary bird, and will also do very well in a cage. They are bred regularly, the adult pair often rearing two or even three broods in a season, and have been bred in roomy cages. They are obviously encouraging birds for a beginner since they are not very demanding in food requirements when rearing. In addition to soaked seeds and the other foods recommended in the introduction to this chapter, a little small live food will help. Ants' egg and greenfly will help. If breeding in a cage, particular attention to some dietary supplement is suggested although they have reared on a non-live food menu. They can be very aggressive for their size and, if attempting to breed in a small area, can terrorize any small companion who gives offence. They ought therefore to be kept in a large roomy aviary, preferably planted, where fighting will be greatly reduced, or given an enclosure to themselves.

Black-and-white Mannikin
(*Lonchura bicolor*)

Description: *About 3½ in. (88·9 mm.). Adult has head to chest, mantle, wings and tail glossy black washed with violet; outer webs of flight feathers, rump and uppertail-coverts barred black and white; chest to undertail-coverts white; flanks black, scalloped with white. Sexes alike. Juvenile is dusky above; chin to breast grey; rest of underparts buff; faint barring on flights.*

The above race is also known as Fernando Po Mannikin, or Black-breasted Mannikin; it ranges from the Cameroons to Angola and across to East Africa. The nominate race, *bicolor*, from West Africa lacks the barring on wings and rump and perhaps better deserves the name Black-and-white Mannikin. It is also called Blue-billed Mannikin. They are not often imported but do turn up from time to time. It is a bird of forest clearings

Fernando Po Mannikin (*Lonchura bicolor poensis*); Black-and-white Mannikin (*L. b. bicolor*)

and forest edges, and as such is less liable to get trapped than the birds that flock in the grasslands.

Another race, sometimes regarded as a full species, is the Rufous-backed Mannikin, *nigriceps*, which differs from *poensis* in having the mantle, wing-coverts and tertiaries chestnut brown. The sexes are alike; the juvenile resembles a juvenile *poensis* but is browner above. It ranges

from Kenya to Natal, but is also found in southern Arabia. The Rufous-backed Mannikin has been regularly available in recent years and has proved to have all the attributes of the Bronze-winged Mannikin, but is much less aggressive and has bred quite peacefully in the company of wax-bills.

Bib Finch
(*Lonchura nana*)

Description: $3\frac{1}{2}$ in. (*88·9 mm.*). *Adult has lores, chin and throat black; rest of head olive grey; mantle, wing-coverts, rump, uppertail-coverts olive brown; wings and tail blackish; underparts light brown with pink wash; undertail-coverts barred fawn and brown; bill is black above, wax red below, legs pink. Sexes alike. Juvenile not recorded but probably has black bill, and possibly lacks black bib.*

This lovely little munia from Madagascar is virtually unknown to modern aviculture, and I have never seen one, nor ever seen it on offer. According to Rutgers it should be treated just like the Bronze-wing, is a very free breeder in captivity, and has hybridized with other munias, including Bengalese and Silverbills. Any contemporary notes published would obviously be of the greatest interest.

The Bib Finch is sometimes called Dwarf Mannikin.

Black-headed Munia
(*Lochura atricapilla*)

Description: $4\frac{1}{2}$ in. (*114·3 mm.*). *Adult has entire head and upper breast, vent and undertail-coverts black; remainder of body chestnut, reddish on uppertail-coverts. Sexes alike.*

Sometimes called the Chestnut or

Chestnut-bellied Munia, or Black-headed Nun, this bird is often considered to be con-specific with the Tri-coloured. I once kept a medium-sized aviary with a lot of different munias and they frequently separated into their own individual species, the Black-headed sitting together in a different bush from the Tri-coloured, so I don't have very much sympathy with this idea. They come from India, where they are commonest in the southern regions and show a preference for swampy areas where grasses grow lank and plentifully: when the rice is ripening they descend in large flocks on the paddy fields and constitute a pest.

Breeding reports are rare and, in contrast to most munias, in my aviaries they have never come closer to it than displays and a little grass-carrying. However, they have bred on occasion and appear to have been quite typical, and have reared on a non-live food diet.

Tri-coloured Munia
(*Lonchura malacca*)

Description: *4½ in. (114·3 mm.). Adult has entire head, upper breast, centre of belly and undertail-coverts black; remainder of upperparts chestnut brown, reddish to maroon on tail-coverts and tail; lower breast and flanks pure white. Sexes alike.*

The Tri-coloured Munia is one of the most commonly imported munias and is a very smart and attractive bird. It is found over much of India, showing a preference for grassy and wet areas, and also turns up in the paddy fields in large numbers when the season is right. In captivity they are very easy birds to maintain, and a few will make a nice addition to a collection of small exotics. A small flock will make a pretty sight in a large aviary that is designed for pheasants, and should this contain a stand or two of bamboo then the chances of the munias breeding will be considerably enhanced. Like the Black-headed they have been bred only infrequently and do not share the eagerness to reproduce that some munias have. It may be that many comparative newcomers to the hobby of bird-keeping, who find that their munias have bred (it usually comes as a surprise), imagine that with such common birds such an occurrence can hardly be noteworthy.

Javan Munia
(*Lonchura ferruginosa*)

Description: *4½ in. (114·3 mm.). Adult has top of head to nape, lores, sides of head and neck, and mesia dull buffish white merging into chestnut on the back; wings, back to tail dull chestnut; chin to throat, centre of belly and undertail-coverts black; breast and flanks dull chestnut. Sexes alike.*

The common name of this species derives from the bird's origins, being Java and Bali. It should not be confused with the Java Sparrow, and the alternative name of Black-throated Munia is better. It resembles the Maja Finch with a black bib added and dealers sometimes call it the Javan Maja. There are many subspecies, variations including *sinensis* from Malaysia and the lowlands of Sumatra, *batakana* from the Sumatran highlands, and *jagori* from Borneo, Natunas, Palawan and the Philippines. All the races have darker heads and some have brown bibs in place of black. In his revision of the Estrildinae in 1943, Delacour added *atricapilla* and *malacca* as races of *ferruginosa*.

One of the nice things about keeping munias is that they soon settle down to become really good aviary birds. They will roost in an aviary shelter regularly every night, and never have to be driven inside. They will keep to regular routines, bathing every day at mid-morning and, in the summer, again in the afternoon. The Javan Munia is no exception and will behave exactly as the other species.

White-headed Munia
(*Lonchura maja*)

Description: *4½ in.* (*114·3 mm.*). *Adult has entire head white, graduating into dull chestnut above and black below. Males sometimes have brighter white heads, but generally the sexes are alike. Juveniles are dull versions of the adults.*

This species is also called Pale-headed Munia, Maja Munia or Mannikin, and White-headed Nun. It is a bird of the cultivated grasslands and paddy fields, and has a wide range extending from Malaysia to New Guinea. Delacour included under *maja* all the pale-headed forms that one might find through an exhaustive study of the literature: *pallida, subcastanea, vana, caniceps, kumisi, strachleyana* and *flaviprynna*. The latter has been retained as a separate and good species by Immelmann and I agree with that.

In captivity it is a perfectly typical munia and has bred from time to time, rearing the young on fresh seeding grasses and soaked seed. They are fairly dully coloured, lacking the sharp and bright plumage of the Tricoloured Munia but none the less are attractive. Breeding is much more likely to take place in an outdoor planted aviary; they seem to prefer to build their own nest rather than use a basket or box.

Dusky Munia
(*Lonchura fuscans*)

Description: *4 in.* (*101·6 mm.*). *Adult dark dusky chestnut all over, slightly darker on wings and tail. Sexes alike.*

This species comes from Borneo and adjacent islands where it frequents rice cultivations and open grassland. It appears to differ from other munias in that it has great curiosity and, when alarmed or frightened, it sits quite still, in contrast to other species that will fly off in a twittering flock. This behaviour confounds the peasants, who take much trouble to construct bangers and rattling scarecrows to scare marauding birds away. Another unusual aspect of this species is that, while it builds a typical spherical nest of dry grasses, etc., it builds high in a tree, the record height being 250 ft. (76·2 m.) above normal ground-level!

It is mentioned in the literature as Black, Black Borneo, Brown, or Sooty Mannikin. It has apparently been bred in Denmark, New Zealand and Australia, but no details are available. There are no British records of it to my knowledge, but it seems to me to be completely typical in captivity.

Spice Bird
(*Lonchura punctulata*)

Description: *4–4½ in.* (*101·6–114·3 mm.*). *Adult has entire head, back, wings and tail dull chocolate brown with pale shafts to the feathers of the mantle; uppertail-coverts and tail feathers have straw-coloured wash; breast and flanks creamy white spotted and barred with dark brown; belly and undertail-coverts creamy white. Sexes alike.*

There is a subspecies of the Spice

Bird, *topela*, known as the Topela Finch or Chinese Spotted Munia, which may be distinguished by its grey-green rump and more yellow tail. It is rarely imported. The Common Spice Bird – also called Spotted Munia, Nutmeg Finch, or Mannikin or Mascot Finch – is frequently imported. It ranges from Ceylon, through India to the Himalayas, to Burma and Malaysia, to Indo-China. It moves around in pairs or small flocks, and is particularly

Spice Bird (*Lonchura punctulata*)

fond of luxuriant undergrowth. Spice Birds have bred many times in confinement, and have hybridized with several other munias, but it would be unfair to suggest that they are easy to breed. For a start they are choosy about a nest-site and in my experience most readily accept a nest-basket placed on a wall in a protected spot with surrounding cover, such as a growing clematis. They are also fairly insectivorous and, although the odd pair may well rear successfully without live food being supplied, I have experience – and have reports of – parent birds deserting their brood, apparently because they had no insects with which to feed the young.

Striated Munia
(*Lonchura striata*)

Description: *4½ in. (114·3 mm.). Adult male has entire body dark brown with exception of rump and underparts, which are dirty off-white; feathers of mantle have pale shafts; tail is longer than normal for a munia, and tapered.*

In Ceylon and India the nominate race, *striata*, is generally known as White-rumped Munia, and its plumage is more contrasting. To the north and eastwards in Burma the colours are duller and the race *acuticauda* is known as Sharp-tailed Munia. It is a gregarious bird found in small flocks in forest clearings and grassland bordering forests. In the southernmost extremes of its range it is commonly found in the company of the Pintailed Nonpareil. They feed mainly on the seeding grasses of the forest glades, but although it is sometimes found in the paddy fields with other munias the lure of ripe seeding bamboo in the forests is much greater.

A fine pair, once settled in, will generally breed and a good breeding pair will be quite prolific in their output. They will happily rear on green seeds, chickweed, soaked seeds, etc., and need not be given any live food. I had a few that would chew and mumble mealworms, but I think that they were only copying the Spice Birds.

Bengalese
(*Lonchura striata,* dom.)

Description: *About 4 in. (101·6 mm.). As for the Striated Munia, only pied.*

There are two varieties, chocolate and white, and fawn and white.

The Bengalese is a domesticated Striated Munia. Its origins are fairly obscure, but it was probably originally domesticated by the Chinese, and subsequently developed by the Japanese. In addition to the two basic colour-varieties there is an all-white bird, reputed to be weaker and to have poorer eyesight, and a rare chocolate, fawn and white. The varieties are then permutated by a crested variant. Aviculturists who specialize in Bengalese strive to breed birds in which the distribution of markings is consistently in the same pattern, as well-matched pairs score higher in bird-show competitions. One of the problems with this is that the better the fixing the nearer they get to the original wild *striata*, and I have seen a winning pair of identical chocolate and white Bengalese that were almost indistinguishable from a pair of Indian Striated Munias. Over the centuries Bengalese have been developed as extremely efficient breeding 'machines'. So strong is the instinct that one can place two immature males in a strange cage, with nest and eggs from some other species, and there would be a very good chance that they would begin brooding almost at once, and attempt to rear the young. Breeders of Australian finches, Parrot-finches, and rare waxbills generally have a couple of pairs of Bengalese in cages to use as standby foster-parents. Used in this way one can often avoid the unhappiness of a 'near-miss' caused by the proper parents deserting. There are dangers of imperfect fostered birds resulting if use of Bengalese becomes routine. One danger is that the Bengalese will rear on an inadequate diet, and the fostered individuals may grow up sterile or not properly developed in some subtle way. The main risk is that the fostered young become imprinted on to Bengalese and grow up 'thinking' that they are Bengalese but end up as being neither one nor the other, and in turn are effectively sterile.

For me the joy of Bengalese is the certainty with which they will breed, and after a series of failures with rare

Bengalese (*Lonchura striata*, dom.)

or difficult species to *know* that at least one pair in your collection will produce young is most encouraging. They also have endearing personalities, and deserve to be kept for their own sakes. They have, incidentally, hybridized with a large number of munias, grassfinches and waxbills.

Chestnut-breasted Finch
(*Lonchura castaneothorax*)

Description: *About 4 in. (101·6 mm.). Adult has from forehead to nape greyish brown lightly flecked with brown; mantle and wings dark brown;*

*rump and uppertail-coverts straw
yellow; tail yellowish; lores, sides of
face and chin, throat black; breast
chestnut; lower edge of breast, sides
of lower breast black; flanks scalloped
cinnamon and black; belly and
undertail-coverts white. Sexes alike.
Female may be paler or have less extensive black markings below, but the
species is too variable for this to be
a sure guide. Juvenile, typical munia
but has whitish streaks on cheeks,
buff white on throat, and is paler below.*

Also called Chestnut Finch and
Chestnut-breasted Munia or Mannikin. It was previously listed in a genus

Chestnut-
breasted Finch
(*Lonchura
castaneothorax*)

Donacola, and appears as such in all
the earlier handbooks. It is a bird of
reed-beds, cane fields, and grasslands
along the coastal districts of tropical
northern Australia. During the breeding season it pairs off and is much
less gregarious, but out of season it
congregates in large flocks and does
much damage in the cultivated areas,
where it gets the local names Barley
Bird and Barley Sparrow.

It has bred frequently in Australia,
South Africa and America, but there
are few records in Britain and the
stock is barely keeping level, and then
only with the help of birds imported
from the Continent. Some pairs will

rear successfully on a seed and
green-food diet, others will take some
soft food, others still will only rear if
live food is available. In a well-planted
and uncrowded aviary not only are
chances of breeding improved, but
possible problems of a dietary nature
will be reduced. It is a wise precau-
tion to find out if possible what the
parent birds took when rearing. There
are several subspecies of this munia
on New Guinea and since a few
traders specialize in Australasian
island-birds there is a chance that
the birds are in fact wild caught. In
this event I recommend offering some
live food when breeding.

Yellow-rumped Munia
(*Lonchura flaviprymna*)

*Description: 4 in. (101·6 mm.). Adult
has head grey, whitish on sides of
face and bib; mantle chestnut; rump
and uppertail-coverts yellow; tail
yellowish; breast and belly white,
tinged yellow on the flanks; undertail-
coverts black. Sexes alike.*

This munia, also called Yellow-
rumped Finch, Yellow-tailed Finch,
or even White-headed Munia, ranges
across north-western Australia and
the North-West Territory. It is found
in pairs or small flocks inhabiting the
tall cane-grass areas on the fringes of
swamps and rivers. It is an inland
bird, moving to coastal areas only in
times of drought. It is sad that population levels in Europe are so low as
to guarantee that in time the species
will die out, for it is a pretty little
bird, utterly peaceful, with a small
but sweet song, completely hardy,
and is a free breeder. It is likely that it
is too degenerate now, but any last-
ditch effort to re-establish a breeding
strain should be done with several
pairs in a large well-planted aviary to
help develop the fittest birds possible.

III · ERYTHRURAE

GRASSFINCHES AND PARROT-FINCHES

Grassfinches and parrot-finches form a small group of brightly coloured beautiful little birds that are in great demand with aviculturists all over the world. The grassfinches come from Australia, from where export is banned, and as world supplies depend on aviary-bred stock, demand invariably exceeds supply. The parrot-finches range from Australia to Malaya and Burma but, with the exception of the wide-ranging Pintailed Nonpareil, are inhabitants of far-flung islands or are protected and so have great rarity value; again demand exceeds supply. The grassfinches tend to be birds of open country, but there are exceptions, and parrot-finches tend to be birds of bamboo groves. The sexes are nearly always alike, or very nearly. There are some twenty-four species in the subfamily, of which about half are well known in captivity.

The Gouldian Finch holds a slightly anomalous position. It was always considered to be a grassfinch, but gradually opinion swung towards positioning it as a parrot-finch. Then Immelmann argued that it could not be included in the *Erythrura* because of various behaviour patterns which place it as a link between the parrot-finches and the munias. For my money it is a parrot-finch.

HOUSING

Some of these species are so adaptable as to be able to breed readily in cages. A friend of mine on an expedition in the outback of Australia caught some wild Zebra Finches which tried to breed in their cage on the back of the Land-Rover. I have experimented with this species and successfully reared three young in a cage measuring 15 × 10 × 8 in. (381 × 254 × 203·2 mm.). Of course this is not to be encouraged, since the stamina of the stock is bound to deteriorate fairly rapidly, but it is not surprising that the Zebra Finch has become domesticated. In contrast the Red-eared and Beautiful Firetail Finches are not even easy to keep in

good condition, let alone breed. The exceptions will be mentioned
in the text, but as a generalization they do well in large roomy
cages or indoor flights, and will do even better in outdoor aviaries.
Most of them will take some live food when rearing, and it can
be seen that a planted aviary will ease the worry of supplying
insects considerably. Most keepers of grassfinches and parrot-
finches today seem intent on avoiding the live-food issue and
will make every effort to get youngsters reared on a non-live diet.
If strong breeding stock can be perpetuated in this way I am all
for it, but I cannot help feeling that it is always better if insects in
some form can be provided. Most grassfinches and parrot-finches
that are available these days are imported from the Continent,
where they are bred. Most Continental dealers keep these birds
in near hot-house conditions and often at 70° F. (21° C.). This
means that newly-bought birds must be kept warm and gradually
acclimatized.

FOOD

All the species normally live on grass-seed throughout the year.
Most of the grassfinches take termites when they are flying, and
will feed termites to their young; the Gouldian Finch is a keen
hawker of flying termites. The feeding requirements of the better-
known parrot-finches are similar, and they too relish ants' pupae,
termites, etc. The Royal Parrot-finches also take fruit-seeds,
particularly figs, and will eagerly deal with the pips out of the
centre of a fresh apple. The requirements of the lesser-known
parrot-finches are not recorded but are likely to be similar.

Apart from live food when rearing, most of the genus will take
a little live food throughout the year. They will take various millet
seeds, both loose and on the spray, a little Canary seed, and a lot
of half-ripe seed. Japanese millet can be given, and is very good
if soaked, also soaked millet sprays. Cuttle-fish bone should be
crushed and sprinkled over a grit or sand mixture. If the birds do
not have access to a planted aviary they will appreciate a regular
freshly pulled sod of grass to pick over.

BREEDING

Normally, most species in the group will build a typical estridine
spherical nest with a side entrance, placed low down in a shrub or
among bamboo, but the odd species will nest high up, and, being

opportunist breeders that respond to food supply, etc., some species will take a hole or crevice and nest in that. Both sexes share the job of building the nest and make a good team, the female sitting inside and working the material which the male collects and works from the outside. The main material is fresh grass bitten from growing plants, but the cavity is lined with soft fine bents, hair, etc.

Both sexes share the incubation, and rear the young together. Incubation of the average clutch of four to six eggs takes twelve or thirteen days, and the young fledge within three weeks. They are fed on regurgitated unripe grass-seeds and insects. The juveniles are extremely precocious and in at least three species (the Zebra, Gouldian and Painted Finches) may start breeding behaviour at three months old.

They will all accept one of the commercially produced wicker or rush nest-baskets, but in the absence of these may take a half-open box, a roll of wire mesh stuffed with hay, or may prefer to build their own nest if a suitable site exists. Some strains of Gouldian Finches, and some other species, might still adhere to an Australian breeding schedule, and want to begin breeding in November. This is not very helpful if one is counting on breeding them in the summer in a well-planted garden aviary. It is a point worth inquiring about if you buy direct from a breeder.

Diamond Sparrow
(*Zonaeginthus guttatus*)

Description: *4½ in. (114·3 mm.). Adult has head to nape grey, whitish on cheeks and whiter on throat; lores black; mantle and wings brown; rump and uppertail-coverts crimson; tail black; below, centre of breast black; sides of breast and flanks black, each feather carrying a large white subterminal spot; belly and undertail-coverts white; bill red. Sexes alike, but older females tend to be smaller, have narrower breast-band and lores brownish. Juvenile, similar to adult but more olivaceous; flanks olive brown barred with whitish.*

The Diamond Sparrow is also called Diamond Fire-tail or Spot-sided Finch, and comes from eastern Australia where it is a bird of open forest, mallee scrub and tree-dotted grasslands. It feeds on the ground, spends a lot of time hopping about

Diamond Sparrow (*Zonaeginthus guttatus*)

looking for seeds, and is frequently seen in small flocks. It is a sociable bird which will breed in loose colonies.

In captivity it has several bad reputations: first, of wanting to breed in the middle of a European winter; secondly, of being very lazy, growing fat and consequently never coming into breeding condition; and thirdly, of being liable to be aggressive, especially the males when they are in breeding condition. I have only experienced the second of these three problems but overcame it by placing the birds in an outdoor flight. I can only suggest that if one does get a problem pair it is better to give them an enclosure to themselves. A good compatible pair are excellent breeders, but one has to be careful not to get somebody else's rejects.

Red-eared Fire-tail Finch
(*Zonaeginthus oculatus*)

Description: *About 4½ in. (114·3 mm.). Adult male, from forehead to lower back and wings olive brown finely barred with blackish brown; rump and uppertail-coverts bright crimson red; tail olivaceous, barred with black, crimson at base and on outer edges; chin to breast pale buffish grey, finely barred with black; lores and line around eye black; small patch behind eye bright red; belly and flanks to undertail black spotted with white; bill red; eye-ring pale blue. Sexes alike when not breeding; in breeding condition male a lighter, brighter colour with scarlet ear-spot, while that of the female is orange.*

The ring of blue skin in the Red-eared Fire-tail (or Red-eared Finch as it may be called) is a brighter blue than in the Common Fire-tail (*bellus*). It is a beautiful little grassfinch that is rarely met with in captivity, and like

all fire-tails is a bad traveller. Since no breeding stocks exist in Europe it is unfortunately quite unlikely that we shall ever see it here again. I remember seeing a few, along with other fire-tails, Gouldians and Red-browed Finches round about 1950. They all died within weeks of arrival and we were very wary about taking them.

The only worthwhile reference I have to them is an excellent and long article by Alwyn Pepper in *Cage and Aviary Birds* in 1966. Mr. Pepper obtained four eggs from a nest that was discovered in a felled sapling, and placed them in a Bengalese nest. Two youngsters were raised, proving to be a pair. These birds in turn bred successfully (no problems of imprinting, Gouldian breeders should note) and raised six in their first successful nest when two years old. By this means, in a well-planted and secluded aviary measuring 36 × 30 × 10 ft. (11 × 9·1 × 3·1 m.) that contained a few other grassfinches and small softbills, Mr. Pepper established a perpetuating strain of Red-eared Fire-tails. That they are delicate, or rather very sensitive, is evidenced by the fact that they always deserted whenever their surroundings were disturbed at all (for example the pruning of a creeper). Pepper refers to a friend who successfully kept four of the species in a large aviary for two and a half years, but when moved to another aviary they all died within a week. The males are territorially aggressive to other male Red-ears when breeding, but tolerant of other species.

Fire-tail Finch
(*Zonaeginthus bellus*)

Description: *4½ in. (114·3 mm.). Adult male, from forehead to lower* back, wings and lower tail olive brown with fine blackish barring; rump, uppertail-coverts and basal edges of tail bright crimson red; lores and through the eye, centre of abdomen and undertail-coverts black; rest of underparts light grey, finely barred with black; bill red; eye-ring pale blue. Female resembles male but has abdomen barred, not black. Juvenile not described.

Also called Beautiful Fire-tail, this is a species of open woodland and scrub; it is rarely seen away from tree country. It feeds on grass-seeds, and also seeds of trees and shrubs, and has been seen feeding on small insects including snails. In his book on Australian Finches Immelmann quotes Gordon as follows: '... the building of a roosting-nest is the first sign that fire-tails are settling down to aviary life. Birds that fail to acquire a "campsite" in an aviary are either sick or finding their surroundings too disturbing. In either case they do not live very long.' I have never kept the Fire-tail, and notes on its behaviour in captivity are so rare that one must accept Immelmann's advice that they need large, well-planted aviaries with corners of dense cover affording complete seclusion.

Painted Finch
(*Zonaeginthus picta*)

Description: *4–4½ in. (101·6–114·3 mm.). Adult male, from forecrown to lower back, wings and tail brown; rump and uppertail-coverts, forehead, lores, side of head, chin and throat scarlet; breast to undertail-coverts black with subterminal white spots on sides of breast and flanks; vertical streak of scarlet on centre of breast; bill, upper mandible black-tipped and edged with red, lower mandible red*

with blue base. Female has red of face restricted to lores and superciliary. Juvenile lacks red on head and breast or bill, is duller, and spots on breast are dirty white.

This lovely bird is sometimes called Painted Fire-tail, and Mountain Finch. It is usually placed in its own genus of *Emblema*, but Delacour agreed that its pointed bill was simply an adaptation for picking out fallen seeds between the tussocks of spinifex grass, and indeed it is a ground-feeder in preference to taking seeding grass-heads. It is the species of grassfinch that has penetrated the furthest into the arid areas of central Australia and

Painted Finch (*Zonaeginthus picta*)

is apparently an inhabitant of spinifex-covered hills, small groups being resident in the vicinity of water-holes in the rocky gorges.

It is an excellent aviary bird, being lively, dainty and beautiful, but shows off better in a large sparsely planted flight where it will spend a lot of time on the ground. The nest is naturally built in a clump of spinifex a foot or two from the ground, and the birds first prepare a base – possibly to provide some kind of barrier from the spines – made of bits of bark, small stones, earth, etc., upon which the nest is built. It does not readily take to a nest-basket (though if some are placed low-down in suitable cover the story might be different) and prefers to build its own nest in a clump of spiny grass. Apparently, if there are inadequate materials available for the construction of the base the birds might stop building altogether.

It is rarely bred in Britain, but surplus birds are occasionally available on the Continent. Every effort should be made to find out how they have been bred. In Australia and the U.S. it breeds freely and readily in roomy planted aviaries, rearing young on seeds, green food and some insects. It has been hybridized with the Sydney Waxbill.

Sydney Waxbill
(*Aegintha temporalis*)

Description: *About 4 in. (101·6 mm.). Adult male, grey on top of head to nape; broad red stripe of lores and superciliary; sides of head and neck pale grey; back and wings olive; rump and uppertail-coverts crimson; tail dark brown; below whitish with buff-ash wash on flanks; bill red with black culmen. Sexes alike. Juvenile lacks red eye-stripe, otherwise a dull browner version of adult.*

Since the Sydney Waxbill is a grassfinch it is argued that the alternative name of Red-browed Finch should be used. If one is to be pedantic one might suggest that it be called Red-browed Grassfinch; however, I find Red-browed suggestive of the common grey waxbills, and Sydney has to be Australian. Other names include Temporal Finch and in Australia it is invariably called Red-head or Red-headed Finch. It is a bird of coastal eastern Australia, from Cape York in the north round to Kangaroo Island, off-shore from Adelaide. The northern race, *A. temporalis minor*, known as the Lesser Red-brow or Red-head, is a good half-inch smaller, is paler on cheeks and below, has a more yellowy-brown back, and has blackish undertail-coverts.

I kept a pair of these birds years ago before the Australian ban, and found them to be perfectly normal, albeit rather retiring, grassfinches as far as they went, but I realize now that they cannot be kept like Zebra Finches. Mine showed no signs of breeding at all. They are not willing to accept a box or nest-basket, preferring to build their own nest low down in a thick shrub. They are not reputed to be free breeders in Australia although strains are being built up, and do apparently need a lot of natural cover in which to relax; they are said never to lose their nervousness. One Australian breeder told me that he had bred them and recommended a diet largely of seeding grasses when breeding; some dry seeds should always be available of course, but live food was considered to be an extra just to complement the green seed. They seem to do better in small planted aviaries up to 8 ft. (2·4 m.) long rather than larger ones.

Star Finch
(*Poephila ruficauda*)

Description: *About 4 in. (101·6 mm.). Adult male has entire front of head, ear-coverts and throat crimson; ear-coverts, mesia and throat profusely dotted with white spots; nape to rump and wings olive; uppertail-coverts dull carmine with large white spots, tail dull carmine; breast and flanks olivaceous grey each feather with subterminal white spot; belly yellowish white; undertail-coverts white; bill red. Female is very similar but slightly duller and less extensive red on face. Juveniles are much duller and greyer,*

Left: Long-tailed Grassfinch (*Poephila acuticauda*): the sexes are alike.
Right: Star Finch (*Poephila ruficauda*): male

paler below, and have red of face restricted to lores, or not showing.

This is a very distinctive-looking bird which, for some connotation of its white-spotted red face, always reminds me of a naughty schoolboy (blushing and freckled, I suppose). It is often called Ruficauda in Europe, but in Australia is apparently often referred to as Red-tailed or Rufous-tailed Finch, or Red-faced Finch. Early systematists put the species in its own monotypic genus, like so many Australian grassfinches, in this case *Bathilda*. I have followed Delacour's simplification here. It is a bird from northern and eastern Australia

and according to Immelmann is very closely bound to surface water. It occurs mainly among tall rank grasses and rushes around swamps, rivers and creeks, and has a distinct preference for the growing seeds, which it takes from the stems. It only takes fallen seeds from the ground during the dry season when the grasses have died off. 'During the breeding season it also takes insects on the wing (mostly flies, flying ants, flying termites and moths) as well as from the leaves and grasses. The species seems to become insectivorous to a much greater extent than other grassfinches.' Under his Aviary Notes Immelmann also states that when breeding in captivity live food is a 'must'.

I kept and successfully bred wild-caught Star Finches in the early 1950s and never supplied any live food at all, and neither was the aviary heavily planted (it had a convolvulus climbing up one side, and no other plant at all). In the literature reports on this are mixed; one breeder, for example, raises young in cages 24 × 18 × 15 in. (609·6 × 457·2 × 381 mm.) and, when the young hatch, provides one mealworm per bird three times a day, increasing this by one mealworm a day until they fledge. The grubs are cut up. Others report that live food is available but isn't touched. Bengalese have reared on an all-seed diet. As with most of the grassfinches it is really a matter of discretion for the keeper; if one does not want to supply live food then try the birds without. Personally I would prefer to let the birds breed in a roomy well-planted aviary with strong-winged and vigorous stock in mind as my ambition.

Hybrids have been recorded with the Zebra and Crimson Finches. There is a tendency towards yellowing of the plumage, and yellow sports have also been recorded, but a perpetuating strain of 'yellow' Star Finches has not been reported yet.

Crimson Finch
(*Poephila phaeton*)

Description: *4½–5 in. (114·3–127 mm.). Adult male, from forehead to rump and wings earth brown, blackish gloss on the head, with some crimson wash on mantle, more noticeably on the wings; uppertail-coverts bright crimson, tail dull crimson; lores, superciliary, sides of face, chin to breast, flanks bright crimson with a little spotting of pure white on flanks;*

centre of belly, undertail-coverts black; bill red. Adult female paler above than male; red restricted to face and throat, rest of underparts ashy with white dotted flanks. Juvenile duller version of female and lacks any red on head; bill black.

This species has also been placed in a monotypic genus by early workers, *Neochmia*, and has the alternative common name of Blood Finch. It ranges over northern Australia and occurs also in southern New Guinea. There is a race from the Cape York peninsula, *albiventer*, which is suffi-

Crimson Finch (*Poephila phaeton*)

ciently distinct as to collect its own common names of Pale or White-bellied Crimson Finch. Where *phaeton* has the belly and undertail-coverts black, *albiventor* is white; it also has the base of the bill grey. The female is paler below and shares the bill difference. This race is slightly smaller than the nominate.

The Crimson Finch is a bird of well-watered grassland and is rarely found far from water. It has adapted very well to the onslaught of man, recognizing him as a secure source of water, and is generally to be found around the homesteads in the north. It is similar in its behaviour to its relative the Star Finch (with which, incidentally, it has hybridized on several occasions in captivity), preferring to keep to grasses for feeding, and not taking seeds from the ground except when the seed was not available elsewhere. Insects, which it takes naturally, are included in the diet of the nestlings. I have not bred the species, and it is many years since we kept any, but various notes that I have indicate that not many mealworms or maggots will be taken by rearing birds, but spiders and greenfly, midges and other small insects will be taken if offered. Successful breeding does not depend on this, particularly not in a planted aviary, but some live food is recommended. Indeed, a good compatible pair, with the right breeding diet, can be most prolific birds (this is true of all *Poephilae*). I choose the word 'compatible' with deliberation because the Crimson Finch has a reputation for being very spiteful and unpredictably vicious. As a lad I was so frightened by this belief that I never kept it with other waxbills or grassfinches. However, the popular bird literature is singularly empty of such remarks and, with the exception of Immelmann who also records its argumentative nature in the wild, there is nothing to suggest that it is a problem species.

It is a beautiful bird, quite expensive on the rare occasion that it is available, and since breeding will be much more likely in a roomy, planted flight, or a large cage with no other inhabitants, then fighting may not occur. However, I do suggest that if birds are bought separately then they should be watched for quarrelling when introduced, and that other red

or reddish birds are not casually included in the same enclosure.

There are many references in the literature to 'Golden Finches'; these are a yellow mutant that rarely occurs in the wild. It has been established and several strains occur in Australian aviculture. Odd specimens have occurred elsewhere but not established. I have never seen one, but understand that the yellow, which replaces the red of a normal bird, is both variable and generally dull, like the ochre of the face of a Yellow-headed Gouldian Finch.

Zebra Finch
(*Poephila guttata*)

Description: *4–4½ in. (101·6–114·3 mm.). Adult male, forehead to nape grey, graduating into earth-brown back, wings and tail; rump white; uppertail-coverts black, heavily barred with black and almost covering the tail; vertical white bar from lores to mesia, edged with black; ear-coverts orange; chin to breast finely barred black and white; flanks chestnut spotted white; belly and undertail-coverts creamy white; bill vermilion. Female resembles male above; but is creamy white on ear-coverts and entire underparts. Juvenile resembles female but lacks black and white line on face and has bill blackish.*

Universally known as the Zebra Finch, this lively little bird ranges over most of Australia. Races are found on Timor, Flores, Sunda and other small islands near by. They are generally darker, larger, and have much reduced barring on throat and breast. They just might be available from time to time. They would only have curiosity value, however, because the species is thoroughly established in domesticity and many colour variations have been stabilized as true-breeding types. These are too numerous to describe in detail, but include a fawn, which is a little larger and generally considered to be prettier than the normal, or grey; the penguin is a normal or fawn that lacks the black markings altogether and is usually slightly smaller than a normal; the white is pure white but retains the red bill, and a chestnut-flanked white is white but retains the chestnut flank marking, usually in a dilute form. The pied Zebra is a normal or fawn in which patches of white occur erratically over the body. There are other variations, rather subtle ones for the connoisseur.

Zebra Finches are delightful and

Zebra Finch (*Poephila guttata*)

vivacious birds that are not at all aggressive, but have such energy and busy-body characters that they are better kept with munias and weavers than waxbills and grassfinches, since they might cause too much disturbance. They will rear successfully on seed and grasses, and soft foods need only be provided at the personal preferences of the keeper. I have reared Zebras under every possible variation of diet and enclosure, but have never seen one take mealworms or maggots for any reason other than curiosity.

One problem that seems to have reduced, and I have not noticed it at all in recent years, is that of compulsive nest-building. The Zebra has a tendency to fill its nesting receptacle until only a small nest-chamber is left at the top; the problem, however, stems from the fact that it will pause to lay a full clutch but begin building again almost before serious brooding has begun. Such a free-breeding bird as the Zebra Finch has hybridized with many species (Immelmann lists twenty-four distinct crosses) including all the other *Poephilae*, some waxbills and munias. The most striking hybrid I have seen was a lovely Diamond Sparrow and Zebra Finch.

Bicheno's Finch
(*Poephila bichenovii*)

Description: *4 in. (101·6 mm.). Adult male, forehead to rump pale greyish brown finely barred with dark brown; lower rump and uppertail-coverts white; tail dark brown; secondaries and greater wing-coverts blackish, barred white; black line beginning at forehead and edging lores, ear-coverts and throat; another black line edges breast, forming a bar; apart from twin bars, and black undertail-coverts, underparts are creamy white. Sexes alike and since plumage is variable no reliable diagnostics exist. Juveniles are duller; more olivaceous above; barring indistinct.*

The bird that I have described is the nominate race, *bichenovii*, from eastern Australia; it is also known as Banded Finch or White-rumped Bicheno. There is a distinct race from north-western Australia and Northern Territory, *annulosa*, which is known as the Black-winged Finch or White-rumped Bicheno. Other common names for the species are Double-bar

Finch and Owl-faced or Owl Finch. The latter names derive from the circular, owl-like mask-effect given by the black ring that encircles the face. There are plenty of scientific names as well, *Stictoptera* or *Stizoptera* being usual; however, again I join Delacour in rejecting so many monotypic genera and follow him in placing Bicheno's Finch alongside the Zebra Finch in the *Poephila*.

As with many, if not most of the grassfinches, it is difficult to get a good compatible male and female. Odd birds available are so often sole survivors of a pair or small collection, and are old; others are rejects from aviculturists who have found them to be poor breeders. However, a good healthy pair make excellent parents and will cheerfully rear on an all-seed and green-food diet. In a planted aviary it will not be necessary to supply live food at all, but in an unplanted enclosure or indoor flight it might be worth offering a few small mealworms or maggots, and these might be chopped up over soft food. Bicheno's will breed well in mixed company as long as overcrowding is avoided; Star Finches make ideal companions. They have hybridized with most of the other *Poephilae*, and White-headed and Yellow-rumped Munias.

Cherry Finch
(*Poephila modesta*)

Description: *About 4 in. (101·6 mm.). Adult male has forehead, crown and chin dull plum red; hind neck to rump, including wings, brown, with wing- and tail-coverts edged with white; tail blackish; lores black; sides of face and throat to undertail-coverts dull white barred mainly on breast and flanks with brown. Female*

a little paler but very similar; main difference is lack of red on chin. Juvenile like female but lacks any red on head and is paler below.

The Cherry Finch, also known as Plum-headed Finch, Plum-capped Finch, Modest Grassfinch, Plain-coloured Finch or Diadem Finch, is also listed in a monotypic genus, *Aidemosyne*. It is a species of grass country in eastern Australia, and will often be found close to habitation. Cayley found it to be an engaging and friendly little bird that tamed readily, and, like sparrows, it will hop around houses looking for tit-bits. They seem to be equally at ease in tall grass or on the ground looking for fallen seeds.

A compatible pair are usually excellent breeders, but success can only be assured if several pairs are obtained, marked for certain identification, and allowed to pair up according to their own preferences. I have twice taken a male and female at random from a stock cage and on each occasion the pair have not paired. Indeed, the only grassfinches that I have *never* had this problem with at any time are Zebras and Stars. They do not need insects, providing seeding grasses and other green food are available, and as with every grassfinch better breeding results are obtained in planted aviaries. Pairs do not have to be kept segregated from other birds.

Parson Finch
(*Poephila cincta*)

Description: *About 4 in. (101·6 mm.). Adult, from forehead to nape French grey; mantle cinnamon; becoming brown on lower back and wings, to black on rump; uppertail-coverts white; tail, lores, chin, throat black;*

breast and upper flanks cinnamon, the flanks changing to a patch of black which is a continuation of the black rump-bar; cheeks, belly and undertail-coverts white; bill black. Sexes alike. Juveniles resemble adults, though when first fledged look darker eyed; slightly less extensive black and somehow 'softer'.

The nominate race described above is also called the Black-throated Finch and is a bird of the eastern parts of Australia, from central and southern Queensland and New South Wales. The race *atropygialis*, first described by Diggles and thought to be a separate species, comes from Cape York. It is distinguished by having a paler grey on the head, richer brown on mantle and breast, and black upper-tail-coverts. Aviculturists both in Australia and Britain prefer to call this bird Diggles's Finch, but it may also be listed as Black-tailed Grassfinch or Black-rumped Parson Finch. The white-rumped race, the Parson Finch, is the form thoroughly established in captivity in Europe; it is also the commoner form in Australia, but the Diggles's Finch is also established and is not rare. Parson Finches seem to take little insect food when rearing, and will rear on grass-seeds, etc., and are thus firm favourites in aviculture. They are not uncommon, neither are they very expensive, but the majority of stock on the market are Continental-bred birds. Most British enthusiasts seem to prefer to keep one or two pairs of several species rather than specialize in depth. The Parson Finch, like all the *Poephilae*, are perfect subjects for developing a strong strain, but pair-compatibility can only be optimized if a minimum of, say, half a dozen 'pairs' are acquired to begin with. It will readily hybridize with

all the other black-throated *Poephilae* and should never be mixed for this reason. It has also hybridized with the Spice Bird, Cut-throat and Red-headed Parrot-finch among others.

Long-tailed Grassfinch
(*Poephila acuticauda*)

Description: *4½ in. (114·3 mm.), spines of the two central tail-feathers may add up to 1½ in. (38·1 mm.) to this. Identical to Parson Finch but has two central tail-feathers elongated, and yellow or red bill. Juveniles have a blackish bill.*

This popular and very attractive bird is a native of northern Australia, and in its native country is often called Black-heart or Black-hearted Finch. At the westernmost end of the bird's range it has a yellow bill, but at the eastern extremity the bill is coral red. This form is known in aviculture as Heck's Grassfinch and was formerly known as a race *hecki*, but there are so many variations of colour occurring all over the range, and all shades of orange, that *hecki* is not considered as a valid race today. In captivity the red bill has usually been found to be dominant and it is not desirable to cross-breed the two colours for fear of losing the yellow as a pure form, and the loss of both by eventually ending up with orange-billed birds.

The yellow (or red) bill of this species, together with its elongated tail, makes it a more attractive bird than the Parson Finch, and for this reason it was preferred and bred much more extensively than the other. However, rarity value has increased the desirability of the Parson and it is equally sought-after. The initial boost of popularity to the Long-tail during the early 1950s, when Australian birds were still being exported, ensured its firm establishment in captivity. It is undoubtedly on the road to domesticity and is the perfect species for anyone who cares to make a start with the *Erythrurae*, Immelmann has listed sixteen hybrids, but no doubt there are more. Outside the *Poephilae* it has crossed with the Diamond Sparrow, Bengalese and Chestnut-breasted Munia.

Masked Grassfinch
(*Poephila personata*)

Description: *4½–5 in. (114·3–127 mm.). Adult male, forehead to upper rump, and wings cinnamon brown; lower rump and uppertail-coverts white; tail black; sides of forehead, lores, edging to bill, chin black; throat and breast lighter cinnamon; belly and undertail-coverts white; patch on flanks black; bill yellow. Sexes alike, but bill of male sometimes a little darker, and black mask*

White-eared Masked Grassfinch
(*Poephila personata leucotis*)

larger. Juveniles lack face mask and have bill blackish.

This species ranges across tropical north Australia, and the birds of Cape York peninsula – as with so many other species – are separated as a distinct race. This form, *leucotis*, known as the White-eared Grassfinch, is not known in Europe but is regularly bred in small numbers in Australia. They are ground birds, feeding on the ground generally, preferring grassy areas with lots of ground scrub and occasional but regular clumps of eucalyptus trees in which they gather in flocks. In the wild it normally nests low down, frequently on the ground, and both sexes share in the nest-building. Unlike other grassfinches it waits until the wet season is completely finished then rears one brood in contrast to the two or three broods built by most other species. It is extremely fastidious about choosing the nest-site, which may, incidentally, be in a hole, and may take two weeks or more in building the nest.

This is the most frustrating species of grassfinch that I have kept, and has never built a nest, let alone bred. It is clear that the best conditions to keep them under is as a small flock of from ten to twenty birds in a large planted aviary. They are very sociable birds and have a complicated behaviour-pattern that is more fulfilled in a flock situation. I do not recommend keeping them in a mixed flock of grassfinches that contains either of the black-throated species for, although the flock-stimulus value will be greater, so will the risk of cross-breedings increase. They are not the easiest of grassfinches to breed, but a good pair who respond to their keeper's methods will breed as well as any other *Erythrurae*. Some pairs will take a lot of live food, my last 'pair' would each take half a dozen mealworms every day that I gave them the opportunity.

Gouldian Finch
(*Chloebia gouldiae*)

Description: *About 5 in. (127 mm.), but wild birds are longer owing to the greater length of the spines of the central tail-feathers. Adult male, entire front part of head from crown to throat black, edged with turquoise blue; from upper neck to rump, and wings olivaceous green; uppertail-coverts bright turquoise blue; tail blackish; breast purplish lilac; rest of underparts yellow, palest on undertail-coverts. Female similar but noticeably paler on breast and underparts. Juvenile olive green above, paler to whitish below; adult feathering begins to show very soon after fledging.*

There are several colour morphs of the Gouldian Finch; three occur naturally in the wild. The above, known as the black-headed Gouldian, accounts for about 90% of wild populations. The red-headed Gouldian has forehead and crown, lores, cheeks and mesia red; chin and throat remain black, and a black line extends around the head to separate the red from the turquoise. It accounts for about 9% of wild populations. The final 1% is of a yellow-headed morph, in which the red of the red-headed becomes dull yellow. In captivity most breeders concentrated on red-headed birds and these normally changed hands at a 50% premium; the yellow-headed birds were about 25% dearer still. At the time of writing this (early 1974) red-heads are so common that black-heads are now more expensive

because of scarcity value. There appears to be a concerted effort on the part of some breeders to improve the quality of yellow of the yellow-headed form, and to breed more of them. In addition to these three well-known forms, white, albino and fawn Gouldians have appeared, but none has been bred. A new variety, in which the lilac breast is replaced by pure white, has been established and is independent of head colour.

The use of the Bengalese, both by the Japanese who 'factory-bred' tens of thousands of Bengalese-reared Gouldians for twenty years or so, and many breeders both in Britain and on the Continent, has done great damage to strains of Gouldians in Europe and America. Compared to populations in South Africa and Australia, where the Gouldian is generally vigorous, free-breeding and strong, these populations are infertile, sterile, weak and imprinted on to Bengalese. It is not fair to blame the Bengalese entirely for the harmful effects, and these are not necessarily mutually exclusive. The first, imprinting, could mean that some of the instincts of the fostered Gouldian are directed at the Bengalese species instead of at its own; this could mean that the bird fails to respond adequately to breeding signals given by other Gouldians. The second is that the Bengalese only too frequently rear on an all-seed diet and have not been trained to be fed protein-rich soft foods, insects, etc., therefore the young Gouldians grow up suffering from partial malnutrition. Thirdly, in the same way that the Bengalese, the Bantam and some other species have evolved to be super-prolific, so the Gouldian in Europe has tended to evolve as a non-breeding creature; its rearing and feeding instincts have become dulled over generations since there is no need for them.

Another problem with Gouldians is climate, for they are real sun-worshippers and are naturally at their liveliest and most active in hot midday sun, and I do mean hot – around 100° F. (38° C.) – when most other birds become torpid. It is also worth noting that the southernmost limit of the species' range is where the night-time temperature drops to 60° F. (16° C.).

Furthermore, when it breeds it is very prolific, raising three broods of up to eight in each brood; the humidity is in the order of 90%. Finally, there is the question of diet, for the Gouldian is highly insectivorous and seems to have rather specific dietary needs. Diet can be coped with by sprinkling seed and green food with an additive like Squibb's Vionate, *and* adding one of the multi-vitamin/mineral additives to the water. But it is clear that to really succeed with the species one needs a sunny tropical greenhouse with temperature and humidity controls, sun-ray lamps, and fresh growing grasses. In the face of this most breeders seem determined to prove that the Gouldian is no different from a Zebra Finch and maintain it under similar conditions. That being so, it is frankly amazing how many young are raised each year. Whilst most breeders will be inclined to join the 'treat it like a Zebra, and keep Bengalese as insurance' set, I do urge that some consideration be given to the conditions under which the Gouldian positively thrives in the wild.

Pintailed Nonpareil
(*Erythrura prasina*)

Description: *About 5½ in. (139·7 mm.). Adult male, forehead, super-*

ciliary, cheeks, ear-coverts, chin and throat dark blue; lores black; crown to lower back, wings green; rump and uppertail-coverts scarlet; breast, flanks and undertail-coverts straw buff; belly scarlet; bill heavy and black. Female has less blue on face and no red on belly. Juveniles resemble female but have olive rump and uppertail-coverts.

There is a colour morph in which the scarlet of belly and rump is replaced by bright yellow. It occurs throughout the range of the bird at variable incidence, probably no more

Pintailed Nonpareil (*Erythrura prasina*); Bamboo Munia (*Erythrura hyperythra*)

than 5%. The female of this form has the dark red uppertail-coverts replaced by yellow. There is a race from Borneo, *E. p. coelica*, in which the male has the colour of belly and rump noticeably richer. Some other names for the species are Pintailed Parrot-finch, Nonpareil Parrot-finch, Long-tailed Munia, Red-bellied Munia or Bamboo Munia (this latter is the accepted common name for *E. hyperythra*). Dealers who receive the yellow-bellied variant have been known to advertise them as Yellow-bellied Parrot-finch.

It has a wide range, from Burma through Malaysia to Sumatra and Java. It is common among bamboo groves, frequenting paddy fields in large flocks, causing much damage, and yet its nest has never been described. Nothing is known of its natural breeding behaviour. On the Continent it has been bred on several occasions, and Rubner in Bavaria found it to be as prolific and easy to breed as Red-headed, Blue-faced, and Peale's Parrot-finches, and bred hybrids with both the Red-headed and the Blue-faced. Strangely, however, breeding reports from Britain are nonexistent. It is a little delicate on arrival and, from an experience with maybe twenty pairs over about a fifteen-year period, I am sure that they have a tendency to intestinal and liver problems and I recommend that newly imported birds be given a five-day dose of antibiotics. I have also found that they definitely prefer paddy, dry or soaked, to any other seed. They will take clipped oats quite readily and then canary-seed, hemp and millet. It seems silly to force them to take a canary-rich diet which is both expensive and unnecessary, but many bird-keepers do.

Bamboo Munia
(*Erythrura hyperythra*)

Description: *About 4 in. (101·6 mm.). Adult has forehead blackish; crown blue; rest of upperparts green; lores, superciliary, sides of face and all lower parts straw buff; there is some green washing on sides of breast and flanks. Sexes alike, juveniles duller.*

The Green, Green-rumped, Green-tailed or Mountain Parrot-finch seems to be a high-country version of the Pintailed. Visually it looks very much like a female *prasina*, but can be distinguished by its green rump and uppertail-coverts. It also has a similar distribution – Malaysia, Sumatra to the Philippines and Celebes. In evolutionary terms it may well turn out to

be the original parrot-finch. I saw some advertised a few years ago and was very interested in them, but they were fairly expensive and my travelling abroad stopped me buying any new birds at the time. Their dull colouring would reduce their following to real enthusiasts to whom song and bright colours are not everything. But undoubtedly they have been kept by somebody, and possibly bred, but no mention has appeared in the literature.

Blue-faced Parrot-finch
(*E. trichroa*)

Blue-faced Parrot-finch
(*Erythrura trichroa*)

Description: *4½ in. (114·3 mm.). Adult male has front of head, superciliary, cheeks and ear-coverts blue; uppertail-coverts crimson; tail brown edged with crimson; rest of body grass green. Sexes alike, but blue tends to be more restricted and duller. Juvenile green all over, paler below.*

This bird is also known as Blue-headed, Three-coloured and Tri-

The Parrot-finches: 1. Green-faced Parrot-finch (*Erythrura viridifacies*); 2. Red-headed Parrot-finch (*E. psittacea*); 3. Tri-coloured Parrot-finch (*E. tricolor*); 4. Mt. Katanglad Parrot-finch (*E. coloris*); 5. Kleinschmidt's Parrot-finch (*E. kleinschmidti*); 6. Pintailed Nonpareil (*E. prasina*); 7. Gouldian Finch (*Chloebia gouldiae*); 8. Blue-headed Parrot-finch (*E. papuana*); 9. Blue-faced Parrot-finch (*E. trichroa*); 10. Bamboo Munia (*E. hyperythra*); 11. Peale's Parrot-finch (*E. cyanovirens pealei*); 12. Blue-bellied Parrot-finch (*E. c. cyanovirens*); 13. Royal Parrot-finch (*E. c. regia*)

coloured Parrot-finch, but the latter two names are better reserved for *E. tricolor*. It is a bird of the Pacific Islands ranging from Celebes and the Moluccas through New Guinea eastwards to the Loyalty Islands. It is a favourite among enthusiasts of the *Erythrurae* and is bred regularly in good numbers on the Continent. In Britain, however, the preference for cage-breeding grassfinches combined with an unwillingness to buy more than one or, at most, two pairs has meant that the species – like so many others – has never become really established and all advertised birds are imported. Nearly all breeding successes are in aviaries, and planted aviaries – while by no means necessary – certainly seem to improve the output. They are active birds, wild in a cage, but delightfully tame in an aviary. They have bred on many occasions without any live food, but cannot be expected to rear on hard dry seed. If live food is not available they should be given seeding grasses, green food, and rearing food like sponge cake, etc.

Red-headed Parrot-finch
(*Erythrura psittacea*)

Description: *4–4½ in. (101·6–114.3 mm.). Adult male has front of head, from crown to ear-coverts, chin to upper breast, rump and uppertail-coverts scarlet; tail brown washed with scarlet; rest of body grass green. Sexes alike. Juveniles are typically green, but many fledglings show some red face feathers from the start.*

This species, which is sometimes referred to in the literature as Red-faced Parrot-finch, or simply as Parrot-finch, comes from New Caledonia. Like the Gouldian Finch it has a strong tendency to nest in crevices or holes and has a positive preference for adapting a suitable site rather than building a nest of its own. They are long-lived and lively birds, and are extremely suitable as aviary subjects. One aviculturist, Mr. Norman Nicholson, made a lifetime's hobby out of the one species and bred it to more than thirty generations. He found that over the years his birds increased in size and vigour rather than the reverse, a tribute perhaps to the consistency and quality of his husbandry. In addition to canary and millets, they have a liking for apple, and will take the seeds readily. They will also take other small seeds, and many breeders provide mealworms and/or other live food as well as egg-rearing food. They have been successfully bred on a diet of seeds, grass, chickweed and soft food; live food may be regarded as a desirable optional.

Royal Parrot-finch
(*Erythrura cyanovirens*)

Description: *4½ in. (114·3 mm.). Adult has forehead to nape and sides of head bright red; mantle and upper rump, wings, breast and undertail-coverts green; lower rump and upper-tail-coverts scarlet; flight feathers and tail brown; chin, throat and suffusion on to breast and neck blue; bill black. Sexes alike. Juveniles have head blue, body green, uppertail-coverts dull red; red begins to come through on the head from time of fledgling; bill horn-colour.*

There are three distinct races that are generally regarded as distinct species in aviculture. When compared side by side, a plumage progression may be noted. The nominate race, *E. c. cyanovirens*, known as the Blue-bellied Parrot-finch, is the bird described above; it comes from Samoa, and is probably rarely imported. I have no doubt that it would be called Royal Parrot-finch and sold as such. Peale's Parrot-finch (*E. c. pealei*), also referred to as Short-tailed or Fiji Parrot-finch, comes from the Fiji Islands. It is marginally smaller than the nominate race, has less extensive red, and the blue extending from the throat only reaches the upper breast. The Royal Parrot-finch (*E. c. regia*) comes from the New Hebrides; it is slightly larger than the nominate, has

Peale's Parrot-finch (*Erythrura cyanovirens pealei*)

Royal Parrot-finch (*E. cyanovirens cyanovirens*)

a heavier bill, the red hood extends to reach the mantle and the blue wash covers back, wings and breast.

There is no reference to *E. c. cyanovirens* in the avicultural literature at all, but I think it is safe to assume that it can be treated exactly like the other two races, which are well documented. The exact function of the rather heavy bill is not known, but it is assumed that it is an adaptation for taking fruit seeds, particularly wild fig, of which they are very fond. They have been bred in cages and aviaries, and anything from about 4 ft. (1·2 m.) in length up to a full aviary seems to suit them well. In this respect they appear to be the best of the parrot-finches. As with all *Erythrurae*, whether grassfinches or parrot-finches,

pair-compatibility seems to be the first imperative for succesful breeding. It is quite possible that one can buy two males and two females, and find that by arbitrarily separating them into two pairs one gets nowhere but by subsequently changing the males over one gets immediate success. If one imagines buying one of the unbonded pairs, one can easily become frustrated. The solution is either to buy bonded pairs, buy several birds and allow natural selection to take place, or rely on luck. As with other parrot-finches they will rear young on a non-live food diet, but many breeders have found that mealworms have been accepted readily, and other live food, if taken, must be beneficial.

Pink-billed Parrot-finch
(*Erythrura kleinschmidti*)

Description: *$4\frac{1}{2}$–5 in. (114·3–127 mm.). Adult, entire facial mask black, edged with turquoise; upperparts olive green; bright red rump; short blackish-green tail suffused with red; underparts yellowish green; bill bright pink. Sexes alike.*

The Pink-billed, Black-faced or Kleinschmidt's Parrot-finch is restricted to the Fiji island of Viti Levu.

Practically nothing is known about it and it is unknown as a cagebird. However, since optimistic trapping expeditions usually take orders in advance, and optimistic dealers put the ordered species on their lists, it is as well to mention it here.

It was considered at one time to be a bird of high-altitude rain forest, but has recently been seen in the same habitat as Red-headed Parrot-finches at low altitude. It has been suggested that its heavy bill is an adaptation for eating buds, and it may well have similar habits to the Royal Parrot-finches.

Green-faced Parrot-finch
(*Erythrura viridifacies*)

Description: *4½ in. (114·3 mm.). Adult has entire body grass green except rump, which is red, undertail-coverts which are ochreous yellow, and tail heavily suffused with red; bill black. Sexes alike.*

The Green-faced, Green-headed or Manila Parrot-finch comes from Luzon in the Philippines. I have never seen it listed in Europe, but it has been available in the United States. I can find no reference to it, but an acquaintance from the U.S. once told me that it was 'a typical little tropical finch and was no trouble to cater for'.

Tri-coloured Parrot-finch
(*Erythrura tricolor*)

Description: *4–4½ in. (101·6–114·3 mm.). Adult has lores and bib black; remainder of face to flanks and belly blue; undertail-coverts green; crown, back and wings green; lower back to uppertail-coverts red, tail heavily washed with red; bill black. Sexes alike.*

The Tri-coloured, Three-coloured, Blue-fronted or Timor Blue Parrot-

finch from Timor, the South-West Islands and Tanimber should not be confused with *E. trichroa*, which is sometimes called Tri-coloured Parrot-finch. It does appear on dealers' lists occasionally, but in each case that I have investigated it has turned out to be *trichroa*. I have no reference to it in the literature at all.

Red-eared Parrot-finch
(*Erythrura coloris*)

Description: *About 4½ in. (114·3 mm.). Adult like Blue-faced Parrot-finch but has bright red patch on side of neck.*

This species was only discovered a dozen years ago by an expedition to Mindanao. The bird was found on Mount Katanglad and for this reason it has been named Mt. Katanglad Parrot-finch. It was listed by Mr. Hastings a few years ago as *E. coloris*, but my hasty order received the reply that all specimens had already been snapped up on the Continent before the birds arrived in England.

Papuan Parrot-finch
(*Erythrura papuana*)

Description: *5–5½ in. (127–139·7 mm.). Adult like a large, longer-tailed Blue-faced Parrot-finch.*

The Blue-headed or Papuan Parrot-finch is found only in the higher elevations of the mountain ranges of New Guinea and Papua. It is apparently an ecologically isolated sibling of *E. tricolor* which it closely resembles, being larger and duller. It is virtually an unknown species that has not been seen in Europe since before the Second World War, when it was bred by at least two aviculturists in Britain. It is very unlikely that it will appear on the dealers' lists again owing to the rigid laws protecting the fauna of the island.

Part Four
PLOCEIDAE

I · PLOCEINAE

All of the species in this chapter might be embraced by the term 'typical weaver' or 'true weaver'. However, to the average aviculturist the true weavers are those that fall in the genus *Ploceus*. I mention this point at the start in case the term elsewhere should cause confusion. Generally they are sparrow-sized birds, with strong bills and strong sturdy bodies. Most of the males have two distinct plumage-phases in the year; when breeding they are either bright yellow and black, or black with splashes of red and orange, or they display long showy tail-plumes. However, when not in breeding plumage they are very similar to their streaky-brown females. In aviculture the nuptial plumage is known as 'in colour' or i/c, and these words or letters after a bird's name in a dealer's list denote this. Conversely, a male in eclipse plumage is referred to as being 'out of colour' or O.O.C.

The vast majority of the typical weavers are African birds, although a few occur in Asia and the Pacific regions. They are named for the remarkable nests that most of them weave; indeed some are quite extraordinary. The nest of the Social Weaver, for example, may fill an entire tree, although really this is a communal structure, the combined nests of maybe hundreds of pairs. Many species build beautifully complex retort-shaped nests. They do not have well-developed songs, but most of them are quite noisy, and a nest colony can be a raucous, shatteringly chattering affair. All of the colony-breeding species deserve to be kept in colony-type situations in captivity, for then the interaction of social behaviour can best be observed and the birds behave more naturally. Most of them are birds of open bush or savanna country, but a few are frequenters of woodland.

HOUSING

Weavers are active and lively birds. When in breeding condition they chase each other around, with feathers fluffed and voices chattering away like clockwork toys. Some hang upside-down from the loop-framework of a newly started nest and, with wings flapping, call and 'sing'. From this it must be obvious that they are not suitable cagebirds. It must be admitted that their basic requirements may be met in a cage, and some species may live apparently contentedly in one. However, at the risk of being anthropomorphic, I find this akin to a prison sentence for a human being. One has only to compare a group of any particular species in a cage with the same birds when placed in a flight to see the difference.

All weavers undoubtedly do much better in a flight than in a cage, and a large planted aviary is ideal. Unfortunately the proud gardener will find them rather destructive and aviaries that are planted must be developed with care and skill. The problem arises out of the desire of the birds to use strips of soft material with which to weave their nests, and a natural source, for example, is the palm. A male weaver will make a cut near the base of a leaf then, holding the leaf firmly just above the cut, will fly upwards, tearing off a neat long strip. Attractive plants such as the red-hot poker (*Kniphofia*) are utterly ruined in this way. Tough, small-leaved shrubs like privet, *lonicera nitida*, box and others are ideal. Grass will thrive, since it will not be picked until it is long, and then the action is beneficial. Most important is a base for the birds to build on and something is needed if they are to be prevented weaving unsightly and useless half-nests in the wire mesh.

If the enclosure is big enough to support a tree or two this is fine, but the buds may be nipped off in the spring. The ideal suggestion is to suspend several branches beneath the roof of the flight. Many weavers naturally build their nests over water and a couple of inverted dustbin lids used to make substitute wells or ponds will definitely contribute to the overall well-being of the birds. Ideally, of course, a large shallow pond will provide a wonderful stimulus. Many weavers naturally build in rushes and reed-beds over water and some planting to stimulate this environment will also be very helpful. Reeds may be difficult but worth trying if the ground is damp. Bamboo may be a suitable substitute. Nest-building material may be supplied in the form of raffia, cut into variable lengths (8–20 in./203–508 mm.). Some keepers like to give raffia in different colours, but my personal preference is to use the green-coloured variety.

Having stressed how desirable it is to keep the weavers in aviaries or flights, I might add that some people cage them up for the eclipse season, acting from the viewpoint that such dull and uninteresting birds can be put out of sight until they regain the lovely trappings of courtship once more. I disagree. I have found all weavers to be inclined towards irritability when out of season, especially females, and the extra room for manœuvre afforded by an aviary serves to reduce the danger of too much bickering. Secondly, birds that thrive out-of-doors are much more receptive to the urge of spring when it comes. The indoor-cage supporters, however, point out that artificial light can bring forward the 'start of spring' and can also extend the nuptial plumage phase. Indeed I have seen bishops that have stayed in colour for ten months out of twelve through being kept indoors, and a Napoleon Weaver of mine that was kept in the kitchen stayed in colour for thirty months.

If you opt for a cage keep it as big as possible. Breeding behaviour is only developed fully in a roomy flight, and breeding itself will only take place in an outdoor aviary.

FOOD

The weavers are, generally speaking, very easy birds to care for. They will thrive on an all-seed diet and require nothing else apart from the usual grits, etc. Most weavers show a distinct preference for millet seeds and a bowl of various mixed millets may be provided, or each type in a separate pot. Canary-seed can be given separately, thus allowing the birds to select according to their needs – which vary, of course. Personally, I usually give a Canary mixture, throwing the uneaten seeds around the open area of the flight for the birds to pick up later. Weavers feed on grass-seeds at all times of the year. The fresh ripening grain provides a stimulus to breeding and some species are so geared to this that instead of having a calendar-oriented breeding cycle they breed in response to food supply. When the long dry season has been in progress for some time the only seeds available are those hard and dry ones that have fallen to the ground. Therefore, broadcasting seed in an aviary is providing a stimulus for natural food-seeking behaviour.

I have always planted canary and millet deliberately in aviaries containing Ploceidae and Amadinae as this also provides much entertainment, and serves the valuable function of supplying some fresh green seed. Millet sprays may be hung in bunches and will attract a lot of attention.

When breeding, weavers will take soaked and sprouting seeds, fresh growing grass-seeds (try oats and wheat, etc.) and will all require a little live food. It does not appear to be necessary to supplement mealworms and maggots with a mineralized multi-vitamin additive, since their are plenty of breeding reports that indicate that the birds' needs are fairly simple. However, I believe in giving the best available, and if one is fortunate enough to have weavers completing their breeding cycle I would like to ensure that the resulting young are as completely nourished as possible, and that risks of hormone deficiencies are minimized. Mealworms and maggots, of course, may be given at other times, and generally will be appreciated.

BREEDING

Breeding notes have really been covered in the foregoing sections. Specific variations, where known, are mentioned under the individual species, but generally one can say that weavers: (a) are more likely to breed in a socal situation; (b) need a fairly roomy enclosure in which to indulge in their chasing and displaying; (c) might well require natural cover to provide a nest-site; (d) will require either a supply of live food for the young nestlings, or a large and well-planted aviary in which to find their own insects.

Quite a few species appear to have been bred, but details are rarely provided and frequently the species is simply mentioned as one of several bred during the previous season. With very few exceptions, every member of this subfamily could be better covered in the literature, and any aviculturist who has a successful breeding in his collection would help the hobby by writing about it.

PLOCEUS WEAVERS

This is a large genus of attractive and interesting species. In much of the literature some of these species may be found listed under many different genera, including *Hyphanturgus*, *Othyphantes*, *Plesiositagra*, *Hyphantornis*, *Symplectes* and *Sitagra*. With only a few exceptions they are all found within the African continent south of the Sahara. There is great confusion among aviculturists and dealers over identifying them, and it is quite possible to find a species separated by sex in a pet shop, each sex being sold as a different species. Most of the *Ploceus* weavers have two distinct plumage-phases a year and, when in colour, are reasonably easy to identify. When out of colour they become more difficult, and comparisons are usually necessary. Most, but not all, of the males are yellow and black, and many of them closely resemble the females when out of colour. This is true also of the juveniles, which do not mature until their second year, and may have an intermediate plumage when they show some characteristics of the adult. The females are usually rather in the style of female House Sparrows, and are referred to by most writers as being 'sparrowy'. Many, in fact, are significantly different and, I think, much more attractive than a female *Passer domesticus*.

Apart from identifying the species it is often very difficult to identify the sex correctly, what with out-of-colour males resembling females, and juveniles also contributing to the confusion. Many 'pairs' turn out to be an adult male and an immature male, and from my own experiences I know that an out-of-colour pair can easily turn out to be two females.

A few of these species nest solitarily, but most are social and nest in colonies which may range in size from a few nests to, quite literally, millions! The way in which many of these nests are built is very interesting. The male birds first build a frame, a loop which is tied, and is then enclosed by a rough outside wall. The females then begin to take an interest in the colony and the males compete furiously to attract attention, each hanging from its nest, flapping and singing. Having chosen a mate, a female will then help to complete the nest, pulling material in that the male pushes through, and in turn pushing it out at a different place. There is a strong tendency to polygamy on the part of the males, and in some species males are completely polygamous.

Rufous-necked Weaver
(*Ploceus cucullatus*)

Description: *6–7 in.* (*152·4–177·8 mm.*). *Adult male in colour has head black, including lower throat; nape* washed with rufous; neck, rump and all underparts bright yellow; mantle mottled yellow and black; wings black, feathers edged yellow; tail olive edged yellow; eye bright red; bill black. Out of colour, head

Rufous-necked Weaver (*Ploceus cucullatus*): male on the left, female on the right

olivaceous yellow; above ashy with brown streaks; chin to upper breast yellow; rest of underparts white; bill horn-colour. Female in breeding plumage has top of head, sides of face green, above yellowish green to ashy, streaked with dusky; below yellow, sometimes centre of belly white; belly blackish. Out of colour, female is like male but noticeably smaller. Juveniles resemble breeding female but are more olive brown on back.

This common bird, which ranges over much of Africa from Senegal to Abyssinia, Mozambique to South-West Africa, is also known as Village Weaver, Black-headed or Black-headed Village Weaver, V-marked Weaver, Golden Oriole and Spotted-backed Weaver, but the name most often used in aviculture is Rufous-necked Weaver. It is common around native settlements, building its nests in isolated trees over the village water-

hole, and is found in other areas, usually swamps or rivers. There may be hundreds of nests in one tree, each a separate unit, and not forming a united whole as, for example, the Social Weaver. The retort-shaped nest has the entrance-hole at the bottom. The species is parasitized in the wild by the Emerald Cuckoo.

The Rufous-neck has a large sharp bill, and wicked-looking red eyes. It has a bad reputation for being unpredictably murderous, and should not be kept with any bird not its equal. I have kept odd males and pairs in small aviaries with waxbills and munias, but have never had a single incident. Mine all proved to be totally hardy, able to winter outside without heat. Rutgers says that 'they may be induced to breed', but I know of no authentic record in Britain, although it might have been bred on the Continent.

Little Masked Weaver
(*Ploceus luteola*)

Description: *4½ in. (114·3 mm.).
Adult male in colour, forehead, lores,
cheeks, ear-coverts, chin to throat
black; mantle greenish yellow faintly
streaked; wings and tail dusky edged
yellow; rest of body bright even yellow; bill black; eyes red. Out of
colour, top of head green; back buff
streaked with dusky, lores and ear-
coverts to breast buff; belly white;
bill horn-colour. Female in colour resembles eclipsed male but has sides
of face to breast pale yellow; bill
black. Out of colour female resembles eclipsed male but is white
below, washed buff on breast and
flanks, and yellowish on cheeks and
undertail-coverts. Juveniles resemble
eclipsed female.*

Other names for this small bird
include Atlas Weaver (not to be used
since it is used in the trade for any
unidentified black-faced weaver), Little
Weaver (the common name for *Ploceus
monacha*) and Slender-billed Weaver.
Bannerman refers to the nominate
race as Lichtenstein's Slender-billed
Weaver. It is a common little bird
that ranges from Senegal across to
Kenya. It is rather warbler-like in
size and body-colouring, and in activities also, for it is an arboreal bird
of light woodland and searches agilely
for insects among the leaves and
branches. It is not gregarious, but as
many as ten nests have been recorded
in one tree; they are very often placed
alongside wasps' nests. The nest is
retort shaped and has a short
entrance-spout hanging down. It is
one of the smallest weavers' nests.
The Little Masked Weaver has been
bred in captivity, but I cannot find
sufficient evidence to support Rutger's
remark that it is 'one of the most

free-breeding of all the species'.
Shore Baily had a pair in 1914 that
built a nest suspended from a branch
over the pond. These birds reared on
insects that they caught themselves,
supplemented by mealworms. Mr.
Shore Baily's enclosures were not
noted for their smallness.

West African Little Weaver
(*Ploceus monacha*)

Description: *4½ in. (114·3 mm.).
Adult male closely resembles* luteola,
*above. May be distinguished by hav-
ing mantle clear and unstreaked,
below it is a richer yellow, deeper
on the flanks; another point of difference is in the nape; in* monacha *it is
golden yellow but in* luteola *the green
of the mantle edges on to the nape;
the bill of* monacha *is straighter
and finer. Female is different from
female* luteola, *has all upperparts
bright olive yellow, unstreaked,
with clear yellow superciliary, underparts bright yellow; bill black. There
is no eclipse plumage. Juveniles
resemble dull, paler female; bill
horn-colour.*

This beautiful little weaver has a
similar habitat to the Little Masked,
but is less common and is restricted
to West Africa, from the Congo to
Gambia. The nest lacks the entrance-
spout of most species and may be
suspended from a leaf or grass stem,
near by or, more likely, over water.
The species is more colonial in habit
than *luteola*, and is more gregarious
outside the breeding season. I have
no note of it occurring in captivity,
but the chances are very high
that had it appeared (which I think
most probable) it would have been
sold as a Little Masked or Atlas
Weaver.

Half-masked Weaver
(*Ploceus vitellinus*)

Description: *About 5 in. (127 mm.). Adult male in colour, very similar to* luteola *but larger and lacks black on forehead; forehead and crown chestnut which fades into golden yellow on nape; throat strongly washed with orange chestnut; bill black; eye yellow. Out of colour, loses black on head, and is mainly green above, noticeably streaked blackish; pale yellow below, whiter on belly; bill horn-colour. Female, in colour, olivaceous yellow above, streaked with blackish on mantle; chin and throat yellow; breast and flanks yellowy buff; belly whitish, undertail-coverts yellow. Out of colour, less green above, paler below without buff tinges; bill horn-colour. Juveniles similar to eclipsed female but less green above and buffish on throat in place of pale yellow.*

The Half-masked, Ruppell's, Vitelline or Vitelline Masked Weaver is another west African species that ranges from Senegal across to the Sudan. It is a bird of wild scrub, nesting in colonies in acacia groves. The nest, suspended from a twig, is

Half-masked Weaver (*Ploceus vitellinus*): female left, male on the right

shaped like an inverted heart and the entrance tunnel is so short that it is hardly noticed. The species is very similar in appearance to Heuglin's Masked Weaver and the Tanzania Masked Weaver, but to avoid confusion I will describe each briefly.

Half-masked Weavers are imported regularly and do well in captivity, being hardy and more peaceful than most. They are good mixers in a roomy flight and will weave their kidney-shaped nests from the tips of branches. They have been bred on several occasions. Two reports I have are of Shore Baily in 1916 and Canon Lowe in 1959. They take a fair amount of live food when rearing, most of which is apparently done by the female.

Heuglin's Masked Weaver
(*Ploceus heuglini*)

Description: *About 5 in. (127 mm.). Adult male in colour, resembles* vitellinus *but has no chestnut or orange, and black of throat extends to a point in the centre of breast (where there tends to be a suffusion of chestnut-orange), but it does not extend behind the eye as it does in* vitellinus; *bill black; eye pale yellow. Out of colour, greenish above, chin to undertail-coverts yellow; bill horn-colour. Female in colour olivaceous green above with dusky streaks; below bright yellow, ochreous on breast, whitish on belly; bill black; eye cream. Out of colour, green above duller, streaked dusky; duller yellow below; bill horn-colour. Juvenile resembles eclipsed female.*

This species, which closely resembles the Half-masked Weaver, is a bird of dry grass country. It ranges from West Africa to the Sudan and Kenya, is rather shy and avoids areas

of human habitation. It breeds in colonies of four to seven pairs and, like many weavers, often nests in trees where wasps or stinging flying ants are nesting: in these cases a colony may contain more pairs. Like the Rufous-necked Weaver, it is a compulsive nest-builder, and will build as long as there is suitable material available. 'Cocks' nests' are built, or half-built, almost at random.

Tanzania Masked Weaver
(*Ploceus reichardi*)

Description: *About 5 in. (127 mm.). Adult male in colour, very similar to* vitellinus *but chestnut more noticeable and extends over breast and flanks. Female very similar to* vitellinus; *bill is shorter. No descriptions of eclipse or juvenile plumage available.*

This bird is described for comparison with the Half-masked Weaver. It comes from south-western Tanzania and nothing relevant to avicultural needs seems to be known. The species is listed in most of the literature as Tanganyika Masked Weaver.

Masked Weaver
(*Ploceus intermedius*)

Description: *About 5 in. (127 mm.). Adult male in colour, very similar to* vitellinus *but has forehead and fore-crown black also. Out of colour, it is similar to* vitellinus *again but yellower on sides of face, with clear yellow superciliary. Female resembles eclipsed male but more olivaceous green, less yellowy; bill black. Out of colour, it is less yellowy still, duller and more streaked above. Juveniles are duller than adult female, browner above and white below, chest buff yellow.*

This is a bird of East and southern Africa. The eastern bird, *P. i. intermedius*, is semi-gregarious, nesting in small colonies up to ten pairs, according to Praed and Grant, in any kind of country, but usually near water though not necessarily over it. The nests may be built in tall trees, bushes or even reeds. The southern bird, *P. i. cabanisii*, is sometimes called Cabani's Weaver or Lesser Masked Weaver. It is apparently more of a waterside bird, and the nests are usually low over water. The nest is round with a short, hanging tubular entrance-spout. It is a great weaver and will produce endless nests. I do not think it has been bred in captivity.

Baglefecht Weaver
(*Ploceus baglafecht*)

Description: *About 6 in. (152·4 mm.). Adult male in colour, forehead and forecrown yellow; crown and nape yellowish green; mantle green with faint streaks; rump green; tail brown washed green; lores to ear-coverts black (chin sometimes black also); sides of face, chin to undertail-coverts yellow, belly whitish; bill black. Out of colour, above ashy washed buff, and streaked with black on back, blackish streaks in place of mask; below buff; bill still black. Female, in colour resembles male but has forehead greenish, and mask duller. Out of colour, resembles male. Juveniles resemble female but lack mask; young males are yellow on throat and breast, young females buff.*

This is a common bird of the high plateau of Abyssinia but is a rare one in captivity. I have only seen it on two occasions. It is not gregarious so one need not feel the need to establish a small colony in order to breed them; settles well, is quite hardy, and moderately insectivorous when breeding.

Black-headed Weaver
(*Ploceus melanocephalus*)

Description: *5½ in. (139·7 mm.). Adult male in colour, entire head and upper breast black; neck, uppertail-coverts, chest to undertail-coverts golden yellow; back yellowish green; wings black with yellow edges; tail green; bill black; eye brown or yellow. Out of colour, head olivaceous; back brown streaked dusky; rump plain brown; uppertail-coverts greenish; faint yellow superciliary; below buff, whitish on throat and belly; bill horn-colour. Female resembles eclipsed male throughout the year, but is smaller. Juveniles resemble female.*

This lovely little weaver is found in western and South Africa, and is particularly fond of swampy country; in West Africa it seems to prefer mimosa groves, and in east papyrus swamps or near rivers and lakes. I once bought five of these birds, apparently three males and two females, but the latter eventually moulted out to be males. What is frustrating about this – with any weaver – is that the weaving is never finished off, and one's flight becomes filled with half-finished 'cocks' nests'. This is because the female is needed, as the male's partner, to complete the nest. I kept them in a large unplanted flight with breeding Budgerigars, Cockatiels and Lovebirds, and they successfully provided action and entertainment. They thrived on the parakeets' seeds and millet sprays. They never seemed at all aggressive. It was first bred in 1912, and I expect that a few breedings have occurred since then.

Southern Masked Weaver
(*Ploceus velatus*)

Description: *About 5½ in. (139·7 mm.). Very similar to* vitellinus *but has narrow line of black on front of forehead; crown saffron, not chestnut, black extends to touch breast; breast flushed with saffron, not chestnut; eye orange red. Out of colour, mantle streaked dusky, not blackish. Female differs from female* vitellinus *by having dusky streaks on mantle, not black. Juveniles resemble eclipsed female.*

This bird is known in South Africa as simply Masked Weaver. It is common in many urban areas, making its presence known by stripping foliage from the trees and suspending its round nests at the end of the bared stems. Like all weavers it is a chattering, fizzing, noisy creature when breeding. It is an omnivorous bird, taking seeds, insects, fruit, and soft parts of flowers and buds. It was first bred in captivity at the Zoological Society gardens in London in 1892.

Baya Weaver
(*Ploceus philippinus*)

Description: *6 in. (152·4 mm.). Adult male in colour, forehead, lores, sides of head, chin and throat dark blackish brown; remainder of head and breast bright yellow; upper plumage brownish black, the feathers margined with yellow; rump and rest of underparts fulvous; wings and tail blackish brown edged with fulvous; bill dark brown. Out of colour, fulvous above, streaked with blackish brown; rump unstreaked; superciliary fulvous; cheeks, breast and flanks brown; rest of body fulvous. Females and juveniles resemble eclipsed male.*

The Baya Weaver does look very much like a female House Sparrow when out of breeding plumage, and in this condition is not very popular in the trade. It ranges over most of India and Ceylon and also occurs in Burma, extending to Thailand, throughout the Malay Peninsula, Java and Sumatra. During the winter it does a lot of damage to seed-crops, but when breeding it feeds its young on a great deal of live food and so redresses the balance somewhat. It prefers grassland or open cultivated, arable land which is dotted with copses and clumps of trees, in which the colonies are developed. A colony, which may amount to a dozen or so pairs – but on occasion may include a hundred – is started by a few male birds. These unmated birds begin their nests, stimulated by each others' performances, and the nearer completion the more attempts are made to attract females. The nests are in fact almost completed before the females get in on the act and, apparently, select a

Male Baya Weaver (*Ploceus philippinus*)

nest. The male is subsequently accepted, and together they finish the nest off. The female lines the nest chamber while the male completes the long pendant entrance tunnel.

The males are often recommended as subjects for a bachelor collection and as such are good value, for they advance their nests to near-completion alone. I have only kept them as pairs and have found them to be invariably spiteful and too aggressive for ordinary mixed collections. In my opinion they are ideal for the kind of large planted aviary in which pheasants and pigeons are normally kept together. A small flock is wonderfully entertaining and the nests – providing adequate material is available – are spectacular, up to 3 ft. (914·4 mm.) in length has been recorded, but mine never got past 12 in. (304·8 mm.).

Striated Weaver
(*Ploceus manyar*)

Description: *About 6 in. (152·4 mm.). Adult male in colour has forehead and entire crown golden yellow; rest of upperparts dark brown; chin and throat brown; breast and flanks light fulvous heavily streaked brown; bill black. Out of colour, entire upper-surface dark brown streaked by fulvous edges to feathers; superciliary and short transverse line across neck yellow; below, pale fulvous washed with yellow on throat; bill horn-colour. Female in colour resembles male but lacks yellow crown; out of colour resembles male completely. Juvenile resembles out-of-colour adult.*

The Striated Weaver reminds one of a less colourful Baya Weaver. It is widely distributed from Ceylon and India to Burma and Java. The Indian race described above, *flaviceps*, is replaced in Burma by *pequensis*, which apparently is much more richly coloured. The nominate race, *manyar*, comes from Java. It is a bird of thick reed-beds along riversides, or marshy land where it breeds in small colonies of half a dozen or so pairs. It builds a similar nest to the Baya, but is thicker and less elegant. It is identical to the Baya in captivity, but is maybe less aggressive, and has successfully bred.

Black-throated Weaver
(*Ploceus bengalensis*)

Description: *5½ in. (139·7 mm.). Adult male in colour, very similar to* P. manyar *(above) but has blackish band on sides of throat tending to form a bar; reddish brown below. Out of colour, lacks yellow on throat. Female resembles female* manyar *in both plumages. Juveniles resemble female.*

Possibly more commonly known as the Bengal Weaver, this species comes from northern India, and is equally dully coloured out of season. However, when in breeding condition it more than compensates by its energetic and tireless nest-building. Unmated birds will not complete their nests. When breeding, as with all weavers, live food is essential.

Chestnut Weaver
(*Ploceus rubiginosus*)

Description: *About 6½ in. (165·1 mm.). Adult male in colour, head black; rest of plumage chestnut; wings and tail black edged buffish; bill black. Out of colour, light earth brown above, broadly streaked with black except on rump; wing-feathers edged pale buff; sides of face and all* underparts fawn, except throat and belly which are whitish; bill horn-colour. *Female similar to eclipsed male but smaller, and greyer on breast and flanks. Juvenile birds resemble eclipsed male, but young males have an intermediate paler version of adult male plumage.*

This interesting weaver is found over much of East Africa, and has rather strange poorly recorded breeding habits. It appears that having built the nests the males go off and form their own bachelor colonies, leaving the females to get on with the family business. The colonies are densely packed and very noisy. I have only seen males in captivity and suppose that this sexual segregation is the reason, for not only would a native trapper be inclined to ignore a colony of sparrow-like birds, but would probably regard an all-male colony as containing both sexes, since immature males would be mistaken for females. In captivity it should not be kept with small finches or waxbills. It will do well in a roomy cage, but behaves rather more naturally in a roomy flight.

Golden Palm Weaver
(Ploceus bojeri)

Description: *About 5½ in. (139·7 mm.). Adult male, entire body golden yellow, head and throat orange; breast saffron; mantle, wings and tail washed with olive; bill black. Female mustard yellow above, lightly streaked with dusky on back; wings dusky edged yellow; tail olivaceous yellow; below bright yellow; bill horn-colour. Juvenile like female but paler below. No eclipse plumage.*

This species is a bird of coastal East Africa, ranging from the Somali Republic to Tanzania; it is not common but is gregarious and forms noisy chattering colonies in palm trees. Like the Golden Weaver a small flock in a roomy aviary will be both very attractive and entertaining.

Spectacled Weaver
(Ploceus ocularis)

Description: *About 6 in. (152·4 mm.). Adult male, forehead and crown golden yellow, rest of upperparts yellowish olive, paler on rump; cheeks golden yellow; lores black, extending to behind the eye; chin and centre of throat black; entire underparts bright yellow, flushed orange on breast; bill black; eye pale yellow. Female resembles male but lacks black of chin and throat. Juvenile resembles female but has bill horn-colour. There are no seasonal changes of plumage.*

The Spectacled Weaver has previously been placed in the genus *Hyphanturgus*. These birds are noteworthy for the fact that they have no change of plumage into and out of the breeding season. The Spectacled Weaver, the widest-spread member of the group, is found over most of central Africa except in the tropical rain forest, and in East Africa down to the Cape. It is usually seen singly or in pairs, and is rather a shy weaver which normally keeps to matted bush or the tree canopy where it creeps about the foliage hunting insects. The retort-shaped nest may have an entrance-spout hanging down for a few inches or a few feet! It is built of green grasses and shredded palm leaves, etc., and is usually suspended from papyrus leaves, creepers or branches, often low over water. It is very insectivorous, as its finely pointed bill might suggest, but it also takes berries and flowers. In captivity it will take the usual seeds, mostly millet, but will thrive best if given some mealworms and/or maggots regularly. It may be persuaded to take a little universal soft food. I do not know if it has bred in captivity.

Reichnow's Weaver
(*Ploceus reichenowi*)

Description: *About 6½ in. (165·1 mm.). Adult male has forehead and forecrown yellow, continued as a line behind the ear-coverts and nape to join the underparts, which are entirely yellow, washed with orange on throat and upper breast; lores, round*

the yellow line between ear-coverts is often broken in both sexes. *P. r. nigrotemporalis* ranges from southern Abyssinia to north-west Kenya, and lacks the yellow line entirely. Incidentally there is no eclipse plumage at all. The species may be encountered in pairs or small parties (possibly family groups) in various kinds of country, but is fairly common in woodland clearings, the edges of forests or bushy scrub. *Nigrotemporalis* is an upland race occurring above 6,000 ft. (1,828·8 m.). It is said to be practically omnivorous and is recorded as taking grass-seeds,

Reichenow's Weaver
(*Ploceus reichenowi*)

eyes, ear-coverts and rest of upperparts black; wing-feathers edged with yellow; uppertail-coverts mixed black and yellowish olive; tail olive green. Female has entire top of head black. Juveniles are olive green above, streaked with black.

There are three races of this bird, all from East Africa. The most widespread is the nominate described above. *P. r. fricki*, from southern Abyssinia, which is distinguished by having olive green on the mantle and

berries and insects. It is not a colonial species and is a solitary nester, so the aviculturist can dismiss thoughts of needing several pairs for breeding. The nest is a solid-looking affair suspended from a palm leaf or a twig, and is built out of green material by the male, lined with seed-heads by the female.

The only breeding in captivity that I know of was by Creed in London in 1954. The pair were kept in an aviary with a couple of dozen breeding Border Canaries, and a few British birds. The young were fed on mealworms, maggots, fruit, bread and milk, and flies. Mr. Creed, as an aquarist, successfully experimented with *enchytrae* (white worms). An interesting point in the report was that the male weaver, not content with doing most of the feeding, also fed young Canaries with mealworms.

Forest Weaver
(*Ploceus bicolor*)

Description: *About* $6\frac{1}{2}$ *in. (165·1 mm.). Adult male has entire head and throat, all upperparts black; breast to undertail-coverts golden yellow. Sexes alike; there is no eclipse plumage. Juvenile has chin and throat yellow, flecked black; otherwise resembles adult.*

The Forest Weaver is also listed as Dark-backed Weaver, and according to Allen Silver may well have been sold as Reichnow's Weaver, which name tends to be used for any black-backed weaver. It is widespread over most of Africa south of the Sahara, but although Praed and Grant include west Africa in its distribution it is never mentioned by Bannerman. There are several races throughout eastern, South and South-West Africa, but I do not consider it worth while describing each. It is certainly not imported very often, being a bird of arboreal habit, occurring in bush forests and thick cover. It is quite insectivorous, hunting insects with the agility of titmice, but also takes some berries. It is not gregarious, although small parties of up to a dozen birds are found in winter, and is not a colonial breeder.

Golden Weaver
(*Ploceus subaureus*)

Description: $5\frac{1}{2}$ *in. (139·7 mm.). Adult male in breeding plumage entirely yellow, suffused with green above, head and upper breast saffron; bill black; eye red. Out of colour, greener above; saffron much reduced; bill horn-colour. Female in colour resembles out-of-colour male but is lightly striated above, and has bill black. Out of colour, more heavily streaked above; belly whitish; bill horn-colour. Juvenile resembles out-of-colour female but has greener head, more dusky above; young female breast to undertail-coverts white.*

This beautiful bird ranges throughout East Africa from Kenya to Mozambique. It is a common and

Golden Weaver
(*Ploceus subaureus*)

highly gregarious bird that has been confused with the Golden Palm Weaver on many occasions; it has less orange on the head and the upper mandible of the Golden Palm Weaver out of colour is darker. It is, however, more widespread and more often imported. I have not kept it for long, but it struck me as being perfectly suitable for a mixed collection, and very easy to look after. It has been bred a long time ago, but I have no details of the occasions. It is ideal as a colourful bird to have as a flock in a large planted aviary. The nest is a ball with the entrance below, but there is no spectacular pendant tunnel.

Black Mountain Weaver
(*Ploceus melanogaster*)

Description: *About 6 in. (152·4 mm.). Adult male, forehead, crown and sides of face, and a narrow band across the lower throat from cheek to cheek yellow; streak through eye and rest of body black. Female has chin and throat yellow as well as yellow cheeks and forefront of head, remainder of body black. Eye red; bill black. Juvenile has head and underparts greenish olive yellow; upperparts from nape to tail dull black; bill horn-colour.*

The Black Mountain Weaver ranges across eastwards from West Africa to the Sudan where it is replaced by the race *stephanophorus*, which has been called Black-billed Weaver. According to Bannerman it is a bird of mountain country, occurring above 5,000 ft. (1,524 m.) and the East African race also appears to be a highlands bird. Its preferred habitat is thick undergrowth and it is described as skulking, secretive and shy. Little wonder that it is rarely imported. A pair were recently displayed at the London Zoo. It takes seeds, berries and insects, and notes on its behaviour in captivity would be most welcome.

Vieillot's Black Weaver
(*Ploceus nigerrimus*)

Description: *About 7½ in. (190·5 mm.). Adult male, entirely black, faintly brownish on wings and tail; bill black; eye lemon yellow; feet light brown. Adult female, brownish olive above with dark and black centres to the feathers; uppertail-coverts uniform olive brown; below olive, yellowish on belly; bill, upper mandible dark grey, lower yellowish grey; eye ochre; feet light brown. Immature birds resemble female but are lightly streaked below; young males have yellow eye and are blacker streaked above; there are many intermediary plumages. Young female has a brown eye.*

This species may be listed under the genus *Melanopteryx*. The adult male has the base of the nape feathers grey, but these are entirely concealed. Should the owner notice this grey, especially when the bird is held in the hand, it might be concluded that in fact one has a White-naped Weaver, *Ploceus (Melanopteryx) albinucha albinucha*. This latter bird can be distinguished by its eye colour, which is pearly white. The nape feathers of the White-naped Weaver are white with black fringes, the feet are a dirty flesh colour. The females are identical. Maxwell's Black Weaver, *Ploceus (Melanopteryx) albinucha maxwelli*, has the bases of the nape feathers grey, as in *P. nigerrimus*, and these too are concealed; furthermore, the eye is variable depending on the individual, and may be anything from cream white to lemon or greenish yellow. It may be distinguished by the feet, which are brownish black, and a noticeable but very dark brownish cast to the underparts. The plumage of this bird is quite glossy. A very interesting point to note is that the female of Maxwell's Black Weaver has the same black plumage as the male. None of the three species discussed here has an eclipse plumage; once assumed, the adult plumage of black feathering remains all the year round.

Vieillot's Black Weaver is similar in size and shape to the Rufous-necked Weaver (*Ploceus cucullatus*), and has very similar habits. Indeed the two species are often found in each others' company, and may even form mixed breeding colonies. It

ranges from eastern Nigeria across Uganda.

The White-naped Weaver is a bird of Sierra Leone and Liberia, while Maxwell's Black Weaver is found on Fernando Po and in the forests of Cameroon. While the White-Naped bird appears to be similar to Vieillot's in habits, *maxwelli* is a bird of the upper levels of the forest trees.

All three birds are easy to maintain in captivity. De Winter has bred Vieillot's Black Weaver and remarked upon how easy it was to breed. Hybrids with the Black-crowned Weaver were produced but died at five days old. From the avicultural point of view these are typical *Ploceus* species, requiring the same treatment as for *P. cucullatus*.

BROWN WEAVERS

The weavers in this section are those normally grouped in various ways apart from the *Ploceus* and other yellow weavers. What sets them apart as a group is their predominantly brown streaky plumage, which is sometimes relieved by red. In captivity they require the same treatment, deserving to be kept in aviaries where they can build their nests and display in the most attractive way. As a generalization also, they will rear young on unripe seeds and insects. Whilst most of the following weavers are less spectacular, generally being duller in plumage and less colonial in habit, they are extremely interesting birds, and well repay careful attention and close study. As with the previous group, the literature abounds with 'has been bred' remarks, but details are few and far between.

Madagascar Weaver
(*Foudia madagascariensis*)

Description: *5–5½ in. (127–139·7 mm.). Adult male in colour, bright crimson all over the body, with lores and stripe through the eye, and streaks on back and wing-coverts black; wings and tail brown, edged*

with reddish; bill black. Out of colour, brown above, heavily streaked with darker brown; below yellow, washed with brown on breast and flanks. Female resembles eclipsed male.

I have seen this bird on several occasions on the Continent, both in collections and, on a couple of occasions, in pet shops. I have not been able to trace the source of supply, however. It is a native of Madagascar, not occurring on mainland Africa at all, and unfortunately no birds from the island ever seem to turn up in the dealers' lists. I have only studied the species in the company of other weavers and it has appeared to be quite typical in its requirements and behaviour. It is fairly gregarious and flocks descend on crops to make a nuisance of themselves, and do considerable damage in paddy fields, but it also takes fruit in season, berries and a wide variety of foods. It is also known as the Madagascar Fody. Occasionally some xanthochroic specimens show up, when the bright red is replaced by bright yellow. According to Shore Baily it is very quarrelsome in an aviary. Apparently it has been bred in Germany and in France, '. . . in M. Delacour's aviaries, a cock Madagascar Weaver mated to a hen *Hyphantornis vitellinus* (Half-masked Weaver). They mated in 1910 and 1911 in a nesting-box. Three young were reared, two of which were females and quite similar to a hen Madagascar Weaver; the cock, when two years old, developed a pale orange creamy colour.'

Thick-billed Weaver
(*Amblyospiza albifrons*)

Description: *About 7 in. (177·8 mm.). Adult male has forehead white (extent is variable); rest of head to mantle and breast dark brown; rest of upperparts sooty brown; white patch to base of primaries; underparts sooty grey; bill large, blackish. In fresh winter plumage the feathers are all tipped with brown and white, which wears off as spring approaches. Female brown above with lighter*

edges to the feathers; off-white below streaked with blackish; bill horn-colour. Juvenile resembles female; bill yellowish.

This species is known as Grosbeak Weaver, Hawfinch Weaver and White-fronted Weaver. There are about nine races with varying degrees of sootiness to the plumage, white forehead and bill size. Bannerman, as usual, gives each race a distinct common name, i.e. Ashanti White-fronted Grosbeak (*A. a. capitalba*) and Cameroons White-fronted

Head of female Grosbeak Weaver
(*Amblyospiza albifrons*)

Grosbeak (*A. a. saturata*). As the species is distributed in one form or other over most of Africa south of the Sahara I suggest that anyone fortunate enough to own it, and who cares to identify it exactly, should refer to Mackworth-Praed and Grant, and Bannerman.

It is a bird of low-lying swampy areas, living in reed-beds where it also breeds. Despite its large bill it weaves exquisite nests of the finest materials, retort-shaped, but whether there is an extended porch entrance or not depends on the race. It feeds on seeds, berries (cracking kernels of cherry-stone size) and fruit, and apparently rears the young entirely on this diet. In captivity they are shy and retiring until thoroughly settled in and seem to use their awesome bill in defence only. They have been kept with wax-bills with no problems, but this is not to be recommended on two counts: (a) whether peaceful or not their size will unsettle the waxbills, and (b) since no reports are available on breeding behaviour in captivity it cannot be certain that a breeding pair will not be aggressive. They are gregarious, and will often breed in mixed colonies with other weavers in the wild, but this is no guarantee of a peaceful nature. I recently received a pair that lived happily with some Wild Canaries, *Sicalis* finches and a Sky-lark. Unfortunately, the male soon died, but the female continues to live a contented life with these birds. They will take a wide variety of seeds, in-cluding sunflower and oats, and appreciate the odd mealworm (in this case meant for the Skylark) as most weavers in fact do.

Red-headed Weaver
(*Anaplectes melanotis*)

Description: *About 6½ in. (165·1 mm.). Adult male in colour, lores, ear-coverts to chin black; rest of head to chest scarlet red; all upper-surfaces dark greyish brown with red edges to some of the mantle, wing and tail-feathers; underparts whitish; bill red. Out of colour the bird is greyer above with no red on the back. Female, wholly grey above, white below with a grey wash on chest; edges of flight and tail-feathers edged with red; bill red. Juveniles are similar to adult female but rather olivaceous on the head; sides of face and chest buff; edges of flight and tail-feathers orange yellow; bill dusky soon be-coming reddish.*

From a careful comparison of field guides it appears that birds from West Africa are browner above than those from East Africa, which are greyer. Its common name should not confuse it with the Red-headed Quelea, and one is inclined to follow Bannerman and call it Red-headed or Red-winged Anaplectes. A race from south-eastern Africa, *A. m. rubriceps*, is considered by some authorities to be a distinct species. The adult male has little or no black on the head; the edges of the flight and tail-feathers are yellow; the mantle in breeding plumage is black mottled with red, and grey out of colour. It has been called Yellow-winged Anaplectes. A third race, *A. m. jubaensis*, differs by the adult male having the entire underside bright red. It comes from Somalia. It is a large weaver, not often im-ported since it is a bird of the upper levels of the tall trees of the light woodland it frequents. As such it is not often netted.

Red-billed Weaver
(*Quelea quelea*)

Description: *About 5 in. (127 mm.). Adult male in colour, forehead, sides of face, chin and throat black or blackish brown; rest of upperparts buff to earth streaked with blackish; wing and tail-feathers edged buffish pale yellow; breast, sides of neck to belly tawny rose; undertail-coverts off-white; eye-ring and bill red. Out of colour, buff to greyish brown above, streaked with dusky; below buff, whitish on throat; bill red. Female in colour has bill yellow; out of colour the bill is red. Juveniles have the bill horn-colour. In other respects both are indistinguishable from eclipsed male.*

This species, perhaps the commonest in Africa at one time, is very widespread over all of Africa south of the Sahara. It is variously called Quelea, Red-billed Quelea, Common Dioch, Black-faced Dioch. They are highly prolific and are opportunistic breeders, the breeding stimulus being provided by the rainy season, and the great wandering flocks settle to breed at wherever they happen to be at the moment the conditions are correct. Unlike most other weavers they are able to breed at one year old. Nesting colonies may cover areas acres across,

Head of male Red-billed Weaver
(*Quelea quelea*)

but are ephemeral things, the entire colony being vacated at practically the same time. Since the entire flock will move on as soon as the breeding cycle has been completed, the male participates in the whole business. Both birds incubate by day, but only the female broods at night. This is in direct contrast with the majority of weavers, when the males begin building new nests for new females as soon as the first one is sitting tight. The Common Quelea has been so numerous at times, with flocks containing *millions* of birds, that governments have organized ruthless methods of wiping them out. The reed-bed roosts have been bombed with napalm, and tree-roosts dynamited; poisoned grain has also been used. The result, after

a dozen years of determined and co-ordinated effort, has been to reduce this locust-like pest to the population levels of other species. At the date of publication it looks as though this is one problem that may be coming under control, without its control raising fresh problems.

In aviary, the Red-billed Weaver is a rather dull and not very dramatic bird. Even when it is in full colour it tends to be eclipsed by its bright yellow and black cousins. It undoubtedly does better in a small colony than as odd birds. Odd males I have kept have been dismal failures as weavers, aimlessly threading grass and straw through the wire mesh. Half a dozen will weave nests in suitable sites and in a planted aviary may well breed. Several breedings have been reported (nearly always when two pairs were present) and feeding requirements have proved to be reasonably simple, mealworms being the only live food provided on one occasion. Considering the large number of birds imported each year, breedings are extremely rare, however.

There is a morph of this species that is occasionally imported in which the black of the face is replaced by the rose-tawny colour which normally surrounds it. At one time this was considered to be a separate species, or a race, and was called Russ's Weaver.

Red-headed Quelea
(*Quelea erythrops*)

Description: *4½–5 in. (114·3–127 mm.). Adult male in colour very similar to* Q. quelea, *but has entire head red, usually with a black chin; tail is shorter; bill black. Out-of-colour males are darker than* quelea, have horn-colour bills and are washed with yellow on superciliary and sides of face. Female resembles eclipsed male. Juvenile resembles eclipsed adult but has paler edges to feathers on upperparts.

This bird is as widely distributed over Africa as its better-known relative above. It is not so common, however, and is far less frequently imported. I cannot understand why. It is also called Red-headed Weaver and Red-headed Dioch. It should not be confused with the Red-headed Anaplectes. According to Mr. Yealland and Shore Baily it has been bred, presumably only on the Continent (Shore Baily mentioned Germany), for I can find no record. It is a very attractive bird, slightly smaller than the Red-billed Weaver. I have found it to be tamer, much less wild and more suitable for life in cages than its relative.

Cardinal Quelea
(*Quelea cardinalis*)

Description: $4\frac{1}{2}$ in. (114·3 mm.). Adult male in colour has entire head crimson red, back of head and nape streaked with tawny and black suf-fused with red; flanks lightly streaked with dusky; bill black; otherwise like quelea. Out of colour resembles quelea but is streaked on head, tinged olive yellow and often suffused with red; bill horn-colour. Female resembles eclipsed male but never has red on head; may be told from female quelea by smaller size and smaller bill. Juvenile resembles female but is browner and is speckled lightly on chest.

The Cardinal Quelea is another bird that may be called Red-headed Weaver, a term not advisedly used in this case. It may be told from the Red-headed Quelea, when the latter has no black chin, by the streaking on the breast. It is an East African bird, ranging over grassland often in the company of other queleas from southern Abyssinia to north-western Tanzania. It is the smallest of the genus, and a charming gentle bird. I have kept it happily in a cage and have seen it whizzing about a planted aviary with strips of reed in its bill, building its unusual pouch-shaped nest. The entrance is near the top, to one side, and I believe that in suitable cover the nest is placed so that a leaf may be drawn over the top to 'close' it.

· BISHOPS AND WHYDAHS

There are about sixteen species in the group of birds known as bishops and whydahs. They are very closely related, and appear in Peters's checklist as all being in the one genus *Euplectes*. However, nearly all avicultural handbooks and most field guides will place all of these whydahs in one or more distinct genera. For example, the majority are placed under *Coliuspasser*, but a diligent researcher will also find reference to *Drepanoplectes*, *Chera*, *Urobrachya* and others. I have attempted to follow Peters when-

Left: Yellow-shouldered Whydah (*Euplectes macrocercus*). Right: White-winged Whydah (*Euplectes albonatus*). Both are adult males in breeding plumage

ever possible and will do so here, but it is worth stressing that with the exception of Jackson's Whydah, which is generally given the monotypic genus of *Drepanoplectes*, all of the whydahs here are usually to be found under *Coliuspasser*.

All the males here have a dramatic breeding plumage of velvety black, with patches of bright red, orange or yellow. In many, large areas of the body feathers, usually the red/yellow, are fluffed out; in others the feathers of the nape are semi-erect, thereby forming a ruff. Many of the whydahs have elongated tail-feathers, referred to by most writers as 'widow's weeds'. In many works the common name for a whydah is widow or widow-bird. A full explanation of the origins of these names is given in the introduction to the chapter on the brood-parasitic whydahs, the Viduinae, which may be referred to as the 'true' whydahs. Out of the breeding season the males closely resemble the females, which are sparrowy and short-tailed. The females are generally smaller, however, and by no means as difficult to distinguish as most female weavers. They are typical birds of the African savanna and require long grass both for breeding and feeding. Most of them are found in lowland savanna, but there are a few exceptions: *Euplectes afer* inhabits swamp country and reed-beds along river banks, while *E. capensis* ascends to 6,000 ft. (1,828·8 m.) or so in the Cameroons, and East Africa.

For reason of their striking and beautiful plumages they are very popular birds in captivity. Breedings are rare, although not unobtainable; but unfortunately so many aviculturists want variety that few are able to give these birds the conditions that are needed to encourage them to breed. For example, the kind of large aviary that may contain a pair of pheasants, or a few ornamental ducks, may well be planted with a stand of bamboo or reeds. In such an enclosure some of the bishops would undoubtedly thrive. The males become rather territorial and much chasing and pursuing takes place. The smaller bishops remind me of fluffy clockwork toys, and a couple of displaying males certainly do not resemble one's preconceived idea of a bird in display. Each male stakes out its own territory and patrols the boundaries erratically, marking them with a simple display. Often several nests are started by the male, but not finished. The wandering females select their males and finish off their chosen nest. The males are quite polygamous and may manage to maintain harems of half a dozen or more females. If breeding is seriously envisaged an aviary should not be crowded, and it would be better if females outnumbered the males. As a crude generalization, the smaller the species, the more may be accommodated in one enclosure.

Orix Bishop
(*Euplectes orix*)

There are five races of *E. orix*, at least two of which are often treated as being distinct species in some text-books, and they have different common names. The name I have given above is not often used, except in this context. I will therefore describe them individually, giving each the common name most frequently used.

Grenadier Weaver
(*E. o. orix*)

Description: *About 6 in. (152·4 mm.).
Adult male in colour has forehead,
crown, sides of head and chin, lower
breast and belly black; rest of body
bright red to scarlet, brownish on
mantle; wings and tail dusky edged
with buff; bill black. Out of colour,
streaked dusky with buff above;
below, buff streaked with dusky on
breast and flanks; bill horn-colour.
Female resembles eclipsed male but
is more clearly streaked below.
Juvenile resembles non-breeding adult
but has broader buff edges to
feathers.*

This race, which may be called
Grenadier Bishop, Red, Scarlet or
Crimson Grenadier, Red Bishop, or
Red Coffee Tink, comes from South
Africa. It is the largest race, and
much sought after.

Red-crowned Grenadier
(*E. o. sundevalli*)

Description: *About 5½ in. (139·7
mm.). Adult male differs from orix in
having the red a richer reddish orange
that extends to cover the crown and
ear-coverts; the tail-coverts almost
hide the tail completely. It is also
smaller.*

This bird may also be labelled
Red-crowned Bishop, or Sundevall's
Grenadier. It is found in Rhodesia,
Nyasaland and northern Angola.

Black-fronted Red Bishop
(*E. o. nigrifrons*)

Description: *About 5½ in. (139·7
mm.). The adult male is extremely
similar to orix, being a little smaller.
It may be distinguished by its back,
which is darker tawny and is streaked
with black.*

This race might be called Böhm's
Grenadier, Grenadier Weaver or Red
Bishop. It comes from Kenya and
Tanzania.

Orange Bishop
(*E. o. franciscana*)

Description: *About 5 in. (127 mm.).
Adult male has black of crown extending to back of head, but rich
orange of body extends up to chin,
tail-coverts embrace tail but for tips
of outermost feathers.*

Smaller than previously mentioned
races, it is very often called the Orange
Weaver. It is the commonest, ranging
from Senegal to the Sudan, and is the
race most frequently imported.

East African Orange Bishop
(*E. o. pusillus*)

Description: *About 5 in. (127 mm.).
Adult male similar to franciscana, but
is a paler orange to yellowish orange.
The tail is not covered by the tail-
coverts.*

This race is rarely imported and
would probably pass for a pale
Orange Bishop unless the dealer was
astute enough to realize that it might
be distinct. It is found in north-eastern
East Africa.

Apart from the colour differences
between the races, ranging from pale
yellow in *pusillus* to scarlet crimson
in *orix*, the races vary somewhat
within themselves and tend to fade
with subsequent moults in captivity.
Birds that have a rich diet in outdoor
aviaries tend to have better colour.
Rutgers suggests that olive oil in the
diet will maintain colour: no doubt
any proprietary brand of colour food
will do a good job.

The Orange Bishop was first bred
in England in 1913, and the most

recent report I have is from New Zealand in 1969. The Grenadier was first bred in 1912, and again in 1921. In all the reports of these and other breedings it is clear that breeding is not difficult if there is sufficient live food and the male is not crowded by similar species, since it will become quite aggressive. Allen Silver told me of a male Grenadier that he once had that had to be removed from its aviary every breeding season because of its belligerency. I have kept three races, *franciscana*, *pusillus* and *orix*, and never had any trouble at all.

Fire-fronted Bishop
(*Euplectes diademata*)

Description: *5½–6 in. (139·7–152·4 mm.). Adult male in colour has forehead vermilion; mantle yellow, streaked with black; rump, upper- and lower-tail-coverts golden yellow; rest of body black; wings black, buff edgings to all but primaries which are edged yellow; bill black. Out of colour, streaked buff and black above; chin to breast and flanks buff, streaked with darker buff on breast, remainder of underparts white; bill horn-colour. Female similar to eclipsed male but smaller. Juvenile similar to female but is slightly paler and a paler bill.*

This beautiful bishop is found only in eastern Kenya and northern Tanzania. It is recorded by Praed and Grant as being common in the rice fields along the coastal strip or in grass patches, but it appears not to congregate in flocks, and is scarce and local. The only avicultural reference that I have for this species, which I regret I have never seen, is the report by E. Nørgaard-Olesen in the *Avicultural Magazine* for 1970. His birds bred in an outdoor aviary that was grassed over with some *Juniperus chinensis* growing. They shared the aviary with some frugivorous birds, so observations on diet were difficult, but they certainly took seeds and mealworms. They appear to be attractive and interesting birds, and deserve to be studied and written up further.

Zanzibar Red Bishop
(*Euplectes nigroventris*)

Description: *About 5 in. (127 mm.). Adult male in colour, forehead to uppertail-coverts, undertail-coverts deep orange, mantle streaked with dusky; chin to belly black, occasionally streaked with red on the throat, and buff on flanks; bill black. Out of colour, streaked buff and dusky above; buff below; bill horn-colour; very similar to out-of-colour orix but wider buff margins to feathers. Female and juvenile similar.*

This species may also be referred to as Black-bellied Weaver, Black-bellied Grenadier or Black-bellied Bishop. It come from Zanzibar and coastal East Africa from Kenya to Mozambique. It is a common and noisy bird that nests in colonies, but within the colony each male has its own small territory. It is very closely related to *E. orix*, but where the two species occur together there is no interbreeding. It is not often imported but has appeared from time to time.

Crimson-crowned Bishop
(*Euplectes hordeacea*)

Description: *6–6½ in. (152·4–165·1 mm.). Adult male in colour, forehead, lores, ear-coverts, sides of face and chin, wings, tail, lower breast, belly and flanks black; forecrown to upper-*

tail-coverts, throat and upper breast red to orange, mantle brownish and scapulars streaked with black; undertail-coverts buff; bill black. Out of colour, broadly streaked with brownish buff below, and narrow streaks on breast and flanks; also has yellowish wash to underparts; upperparts not so broadly streaked. Juvenile resembles female but has broader margins to streaked feathers.

Crimson-crowned Bishop
(*Euplectes hordeacea*)

The Crimson-crowned Bishop may also be referred to as Blackwinged Red Bishop. Its colouring is variable, from orange to red, and according to Praed and Grant there are occasionally some albinotic specimens found, where the wings and tail are white, and the general body-colour is very pale. The eye and bill, however, remain black. The east African race, *craspedoptera*, differs by having the undertail-coverts white, streaked with black. It is a common bird found in grass country over much of Africa from Senegal to the Sudan, Angola and Rhodesia. It has been imported from time to time, is fairly expensive, but is a popular bird.

It has been bred in England, and has proved to be quite typical.

Black Bishop
(*Euplectes gierowii*)

Description: $6\frac{1}{2}$–7 in. (*165·1–177·8 mm.*). *Adult male in colour, forehead, forecrown, lores, behind eye to ear-coverts, sides of face, chin, wings, tail, and lower breast, flanks and belly black; hindcrown, neck, throat and breast orange red; mantle and rump yellow; lower rump, upper- and undertail-coverts ashy; bill black. Out of colour, head, back and upper rump black broadly streaked with buff; superciliary buff; sides of face buff with black fleckings; below, buff with broad streaks on breast; bill horn-colour. Female similar to eclipsed male, yellowish buff below, with blackish spots on breast. Juvenile resembles female but smaller spots on breast.*

This is a large bishop that I have not come across in captivity, and little appears to be known of it in its natural state. It is an uncommon bird that comes from Angola and parts of east Africa. It is a bird of swamps and riverside reed-beds, and may be referred to in field literature as Gierow's Bishop.

Yellow-rumped Bishop
(*Euplectes capensis*)

Description: 6–$6\frac{1}{2}$ in. (*152·4–165·1 mm.*). *Adult male in colour wholly black; bright yellow patch on corners of wings; rump bright yellow; light edges to wing-feathers; bill black above, whitish below. Out of colour, male retains wings, tail and rump as before; rest of body heavily streaked with blackish above, paler below with narrower dusky streaks; bill dark* horn-colour above, pale below. Female is similar but has rump mustard yellow and is paler to whitish buff below. Juveniles resemble female but lack yellow on shoulder, are spotted rather than streaked below, and young males are naturally larger than young females.

This bird has also been called Yellow, Black and Yellow, and Cape Bishop, or Yellow-backed Weaver. The race from West Africa is referred to by Bannerman as Burton's Black-and-yellow Bishop. There are several races, the larger ones with heavier bills coming from South and South-West Africa. The West African race, *phoenicomera*, is about 6½ in. (165·1 mm.) while the East African one, *xanthomelas*, is about 6 in. (152·4 mm.). It is a common bird in the grasslands but seems to have distinct preference for high country between 4,000 ft. (1,219·2 m) and 8,000 ft. (2,438·4 m.). This no doubt explains its rarity in captivity, for it is only occasionally seen. It is a beautiful bird, well worth having. Shore Baily refers to it as being a powerful bird with a formidable-looking bill, but he found it quite harmless with other birds. According to Russ it is one of the easiest of the bishops to breed.

Napoleon Weaver
(*Euplectes afra*)

Description: *4½–5½ in. (114·3–139·7 mm.). Adult male in colour has forehead to nape, lower back to upper-tail-coverts, sides of neck, band across the breast, flanks and under-tail-coverts bright lemon yellow (the yellow breast-bar may have a few chestnut feathers); frontal edge of forehead, lores, ear-coverts and sides of face, chin and throat, breast and belly black; upper mantle black with*

some yellow markings; wing and tail blackish edged buff; bill black. Out of colour, streaked above black and buff; broad superciliary yellowish white, below whitish, washed with yellow with some streaks on breast and flanks; bill horn-colour. Female in colour is very similar to eclipsed male but less strongly marked above; out of colour, may be told from male by distinctly buffer underparts and heavier streaking on breast and flanks. Juveniles are browner above, buff on throat, more finely streaked below.

Napoleon Weaver
(*Euplectes afra*)

This weaver, one of the commonest bishops to be imported, is also known as Yellow-crowned or Golden Bishop. There are four or five races, distributed over much of Africa south of the Sahara wherever swampy grass or riverside reed-beds are to be found. It frequently nests over water, building a large oval nest, with a porched side-entrance near the top, that is attached to growing reeds. In an aviary a stand of bamboo or maize will be an encouragement; bullrushes or tall sedge might do equally well. The displaying male is one of the most entertaining; fluffing its rump up like a powder-puff it flies around in short straight lines, changing direction abruptly and singing a whirring little song. It looks for all the world like a clockwork toy. The males compete furiously, and in a large roomy aviary stimulate each other tremendously. In a small flight or flight-cage they are sufficiently territorially aggressive to be a nuisance and should be kept with larger birds, like Cockatiels, doves, starlings, etc.

The South African bird, *E. a. taha*, is given its own common name of Taha Weaver. It may be distinguished by having the black of the underparts continuous from chin to vent. The West African race, *E. a. afra*, is the commonest in captivity, and is the bird described above. Three races come from East Africa: *stricta* is the largest, reaching about 5½ in. (139·7 mm.). It is uniform black from chin to vent; and out of colour lacks any yellow wash below. The female is browner than *afra* and more heavily streaked above. It comes from Abyssinia. The race from Kenya and Tanzania, *ladoensis*, is the size of the nominate and has only vestigial yellow markings across the breast. Out of colour, it is very similar to the Orange Weaver, *E. orix franciscana*, but is yellower below and darker striped above.

The Napoleon Weaver was first bred in 1912 by Lord Poltimore, Shore Baily bred it in 1915, and it has been bred several times since then. However, either post-war aviculturists have a different style, or are very modest, for no reports have appeared in recent years. It appears to be fairly easy to breed, but does need a good supply of insects, and is energetically bumptious in defence of its nest.

Red-shouldered Whydah
(*Euplectes axillaris*)

Description: *About 7 in. (177·8 mm.). Adult male in colour, jet black with vermilion-red shoulder-patch, lesser wing-coverts brown, other wing-feathers edged with buff; bill blue black. Out of colour, broadly streaked with black and buff above, wings remain the same but red shoulder not*

Red-shouldered Whydah
(*Euplectes axilliaris*)

so bright; below buffish white, some streaking on breast and flanks. Female resembles eclipsed male but has black shoulder-patch, the feathers edged with red. Juveniles differ from female in having shoulder-patch black edged with buff.

This lovely species is commonly known as Fan-tailed Whydah, and various races have different common names. *C. a. bocagei* is called Bocage's Fan-tailed Whydah, or just Bocage's Whydah; it comes from the

Cameroons to Angola, is a bigger and more heavily built bird that has an orange-yellow shoulder-patch, the primary and secondary coverts all brown, and a bluish-white bill. *C. a. phoenicus* from East Africa resembles *axilliaris* but has an orange shoulder-patch, and the primary and secondary coverts brown. The Niger Fan-tailed Whydah, *batesi*, resembles *bocagei* but has the lesser wing-coverts more reddish orange.

The courtship of the Red-shouldered Whydah is a laboured, almost butterfly-like flight low over long grasses where the female is hidden. In flight the red shoulder-patches are striking. One male maintains a harem of several females, each of which builds its own nest in long grass, a domed affair with grass drawn over the top. The male spends its energies guarding its territory. In an aviary it seems to be one of the most peaceful of whydahs, and is not so aggressive by any means. It has bred, and one report I have says that the nest was built by the male, but all the rearing was done by the female.

Giant Whydah
(*Euplectes progne*)

Description: *Adult male in colour, up to 24 in. (609·6 mm.) long; wholly black; with shoulder vermilion, white wing-bar, wing-feathers edged buff, bill pale blue. Out of colour, about 8 in. (203·2 mm.); streaked above tawny and black, wings as in colour, below pale buff streaked with tawny; bill horn-colour. Female is smaller, less heavily streaked above, shoulder-patch orange with black centres to feathers. Juvenile birds resemble female but have buff shoulder-patch with black centres.*

From the Whydah with the shortest tail to the one with the longest, from which it takes the alternative common name Long-tailed Whydah or Sakabula.

The display flight is remarkably impressive, a slow butterfly-flap with the great tail undulating behind. In rain the tail becomes waterlogged and the bird cannot fly. There is a race from Kenya, *delamerei*, known as Delamere's Giant Whydah, which

Giant Whydah
(*Euplectes progne*)

supposedly has an even longer tail. It is a wonderful bird to keep in an aviary big enough to allow it to fly properly, a minimum of 10 × 20 ft. (3·0 × 6·1 m.) I suggest. I have watched two males in a mixed collection in a flight about this size and they counter-displayed continually. Shore Baily describes 'a fine flock ... flying in a medium-sized aviary', belonging to the Duchess of Wellington. 'At least two pairs had nests at the time of my visit, and the hen birds were continually asking for mealworms which they would take from the feet of Her Grace.'

The species was first bred in 1909 by Teschemaker, and has bred on occasions since. The most recent on record being by R. G. Norris (*Foreign Birds*, 1968). These birds bred in a well-planted flight that measured 36 × 6 × 2·5 ft. (10·9 × 1·8 × 0·7 m.), and the young were reared initially on ants' eggs, then with mealworms and any other insect available. As Mr. Norris remarks, 'All the books say that the Giant Whydah is perfectly harmless, etc., can be kept safely with smaller birds, etc. But to prove the books wrong this bird turned more spiteful every day.' In my experience it is a peaceful bird, but then I have never bred it in a narrow (albeit long) aviary.

Red-collared Whydah
(*Euplectes ardens*)

Description: *Adult male in colour, up to 15 in. (381 mm.); wholly black with red band across upper breast; place edging to wing-feathers; tail long (up to 9 in./228·6 mm.), central feathers the shortest; bill black. Out of colour, tawny above, heavily streaked with black; wings black with pale edges; yellowish superciliary, face and throat; below buff to white; bill dark horn-colour; total length 6–6½ in. (152·4–165·1 mm.). Female similar, not so heavily streaked above; shorter tail; about 5½ in. (139·7 mm.) long. Juveniles resemble adult female but have narrower black streaks above; males are larger.*

The bird described above is the nominate race from East and South Africa; the red crescent on the breast is variable in colour and may be any strength of red from crimson through orange to almost yellow. The west African race, *concolor*, is distinguished by being totally black, with no throat-patch at all. It has the common name of Long-tailed Black Whydah, or simply Black Whydah. In parts of central and East Africa, where the two races meet, intermediates occur. the pale edge to the wing-feathers of all adult males has a tendency to wear off, leaving the bird quite black. It is a common bird in grassland, being quite gregarious, and has a distinctive display flight whereby the courting male will fly slowly, quite near the ground, following or circling any female that enters its territory. The flight is typically 'butterfly', and the tail is deliberately held pointing downwards.

As an aviary bird it has all the desirable, and otherwise, characteristics of the *Coliuspasser* whydahs, displaying well and being easy to maintain. However, it appears to be quite a willing breeder. According to Rutgers, 'Good breeding results have been obtained quite often', and certainly Shore Baily found it an easy breeder. One of his females apparently hybridized quite freely with both Red-shouldered and Yellow-backed Whydahs even though its own male was present. My experience with the species is limited, but I have found it to be belligerent, and very aggressive to any other bird with red in its plumage. It naturally builds a nest low down in long grass or shrubs and perennials, and draws the living grass over the top to form a natural shelter. In an aviary nests have been built in bushes and conifers, but I believe that more natural situations should be provided.

Yellow-shouldered Whydah
Euplectes macrocercus)

Description: *Adult male in colour, about 10 in. (254 mm.), wholly black with shoulder yellow; edges to wing-feathers pale; tail long and graduated; bill black. Out of colour, about 6½–7½ in. (165·1–190·5 mm.); buff above, broadly streaked with black; wings black with yellow shoulder; yellowish on face and throat; buff below; bill horn-colour. Female similar to male but less*

Yellow-shouldered Whydah
(*Euplectes macrocercus*)

black above; length about 6 in. 152·4 mm.). Juvenile similar to female but has shoulder fawn; bill pale horn-colour.

This species is not very often imported, possibly because it is restricted mainly to the high plateaux of Eritrea and Abyssinia. It may be separated from the Yellow-backed Whydah by its larger size and longer tail. I cannot accept Rutgers's suggestion that yellow on the shoulder of out-of-colour birds may indicate a male since females also have yellow shoulders; furthermore females of this species have a tendency to melanism.

Birds that have this tendency seem to be even more melanistic in captivity, so even the appearance of black feathers cannot be a certain diagnostic. It is not an aggressive bird, but may become very territorial against other black-and-yellow birds if breeding activities get under way.

Yellow-mantled Whydah
(*Euplectes macrourus*)

Description: *Adult male in colour, about 9 in. (228·6 mm.); wholly black except for yellow shoulder, scapulars and mantle yellow. Out of colour,*

Yellow-mantled Whydah
(*Euplectes macrourus*)

about 6½ in. (165·1 mm.); similar to male Yellow-shouldered but duller above, black streaks not so dense. Female, similar to foregoing species but yellowish suffusion over all below, and rump browner. Juveniles yellower below than macrocercus.

Also known as Yellow- or Gold-backed Whydah, this species is widely distributed from Senegal across to the Sudan, Angola to Mozambique, and is regularly imported. It is a common bird, but local, showing a preference for low-lying or swampy grassland. Both sexes have yellow shoulders when in eclipse plumage and the presence of yellow on an eclipsed 'male' is no guarantee of success. As with most whydahs females are in short supply because so many 'females' turn out to be either an immature or eclipsed male, and since the presence of several females will stimulate the male to much greater performance of display and nest-starting (and thereby stimulate the females to ovulation) the serious aviculturist will not find it too easy to get started. According to Boosey they are 'fairly ready to go to nest in confinement', but I have no records in my file. I see no reason why they should not breed in a roomy, well-planted flight.

White-winged Whydah
(*Euplectes albonatus*)

Description: *Adult male in colour, about 9 in. (228·6 mm.); identical to Yellow-backed in size and shape, and Yellow-shouldered in colour, but distinguished by white patch at base of primaries. Out of colour, similar to Yellow-shouldered but may be identified by white wing-patch. Female very difficult to tell from female Yellow-shouldered but is smaller. Juveniles like female but darker below.*

There are three distinct races of the White-wing; the Angolan bird, *asymmetrurus*, differs from the nominate race described above by having a longer tail; the East African race, *eques*, has the shoulder cinnamon instead of yellow, and is slightly larger. Where identification is difficult but important, the species may be distinguished by white underwing-coverts, as opposed to brown or buff in other

species. It is a bird of open grassland, noted by its habit of spreading its tail wide. It has been bred several times in captivity; the only case that is well detailed, however, being from the (then) Belgian Congo when four males and several females were kept in a large aviary with a great many weavers of various kinds. Breeding results improved noticeably when the quantity of inmates was significantly

White-winged Whydah (*Euplectes albonatus*)

reduced. The young were raised on mixed seeds, soaked bread, wild seeding grasses and termites; the breeder reported that the termites were not usually taken. The species is naturally territorial of course, but I think that the area required by a male is much smaller than with some species, and it is definitely less aggressive than most whydahs.

Marsh Whydah
(*Euplectes hartlaubi*)

Description: *Adult male in colour, 11–12 in. (279·4–304·8 mm.); wholly black with long graduated tail; shoulder orange yellow; median wing-coverts buff; bill bluish white. Out of* colour, 8–8½ in. (*203·2–215·9 mm.*); broadly streaked above with black and brown; wings as in breeding plumage; below buff, streaked with brown on breast and flanks; bill horn-colour. Female resembles male out of colour but less black above, and shoulder dull yellow. Juvenile less heavily streaked above than female, unstreaked and browner below; bill flesh-colour; length 7½–8 in. (*190·5–203·2 mm.*).

This is the largest of the whydahs, and may be distinguished when out of colour from the Giant Whydah as it is slightly larger and more heavily streaked in both sexes and has a shorter wing. When positive identification is critical it will be found that the underwing-coverts are white. It is not a common bird either in the wild or in captivity. I have not seen it; neither have I seen mention of it in the literature.

Red-naped Whydah
(*Euplectes laticauda*)

Description: *Adult male in colour, 9–10 in. (228·6–254 mm.); wholly black with red band running from crown around the side of neck across the upper breast; the mantle may be spotted with buff, bill black. Out of colour, about 6 in. (152·4 mm.) and almost identical to Red-collared Whydah. Female and juveniles are also very similar to* E. ardens, *but are less heavily streaked, and more evenly brownish all over.*

This species is sometimes regarded as a race of *E. ardens*, but may be distinguished by its shorter, broader and less flexible tail and of course, the red band which carries on to encircle the head. It may be called Crimson-ringed Whydah. It is an East African bird, rarely imported. I cannot

find any reference to a successful breeding. It appears to be a typical *Euplectes* in its habits in captivity, being nowhere near as belligerent as the Red-collared Whydah.

Jackson's Whydah
(*Euplectes jacksoni*)

Description: *Adult male in colour, about 13 in. (330·2 mm.) long; wholly black with brown to yellowish shoulders and wing-feathers edged with light brown; tail-feathers long, broad and curved; bill blue to blue black. Out of colour, brown streaked with blackish above and brown on breast and flanks and is very similar to out-of-colour Giant Whydah but lacks any red on shoulder. Female as female Marsh Whydah but brown underwing-coverts. Juvenile resembles female but young male is larger.*

This lovely bird comes from a small area around the border between western and central Kenya, and Tanzania. It is a common bird in this area, being found in the highlands in grass country. The male in breeding dress is noticeably different, for when it is standing the tail is generally held clear of the ground, and when displaying is like an elongated cockerel's tail. The display is amazing. The male selects a particular tuft of grass out of acres of tall grass, and proceeds to flatten an area around this by jumping upon it. The display consists of the male hopping round and round this tuft on what may eventually be worn down to bare earth, all the while leaping high into the air. This attracts passing females who alight upon the central tuft and may or may not accept the male as a mate. In between those jumping displays the male will fly back and forth across his surrounding territory, chasing away any

Jackson's Whydah (*Euplectes jacksoni*)

intruders. It is in this surrounding area that the females (up to eight have been recorded), will build their nests and rear their families. The sight of a long view of endless grass, with a male Jackson's Whydah spasmodically rising up momentarily from an unseen arena then falling back, is quite unforgettable.

A few Jackson's Whydahs are imported each year, but known suppliers often have waiting lists of customers and, despite high prices, these birds are usually sold before reaching the advertisements. This is one of those species for which a determined buyer must get his name on to importers' mailing-lists. It has been bred in captivity on a few occasions, and reports differ about feeding requirements. It appears that live food may not be necessary. However, it does seem that breeding is contingent on a decent area of long grass. As with all the larger whydahs and bishops it is clear that natural behaviour and breeding success is only likely in a large planted aviary.

II · VIDUINAE

PARASITIC WHYDAHS

That there are two distinct groups of weavers known as whydahs is a fact that will not have escaped the reader. The first, often placed in the genus *Coliuspasser* but now included in *Euplectes* with the bishops, are typical weavers in the sense that they build their own nests, and raise their own families. The group dealt with here, however, is sufficiently different to warrant status as a subfamily. The viduines are distinguished by being brood-parasitic; that is to say they lay their eggs in other birds' nests in the manner of the Common Cuckoo, and allow the foster-parents to rear their young. Unlike the Cuckoo, however, the young whydah does not eject its foster-brothers and sisters but is raised with them, and successfully imitates them until it is weaned and independent, when it wanders off to join its own kind.

Whydahs are often called Widows or Widow-birds, and they are characterized by the long black caudal plumes that the males grow in the breeding season, but which are subsequently lost. I have always been interested in the way in which birds are named, and was delighted to discover the following story in a nineteenth-century book of engravings:

'With regard to the name widow, the author of *Gardens and Menagerie Delineated* informs us that Edwards, the first modern writer by whom this interesting bird was figured and described, happened to say that the Portuguese called it the Widow from its colour and long train; Brisson took the hint, and gave it the name of Veuve in French and Vidua in Latin.

'The French naturalist had, however, overlooked the fact that Edwards had himself corrected the mistake, for such it was in the following terms: "In my description of this bird I have said that it is called the Widow by the Portuguese; but I am since informed that it is called the Whidah-bird, because it is brought

frequently to Lisbon from the Kingdom of Whidah, on the coast
of Africa."'

The name Widow, accidentally given, has now been adopted
both in popular and scientific ornithological language. Interestingly, however, it is commonly spelt Whydah in British aviculture.

There are nine species of *Vidua*, normally divided into three
subgenera, which I shall retain here to avoid causing confusion.
All are imported more or less regularly, but identification of the
Paradise Whydahs and Combassous is usually superficial and
many an interesting race is 'lost' in this way. In fact, although
these birds are freely available, inexpensive, attractive, popular,
and often dealt with in the popular-cagebird press, they seem
never to be taken seriously and all the breeding records are
accidentals. The only times that the species has been bred by
design have been by serious scientific research workers.

HOUSING

When in nuptial plumage all viduines, except the three Combassous,
grow long tails. These may be anything up to 12 in (304·8 mm.)
long. It must be obvious that this makes them rather unsuitable to
be kept in usual cages, where the tails get snagged on the wires
and cage floor. If they are to be kept in a cage, this must be of
suitable dimensions and I suggest a minimum length of 36 in.
(914·4 mm.) (but longer would be much better) and a height of
30 in. (762 mm.). The basic needs are (a) for the male to be able
to turn round on the perches at either end of the cage without the
sides of the cage rubbing the tail, and (b) for the bird to be able to
hop about the floor (they are ground feeders) and have sufficient
room to be able to keep its tail free from snags. A minimum
floor area of 2 × 4 ft. (0·6 × 1·2 m.) is therefore suggested. Of
course they look so much better in aviaries, or at least roomy
flights. The males will perform courtship displays, hovering before
their mates, or bobbing and twisting before them. One is most
unlikely to see this in a cage. In an aviary they may be kept with
all manner of other species and generally speaking are not harmful
unless the enclosure is crowded, when unnecessary bullying may
take place. Some species have a reputation for being spiteful,
others for being 'safe', but in my experience all may give cause
for concern if kept in too close proximity with waxbills.

FEEDING

These birds will live quite comfortably on a mixture of various millet seeds, and a few other seeds which may be supplied in a separate pot or sprinkled on the floor. A Canary mixture will be of interest in this respect. They will take millet spray, soaked and germinating seed, and green food such as chickweed and lettuce, the universal favourites. Crushed cuttle-fish bone may be sprinkled on the floor or mixed with the grit, and a multi-vitamin may be added to the drinking water from time to time. However, they are not problem birds in any way, and are the classic 'seed-eaters' for the beginner.

BREEDING

When it comes to breeding, the viduine Whydahs are another matter, and are not at all easy to breed. The problem is not difficult to see; it is because one first needs to be successfully breeding the respective host species at the time. Since waxbills are not easy to breed under the average aviary conditions it might be worth spelling out the ideal situation here. The first necessity is a roomy well-planted aviary, something like 10 × 6 ft. (3·1 × 1·8 m.). This could house two or three pairs of say, St. Helena Waxbills. There should be a shelter attached, or at least a partitioned-off feeding area. Nest-boxes should be placed in secluded and sheltered spots, for example in the clematis, or shielded by a bunch of heather. Naturally, the keeper should be prepared to give out pupae, mealworms, gentles, etc., according to supplies available. Either a pair or a trio of Pintailed Whydahs could be kept in an adjoining flight and introduced when the waxbills begin nest-building, or they could be placed in the same enclosure from the start.

The female whydah comes into breeding condition through watching the breeding activities of the host species, and only ovulates through the stimulus of seeing the host species mating. The male whydah combines phrases of its own song with the song of the host species and so compounds the complex interrelationship. The female whydah lays her egg very secretively in the nest of the selected host, and this is why plenty of cover is necessary (apart from encouraging insects) to hide her and screen the nest from the true owners. A feeding house serves a similar function.

Accurate host selection may not be critical, since there are records of whydahs laying in non-host species' nests, but this may be explained in many ways, and accurate pairing is to be advised if serious breeding is to be attempted.

Paradise Whydah
(*Steganura paradisaea*)

Description: *Adult male in colour, 12–20 in. (304·8–508 mm.); head, including throat, black; hind and sides of neck golden buff; breast chestnut; remainder of upperparts and undertail-coverts black; flanks and belly white; bill black. Out of colour, 5½ in. (139·7 mm); head creamy buff streaked with black; wings and tail black, broadly edged with tawny or ashy; below, chest and flanks deep tawny with black streaks; breast to undertail-coverts white. Female similar to eclipsed male but is duller, less tawny and more earth to buff. The juvenile is more earthy above and below, and less streaked on breast and flanks; bill horn-colour.*

This species may be told from the other species by the shape of its tail, for the two central feathers are *graduated*, and for their last two-thirds of length they gradually narrow. The female is not easy to tell apart from an eclipsed male, but the male seems to have longer and blacker tertiaries and often seems to be longer. With one pair that I had I could sex them at a glance when they were together (just like a well-known pair of Goldfinches) but if one bird was alone it became more difficult.

Normally the Paradise Whydah is considered to be a peaceful bird, and many writers recommend it for a waxbill collection, but I had one male who was very irritable and which would snap at and bite birds up to Canary size. A fit male in colour

Paradise Whydah (*Steganura paradisaea*): adult male in breeding plumage

will display continually, and makes a very attractive aviary bird.

The Paradise Whydah parasitizes three races of the Melba Finch (*Pytilia melba*), which are *melba*, *grotei* and *soudanensis*, and this large and beautiful waxbill is well worth anyone's time and effort. The first recorded breeding of the species in Britain was in 1955 when a single chick was raised to maturity in a family of Firefinches. The two species formed part of a collection of various waxbills and small foreign birds in a large well-planted aviary owned by Mrs. Lloyd of Bannockburn. It is of interest that conditions were such in this aviary that the behaviour of a pair of Pin-tailed Whydahs suggested that they may have bred also. However, they were removed to safeguard the rather nervous Firefinches. There are several records from Rhodesia and South Africa where the foster-parents have always been Melba Finches. One breeder raised young successfully for four consecutive years.

Broad-tailed Paradise Whydah
(*Steganura orientalis*)

Description: *Adult male in colour, 10–20 in. (254–508 mm.) depending on race; these differ from* paradisea *in colours of neck and breast, and shape of tail as detailed below. Out of colour, is paler than* paradisea *with narrower streaks above. Female and juveniles are also paler with narrower streaks.*

While I lived in Spain I saw many Paradise Whydahs in the pet shops, and all of them were one form or other of the Broad-tailed. If I had had the facilities it would have been fun to try to collect them. Here is a rough word description of the difference for each race, and its corresponding host species.

1. Broad-tailed Paradise Whydah, *S. o. orientalis.* Hind and sides of neck golden buff, upper breast chestnut; tail, two central feathers short and oval, long pair only

5–6 in. (127–152·4 mm.). Host species is the fourth race of the Melba Finch, *Pytilia melba citerior.*

2. Golden-naped Paradise Whydah, *S. o. kadugliensis.* Hind and sides of neck yellow, breast chestnut; tail fairly long and recurved. Host species is *P. m. citerior.*

Broad-tailed Whydah
(*Steganura orientalis obtusa*)

3. West African Paradise Whydah, *S. o. aucupum.* Entire neck around to include upper breast tawny; tail similar to *paradisea* but not so long and not tapered. Host species is *P. m. citerior.*

4. Broad-tailed Whydah, *S. o. obtusa.* Hind and sides of neck tawny, upper breast pale chestnut; four central tail-feathers very broad and sail-like. Host species is the Orange-winged Pytilia, *P. afra.*

5. Cameroons or Uelle Paradise Whydah, *S. o. interjecta.* Upper mantle, neck and breast tawny; tail long and straight, broadening towards the last part. Host species is the Aurora Finch, *P. phoenicoptera,* in both its forms.

6. Togo Paradise Whydah, *S. o. togoensis.* Neck and breast tawny; tail as long as *paradisea* but not

graduated; it is no broader than that of the Paradise Whydah. Host species is the Yellow-winged Pytilia, *P. hypogrammica.*

Some of these West African forms are undoubtedly wrongly identified as *S. paradisea,* which in fact is a bird of East and South Africa. However, they all require the same care and treatment in captivity.

Pintailed Whydah
(*Vidua macroura*)

Description: *Adult male in colour, 10–15 in. (254–381 mm.); top of head, from lores to nape, black; hind and sides of neck, sides of head, chin to undertail-coverts white (chin may be black); upperwing-coverts white; rest of upperparts black; four central tail-feathers elongated; bill red. Out of colour, about 4½ in. (114·3 mm.); centre of crown tawny with black stripe each side, rest of upperparts broadly streaked black and tawny; wings and tail black edged pale; whitish below streaked somewhat on breast and flanks; bill red. Female resembles male but less tawny, and less boldly streaked above; bill in breeding dress brownish to black, greenish to madder (variable). Out of season, female loses much tawny and bill becomes dull red to pink. Juvenile resembles a dull pale female with little streaking, bill black becoming reddish.*

The Pintailed Whydah is widespread over most of Africa south of the Sahara, from Senegal to Eritrea, and down the east to South Africa. It is not found in the Congo basin or Angola. It is a lively bird with great character that seems irrepressible and calls attention in the pet shop. It is best kept with birds slightly larger than itself unless its enclosure is

Pintailed Whydah
(*Vidua macroura*)

roomy and not crowded. Males have a tendency to become bullies, and may pick on some inoffensive bird and persecute it, or may take exclusive ownership of a perch or food pot. I have only kept them twice, and have had no trouble whatsoever, but there is no doubt that they can be spiteful.

It is the only viduine that parasitizes more than one species, these being St. Helena Waxbill (*Estrilda astrild*), the Red-eared Waxbill (*E. troglodytes*), probably the Rosy-rumped or Sundevall's Waxbill (*E. rhodopyga*) and the Orange-cheeked Waxbill (*E. melpoda*). Friedmann listed some nineteen host species (some of which must have been highly dubious), which caused several later writers to discuss the Pintailed Whydah as though it were some kind of reckless Cuckoo. Clearly, however, it is not, and it is the species about which we know the least.

Queen Whydah
(*Vidua regia*)

Description: *Adult male in colour, 11–13 in. (279·4–330·2 mm.); top of head black; entire neck, sides of head, chin to belly light tawny; rest of upperparts and undertail-coverts black; bill and feet red. Out of colour, about 4½ in. (114·3 mm.); buff or tawny above, streaked with black; underparts buffish to white. Female similar to male but is duller and slightly paler; juvenile is browner.*

Queen Whydah
(*Vidua regia*)

This is a lovely bird from South Africa that is not often imported, but a few birds do turn up from time to time. The four central tail-feathers are elongated, and rather narrow until they widen out to feathery tips and give rise to the alternate common name of Shaft-tailed Whydah. It may be distinguished from the Pintailed Whydah when in eclipse by its red legs. The host species is the beautiful,

and equally sought-after, Violet-eared Waxbill (*Uraeginthus granatina*). My guess is that most breeders who are fortunate enough to obtain these waxbills will try to concentrate on breeding them alone, and hardly go out of their way to get a pair of Queen Whydahs. It is believed by some authorities that the Cordon-bleu may also act as a host on occasion, and although the entire repertoire and learning of captive birds studied have reinforced the Violet-ear belief there is no doubt that the Cordon-bleu (*Uraeginthus bengalus*) *has* been a natural substitute. The first breeding recorded was in London in 1963 when in fact Cordons-bleu successfully reared a young Queen Whydah on a diet of maggots and various seeds. Another breeding, in South Africa in 1967, took place in a large well-planted aviary when three young Queens were raised by a family of Violet-eared Waxbills. Termites formed a large part of the diet.

Fischer's Whydah
(*Vidua fischeri*)

Description: *Adult male in colour, 10–13 in. (254–330·2 mm.); forehead and crown, breast to undertail-coverts buff; rump buff streaked with black; rest of body black; four central tail-feathers elongated buff; bill red; feet orange. Out of colour, about 4½ in. (114·3 mm.); above, tawny streaked with dusky on head, rest streaked with black; below, buff to white. Female resembles eclipsed male. Juvenile earth above, streaked dusky; tawny below; belly white; bill black.*

This species comes from east Africa and is also known as the Straw-tailed Whydah and is said to be a peaceful and gentle bird in a mixed collection. It parasitizes the

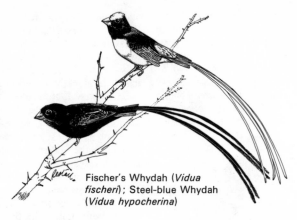

Fischer's Whydah (*Vidua fischeri*); Steel-blue Whydah (*Vidua hypocherina*)

beautiful Purple Grenadier (*Uraeginthus ianthinogaster*), and the male Fischer's will attract his mate's attention to the breeding behaviour of a pair of Grenadiers by uttering pure Grenadier song. I do not think that they have been bred in captivity.

Steel-blue Whydah
(*Vidua hypocherina*)

Description: *Adult male in colour, about 12 in. (304·8 mm.); violet blue black all over, including tail; white spot on either side of rump; bill grey. Out of colour, 4–4½ in. (101·6–114·3 mm.); closely resembles eclipsed Pintailed Whydah but has bill brownish grey, and feet are dusky flesh. Female resembles eclipsed male. Juvenile is a paler ash brown above than immature* macroura, *and has a smaller bill.*

Also known as Long-tailed Combassou, some authorities have placed this bird in the same subgenus as the Combassous. A male that has dropped, or lost its elongated four central feathers may be told from a Combassou by the white underwing-coverts. It is a bird of dry country from East Africa, but little is known

about it either in the wild or in captivity. Nicolai was unable to isolate any waxbill song-phrases from its song, but it is thought to parasitize the Rosy-rumped Waxbill (*Estrilda rhodopyga*).

Senegal Combassou
(*Hypochera chalybeata*)

Description: *About 4 in. (101·6 mm.). Adult male in colour, dull violet blue black all over, wings and tail ashen; white patch on either side of rump; bill whitish; feet light brownish plum. Out of colour, top of head black with a broad central buff stripe, sides of face and stripe over eye buff; blackish streak behind eye; back brown and black streaks; below buff to white. Female and juvenile similar to eclipsed male.*

The Combassou, or Indigo Bird is one of about a dozen races that form between them anything from three to seven species, depending on which authority one refers to. The differences between each are subtle and often overlapping; they are probably separated and/or restricted by the distribution of their various host species, or races. All the *Hypochera*

Senegal Combassou (*Hypochera chalybeata*)

are brood-parasitic on the *Lagonosticta*, the Firefinches. Nicolai proved that the nominate form of *H. chalybeata* mimics the song, distance call, contact notes, nest-calling, and the begging chorus of a group of young birds of the host species *Lagonosticta*

senegala senegala, the Common Firefinch. The geographical races of the Combassou *ultramarina* (coral feet) and *amauropteryx* (feet salmon to orange) similarly mimic the corresponding notes of the races *bruniceps* and *rendalli*. Much work has to be done, and there is little concrete to guide the aviculturist.

There are several records of the Combassou breeding, three from Denmark including one where the birds built a rather poor nest of their own and raised three young. Neunzig had a pair which, having failed in their attempts to parasitize Firefinches, adopted a Zebra Finch nest and raised one youngster themselves from three eggs. These reports cannot be ignored, but it does seem fairly obvious that the genus is primarily brood-parasitic.

They are delightful birds, lively, alert and very like Zebra Finches in their perky behaviour. They certainly deserve a place in any collection that contains breeding (or would-be breeding) Firefinches.

III · PASSERINAE

SPARROWS AND PETRONIAS

The term 'sparrowy' in bird literature is meant to suggest that the particular bird in question resembles a female House Sparrow: it is a kind of shorthand to avoid a detailed description that, if it were to be really accurate, would inevitably take up a lot of space. It is unfortunate that the term has become synonymous with 'dull, drab, uninteresting'. Whether sparrows in general are dull and drab is a matter of opinion; I personally feel they are really quite attractive, and they are all undeniably interesting. However, to many bird-keepers, the sin of lacking pretty colours can only be mitigated (and then only partly) by a lovely song. In this area the sparrows also score badly. I have tried to avoid the use of the terms 'sparrowy' or 'sparrow-like' in this book, but when I have they are meant to suggest similarity with the female House Sparrow, *Passer domesticus.*

I have kept many sparrows, from the common House Sparrow, which I have hand-reared on many occasions, to the Scaly-crowned Weaver. Without exception I have found them to be easy to maintain in good condition on a mixed seed diet with little in the way of extras. I have not kept the Snow Finches (*Montifringilla*), nor have I found any reference to them in avicultural literature, but despite their rarefied habitat preference, of high altitudes (up to 16,000 ft. (5,120·6 m.) in Tibet), they seem to me to be quite typical in their habits, being confident near man, and opportunistic in their feeding and breeding. Some of the species in this chapter might seem out of place to some readers, who might expect to find the *Sporopipes* along with the weavers, and the petronias with the buntings. All birds are interesting and worth study and care, the sparrows no less than any other. I sincerely hope that the following notes suggest that sparrows are not simply a few dull, drab and uninteresting species not worth considering.

HOUSING

As a generalization I have not found any sparrows to be happy in cages. A few settle down fairly quickly, like the Rock Sparrow, but most never seem to lose their wildness. Maybe it can be argued that all birds will settle sooner or later, but I find that my will is generally the weaker and I either give them aviary space, or present them to somebody who can do likewise. In an aviary they thrive, and if only more species were kept no doubt more breeding records would exist. It is unfortunate that because of the low interest level in sparrows only indifferent attempts have been made to breed them. In fact it might be generalized that only those species not thought of as being sparrows, *Sporopipes* and the Yellow Sparrows from Africa, are ever bred. Even so, an aviary appears to be a requisite, though it need not be big, nor need it be planted. The nest-site itself, however, should be secluded.

FOOD

In the wild they are seed- and grain-eaters, in general being highly opportunistic and taking full advantage of the best source to hand. The European species, or those from colder climes, show a preference for Canary-seed, while the hot-country birds are inclined towards millets. In captivity they may be given complex or simple mixtures, and I have found the opportunities to experiment far greater than my time or facilities allow. It is certainly sensible to offer the seeds which are cheaper to buy and not automatically give a Canary-rich mixture. When rearing young they feed exclusively on insects for the first few days, then increasingly add other soft foods and, quite soon, seed. I do not consider any of the sparrows to be demanding or difficult in this matter.

BREEDING

As mentioned under 'housing', sparrows do not seem to settle very well in cages and in my experience do very much better in aviaries. All of the few breedings that I know of have been aviary ones, but it depends on your definition of 'cage' and 'aviary', I suppose. In this context I think I would define an indoor flight of, say, 9 × 3 × 6 ft. (2·7 × 0·9 × 1·8 m.) high as an aviary but would not expect breeding results to follow automatically. While a few weave nests (rather badly) in true weaver fashion, others nest almost exclu-

1. Sociable Weaver (*Philetairus socius*); 2. House Sparrow (*Passer domesticus*); 3. Spanish Sparrow (*Passer hispaniolensis*); 4. Golden Sparrow (*Passer luteus*); 5. Arabian Golden Sparrow (*Passer euchlorus*)

sively in holes, most are opportunistic and will take advantage of circumstances. For example, the Scaly-fronted Weaver will readily take a disused or discarded weaver's nest and reline it, or will happily set up home in a nest-box. The House Sparrow often builds nests in trees in hot countries, and I know of a case in England where a Tree Sparrow (*Passer montanus*) built a nest in a bush; this happened in a friend's large, well-planted aviary where all the boxes had been taken. Such adaptability augurs well for the aviculturist.

Sparrows are gregarious, and breed in colonies, or on a loose colony system. It seems very likely that breeding performances from isolated pairs will be poorer than from pairs formed within a community. I would suggest keeping several pairs, and putting more than enough nest-boxes up. Summers-Smith remarks that for a female House Sparrow to reach ovulation in an aviary it was necessary not only to provide a male, but also a nest and nesting material. Pair-formation and nest-building may precede breeding by many months, so that some separate courtship behaviour is very important. The fact that this courtship is a communal one results from the social behaviour and colonial nesting of the bird, so that a male, inviting a female to coition, must do this in the sight of other sexually mature males, which are stimulated to join in.

I have not found sparrows ever to be actively aggressive or belligerent, but they can certainly be anti-social in their efficiency at stealing other species' nest-sites, and will jab irritably at other birds at feeding tables, or on favourite perches. Unless they are overcrowded they are not normally aggressive when breeding.

Sociable Weaver
(*Philetairus socius*)

Description: *About 5½ in. (139·7 mm.). Adult has crown to nape earth brown; sides of neck, mantle and scapulars blackish with buff edges; rump and uppertail-coverts earth brown with buff edges; wings and tail dusky to blackish with buff edges; lores to chin, and stripe through eye black; cheeks and all lower parts pale buff, with black patch on flanks, edged buff. Sexes alike. Juvenile similar but lacks black on face and chin.*

The Sociable or Social Weaver of South Africa is the most specialized of all the sparrows in its breeding behaviour, for its nests are one joint communal effort that may fill a tree, and may be mistaken for a native hut from a distance. Up to 300 pairs may, in true co-operative manner, construct the single tenement which may measure up to 10 ft. (3 m.) high and 15 ft. (4·6 m.) across. It is usually built high in the branches of a strong solitary tree. The birds begin by building the communal roof, which resembles a straw thatch in many ways; this is a truly co-operative

effort. Each pair then makes its own nest underneath, a circular chamber with an entrance tunnel pointing down.

I have not seen the species in captivity, but it is undoubtedly of the greatest interest to know how the breeding behaviour might be modified. A new colony is begun by only two or three pairs. They build a small platform of twigs, roofing it with grasses, and finally building their nests below. Other pairs join the colony. No doubt a suitable site with plenty of material is necessary, but little more.

House Sparrow
(*Passer domesticus*)

Description: *About 6½ in. (165·1 mm.). Adult male, crown, rump and uppertail-coverts grey; lores and band under eye black; cheeks and sides of neck greyish; band above and behind eye, neck chestnut; back streaked black and chestnut; wings and tail blackish with chestnut edges; chin, throat and centre of upper breast black; underparts pale grey; bill black. In fresh autumn plumage more ochreous-orange bordering above, below buffish tinge; pale edges on breast almost obscure the black; bill dark brown. Female dull brown above, with pale superciliary and dark brown streaking on back; brownish grey below, palest to white on vent. In fresh plumage the ochreous bordering above is broader and there is an olivaceous tinge above. Juveniles resemble female; young males soon show faint signs of male feathering around head.*

The ubiquitous House Sparrow is really too well known to warrant a detailed description. It is probably the most adaptable and successful species of all birds, adapting to take full advantage of the habitat created by that most successful of all animals – man. Its success lies in the fact that it does not trust man one bit, and even in his midst, plied with crumbs and morsels, maintains a degree of alertness born of profound suspicion. I wonder how many readers would think not only of keeping House Sparrows, but of specializing in them. Summers-Smith did, and has made a life-study of this highly intelligent bird; his book on the species dramatizes more than anything I could say that even the dullest species can prove to be a gold-mine of interest.

I have kept many House Sparrows, mostly hand-reared waifs, or rain-water-logged newly-fledged birds. For some odd reason, every one that I kept until it was adult proved to be a female. Even the tamest baby has grown into a wild and untrusting adult and I have always ended by releasing them. They are not very easy to breed, it seems, probably because attempts by most aviculturists have been with wild-caught adults of abnormal feathering – albinistic birds.

Such individuals are possibly even more wary and nervous. However, research workers have successfully bred them on many occasions. The only instances I know of have been in large aviaries where the sparrows have been admitted accidentally, and left unmolested.

Spanish Sparrow
(*Passer hispaniolensis*)

Description: *About 6½ in. (165·1 mm.). Adult male differs from male* domesticus *by having head chestnut from forehead to nape, white scapulars, and black of bib extending to breast and flanks. Female and juvenile similar to* domesticus.

The Spanish or Black-breasted Sparrow ranges over most of the North African coastal areas and the Middle East; it is in fact scarce in Spain and can only be seen with certainty in the marshy grasslands of the south and south-east. Where it exists alongside the House Sparrow, such as in Spain, it is a country bird. However, in parts of North Africa it is the only *Passer* resident and has filled the ecological niche normally taken by the House Sparrow, and its behaviour is practically identical. In Italy there is a *Passer* known as the Italian Sparrow, which is generally considered to be a stabilized hybrid population between Spanish and House Sparrows; it is given subspecific status, *P. domesticus italiensis*. An odd male Spanish Sparrow that I had I sent to Mr. Murray who, at the time of writing, has it in one of his very large aviaries with a female House Sparrow. Our objective is to compare the resulting true hybrid with the supposed hybrid from Italy.

A pair that I acquired in the

Canary Islands lived quite happily in my bird-room with a Starling and a Diuca, and did not cause any trouble. Previously, they had been kept in an aviary with Chaffinches, Trumpeter Bullfinches and Wild Canaries, and had proved to be typical sparrows, intelligent and wary. The lone male had been kept with some buntings and serins, and it behaved perfectly. When the birds were nervous, and all crowding on to the same safest-seeming perch the sparrow was the first to assert its self-interest by pecking at the bird on either side, a typical *Passer* behaviour.

The Canary Island pair were also eventually passed on to Mr. Murray, early in 1973. They were placed in the same large aviary in which the lone *hispaniolensis* was unsuccessfully courting the female *domesticus*. This pair bred successfully, rearing several broods on a mixed diet of soft food and a bit of live food. Incidentally, in the field the Spanish Sparrow is extremely difficult to tell apart from a House Sparrow, but in the hand it is clearly distinct; the double white barring above, whiter cheeks, paler below and more extensive black bib all combine to present it as a cleaner and prettier bird. Its voice is slightly higher and less sharp.

Grey-headed Sparrow
(Passer griseus)

Description: *6–7 in. (152·4–177·8 mm.). Adult male, head and neck buffish grey; rest of upperparts tawny rufous with white edgings to median wing-coverts; below, whitish from chin to breast; sides of body washed with brown, undertail buff; bill black in breeding season, otherwise horn-colour. Sexes alike, but female a little smaller. Juvenile streaked above.*

This sparrow is common and widespread over most of its range, from Senegal to the Sudan. It occupies the House Sparrow niche in many villages and towns, but is also found in the country, especially when seeds are ripe. It may often be found pecking around animal dung, taking undigested seeds and insects. They make good aviary birds, showing themselves off well and often sitting out in the open, sunbathing and preening. They are mildly aggressive, and ought not to be kept with waxbills or manikins. They are rarely available but are worth attention when they do appear, and a modern breeding record would be of great interest. The only breeding that I know of was by Teschemaker in 1909.

Tree Sparrow
(Passer montanus)

Description: *About 5½ in. (139·7 mm.). Adult resembles male domesticus but has forehead to nape chestnut, and a black patch on the ear-coverts. Sexes alike. Juvenile resembles adult.*

The Tree Sparrow, or Field Sparrow as some books may refer to it, is the House Sparrow's country cousin in Britain and western Europe, but it has an immense range, right across the Palearctic land mass to Japan and south-east to Indonesia. We know it as a bird that nests in holes in trees, but in parts of its range it has occupied the niche that in Europe is taken by the House Sparrow. It has occasionally hybridized with the House Sparrow naturally, and also by design. Cheke transferred House Sparrow eggs to a Tree Sparrow nest, and the resulting chicks were reared successfully. A male House Sparrow from this brood was found breeding with a female Tree Sparrow, and the pair successfully raised some hybrid young. The male House Sparrow was therefore content to mate with a smaller bird which resembled a male of its own species, and it was therefore presumably imprinted on to Tree Sparrows. This is a fine example of the effect that the use of foster-parents can have, for if the House Sparrow 'thought' that it was a Tree Sparrow, it would be most unlikely to mate naturally with a female House Sparrow.

All of my Tree Sparrows with one exception have been hand-reared (as a brood together) and whether I have bought one or two they inevitably grew into totally wild creatures. One adult that I bought as a reference for a painting quickly settled down and lived happily with some petronias until I released it. They are neat, pretty little birds, unfortunately ignored by most aviculturists.

Golden Sparrow
(*Passer luteus*)

Description: *About 5 in. (127 mm.). Adult male has entire head and underparts primrose yellow; mantle and edges of secondaries chestnut, rest of wings and tail black with pale to buff edges, thin white wing-bar; bill black when breeding, horn-colour out of season. Female much duller, washed with brown on head, and whitish washed with yellow below. Juvenile resembles female but paler below.*

This bird may be listed as Yellow Sparrow or Sudan Golden Sparrow, although the commonest sobriquet used by most dealers is Golden Song Sparrow, but as the species has no song to mention this is simply trade puffery to sell a sparrow. It is an African species that ranges through desert and scrubland from French Sahara to northern Abyssinia. It is an innocuous bird in a collection, a bit nervous and uninteresting in a cage but rather more interesting in an aviary. It has been bred on several occasions, and hybrids with a House Sparrow have been produced. A single pair have bred, but a small flock of, say, eight or nine birds are much happier and will build several nests in a natural colony close together in a tree or bush.

Arabian Golden Sparrow
(*Passer euchlorus*)

Description: *About 5 in. (127 mm.). Adult male differs from* luteus *in having the mantle yellow; it is also a richer yellow. Out of season it is browner grey above. Female differs from* luteus *in being ashy above, not brown. Juvenile like female, but greyer above.*

The Arabian Golden Sparrow is rarely imported, coming from the Somali Republic and Arabia, but occasionally it does appear. I have only seen it in dealers' cages and do not know it in collections. According to Rutgers it appears to be rather more insectivorous than other sparrows when breeding, but is typically wild, retiring and hardy.

Scaly-crowned Weaver
(*Sporopipes squamifrons*)

Description: *About 4 in. (101·6 mm.). Adult has forehead and crown black with white edging; lores, under eye, chin and stripe running down either side of throat black; white ring around eye; rest of head, cheeks, upperparts greyish brown; wings and tail black, feathers edged white; mesia and* centre of throat white; below, pale ash to whitish. Sexes alike; bill rose pink. Juvenile has dusky streaks in place of 'scaly' forehead; bill yellowish.

Sometimes listed as Scaly-fronted or simply Scaly Weaver, this species comes from southern Africa, ranging across dry thorn country from Angola to Rhodesia and most of South Africa. They are quite remarkable for their ability to survive for long periods – possibly months – without any water. It is a tame and friendly little bird, rather sparrow-like in its habits, and indeed is common around and in many towns and villages. The males have a pleasant twittering song. They are sociable creatures and when not breeding may be found in flocks of up to thirty birds, but even in the breeding season they congregate in small parties, and nests may be sufficiently close to each other to be regarded as forming a loose colony. The nest is a dome-shaped affair, a crudely woven ball with a side entrance, and may be built in a thornbush, or placed under the eaves of a house in a suitable hole or space. In captivity they will accept a nest-box. They also take discarded or unfinished weavers' nests and add their own nesting material. When breeding, the species becomes quite insectivorous, completely so in the wild, and needs an adequate supply of insect food on which to rear its young. The male becomes rather aggressive during this period. According to Shore Baily, 'this bird frequently breeds in captivity', and other writers say similar things. It is unfortunate that I have no references for these, so I cannot verify from personal experience the nuptial belligerency. My own birds have been peaceful members of mixed collections.

Speckle-fronted Weaver
(*Sporopipes frontalis*)

Description: *About $4\frac{1}{2}$ in. (114·3 mm.). Adult has forehead, top of head and mesial stripe black speckled with white; back of head, neck tawny to cinnamon; upperparts dusky ashy brown; wings and tail edged with dull white; lores, superciliary, ear-coverts and side of face dusky grey; chin to breast greyish; rest of underparts white; bill horn-colour. Sexes alike. Juvenile resembles adult, but paler and duller neck.*

Also referred to as Scaly-fronted Weaver or Frontal Weaver, this species is widely distributed over Africa from Senegal to Eritrea and Abyssinia. Like the Scaly-crowned it is a sociable bird, gathering in small flocks and often breeding in loose colonies. In habits it is very similar to its congener, and the male also has a pleasant twittering song. However, in an aviary it is quieter and more peaceful and doesn't become aggressive except in defence of its nest when breeding. In fact it is rather dull and easily becomes inactive. In a cage it gives an impression of rapidly becoming tame and steady, but I put this down to lethargy. It will also take a nest-box in an aviary, and has been bred on several occasions, the young needing plenty of insects.

Rock Sparrow
(*Petronia petronia*)

Description: *6–$6\frac{1}{2}$ in. (152·4–165·1 mm.). Adult, buff to earthy brown all over, paler below; pale superciliary with dark brown line above and below; back streaked with dark brown; terminal white spot on inner web of tail-feathers; yellow patch at* base of throat; bill dark above, horn-colour below. Sexes alike. Juvenile resembles adult but lacks yellow spot.

All the petronias are very similar, being large heavily built, rather upright-standing sparrowy birds. Desert races of this species and desert species are paler, but to most dealers they are all simply Petronia or Yellow-throated Petronia. Few dealers use the name Rock Sparrow, since the name sparrow has low commercial value. The Rock Sparrow ranges from southern France and Spain eastwards to China. It is a bird of hot dry country and it has been suggested that the increase in damp or humid weather in France and Germany has been the cause of the receding distribution southwards, the species falling back on Spain and north Africa. It is rarely available in fact, for despite its wide distribution it does not occur in those areas where bird-trapping is prevalent.

My birds have all been Spanish. I have kept them in cages with various other species of seed-eaters and have found them easy to maintain in excellent condition. I sent a few birds back to England for breeding possibilities, but despite near ideal conditions they have not successfully bred yet. Naturally they nest in holes or crevices in rocks, tree stumps or up in trees. On occasion they will nest in houses as part of a House Sparrow colony. In an aviary they will accept a box in a secluded and tucked-away corner. To my knowledge they have not been bred in captivity yet.

Bush Petronia
(*Petronia dentata*)

Description: *About 6 in.* (*152·4 mm.*). *Adult male, similar to Rock Sparrow but more uniform colour above and more greyish on head, whiter below; bill black in breeding season, otherwise horn-colour. Female similar but more streaked above and browner on head. Juvenile resembles female but yellow throat-spot usually absent.*

This bird may be listed as the Lesser Rock Sparrow. It is an African species that ranges right across Africa from Senegal to southwestern Arabia and northern Uganda. According to Praed and Grant it is a lowland species found either on plains near water or in hot lowland forests. It is a tree bird, and does not settle on rocks for choice, although it generally feeds on the ground. It nests in holes in trees. Of the African petronias this is the species most likely to be imported, although I have not seen it. It was bred most successfully in 1955 in Finland, where four broods were recorded, and previously it bred in Holland in 1933. It appears to be a shy breeder, and this is a characteristic of the genus I believe.

Yellow-throated Sparrow
(*Petronia xanthocollis*)

Description: *About 5½ in.* (*139·7 mm.*). *Adult male, ashy brown above, wings darker on quills with two paler wing-bars and a chestnut patch on lesser wing coverts; chin dull white; noticeable yellow patch on throat; rest of underparts pale ash brown. Female similar but chestnut on shoulder is duller, and yellow throat-spot much smaller. Juvenile similar to female, lacks yellow on throat.*

The Yellow-throated Sparrow or Petronia is the species most likely to appear when petronias are advertised. It ranges from Persia across to India where it is common around cultivated and open scrub country. It avoids forests, but has a great liking for trees and only descends to the ground to feed. It nests in holes or crevices and will readily take to a well-situated box in an aviary, the site being more important than the box. To my eye it is the prettiest of the petronias and a bird that deserves to be taken seriously. Butler suggested that petronias were aggressive, besides being uninteresting. Interest is a matter of opinion, but I have not found them to be aggressive. I kept a pair of the Indian Yellow-throated Sparrows in a smallish aviary one summer with a few other miscellaneous birds and they never struck me as being anything but normal in their behaviour. Like all my petronias they readily took mealworms and soon became tamed by their strategic use.

IV · BUBALORNITHINAE

BUFFALO-WEAVERS

This fascinating subfamily comprises two genera, *Bubalornis* and *Dinemellia*, that contain a total of only three species together. The two *Bubalornis* species are well written-up in the field literature, *Dinemellia* less so, but the latter is better known in aviculture. The common name is taken from the habit of the birds of attending herds of buffalo and other large game, feeding on the ground around the grazing animals. They are quite omnivorous, taking many insects, as well as fruit and seed. They will perch on the backs of buffalo and search for ticks, but are not so specialized in this function as the Ox-pecker. However, they are best known for their nests, which are enormous, being built of large twigs and sticks and sometimes filling the centre of a tree; there are differences between the two genera, but both may be described as being colonial nesters. They are large birds, not very weaver-like in appearance or behaviour, and certainly of interest to aviculture.

HOUSING

These birds may certainly be kept in cages, but as they tend to be large, getting on for ten inches long, they cannot be kept in an ordinary cage for long. A reasonable cage for this kind of bird, which allows a couple of perches to be placed at either end with newspaper on trays below, together with a generous food-tray in the centre, is about 6 ft. (1·8 m.) long × 2 ft. (0·6 m.) high and wide. They are excellent aviary birds, are not quarrelsome and seem to share well with other birds. Here I must say that I have never seen one kept with waxbills or small finches, and would not advise keeping them with such birds because, peaceful or not, the waxbills become more nervous and less likely to live either as naturally or as long unless the quarters are really spacious. They feed in mixed flocks, with other species of similar habit, and are frequently seen in the company of *Spreo* starlings. The ability of these two to cohabit is evidenced by the fact that spreos of one species or another have been found breeding in unused nests in buffalo-weaver colonies. This suggests that *Spreo* starlings might make appropriate companions to buffalo-weavers in captivity and they would need similar care and feeding.

FOOD

The basis of the varied diet of the buffalo-weavers is seeds and grain, but they are known to take a wide variety of insects including termites, beetles, locusts, grubs, worms, ants, mole-crickets and spiders. They also take some fruit and berries. In captivity they may be given a mixture of millet seeds, Canary, sunflower, hemp, wheat and oats. A universal grade of softbill food may be given separately, and also vegetable and fruit. They will willingly take mealworms and other live food, and of course live food is quite important when breeding is under way. Buffalo-weavers are enthusiastic bathers, and this should be remembered when providing watering facilities – a broad pan about $1\frac{1}{2}$ in. deep for a cage and a bowl in an aviary.

BREEDING

The only species of buffalo-weaver that I know of to have bred in captivity is Dinemelli's. This bird does not breed in quite as concentrated a way as the two *Bubalornis* species, so it might be wrong to draw conclusions from one to apply to the others. However, it seems as though all three species are enthusiastic and incorrigible nest-builders. They do not weave pendant nests out of grass and palm leaves, but use sticks that may at times appear to be too big for the bird to carry. The nest-site is a veritable rookery, and the din and squabbling, enriched by twig-stealing among neighbours, puts a European Rook to shame. It is not clear from the literature whether the nests cause the parts of the trees where they are built to die or whether the birds build mostly in dead parts of trees. While a single pair of Dinemelli's will build individual nests, and a few pairs will build separate nests in one tree, the *Bubalornis* species are fairly co-operative birds, and a party of up to a dozen adult males and juveniles from the last brood will work together in co-operation and build a single multi-nest structure, a tenement nest block which may house up to a dozen females who build the nest cavities and line them with soft grasses and leaf debris. There may be several of these nest conglomerates in one tree. Starlings of the *Spreo* genus are often found nesting in, presumably, surplus or unused nests within a nest complex.

The *Bubalornis* buffalo-weavers have not bred in captivity to my knowledge. My guess is that they would do so readily if there were several birds, let's say a dozen, and they had an enclosure like the northern or Snowdon Aviary at the London

White-billed Buffalo-weaver (*Bubalornis albirostris*); Dinemelli's Weaver (*Dinemellia dinemelli*)

Zoo. Whether they would breed in a typical garden aviary or not I don't know, but I imagine that anything less than 20 × 12 ft. (6·1 × 3·7 m.) would be too small to provide sufficient space for these large birds to behave naturally. A live tree would not be essential, but a suitable nest framework and plenty of material should be. When rearing, the nestlings are fed on insect food and various soft foods; they take hard seed very shortly after fledging and no doubt the parents include seed in their weaning diet.

White-billed Buffalo-weaver
(*Bubalornis albirostris*)

Description: *About 9½ in. (241·3 mm.).
Adult male, wholly black, with white
bases to the feathers that are normally obscured; fine white leading
edge on primaries; bill in breeding
season bright white and swollen at
base; out of season is black. Female
similar but duller and has blackish
bill. Juvenile dull black or blackish
brown, streaked darker above, paler
below; bill horn-colour.*

This bird may be listed simply as
Buffalo Weaver. It ranges from
Senegal across to Uganda and Eritrea,
and is a bird of dry country. Bannerman mentions its preference for
building in large trees in villages, and
many visitors to Africa will be struck
by the buffalo-weavers' nests in the
trees by the runways of many air-
ports. While some writers speculate
that the species might take small
animals or birds in addition to locusts
and other large insects, it appears
that Cordons-blue and Cut-throats
are able to build their own nests
within the colonies, much like sparrows in storks' nests, and go unmolested. So any shrike-like habit
may be discounted. Dr. Bannerman
mentions that this species is unique
among the entire order Passeriformes,
in that the male in full breeding condition develops a penis. I mention
this in the event of its discovery causing undue alarm to an unsuspecting
bird-keeper. It might prove to be a
useful indicator of sex should there
be other doubts (though its absence
will not indicate a female).

Red-billed Buffalo-weaver
(*Bubalornis niger*)

Description: *9–9½ in. (228·6–241·3
mm.). Adult bird resembles white-
billed species, but male is richer black,
and has a red bill. The female is
duller, browner above and mottled
below; bill horn-colour. Juveniles
resemble female, but male has bill
reddish, female horn-colour with
orange tip.*

This species comes from East and
South Africa. The red bill is very
variable and may be anything from
yellow to true red. I do not know
if it has ever been imported, but it
appears to have exactly the same
needs and behaves the same as the
above species.

Dinemelli's Weaver
(*Dinemellia dinemelli*)

Description: *9–9½ in. (228·6–241·3
mm.). Adult has entire head and
underparts white or off-white; mantle,
wings and tail dusky brown with
white edge to greater wing-coverts
and flight-feathers, white patch to
base of primaries; lower back, rump,
upper- and lowertail-coverts orange
red. Sexes alike. Juveniles similar,
but orange is dull and not reddish.*

This bird may be called White-
headed Buffalo-weaver or Dinemelli's
Buffalo-weaver: many writers refer to
it as Dinemelli's Weaver, preferring
to keep the name buffalo-weaver solely
for the *Bubalornis*. It is a bird of East
Africa, and is found in thorn scrub
and dry bush, nesting in thorn trees.
The multi-nest unit is not so well
developed with this species, and it
is monogamous as opposed to polygamous like the *Bubalornis*.

It bred at Pittsburgh in 1957 and
an excellent report, complete with
photographs, appears in the *Avicultural Magazine* for 1958. Two birds
had been purchased in 1954, built
a lot of nests during the following
two years and finally bred properly.

They built in the curtain vine (*Cissus sicyoides*) with which their conservatory-aviary was well planted, and reared a fine healthy youngster on mealworms, fruits, and insectivorous mixture. They were not at all aggressive at any time, not even in defence of the newly fledged young, but would fiercely defend the nest cavity against invaders of any size.

BIBLIOGRAPHY

In this book I have made many references to the words of individuals, some long dead, and others happily very much still with us.

Without them a book like this simply would not be possible, for there are far too many species for one person ever to have sufficient experience of to enable him to write everything from first hand. Rather than give a detailed list of all my references as if for a scientific paper (which, not being selected, do not guide the reader) I have decided to present two lists. The first is this short bibliography, with some personal comments of my own. The second is a list of references for first breedings, breeding reports of interest, and a handful of articles of wider scope than simply reports of breedings.

AVICULTURAL BOOKS

Aviculture
This was a treatise on the management of foreign and British birds in captivity, published in three volumes from 1925 to 1927 by the Avicultural Society. Volume 1, 1925, deals with passerines and is the only volume that concerns us here. The work was published under the auspices of the Avicultural Society of London, *La Société Nationale d'Acclimatation de France* by a mixed committee, and the editors of the *Avicultural Magazine* and of *L'Oiseau*.

The chapter on 'Typical finches' was contributed by Arthur G. Butler, Ph.D., and covers a large number of finches, buntings and weavers, and is extremely variable in the quality of its content. As a rule a full description is given, plus reference to song and habitat or distribution and a remark such as that concluding such notes on the Scarlet Rose-finch (*carpodacus erythrinus*): 'An example which a sister brought home for me from India never sang, but often uttered its call note; it died the winter after I received it.' The chapter on 'Grosbeaks' was contributed by M. A. Decoux, who covers hawfinches, American cardinals and *Sporophilae* seed-eaters among others, with the same quality as Butler on 'finches'. M. Decoux's chapters on 'Grassfinches' and 'Waxbills' are very good. W. Shore Baily wrote on whydahs and weavers with a lot of useful remarks.

In general this is a book of historical interest, and is much sought after by aviculturists today. Most specialist booksellers have a waiting-list for it. It was never reprinted because the editors of the *Avicultural Magazine* at the time, worried about loss and damage, packed all the plates (by Roland Green, Grönvold, and others) and put them on a ship to Canada to escape bomb damage during the war. The ship was sunk by a Nazi U-boat. The book is full of inaccuracies which on occasion could seriously mislead a beginner; many species are placed in the wrong family, given scientific names which are no longer used and difficult to trace, and there are a few wrong identifications. To an experienced bird man it is a book of great charm, and makes reference to many species that are not to be found anywhere else (except this book).

Foreign Bird-keeping
Written by A. G. Butler, this is a re-write of a series of articles the celebrated bird-keeper wrote for *The Feathered World* in 1892. It was intended to be produced in two volumes, but in fact is in two parts forming one volume. My volume has no date, but it could have been published around 1912. Part One deals with seed-eating and insectivorous birds, and is a collection of personal reminiscences that has to be read rather than referred to (for instance under 'Madeiran Chaffinch' he discusses sparrows and the Pine Grosbeak), but it is a very interesting and useful section, much better for avicultural reference in fact than the same author's equivalent chapters in *Aviculture*. Part Two deals with parrots, crows, pigeons, larks and starlings. Throughout there are useful notes and references to other great aviculturists and their achievements which one rarely finds in the literature of today. Most of the illustrations are done by Dr. Butler, or A. F. Lydon, staff artist of *The Feathered World*. This is a very useful work of reference, by no means complete, or totally accurate, but worth having.

Foreign Finches in Captivity
My copy of this classic work by A. G. Butler is the second edition, dated 1899. It is a 'quality' work, with each of the eighty species dealt with having its own colour plate by F. W. Frohawk. It is a large thick book, over 300 pages, full of lengthy quotations from other authors. Somehow it doesn't invite reference; I only referred to it once in the six months it took me to write this book, and yet it contains a lot of interesting information. I paid four times as much for it as I did for Butler's *Foreign Bird-keeping*, but I find the latter book at least four times as useful. I would certainly recommend it to the serious bird-keeper who wants to expand his library and build up works of reference. To the beginner or specialist it has less value.

The Foreigner
During the 1930s the Keston Foreign Bird Farm published a series of pocket magazines or pamphlets entitled *The Foreigner: A practical guide to the keeping, breeding and showing of all kinds of Foreign Birds and Budgerigars*. These journals have been bound as proper books, and sets, or part-sets, of the six volumes occasionally come on to the market. I have the first three (1934–6) and find them interesting bedside reading, since they are charming and nostalgic and take one back to a different age altogether. The contents are a collection of articles, notes, letters and even poems written by some of the leading aviculturists of the day. The authors represent the great interwar era (as Butler represented the Victorian age of aviculture). As a work of reference they are not of much use, since most if not all of the contents will be duplicated in essence in other sources.

Foreign Bird-keeping
Written by Edward J. Boosey, published by Iliffe Books in 1956 (second edition 1962), this book reflects a life of commercial aviculture by a man who was the joint proprietor of the Keston Foreign Bird Farm. For decades this establishment was the leading importer and retailer of foreign birds in Britain, and as such gave its owners a golden opportunity to observe and study the birds they handled. Unlike many trade establishments Keston maintained a large private collection for breeding, and the gratification of its owners, and Boosey's book reflects this. It is quite a good guide to the birds that it deals with, and is quite comprehensive in its scope. There are five main parts: seed-eaters, parrots, softbills, pigeons and general husbandry. The first section, entitled 'Waxbills, Finches and other Seed-eaters', covers some ninety-six birds. Some thirty-eight species are illustrated by passable black and white photographs, and a further thirty in colour, but there is no index of illustrations and one never knows from the text whether a bird may be illustrated or not. The weakness of what is almost an excellent reference book is that the author missed an opportunity to describe the behaviour, or habits, of so many rarely imported species. The only rarely imported birds about which any really helpful notes are given are those that were bred at Keston. If a bird did not soon show signs of breeding it was sold and is represented in the book by such remarks as 'it is imported from time to time, but never at all freely' (Himalayan Goldfinch, *C. carduelis caniceps*).

Foreign Birds for Garden Aviaries
By Alec Brooksbank, published by Cage Birds in 1949. Mr. Brooksbank was Boosey's partner at Keston, and in this book he wrote of his personal experience or knowledge of some sixty birds of all kinds,

including thirty-nine seed-eating birds, mostly waxbills and munias. It is a charming book, and very helpful to a beginner just starting out with his first small collection of waxbills and finches. Every species is illustrated with one of the author's personal photographs, and the text gives origin, feeding, behaviour and breeding prospects all in a short and very easily read manner, free from technicalities or pretensions. An updated version of this book would be most welcome.

Cagebirds in Colour
Written by John J. Yealland, published by Witherby in 1958. Mr. Yealland was head keeper of birds to the old Duke of Bedford (a world-famous animal-keeper) and latterly Curator of Birds at the Zoological Society of London. As such the author was well qualified to produce a handbook on foreign birds. It is a small concise pocket-book dealing with some 157 species (of which about ninety-three are seed-eaters). Every species is clearly illustrated in colour and the text is excellent, giving short, to the point, objective notes on origin, habitat and habits, feeding and behaviour in captivity and breeding in captivity. This modest little book is probably the most accurate and useful source of reference to a beginner. Its only limitation is that it only embraces 157 birds, but they should be enough for any non-specialist!

Aviary Birds
By Rosemary Low, published by Arco Publications in 1968. Miss Low is well known as a parrot specialist and as sub-editor and regular con-tributor to *Cage and Aviary Birds*. Among her bird hobbies is visiting zoos, and she has visited most zoos in Europe. This book is an introduc-tion and a general guide to what is known as 'The Fancy', the world of bird-keeping and bird-exhibiting. There are sensibly written chapters on accommodation, feeding, sickness, etc., and among the bird chapters are British Birds (fifteen finches and buntings), Foreign Seed-eaters (forty-nine species) and within each chapter are notes on feeding, accommodation, breeding hints, show procedure, and points that count in exhibitions. A separate chapter is given to the two domesticated species, the Zebra Finch and Bengalese, and a full chapter is devoted to exhibiting. This is a first-class guide for the newcomer and beginner in bird-keeping. The book's weakness is that it is virtually not illustrated, only ten species appear in photographs.

Cage and Aviary Birds
Written by D. H. S. Risdon, published by Faber and Faber in 1972. Mr. Risdon is proprietor of the Tropical Bird Gardens at Rode; prior to that he was general manager at Dudley Zoo, and formerly a director of the Keston Foreign Bird Farm. Clearly, another person with birds

right in his system. In this book he has written an introduction to just about every aspect of practical bird-keeping. There are chapters on housing, feeding, general management, ailments, and a set of chapters on birds. No distinction is made between British and foreign, and no mention is made of exhibiting. The seed-eating birds are presented in four groups, the species within each group being compatible with each other. The book is an excellent guide for a newcomer and will help him to master those first rudimentary steps to becoming an aviculturist. There are quite a few excellent photographs, including ten of seed-eating birds.

Breeding British Birds in Cage and Aviary
By R. B. Bennett, published by Cage Birds in 1959. This is a useful work of reference, well illustrated by the author, and is the only book of its kind, dealing solely with British birds in captivity. Where the author clearly has personal experience of a species his advice is clear and sound. But, when dealing with a species that he has not bred, or worse still has not kept, the notes are very weak and often of no use at all. If the word 'breeding' were omitted from the title the complaint would be much less felt. An up-to-date and well-researched modern edition is definitely called for.

Cage and Garden Birds
By Georg Steinbacher, published by Batsford in 1959. I think this book first appeared in German. It is very well illustrated by some forty-eight colour plates, each showing several birds, accurately painted by R. Scholz. In addition there are innumerable line drawings. This book is an excellent discourse on aviculture, thoroughly comprehensive in its discussion on every aspect of a general nature. It is not any kind of checklist, and not one single bird is given specific treatment. Don't buy it to refer to any particular bird, but do buy it as a very educative bedside book.

The Handbook of Foreign Birds in Colour
By A. Rutgers, published by Blandford in 1964, the English edition edited by K. A. Norris. This book is derived from material published in Holland in Tropische Volière Vogels. It is basically in two parts, sixty-four pages of colour photographs, and some 120 pages of text on the birds illustrated. The photographs are very variable, a few are excellent, but many are decidedly unhelpful in identifying the birds depicted. A few are incorrectly captioned and the platemaker's retouching sometimes looks as though it was done with two left feet. However, it is excellent in the text, similar to Yealland's book, much more

extensive, but variable in quality and accuracy. None the less, it is probably the work that I referred to most often when writing this book. My first thought on any poorly known species was always 'I wonder if Rutgers has it' and often there was the bird. Species that are not mentioned anywhere else are given detailed commentary, and some 147 seed-eaters are dealt with, including all the common ones and many uncommon. In spite of the faults mentioned above, this handbook is probably the most useful practical reference to the experienced bird-keeper or beginner alike.

ORNITHOLOGICAL WORKS OF REFERENCE, INCLUDING FIELD GUIDES

The Song and Garden Birds of North America
This is a glossy all-colour book produced and published by the National Geographic Society in the U.S., undated. Every species is given, and illustrated in colour, and all the North American seed-eaters are there. Unfortunately the text is intended more for the general public and is not very technical, and no subspecies are named or described. As a work of interest it is very good, and the coloured plates, whether photograph or painting, are outstanding.

Birds of North America
By Robbins, Bruun and Zim, illustrated by Arthur Singer, and published by Golden Press, New York. This is an excellent paperback field guide that will facilitate accurate identification of any North American bird within minutes (if not seconds): it only gives major races or colour phases.

Life Histories of Central American Birds
By Alexander Skutch, published by the Cooper Ornithological Society in 1954. This volume is one of a series, and deals with members of Fringillidae, Thraupidae, Icteridae, Parulidae and Coerebidae. The following seed-eating birds are dealt with, in great detail: Variable Seed-eater, White-collared Seed-eater, Yellow-faced Grassquit, Blue-black Grosbeak, Streaked Saltator, Striped Brush-finch, Orange-billed Sparrow and Black-striped Sparrow. Thirteen species of Tanager are dealt with among the others. This is a book to buy if it happens to include a species that one is studying and attempting to breed. It is adequately illustrated by Don Eckleberry, and has many photographs. It is a book of outstanding merit that gives a detailed commentary on the natural life history of various species.

The Birds of Colombia

By R. Meyer de Schauensee, published by E. & S. Livingstone in 1964. This book is really a checklist of the birds of Colombia, all 1,556 of them. With subspecies there are 2,640 forms, but descriptions and mentions of the races are often inadequate. Every family has one species illustrated by a good line drawing, and although there are twenty plates, each one showing a number of birds or heads of birds, eight are in black and white (thus rendering them of little use) and of the South American seed-eaters dealt with in my book I could find only six in colour (none in black and white) in Schauensee's book. The text is restricted to description of the nominate race with mention of diagnostic point of difference of a race, range of the species in South America, range and habitat in Colombia. At best it is a guide to the aviculturist to identification.

Guide to the Birds of South America

By R. Meyer de Schauensee, published by Oliver & Boyd in 1971. This book is an extension of *The Birds of Colombia*. The author has deleted all reference to races, and kept only nominate race description, and known distribution limits, but it lists *all* the birds of South America. It has the same format and layout as the Colombia book, and uses the same illustrations, with a few more plates added. Specialists from South America have told me that the book is a masterpiece of desk research but lacks accuracy. Personally I find it at best only a guide in identifying birds that I already have a good idea about. An example of its inadequacy is Pelzeln's Saffron Finch. This bird is listed by all earlier writers as a separate and good species, *Sicalis pelzelni*; even Rutgers presents it as such. But the word *pelzelni* does not appear in this book, and it was only by referring to the British Museum that I was able to confirm that it is now considered to be a race of the Saffron Finch, *Sicalis flaveola*. It is essentially a checklist.

The Birds of Surinam

By Francois Haverschmidt, published by Oliver & Boyd in 1968, and illustrated by Paul Barruel. This is a beautifully illustrated, well-produced field guide with forty colour plates, each depicting half a dozen or so birds. Of the seven *Sporophila* dealt with, four are illustrated in colour and three by line drawing. In addition to description, habitat and habits there are details of nesting, food and total range. The only drawback of the book, which is easily the best of any to do with Central or South America, is that it is limited to Surinam.

The Birds of the British Isles: Volume 1
By David A. Bannerman, published by Oliver & Boyd in twelve volumes in 1953. We are only concerned here with the first volume of a superb production on the birds of Britain. It embraces the crows, starlings and oriole, and all the finches, buntings and sparrows that occur in the British Isles. Several pages are given to each species, and lavish detail about description, migration, habits and breeding habits is presented elegantly and lovingly. Each species has a full-page colour plate painted by George Lodge. With a field guide in hand and this book at home, one is just about perfectly equipped for British seed-eaters.

The Birds of Britain and Europe: with North Africa and the Middle East
By Heinzel, Fitter and Parslow, published by Collins in 1972. This is a slightly bulky paperback pocket guide. It is one of three excellent British field guides currently available, but since our criterion here is an avicultural one I have to single this book out as being the best, for it has more pictures. Pictures are what the aviculturist needs so often. For instance this book contains accurate colour plates of the Rock Sparrow, Yellow-throated Sparrow, Pale Rock Sparrow, St. Helena Waxbill, four Rosefinches, the Wild Canary compared with the Serin, and various other species and/or races not easily found elsewhere.

Birds of the Soviet Union: Volume 5
Produced by G. P. Dement'ev and others. Translated into English and published in six volumes by Israel Programme for Scientific Translations, Jerusalem, 1970. The fifth volume of this mammoth work deals with the crows, starlings, orioles, finches, sparrows, buntings, larks, wagtails and pipits, American warblers, tree creepers and nuthatches, and the tits. It runs to nearly 1,000 pages, and goes into enormous detail on each species, describing the type and world distribution, and giving full treatment to every subspecies that occurs within the Soviet Union. It is unique, and is very useful to the aviculturist for it embraces all of those Himalayan birds that are occasionally imported, and the Asian Greenfinches, Siskins, Goldfinches and Hawfinches. Here too are details of Rosefinches and Petronias, and full details on the Red-fronted Serin. The text deals with distribution; habitational status, biotope, subspecies; ecology, moult, diet, field marks, song, description, colouration; and every race is given individual treatment.

The African Handbook of Birds
By Mackworth-Praed and Grant, published by Longman in three series: *Birds of Eastern and North Eastern Africa*; *Birds of the Southern Third of Africa*; and *Birds of Western Africa*. Each series is in two volumes, Volume 2 always dealing with passerines. The first series was

published in 1955, and Volume 2 of the third series appeared in 1973. It is an excellent field guide, with every species either illustrated in colour or by a black and white line drawing, and has proved to be invaluable to the bird trade, and many aviculturists who keep African birds. In addition to descriptions of every race of a given species, details are given on general distribution, range within the area covered by the volume to hand, habits, nest and eggs, recorded breeding, food and call. The volumes on East and South Africa are now somewhat in need of updating, particularly East Africa, since much new information on breeding and feeding has come to light in the last fifteen years, and some of the nomenclature is a bit rusty. However, it remains the definitive guide on African birds and may take precedence in the birdkeeper's bookshelf over all other African books as a ready reference to identification.

The Birds of Tropical West Africa: Volume 7
By David A. Bannerman, published by Oliver & Boyd in 1949. What Bannerman did for British birds in a previously mentioned book he also did for West African birds in eight superb volumes, with every species illustrated by George Lodge and Roland Green. The colour plates are excellent. Volume 7 deals with all the weavers, whydahs, bishops, waxbills and mannikins that occur in West Africa. The detail and qualitative comment are exhaustive and should satisfy the most inquiring reader. The full set of volumes is now prohibitively expensive, but for some reason copies of Volume 7 crop up on the market at regular intervals.

The Birds of West and Equatorial Africa
By David A. Bannerman, published in two volumes by Oliver & Boyd in 1953. All eight volumes of the original work have been compressed into two; in the process one is given a much tighter and more economical work that only serves to demonstrate how superb the original was. All the original illustrations have been kept, but they are now almost a quarter of the original size. I prefer this to Praed and Grant for West African birds, but it is not so quick and easy to use.

The Canaries, Seed-eaters and Buntings of Southern Africa
Written by C. J. Skead and published for the South African Bird Book Fund by the Central News Agency, South Africa, 1960. The main part of this book is a superbly detailed account of the thirteen finches and buntings that occur in South Africa. As an identification guide it is a luxury, but as an in-depth study it must be of great interest to anyone intent on getting the maximum enjoyment from his birds. There are many photographs of birds, nests and habitat and there are colour plates of every species, many by D. M. Henry.

The Popular Handbook of Indian Birds
By Hugh Whistler, published by Oliver & Boyd in 1928 (fifth edition, 1963). A good field guide, well illustrated with many colour plates and line drawings, and giving details of description, field identification, distribution, habits, etc., breeding, nest and usually food. A modern edition is called for with updated scientific names, but even so with little difficulty the researcher can find useful information on many of the commoner Indian birds, including some sixteen species of weaver, finch, bunting and sparrow.

The Birds of Sikkim India
By Salim Ali, published by Oxford University Press in 1963. Copies of this book are extremely hard to come by. I understand that Dr. Ali's multi-volume work on the birds of India will make a reprinting unnecessary, but it will be some time yet before the volumes on seed-eaters are published. This book is a comprehensive, concise work, dealing with the 200 or so species of the region – although rare species and vagrants receive scant attention – and for each species gives notes on habitat, distribution and description, together with notes on habits. The notes on nesting are good, but no mention is made of food, a key item for aviculturists. The illustrations are fairly accurate but of indifferent quality.

Birds of Borneo; Birds of Burma
By Bertram Smythie, published by Oliver & Boyd. These two books are typical field guides from a well-known ornithological publisher. As such they give useful notes on identification, habitat and range, but do not help the aviculturist much past identification.

Australian Finches
By Klaus Immelmann, published by Angus & Robertson in 1965. Like the book by Skead on South African finches this book is confined to seed-eaters only, namely the Australian estrildids. From the avicultural point of view this must be the best reference book. Each bird is given about ten pages of totally useful information about it. A typical chapter would be subdivided as follows: References, introduction, names, descriptions, distribution, geographical variation. Field Notes: food and feeding habits, calls, courtship and mating, site and nature of nest, breeding, social activities. Aviary Notes: housing, food, breeding and hybrids. The avicultural notes alone are more comprehensive than can be found in any avicultural handbook, and they admirably supplement the field notes. Frankly, I suggest that this book is essential for any serious Australian 'Finch' enthusiast.

MONOGRAPHS
There are three monographs, each a full-length book, worthy of the serious attention of a specialist and I personally could not imagine taking up any of the three birds mentioned without reading the book. Each is as different as the three birds are from each other, and the three authors. Each contains a mine of information. The books are:

The House Sparrow
By J. D. Summers-Smith, No. 19 in the New Naturalist Monograph series published by Collins in 1963 (reprinted in 1967).

The Hawfinch
By Guy Mountfort, No. 15 in the same series, Collins.

The Snow Bunting
By Desmond Nethersole-Thompson, published by Oliver & Boyd in 1966.

Finches
By Ian Newton, published by Collins in 1973. *Finches* deals with the eighteen species of Fringillidae that occur as residents in Europe. While it has far less of an avicultural slant than Immelmann's *Australian Finches*, it is a handbook that must be of equal value to the aviculturist who is genuinely interested in European finches. The detailing on natural food and food-seeking behaviour alone makes the book worth its price. The first three chapters summarize the characteristics, habits and distribution of the individual species. A further fourteen chapters discuss various particular aspects of the biology of the finches dealt with, some general like 'Feeding ecology' and others quite specific like 'Bullfinches and fruit buds'. A chapter of great interest to finch-breeders is the one on moult.

PERIODICALS

Avicultural Magazine
The journal of the Avicultural Society is published bimonthly and is sent free to members of the society. Length is variable, but there are more or less forty pages to each issue; usually there is a colour plate of first-class quality and often there are black and white photographs and line drawings. The contents consist of contributions from members, usually breeding reports, and often of 'near misses', and progress reports from large or well-known collections and zoos. The *Avicultural Magazine* is probably the premier avicultural journal in the world and is recognized in the scientific world to the extent that items are occasionally reviewed in *Ibis*.

The society, and its journal, have existed for nearly eighty years, and many first breedings appear in those early years (see the reference section following), but the early volumes are very difficult to obtain today. A complete set of volumes may be currently priced at £1,000. Post-war volumes are more easy to obtain however.

Membership applications should be sent to the Hon. Secretary, Harry J. Horswell, Sladmore Farm, Cryers Hill, Nr. High Wycombe, Buckinghamshire.

Foreign Birds

The magazine of the Foreign Bird League is the journal of a society which exists to further the interests of the Foreign Bird Fancy, that is to say, it is concerned to some extent with exhibiting and its annual show is a major event in the calendar. The F.B.L. has been in existence for about forty years. Its journal has never achieved the recognition of the *Avicultural Magazine*, and the proliferation of specialist societies within the fancy in recent years has resulted in a great fragmentation of activities, and a lot of material that might have been channelled into this journal now appears in specialist society magazines and bulletins. Formerly bimonthly, the journal is now published quarterly. Enthusiasts are particularly keen to collect the volumes of the late 1950s and early 1960s as these were very rich in breeders' reports.

Applications for membership should be addressed to Mr. and Mrs. C. W. Stevens, Spen Cottage, Greenmoor, Woodcote, Reading, Berks. RG8 0RB.

The Australian Finch Society

This society was formed in 1971 by a group of enthusiasts to encourage the breeding and exhibiting of all Australian finches (excluding the Zebra Finch) and all parrot-finches. It publishes a journal every three months containing news and views about these delightful and interesting little birds. A high level of interest and an ever-growing membership that extends right around the world have resulted in contributions about the behaviour of various species that have not appeared elsewhere. It is well worth the small trouble involved for an enthusiast for Australian finches or parrot-finches to join this society.

Applications for membership should be addressed to the Secretary, Mr. Barrie R. Thomas, 14 Green Lane, Rainford, Lancs.

Cage and Aviary Birds

This is a weekly newspaper published by I.P.C. Business Publications and is available through newsagents. It contains a wide variety of articles ranging from reports of observations of birds in the wild, not only from Britain but all over the world, to more specialized matter. There is a tendency for the editorial bias to be seasonal, responding to the bird-keeper's calendar. For example, the autumn issues contain a great deal of coverage of bird shows; the winter has many articles on preparing Canaries and Budgerigars for the coming breeding season; spring brings an increase in the number of foreign birds imported, and many aspects of their care in captivity are catered for. Whilst much of the material is essentially ephemeral there are many reports that do not appear anywhere else. A further function of *Cage and Aviary Birds* is that it contains a lot of advertising, and is the main source of information for what species are available. It is a paper that is distributed to aviculturists all over the world and in its turn has many contributors from overseas.

RECORDS OF BIRDS BRED
IN CAPTIVITY

It was my original intention with this section, to prepare a list of postwar breeding reports that I thought would be of value to the reader. However, when Dr. C. J. O. Harrison began his series of lists* of records of first breedings in Britain I was inspired to enlarge the list to make it as comprehensive as possible. I have gone back to *Records of Birds Bred in Captivity* that Dr. Emilius Hopkinson wrote under fifty years ago (Witherby, 1926), referred to his later notes in the *Avicultural Magazine* in 1930, 1932 and 1944, and cross-referred to Harrison. My own notes of breedings recorded in *Foreign Birds* and *Cage and Aviary Birds* are supplementary to the work of Hopkinson and Harrison, and include some first breedings not included by either.

My objective has been to give the reader a set of references that will serve to inform him should they be taken up. Several are only mentions, I am sorry to say, but they help to fill a picture. Unlike Harrison I have included breedings in other countries, but only those recorded in British literature. This does not make my list a true world list.

For those not familiar with the shorthand used for references here is a key to abbreviations:

A.M. – *Avicultural Magazine*
B.N. – *Bird Notes*, the journal of the Foreign Bird Club from 1903 to 1924
C.&A.B. – *Cage and Aviary Birds*
F.B. – *Foreign Birds*
I.Z.Y.B. – *International Zoo Year Book*
Hopkinson, *Records*, 1926 – *Records of Birds Bred in Captivity*, E. Hopkinson, 1926
L.Z. Repts. – *London Zoo Reports*
Occ. Publ. – *Occasional Publications*, Association for the Study and Propagation of European Birds in Aviaries.

* In the *Avicultural Magazine* in 1972. The list covered *all* breedings recorded in the recognized literature (i.e. excluding *Cage and Aviary Birds* for which no indices exist, *Foreign Birds* and other publications of a popular nature). It appeared in sections in various issues of the magazine throughout 1972 and 1973.

A typical reference might be *A.M.*, 79, 1973, 3–7. This means that the breeding will be found recorded by the name of the person before it, on pages 3 to 7 in the *Avicultural Magazine*, volume no. 79 which appeared in 1973.

I EMBERIZIDAE

Red-headed Bunting (*Emberiza bruniceps*), Chester Zoo, *A.M.*, 79, 1973, 3–7.

Reed Bunting (*Emberiza schoeniclus*), W. E. Teschemaker, *B.N.*, 1910, 363, 368.

Cirl Bunting (*Emberiza cirlus*), W. E. Teschemaker, *B.N.*, 1909, 119, 128, 145.

Yellow-breasted Bunting (*Emberiza aureola*), Chester Zoo, *A.M.*, 78, 1972, 9–11.

Elegant Bunting (*Emberiza elegans*), R. L. Restall, *A.M.*, 76, 1970, 40–6.

Golden-breasted Bunting (*Emberiza flaviventris*), A. Martin (in 1911), *A.M.*, 1930, 340. *Also*, J. Strachan, *F.B.*, 21, 1955, 70.

Cinnamon-breasted Rock Bunting (*Emberiza tahapisi*), M. S. Aldham, *A.M.* (5), 2, 1937, 311. *Also*, R. L. Restall, *C.&A.B.*, 1/9/1966.

Snow Bunting (*Plectrophenax nivalis*), A. F. Moody, *A.M.*, 52, 1946, 18–19. *Also*, F. C. Astles, *Occ. Publ.*, 3, 1969, 4–5.

Lark-like Bunting (*Emberiza impetuani*), K. S. Harrap, *A.M.*, 76, 1970, 4–5.

Slate-coloured Junco (*Junco hyemalis*), London Zoo, Hopkinson, *Records*, 1926.

White-crowned Song Sparrow (*Zonotrichia leuchphrys*), London Zoo, 1921, Hopkinson, *Records*, 1926.

Rufous-collared Sparrow (*Zonotrichia pileata*), W. E. Teschemaker, *A.M.* (6), 26, 1921, 62. *Also*, B. Bennett, *F.B.*, 25, 1959, 189. *Also*, H. Murray, *A.M.*, 72, 1966, 131–2.

Harris's Sparrow (*Zonotrichia querula*), W. Shore Baily, *A.M.* (4), 9, 1931, 252–4.

Diuca Finch (*Diuca diuca*), 'Bred at the Zoo in 1887 and by Miss Alderson in 1900', A. G. Butler, *Foreign Birds for Cage and Aviary*, c. 1906, 1, 132. *Also*, W. Shore Baily, *Diuca diuca minor*, *B.N.*, 1921, 152.

Rufous-sided Towhee (*Pipilo erythrophthalmus*), 'Has been repeatedly bred', Hopkinson, *Records*, 1926.

Spotted Towhee (*Pipilo maculatus oreganus*), C. M. Payne, *A.M.*, 61, 1955, 224–6.

Black-crested Finch (*Lophospingus pusillus*), C. af Enehjelm, *A.M.*, 60, 1954, 11–15. *Also*, Miss L. Leitch, *A.M.*, 76, 1970, 174–6.

Dickcissel (*Spiza americana*), W. E. Teschemaker, *B.N.*, 1911, 238, 268, and 1912, 143.

Red-crested Finch (*Coryphospingus cristatus*), Decoux, *A.M.*, 1927, 22. *Also*, J. Trollope, *A.M.*, 72, 1966, 149–53. *Also*, G. A. Petrie, *F.B.*, 36, 1970, 87–8.

Pileated Finch (*Coryphospingus pileatus*), Mrs. H. Williams, *A.M.* (2), 4, 1905–6, 30, 49. *Also*, Easton Scott in Page, *B.N.*, 1911, 184. *Also*, B. C. Thomasset, *A.M.* (4), 9, 1931, 303–4.

Crimson Finch (*Rhodospingus cruentus*), 'Neunzig says it has been bred several times', Hopkinson, *Records*, 1926.

Saffron Finch (*Sicalis flaveola*), 'Often bred', *B.N.*, 1904, 247. *Also*, *Sicalis flaveola pelzelni*, W. E. Teschemaker, *A.M.* (3), 1, 1909, 226; (3), 3, 1911, 298. *Also*, Corcoran and Southon, *F.B.*, 22, 1956, 13. *Also*, R. L. Restall, *C.&A.B.*, 18/1/1968.

Yellowish Finch (*Sicalis luteola*), D. Seth Smith, *A.M.*, 1906, 340. *Also*, *Sicalis luteola luteiventris*, W. Shore Baily, *B.N.*, 1922, 179. *Also*, *Sicalis luteola minor*, M. Amsler, *B.N.*, 1915, 320, 329, and *A.M.*, 1916, 25.

Cuban Finch (*Tiaris canora*), Hawkins, *A.M.*, 7, 1900–1, 29, and *A.M.*, 8, 1901–2, 37. *Also*, J. Clement, *F.B.*, 28, 1962, 158.

Grassquits (*Tiaris* Spp.), R. L. Restall, *C.&A.B.*, 21/3/1968.

Olive Finch (*Tiaris olivacea*), Hawkins, *A.M.*, 7, 1900–1, 30. *Also*, D. Seth Smith in A. G. Butler, *Foreign Birds for Cage and Aviary*, c. 1906, 1, 150. *Also*, J. Mander, *C.&A.B.*, 137, 1970, 75.

Black-faced Grassquit (*Tiaris bicolor*), Willford, *B.N.*, 1910, 231. *Also*, R. Goodwin, *A.M.*, 65, 1959, 131–4.

Jacarini Finch (*Volatinia jacarina*), Suggitt, *B.N.*, 1910, 363. *Also*, S. A. Quilina, *F.B.*, 27, 1961, 205. *Also*, I. Millar, *F.B.*, 28, 1962, 112.

White-throated Finch (*Sporophila albigularis*), R. Farrar, *A.M.* (2), 4, 1905, 358. *Also*, C. Elliott, *F.B.*, 27, 1961, 169.

Grey Seed-eater (*Sporophila intermedia*, formerly *S. grisea*), W. Page, *B.N.*, 1912, 338, and 1913, 139.

Rusty-collared Seed-eater (*Sporophila collaris cucullata*), 'Has been bred in Germany', Decoux, *A.M.*, 1921, 116.

Gutteral Finch (*Sporophila gutteralis*), W. Page, *B.N.*, 1912, 338, and 1913, 139.

Cayenne Seed-eater (*Sporophila frontalis*), W. R. Partridge, *A.M.*, 70, 1964, 111–13.

Grosbeak Seed-eater (*Sporophila peruvianus*), R. L. Restall, *A.M.*, 73, 1967, 68–76.

Pretty Warbling Finch (*Poospiza ornata*), Keston Foreign Bird Farm, *A.M.*, 66, 1960, 171–2. *Also*, R. Zackrisson, *A.M.*, 78, 1972, 112–17.

Mourning Sierra Finch (*Phrygilus fruticeti*), M. Amsler, *A.M.*, 52, 1946, 75.

Pope Cardinal (*Paroaria dominicana* as *larvata*), Lady E. D. Pennant, *B.N.* (2), 3, 1912; 156–7 and 338. *Also*, R. L. Restall, *F.B.*, 29, 1963, 202.

Red-crested Cardinal (*Paroaria cucullata* as *coronata*), 'Frequently bred', according to Neunzig in Hopkinson, *Records*, 1926. Hamilton Scott, 'Most seasons a few are reared' in W. Page, *B.N.*, 1913, 285. *Also*, Kostermeyer, *F.B.*, 27, 1961, 62. *Also*, R. Garner, *F.B.*, 28, 1962, 158.

Yellow-billed Cardinal (*Paroaria capitata*), M. Amsler, 1911, *A.M.* (3), 13, 1921–2, 160. *Also*, A. Ezra, 1937, vide *F.B.*, 28, 1962, 221.

Black-throated Cardinal (*Paroaria gularis*), A. Ezra, *A.M.* (5), 2, 1937, 251.

Green Cardinal (*Gubernatrix cristata*), Farrar, *A.M.*, 3, 192. *Also*, E. M. Boehm, *F.B.*, 27, 1961, 8.

Orange-billed Saltator (*Saltator aurantiirostris*), Bright, *B.N.*, 1921, 203, and *A.M.*, 1921, 161.

Virginian Cardinal (*Cardinalis cardinalis*), 'Has been bred in captivity from early times and fairly frequently', Hopkinson, *Records*, 1926. Gedney, *A.M.*, 1, 124. *Also*, R. L. Restall, *C.&A.B.*, 3/6/1965. *Also*, G. Gjessing, *A.M.*, 62, 1956, 71–3.

Red-crested Cardinal (*Paroaria cucullata*) × Virginian Cardinal (*cardinalis cardinalis*), M. Baxter, *F.B.*, 26, 1960, 75.

Rose-breasted Grosbeak (*Pheucticus indovicianus*), F. Astley, *A.M.*, 1911, 33, 370, and *B.N.*, 1911, 214, 234. *Also*, D. T. Spilsbury, *F.B.*, 35, 1969, 138.

Black-headed Grosbeak (*Pheucticus melanocephalus*), W. Teschemaker, *B.N.*, 1912, 328.

Yellow Grosbeak (*Pheucticus chrysopeplus*), E. J. Brook, *A.M.* (3), 8, 1916–17, 28–9.

Lazuli Bunting (*Passerina amoena*), G. A. Coleman, *F.B.*, 21, 1955, 180. *Also*, R. L. Restall, *C.&A.B.*, 20/4/1967.

Indigo Bunting (*Passerina cyanea*), R. Farrar, *A.M.*, 1900, 270. *Also*, R. L. Restall, *C.&A.B.*, 17/11/1966.

Nonpareil Bunting (*Passerina ciris*), R. Farrar, *A.M.*, 5, 1898–9, 165–7; 1902, 37.

Varied Bunting (*Passerina versicolor*), 'Only bred abroad', Hopkinson, *Records*, 1926.

Rainbow Bunting (*Passerina leclancheri*), 'Bred in France', Hopkinson, *Records*, 1926. *Also*, R. L. Restall, *C.&A.B.*, 17/11/1966.

Brazilian Blue Grosbeak (*Cyanocompsa cyanea*), W. E. Teschemaker, *A.M.*, 1910, 64, 198.
Blue Grosbeak (*Guiraca caerula*), London Zoo, 1921, *L.Z. Repts.*, 1921.

II FRINGILLIDAE

Chaffinch (*Fringilla coelebs*), R. James, *A.M.* (5), 3, 1938, 142–3, 161. *Also*, D. Washington, *Occ. Publ.*, 3, 1969, 5–9.
Blue Chaffinch (*Fringilla teydea*), E. Meade-Waldo, *A.M.*, 1, 1894–5, 103–4.
Brambling (*Fringilla montifringilla*), R. Suggitt, *B.N.* (2), 8, 1917, 234–6.
Serin (*Serinus serinus*), G. C. Swales, *A.M.*, 4, 1898, 14–15.
Sulphury Seed-eater (*Serinus sulphuratus*), W. Shore Baily, *A.M.* (2), 5, 1914, 264–5. *Also*, A. W. Fletcher, *A.M.*, 1967, 169.
Green Singing Finch (*Serinus mozambicus*), 'I know it has been bred', E. Hopkinson, *Records*, 1926. *Also*, R. L. Restall, *C.&A.B.*, 20/1/1966.
Black-faced Canary (*Serinus capistrata*), B. Dormer, *F.B.*, 27, 1961, 168.
St. Helena Seed-eater (*Serinus flaviventris*), W. Shore Baily, *A.M.* (4), 4, 1926, 328–9. *Also*, J. Nicolai, *F.B.*, 22, 1956, 110.
Yellow-rumped Serin (*Serinus atrogularis*), W. E. Teschemaker, *A.M.* (2), 5, 1906–7, 198–200. *Also*, D. Delanty, *A.M.*, 57, 1951, 127.
Natal Linnet (*Serinus scotops*), G. Cooke, *F.B.*, 21, 1955, 161.
Grey Singing Finch (*Serinus leucopygius*), E. Allen, *A.M.*, 3, 1896–7, 147.
Alario Finch (*Serinus alario*), H. R. Fillmer, *B.N.*, 2, 1903–4, 30. *Also*, R. L. Restall, *C.&A.B.*, 23/3/1967.
Red-fronted Serin (*Serinus pusillus*), Z. Veger, *A.M.*, 74, 1968, 156–9. *Also*, R. L. Restall, *C.&A.B.*, 5/8/1965 and 11/11/1965.
Citril Finch (*Serinus citrinella*), W. E. Teschemaker, *B.N.* (2), 4, 1913, 322.
Goldfinch (*Carduelis carduelis*), R. Suggitt, *B.N.*, 3, 1904, 70.
Black-headed Siskin (*Carduelis magellanicus*), W. E. Teschemaker, *B.N.* (2), 3, 1912, 4–9.
Siskin (*Carduelis spinus*), W. T. Page, *B.N.*, 8, 1909, 202.
Hooded Siskin (*Carduelis cucullatus*), M. Amsler, *B.N.* (2), 3, 1912, 278–81.
Himalayan Greenfinch (*Carduelis spinoides*), W. E. Teschemaker, *B.N.* (2), 5, 1914, 278. *Also*, *C. spinoides* × *C. tibetanus*, W. Shore Baily, *B.N.* (3), 2, 1919, 214.

Greenfinch (*Carduelis chloris*), J. Sergeant, *A.M.*, 1, 1894–5, 124.
Chinese Greenfinch (*Carduelis sinica*), W. Shore Baily, *B.N.* (2), 6, 1915, 334–6.
Tibetan Siskin (*Carduelis tibetanus*), W. E. Teschemaker, *B.N.* (2), 5, 1914, 278. *Also, B.N.* (3), 2, 1919, 214–15.
Bullfinch (*Pyrrhula pyrrhula*), J. Sergeant, *A.M.*, 1, 1894–5, 124. *Also,* G. De Pass, *A.M.* (4), 12, 1934, 105–8.
Red-headed Bullfinch (*Pyrrhula erythrocephala*), W. St. Quintin, *A.M.* (3), 8, 1916–17, 250.
Trumpeter Bullfinch (*Rhodopechys githaginea*), E. Meade-Waldo, in A. G. Butler, *Foreign Birds for Cage and Aviary*, c. 1906, 1, 98.
Common Crossbill (*Loxia curvirostra*), A. Silver (per J. L. Bonhote), *A.M.* (3), 2, 1910–11, 109–17. *Also,* D. M. Birch, *Occ. Publ.*, 2, 1968, 5–8.
Pine Grosbeak (*Pinicola enucleator*), W. St. Quintin, *A.M.* (2), 5, 1907, 55–76.
House Finch (*Carpodacus mexicanus*), W. E. Teschemaker, *B.N.* (1), 1, 1910, 363. *Also, C. m. frontalis*, W. Shore Baily, *A.M.* (4), 3, 1925, 278–9. *Also,* G. C. Lynch, *F.B.*, 22, 1956, 240–1.
Common Rosefinch (*Carpodacus erythrina*), G. De Pass, *F.B.*, 21, 1955, 179, and *F.B.*, 22, 1956, 14.
Purple Finch (*Carpodacus purpureus*), G. C. Lynch, *A.M.*, 64, 1958, 137–9, and *F.B.*, 25, 1959, 10.
Pink-browed Rosefinch (*Carpodacus rhodopeplus*), W. St. Quintin, *A.M.* (3), 8, 1916–17, 251.
Linnet (*Acanthis cannabina*), W. T. Page, *B.N.* (2), 7, 1916, 19. *Also* W. H. Potter, *A.M.* (4), 13, 1935, 57.
Redpoll (*Acanthis flammea*), B. Carpenter, *A.M.* (2), 6, 1907–8, 160–1.
Lesser Redpoll (*Acanthis flammea cabaret*), G. C. Swales, *A.M.*, 3, 1896–7, 69, bred 1895.
Mealy Redpoll (*Acanthis flammea flammea*), W. E. Teschemaker, *B.N.* (2), 3, 1912, 181–3.
Twite (*Acanthus flavirostris*), G. C. Swales, *A.M.*, 1, 1894–5, 118.
Hawfinch (*Coccothraustes coccothraustes*), W. E. Teschemaker, *A.M.* (3), 3, 1911–12, 28–34. *Also,* A. A. Prestwich, *A.M.*, 52, 1946, 224–5.
Evening Grosbeak (*Coccothraustes vespertina*), C. M. Payne, *A.M.*, 62, 1956, 167–70. *Also, F.B.*, 22, 1956, 246.
Black and Yellow Grosbeak (*Coccothraustes icteroides*), Decoux, *A.M.*, 1924, 73.
Chinese Hawfinch (*Coccothraustes migratoria*), Hartwig, 1886, in Hopkinson, *Records*, 1926.

III ESTRILDIDAE

Red-eared Waxbill (*Estrilda troglodytes*), W. A. Bainbridge, *A.M.* (3), 5, 1913–14, 83–5.

Black-crowned Waxbill (*Estrilda nonnula*), Mrs. N. Wharton-Tigar, *A.M.* (5), 1, 1936, 323–5. *Also,* D. Goodwin, *A.M.,* 69, 1963, 149–57.

Black-cheeked Waxbill (*Estrilda erythronotos*), C. af Enehjelm, *F.B.,* 33, 1967, 77. *Also,* D. G. Osborne, *A.M.,* 80, 1974, 17–19.

Rosy-rumped Waxbill (*Estrilda rhodopyga*), O. Rouse, *F.B.,* 1, 1935. *Also,* K. Edwards, *F.B.,* 27, 1961, 247.

Fawn-breasted Waxbill (*Estrilda paludicola*), B. P. Dormer, *F.B.,* 25, 1959, 131.

Dufresne's Waxbill (*Estrilda melanotis*), E. Robinson, *A.M.* (4), 12, 1934, 249. *Also,* Dulanty, *A.M.,* 55, 1949, 9. *Also,* Miss O. Merry, *F.B.,* 37, 1971, 51–2. *Also,* R. L. Restall, *F.B.,* 35, 1969, 162–9.

St. Helena Waxbill (*Estrilda astrild*), Reeve, *B.N.,* 1910, 343. *Also,* Mrs. C. Lambert, *F.B.,* 25, 1959, 12.

Orange-cheeked Waxbill (*Estrilda melpoda*), Miss R. Alderson, *A.M.,* 8, 1901–2, 65–70. *Also,* D. Delanty, *A.M.,* 57, 1951, 128.

Red Avadavat (*Amandava amandava*), R. Farrar, *A.M.* (2), 1, 1902–3, 407. *Also,* D. Goodwin, *A.M.,* 66, 1960, 174–99. *Also,* R. L. Restall, *C.&A.B.,* 27/4/1967.

Green Avadavat (*Amandava formosa*), W. E. Teschemaker, *A.M.* (2), 4, 1905–6, 70–2. *Also,* Miss O. Ponfick, vide A. G. Butler, *Foreign Finches in Captivity,* 1899, 103.

Golden-breasted Waxbill (*Amandava subflava*), Dunleath, *B.N.,* 2, 248. *Also,* D. Goodwin, *A.M.,* 66, 1960, 174–99.

Quail Finch (*Ortygospiza atricollis*), R. Philipps, *A.M.* (3), 1, 1909–10, 37–47.

Cordon-bleu (*Uraeginthus bengalus*), R. Farrar, vide A. G. Butler, *Foreign Birds for Cage and Aviary,* c. 1906, 1, 159.

Blue-headed Waxbill (*Uraeginthus cyanocephala*), ? J. Cranna, per A. R. Hynd, *A.M.,* 69, 1963, 40. *Also,* D. Goodwin, *A.M.,* 68, 1962, 117–28.

Blue-breasted Waxbill (*Uraeginthus angolensis*), R. Philipps, *A.M.,* 7, 1908–9, 339–50. *Also,* D. Goodwin, *A.M.,* 65, 1959, 149–69.

Violet-eared Waxbill (*Uraeginthus granatina*), Mrs. K. Drake, *A.M.* (5), 1, 1936, 325–7. *Also,* H. Shute, *F.B.,* 24, 1958, 112 and 204, and *F.B.,* 25, 1950, 58.

Purple Grenadier (*Uraeginthus ianthinogaster*), Keston Foreign Bird Farm, E. J. Boosey, *A.M.,* 64, 1958, 164–6.

Common Firefinch (*Lagonosticta senegala*), R. Farrar, *A.M.,* 4, 1898–9, 212. *Also,* C. J. O. Harrison, *A.M.,* 62, 1956, 128–41.

Vinaceous Firefinch (*Lagonosticta vinacea*), Mrs. N. Wharton-Tigar, *A.M.* (4), 11, 1933, 437–9. *Also*, Sir R. Cottrell, *A.M.*, 70, 1964, 106–8.

Lavender Finch (*Lagonosticta caerulescens*), Miss R. Alderson, *A.M.*, 7, 1900–1, 45–9. *Also*, C. J. O. Harrison, *A.M.*, 62, 1956, 128–41. *Also*, C. af Enehjelm, *F.B.*, 24, 1958, 140.

Black-bellied Firefinch (*Lagonosticta rara*), Sir R. Cottrell, *A.M.*, 68, 1962, 27–9. *Also*, J. Howard, *F.B.*, 27, 1961, 249.

Brown Firefinch (*Lagonosticta nitidula*), B. P. Dormer, *F.B.*, 25, 1959, 130–1. *Also*, A. Kirkwood, *F.B.*, 23, 1957, 189.

Jameson's Firefinch (*Lagonosticta jamesoni*), F. Johnson, *A.M.* (4), 13, 1935, 50–1. *Also*, D. Goodwin, *A.M.*, 75, 1969, 87–94.

Dark Firefinch (*Lagonosticta rubricata*), F. G. Dix, *F.B.*, 28, 1962, 174, 209. *Also*, B. P. Dormer, *L. r. haematocephala*, *F.B.*, 25, 1959, 131. *Also*, D. Goodwin, *A.M.*, 70, 1964, 80–105.

Bar-breasted Firefinch (*Lagonosticta rufopicta*), C. J. O. Harrison, *A.M.*, 62, 1956, 128–41.

Peter's Twin-spot (*Hypargos niveoguttatus*), Mrs. K. Drake, *A.M.* (4), 13, 1945, 198–9. *Also*, R. W. Burton, *C.&A.B.*, 38, 1972, 2.

Green-backed Twin-spot (*Mandingoa nitidula*), W. Northwood, *F.B.*, 25, 1959, 136.

Dusky Twin-spot (*Clytospiza dybowskii*), B. Parry, *F.B.*, 36, 1970, 149.

Melba Finch (*Pytilia melba*), Willard, *B.N.*, 1915, 261, 323. *Also*, C. af Enehjelm, *F.B.*, 33, 1967, 77.

Aurora Finch (*Pytilia phoenicoptera*), Willford, *B.N.*, 1909, 194. *Also*, Sir R. Cottrell, *A.M.*, 66, 1960, 161–4. *Also*, W. Langberg, *P. p. lineata*, *F.B.*, 30, 1964, 98–9. *Also*, Miss R. H. Low, *F.B.*, 29, 1962, 17.

Orange-winged Pytilia (*Pytilia afra*), A. J. Clare, *F.B.*, 28, 1962, 164.

Cut-throat (*Amandina fasciata*), R. Farrar, *A.M.*, 3, 1896–7, 63–6.

Red-headed Finch (*Amandina erythrocephala*), W. E. Teschemaker, *A.M.* (2), 4, 1905–6, 354–7. *Also*, Dr. H. Wildeboer, *F.B.*, 23, 1957, 84.

Java Sparrow (*Padda oryzivora*), 'Frequently bred', vide Hopkinson, *Reports*, 1926. *Also*, D. Goodwin, *A.M.*, 69, 1963, 54–69. *Also*, J. B. Newell, *F.B.*, 23, 1957, 124.

Pectoral Finch (*Lonchura pectoralis*), Mrs. H. Williams, *A.M.* (2), 4, 1905–6, 68–70. *Also*, D. Lofts, *F.B.*, 27, 1961, 83.

Spice Bird (*Lonchura punctulata*), Dunleath, *B.N.*, 2, 1911, 152, and 8, 13. *Also*, Gill, in Dart, *B.N.*, 4, 45.

Striated Munia (*Lonchura striata*), Willford, *B.N.*, 8, 1909, 228 (includes *L. s. acuticauda*, Suggitt, *B.N.*, 1914).

Yellow-rumped Munia (*Lonchura flaviprymna*), W. E. Teschemaker, *A.M.* (2), 5, 1906–7, 113–21. *Also*, E. Day, *F.B.*, 24, 1958, and *F.B.*, 25, 1959, 113.

White-headed Munia (*Lonchura maja*), C. W. Scheimer, *F.B.*, 30, 1964, 50. *Also*, W. A. Pope, vide J. R. Hodges, *A.M.*, 78, 1972, 25–27.

Dusky Munia (*Lonchura fuscans*), W. Langberg, *A.M.*, 61, 1955, 229–230. *Also*, P. Frampton, *F.B.*, 30, 1964, 12.

Chestnut-breasted Finch (*Lonchura castaneothorax*), W. E. Teschemaker, *A.M.* (2), 5, 1906–7, 121–4. *Also*, F. Holbek, *F.B.*, 36, 1970, 164–8.

Tri-coloured Munia (*Lonchura malacca*), P. Frampton, *F.B.*, 30, 1964, 12. (*L. m. atricapilla*), Easton Scott, *B.N.*, 1912, 338; 1913, 266. *Also*, F. George, *F.B.*, 27, 1961, 168. *Also*, M. W. Stilwell, *A.M.*, 72, 1966, 47.

Timor Sparrow (*Padda fuscata*), A. Martin, *A.M.*, 67, 1961, 89–90.

Bib Finch (*Lonchura nana*), A. Farrar, *A.M.*, 2, 1895–6, 138. *Also*, Suggitt, *B.N.*, 1914, 374.

Magpie Mannikin (*Lonchura fringilloides*), Weiner, in Fillmer, *Waxbills, Grassfinches and Mannikins*, 1897, 61. *Also*, Smith, *B.N.*, 1914, 376.

Bronze-winged Mannikin (*Lonchura cucullata*), Suggitt, *B.N.*, 3, 70. *Also*, R. L. Restall, *C.&A.B.*, 2/3/1967. *Also*, F. W. Wheeler, *C.&A.B.*, 136, 1962, 375.

Rufous-backed Mannikin (*Lonchura nigriceps*), W. Teschemaker, *A.M.* (2), 7, 1908–9, 321–3.

Black and White Mannikin (*Lonchura bicolor*), G. Taylor, *F.B.*, 37, 1971, 53.

African Silverbill (*Lonchura cantans*), R. Farrar, *A.M.* (2), 1, 1902–3, 407. *Also*, R. L. Restall, *C.&A.B.*, 2/6/1966, 336.

Indian Silverbill (*Lonchura malabarica*), W. Teschemaker, vide A. G. Butler, *Foreign Birds for Cage and Aviary*, c. 1906, 1, 174. *Also*, R. L. Restall, *C.&A.B.*, 2/6/1966, 336.

Pearl-headed Silverbill (*Lonchura caniceps*), W. Langberg, *A.M.*, 69, 1963, 97–101. *Also*, P. Scally, *A.M.*, 73, 1967, 81–2. *Also*, K. Cross, *F.B.*, 33. 1967, 76.

Introduction to the Munias and Mannikins, R. L. Restall, *F.B.*, 35, 1969, 4–9, 44–50, 84–7, 124–30, and *F.B.*, 36, 1969, 162–9.

Red-eared Firetail (*Zonaeginthus oculatus*), A. Y. Pepper, *C.&A.B.*, 130, 1966, 77.

Diamond Sparrow (*Zonaeginthus guttatus*), Page, Suggitt and others, *B.N.*, 1914, 374. *Also*, R. L. Restall, *C.&A.B.*, 4/1/1968.

Crimson Finch (*Poephila phaeton*), Mathias, *B.N.*, 8, 207, 221. *Also*, Hetley, *B.N.*, 8, 227. *Also*, A. R. Hynd, *F.B.*, 4, 1938, 5. *Also*, Mrs. K. M. Scamell, *A.M.*, 63, 1957, 214.

Star Finch (*Poephila ruficauda*), A. E. Nicholson, *A.M.*, 7, 1900–1, 219–23. *Also*, yellow phase, *F.B.*, 34, 1968, 182. *Also*, white phase, J. Hofmeyer, *F.B.*, 26, 1960, 200.

Painted Finch (*Zonaeginthus picta*), Willford, *B.N.*, 1910, 231, 363. *Also*, A. J. Patterson, *A.M.* (4), 13, 1935, 300–61. *Also*, L. Webber, *A.M.*, 52, 1946, 149–58. *Also*, F. Holbek, *F.B.*, 37, 1971, 90–1.

Sydney Waxbill (*Aegintha temporalis*), R. Phillips, *A.M.*, 8, 1901–2, 289–93. *Also*, P. H. Tancred, *F.B.*, 23, 1957, 164.

Long-tailed Grassfinch (*Poephila acuticauda*), Todd, *A.M.*, 3, 1896–7, 210. *Also*, Red-billed form (*P. a. hecki*), W. E. Teschemaker, 1913, vide W. Page, *B.N.*, 1913, 332. *Also*, R. L. Restall, *C. & A.B.*, 30/6/1966, 303.

Masked Grassfinch (*Poephila personata*), Hawkins, *A.M.*, 7, 1900–1, 32.

Parson Finch (*Poephila cincta*), 'Easily bred, often many broods', vide Hopkinson, *Records*, 1926, 40. *Also*, R. L. Restall, *C.&A.B.*, 30/6/1966, 303.

Zebra Finch (*Poephila guttata*), R. Farrar, *A.M.* (2), 1, 1902–3, 407.

Bicheno's Finch (*Poephila bichenovii*), G. D. Glasscoe, *A.M.*, 6, 1899–1900, 35. *Also*, Black-rumped form (*P. b. annulosa*), Mrs. H. Williams, *A.M.*, 8, 1901–2, 264–6.

Introduction to the Parrot-finches, R. L. Restall, *F.B.*, 37, 1971, 48–56, 92–6, 124–9, and *F.B.*, 38, 1972, 4–12, 54–61.

Gouldian Finch (*Chloebia gouldiae*), R. Phillips, vide Fillmer, *Waxbills, Grassfinches, and Mannikins*, 1897. *Also*, White-breasted form, F. Barnicoat, *F.B.*, 34, 1968, 18. *Also*, P. W. Teague, *A.M.*, 52, 1946, 132–5 and *A.M.*, 56, 1950, 191–6.

Tri-coloured Parrot-finch (*Erythrura tricolor*), W. R. Temple, *B.N.*, 1910, 150, and *A.M.* (3), 1, 1909–10, 225. *Also*, D. Batley, *C.&A.B.*, 136, 1969, 316.

Royal Parrot-finch (*Erythrura cyanovirens*), Dr. C. H. Macklin, *F.B.*, 1, 1935. *Also*, *E. c. regia*, J. Dahlborg-Johansen, *A.M.*, 72, 1966, 108–11. *Also*, *E. c. pealei*, London Zoo, vide W. N. Page, 1912, 258. *Also*, N. Nicholson, *A.M.*, 68, 1962, 197–8. *Also*, W. Langberg, *F.B.*, 29, 1963, 77.

Blue-headed Parrot-finch (*Erythrura papuana*), M. Amsler, *A.M.* (5), 2, 1937, 364. *Also*, E. Valentine, *A.M.* (5), 2, 1937, 326–8.

Red-headed Parrot-finch (*Erythrura psittacea*), M. Amsler, *B.N.*, 1910, 267, and *B.N.*, 1914, 350, 354.

IV   PLOCEIDAE

Southern Masked Weaver (*Ploceus velatus*), W. Shore Baily, *B.N.*, 1916–25.

Little Masked Weaver (*Ploceus luteola*), W. Shore Baily, *B.N.*, 1914, 305, and 1915, 42. *Also*, M. H. Williams, *C.&A.B.*, 39, 1972, 2.

Reichenow's Weaver (*Ploceus reichenowi*), A. Ezra, *A.M.* (5), 1, 1936, 248–9. *Also*, C. W. Creed, *F.B.*, 21, 1955, 6–8.

Black-headed Weaver (*Ploceus melanocephalus*), Lord Poltimore, *B.N.*, 1912, 338.

Rufous-necked Weaver (*Ploceus cucullatus*), London Zoo, *L.Z. Repts.*, 1905, 1913. *Also*, E. de Winter, *F.B.*, 27, 1961, 207. *Also*, R. L. Restall, *C. & A.B.*, 24/8/1967.

Baya Weaver (*Ploceus philippinus*), R. L. Restall, *C.&A.B.*, 28/9/1967.

Half-masked Weaver (*Ploceus vitellinus*), Revd. J. R. Lowe, *A.M.*, 65, 1959, 27.

Vieillot's Black Weaver (*Ploceus nigerrimus*), E. de Winter, *F.B.*, 27, 1961, 207.

Madagascar Weaver (*Foudia madagascariensis*), A. Ezra, *A.M.* (5), 3, 1938, 220.

Red-billed Weaver (*Quelea quelea*), Rattigan, *B.N.*, 1911, 323. *Also*, Chester Zoo, *A.M.*, 70, 1964, 229. *Also*, R. L. Restall, *C. & A.B.*, 3/8/1967.

Orix Bishop (*Euplectes orix*), De Quincey, *B.N.*, 1912, 201, 260, 338. *Also*, *E. o. franciscana*, London Zoo, *L.Z. Repts.*, 1917. *Also*, Cleghorn, *F.B.*, 35, 1969, 135. *Also*, R. L. Restall, all races, *C. & A.B.*, 22/9/1966.

Napoleon Weaver (*Euplectes afra*), Lord Poltimore, *B.N.*, 1912, 335, 338. *Also*, W. Shore Baily, *A.M.* (4), 1, 1923, 136. *Also*, W. Shore Baily, *E. a. taha*, *B.N.*, 1915, 296.

Fire-fronted Bishop (*Euplectes diademata*), E. Nørgaard-Olesen, *A.M.*, 76, 1970, 94–5.

Crimson-crowned Bishop (*Euplectes hordeacea*), W. T. Page, *B.N.*, 1920, 223–4, and 1921, 228.

Red-shouldered Whydah (*Euplectes axilliaris*), I. V. Hyndman, both *E. a. axilliaris* and *E. a. bocagei*, *F.B.*, 27, 1961, 16.

Yellow-rumped Bishop (*Euplectes capensis*), A. Ezra, *A.M.* (5), 3, 1938, 221–2.

Yellow-shouldered Whydah (*Euplectes macrourus*), Chester Zoo (W. H. Timmis), *Int. Zoo Yearbook* 13, 1973, 314.

White-winged Whydah (*Euplectes albonatus*), W. E. Teschemaker, *B.N.*, 1915, 261. *Also*, I. V. Hyndman, *F.B.*, 27, 1961, 16.

Red-collared Whydah (*Euplectes ardens*), I. V. Hyndman, *F.B.*, 27, 1961, 16. *Also*, Chester Zoo (W. H. Timmis), *Int. Zoo Yearbook* 13, 1973, 314.

Long-tailed Whydah (*Euplectes progne*), W. E. Teschemaker, *A.M.* (3), 1, 1909–10, 198, 225. *Also*, F. G. Norris, *F.B.*, 34, 1968, 109

Jackson's Whydah (*Euplectes jacksoni*), W. Shore Baily, *B.N.*, 1916, 202, 212, and *A.M.* (4), 1, 1923, 115.

Tree Sparrow (*Passer montanus*), W. E. Teschemaker, *B.N.*, 1907, 46.

Cinnamon Sparrow (*Passer cinnamoneus*), W. E. Teschemaker, *A.M.* (2), 7, 1908–9, 205–8, and *B.N.*, 7, 1908, 128.

Cape Sparrow (*Passer melanurus*), D. Seth-Smith, *A.M.*, 7, 1900–1, 165–7, 215.

Grey-headed Sparrow (*Passer griseus*), W. E. Teschemaker, *A.M.* (3), 1, 1909–10, 238–9.

Golden Sparrow (*Passer luteus*), Mrs. H. Williams, *A.M.* (2), 3, 1904–5, 75–7. *Also*, H. Murray, *C. & A.B.*, 128, 1965, 91.

House Sparrow (*Passer domesticus*), J. D. Summers-Smith, *The House Sparrow*, London, 1967. *Also*, A. H. Scott, *A.M.* (5), 6, 1941, 50–57, 94–101. *Also*, D. Washington, *A.M.*, 79, 1973, 109–15.

Spanish Sparrow (*Passer hispaniolensis*), H. Murray, *A.M.*, 79, 1973, 148–51.

Benguela Sparrow (*Passer jagoensis*), W. Shore Baily, *B.N.*, 1923, 44.

Scaly-crowned Weaver (*Sporopipes squamifrons*), W. E. Teschemaker, *A.M.* (3), 4, 1912–13, 362–6.

Rock Sparrow (*Petronia petronia*), E. G. B. Meade-Waldo, *A.M.*, 3, 1896–7, 28–9.

Bush Petronia (*Petronia dentata*), C. af Enehjelm, *A.M.*, 61, 1955, 151, 214, *Also*, P. W. Louwman, in W. W. Diedrich, *A.M.*, 61, 1955, 266.

Paradise Whydah (*Steganura paradisea*), Mrs. T. Lloyd, *F.B.*, 21, 1955, 156–60, 22, 1956, 8–9. *Also*, C. J. Nerrett, *F.B.*, 28, 1962, 85. *Also*, R. L. Restall, *C. & A.B.*, 27/7/1967.

Pintailed Whydah (*Vidua macroura*), W. Curt, *A.M.*, 65, 1959, 25. *Also*, R. L. Restall, *C. & A.B.*, 21/10/1965, 247.

Queen Whydah (*Vidua regia*), Mrs. P. Henderson, *F.B.*, 29, 1963, 221. *Also*, J. Weeks, *A.M.*, 74, 1968, 6–7.

Senegal Combassou (*Hypochera chalybeata*), K. Nielsen, *A.M.*, 22, 1956, 11–13, 104. *Also*, H. Poulson, *A.M.*, 22, 1956, 177–81.

Brood-parasitism in the Viduinae, *Der Brutparasitismus der Viduinae als ethologisches Problem*, J. Nicolai, *Zeit. für Tierp.*, 21, 2, 1964, 129–204.

Dinemelli's Weaver (*Dinemellia dinemelli*), Pittsburgh Conservatory-Aviary, *A.M.*, 64, 1958, 53–5.

INDEX

SCIENTIFIC NAMES

COMMON ENGLISH NAMES